The Idea Magazine For Teachers®

PRIMARY

1999–2000

YEARBOOK

Diane Badden, Senior Editor

The Education Center, Inc.
Greensboro, North Carolina

The Mailbox® 1999–2000 Primary Yearbook

Founding Editor in Chief: Margaret Michel
Senior Editor: Diane Badden
Executive Director, Magazine Publishing: Katharine P. S. Brower
Editorial Administrative Director: Stephen Levy
Curriculum Director: Karen P. Shelton
Editorial Training: Irving P. Crump
Freelance Management: Karen A. Brudnak
Contributing Editors: Amy Erickson, Njeri Jones Legrand, Mary Lester, Sharon Murphy, Hope Taylor
Copy Editors: Karen Brewer Grossman, Karen L. Huffman, Tracy Johnson, Laurel Robinson, Debbie Shoffner, Gina Sutphin
Traffic Manager: Lisa K. Pitts
Staff Artists: Pam Crane, Nick Greenwood, Rebecca Saunders (SENIOR ARTISTS); Cathy Spangler Bruce, Theresa Lewis Goode, Clevell Harris, Susan Hodnett, Sheila Krill, Rob Mayworth, Kimberly Richard, Greg D. Rieves, Barry Slate, Donna K. Teal
Cover Artist: Lois Axeman
Typesetters: Lynette Maxwell, Mark Rainey
Editorial Assistants: Terrie Head, Melissa B. Montanez, Karen White, Jan E. Witcher
Library: Dorothy C. McKinney (ASSISTANT)

ISBN 1-56234-380-7
ISSN 1088-5544

Printed in the United States of America.

The Education Center, Inc.
P.O. Box 9753
Greensboro, NC 27429-0753

Look for *The Mailbox*® 2000–2001 Primary Yearbook in the summer of 2001. The Education Center, Inc., is the publisher of *The Mailbox*®, *Teacher's Helper*®, *The Mailbox*® BOOKBAG®, and Learning® magazines, as well as other fine products. Look for these wherever quality teacher materials are sold, or call 1-800-714-7991.

Contents

BULLETIN BOARDS

Bulletin Boards ....

Propel spelling skills to extraordinary heights all year long! Cover tagboard stars with foil; then attach a laminated card to each star. Mount the stars, the title, a rocket cutout, and a trail of holiday lights. Every week use a wipe-off marker to program the cards with spelling words. Wipe the cards clean before test time. Each child who aces the test adds a star sticker to the display. Illuminate the lights for added spelling inspiration!

Rebecca Kielas—Grs. 1–2, Badger State Baptist School, Milwaukee, WI

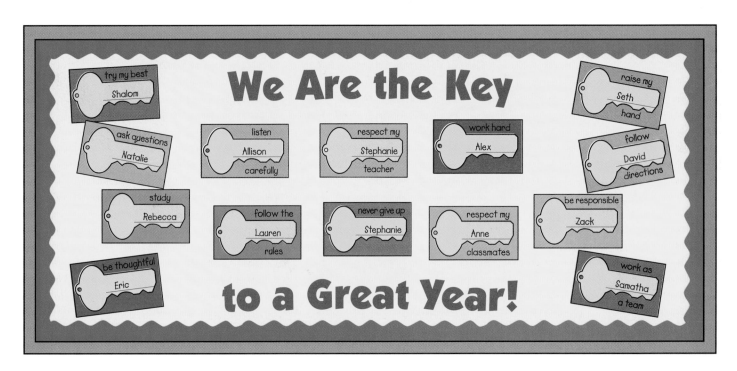

Show students that they each hold a key to success! Enlist their help in naming behaviors that unlock positive learning experiences. Next have each child personalize and cut out a large key pattern (page 20), glue the cutout to a colorful rectangle, and label the rectangle with her goal for a positive year. Mount the projects and title. There you have it, a colorful reminder of what is key for a great year!

Kathie Eckelkamp—Gr. 2, Most Precious Blood School, St. Louis, MO

Bumper-to-Bumper Facts

6 + 8

5 + 8

9 + 5

5 + 7

9 + 4

8 + 4

7 + 7

8 + 9

9 + 7

8 + 8

5 + 5

6 + 7

6 + 6

6 + 5

6 + 9

You'll have bumper-to-bumper traffic at this interactive display! A child draws a driver and one or more passengers on a tagboard car pattern (page 20) and then colors the pattern and cuts it out. Label white rectangles with math facts—one per car. Program the back of each resulting license plate for self-checking. Use Velcro® to secure each plate to a car. Keep students interested in maneuvering the math facts by periodically switching the plates or providing new ones.

Sarah Mertz, Owenton, KY

GET YOUR PAWS ON A GOOD BOOK!

Tia   Paul   Clevell   Marsha   Shelly   Deanna   Kim

Angela   Matt   Beth   Chris   Michelle   Ron   Brian   Kendall

Promote independent reading with this "bone-afide" plan! Trim the top four inches from a class supply of paper lunch bags. Each child writes his name and colors paw prints on a bag. Mount the bags, a canine character, and the title. For each book a child reads, he completes a book review bone (page 21), cuts it out, and stores it in his bag. You can see who's reading what, and the students can sniff out their classmates' favorite books. "Paws-itively" perfect!

Kimberly Hawk—Gr. 3, March School, Easton, PA

Foster friendship with this honey of a display! Write a student-generated list of friendship tips on a large hive cutout. Have each child personalize and color a bee pattern (page 21) and then cut it out. Mount the title, hive, and cutouts. To keep students abuzz with friendship, occasionally read aloud tips from the list and ask students who practice them to buzz! Reward exemplary acts of friendship with bite-size Bit•O•Honey® candy bars.

Jennifer Balogh-Joiner—Gr. 2, Franklin Elementary, Franklin, NJ

Dispense a colorful classroom welcome with this hallway display. A student uses assorted arts-and-crafts supplies to create her self-likeness on a colorful paper circle. Fashion the base of a gum dispenser from colorful paper. Mount the resulting cutout, the student projects, and the title. For the dome, tape a large circle of clear plastic over the projects. By gum, that's a cute display!

Jo Fryer—Gr. 1
Kildeer Countryside School
Long Grove, IL

Fall is a perfect time to snuggle up with a quilt-making project. Each student creates a fall scene on a white paper plate using paper scraps, glue, and other desired supplies. Mount the projects on colorful squares and display as shown. Use a marker to draw stitches. When winter (spring, summer) rolls around, have each student design a new scene for the quilt. Now that's a year-round display that's easy to get comfortable with!

Linda Parris—Gr. 1, West Hills Elementary, Knoxville, TN

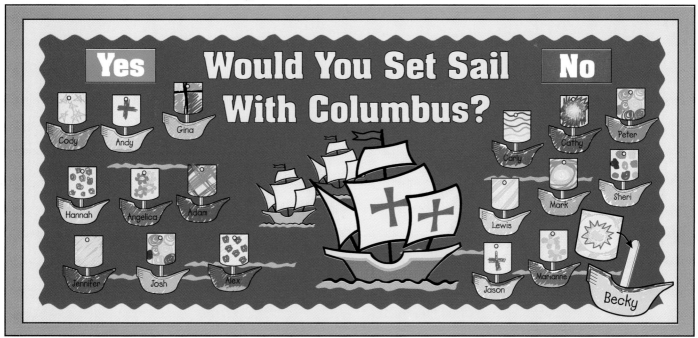

This seaworthy display encourages critical thinking. Prior to investigating the voyages of Columbus, each child colors a ship and sail pattern from page 22, cuts out the patterns, and glues them to opposite ends of a craft stick as shown. Then she uses a pushpin to display her completed project. Revisit the display throughout your study, each time allowing students to keep or change their votes. Encourage plenty of discussion and accept all responses. What a fleet!

Robin Kopecky—Title I Reading Consultant, Lake Louise School, Palatine, IL

There's no monkey business here, just plenty of tasteful suggestions! As students munch on potato chips, lead them in brainstorming ideas for classroom cooperation. Then each child folds a yellow paper rectangle in half and trims away the corners. He writes his name and adds desired potato chip details on the front; then inside he writes his plans for chipping in and cooperating. Mount the projects as shown. Bet ya can't read just one!

Alice Gershon, Kildeer Countryside School, Long Grove, IL

Great gobblers! Have you ever seen such flawless tail feathers? Mount the title and a featherless fowl. Each week, every child who aces the spelling test mounts her paper on a colorful feather cutout. Keep adding these feathers to the bird throughout November and two things are certain to happen: spelling scores will improve, and you'll have a one-of-a-kind gobbler on display!

Gale Kotner—Gr. 2
Southern View Elementary School
Springfield, IL

Light up the holiday season with goodwill wishes! On provided paper, each child writes a wish that will bring happiness to many people. Then he personalizes and cuts out a colorful holiday lightbulb pattern (see page 23) and glues a three-inch square paper base to it. Mount the title and student projects. Use curling ribbon or curled strips of paper to connect the holiday lights. The season definitely looks bright!

Connie Todd—Title I Reading and Math, St. Aloysius Elementary School, East Liverpool, OH

Deck a wall (or hall!) with holiday traditions! Each student illustrates a favorite family tradition from this time of year on a seven-inch square of white paper, glues her illustration on a nine-inch square of black paper, and writes her family name on a 2" x 5" paper strip. Showcase the projects and invite each child to share additional details about her family's tradition with the class. Happy holidays!

Catherine Broome, Melbourne Beach, FL

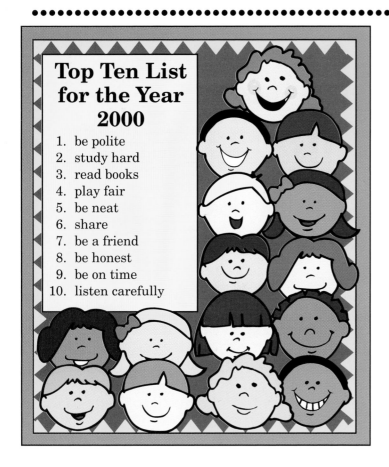

Top Ten List for the Year 2000

1. be polite
2. study hard
3. read books
4. play fair
5. be neat
6. share
7. be a friend
8. be honest
9. be on time
10. listen carefully

Head into the year 2000 with a top ten list of class resolutions! Before holiday break, assist the class in choosing and ranking ten school-related goals for the new year. Write the goals and a desired title on a length of colorful paper. Then provide the supplies that students need to create self-portraits like the ones shown. Mount the projects and top ten list and you're all set to welcome the new year!

adapted from an idea by Nancy R. Poole—Gr. 2
Southland Academy
Americus, GA

Promote creative thinking with a one-of-a-kind winter wonderland! To make a penguin (pattern on page 23), a child completes the sentence starter and signs his name. Then he colors the penguin and cuts it out. Next he fashions winter wear from wallpaper, construction paper, or fabric scraps and glues it on his cutout. Showcase the projects and invite students to ponder the penguins' cool thoughts.

adapted from an idea by Lisa Dorsey—Gr. 2, Garland, TX

LEARNING SCORES!

Spotlight your youngsters' winning plays of the season! A student completes a copy of page 24 and cuts out the football shape. Then he glues his cutout onto a 9" x 12" sheet of brown construction paper and trims the brown paper to create a border. Display the projects as shown. Now that's a midseason game plan guaranteed to boost self-esteem!

Bernadette Hallman—Gr. 3
Annunciation Catholic School
Middleburg, FL

My name is __Allen__
This year I have learned how to write in cursive!
I am also learning how to multiply. I can spell sandwich, Florida, and tackle. I learned that bats are not really blind. I learned that spiders have eight legs. I also learned that Ms. Hallman has a sweet tooth.

Measurement skills live happily ever after at this interactive display! Mount the title, a tower cutout, a likeness of Rapunzel, and a laminated growth chart. Use yellow yarn and tape to make five hair extensions of varying lengths. Display one extension on Monday and secure a hair bow at the top; then add one extension per day. Every day students measure carefully to find out how much Rapunzel's hair has grown. Conclude each day by writing on the growth chart (with wipe-off marker) a class-provided measurement. Next have the students refer to the information on the chart to answer measurement-related questions. To repeat the weeklong activity, wipe off the chart. Then remove the hair extensions and return them to the display in a different order.

Spring Bailey—Gr. 2
Frances Mack Elementary School
Gaston, SC

Measuring Rapunzel's Hair

Growth Chart

Monday   = _10 inches_

Tuesday   = _16 inches_

Wednesday = _____

Thursday   = _____

Friday   = _____

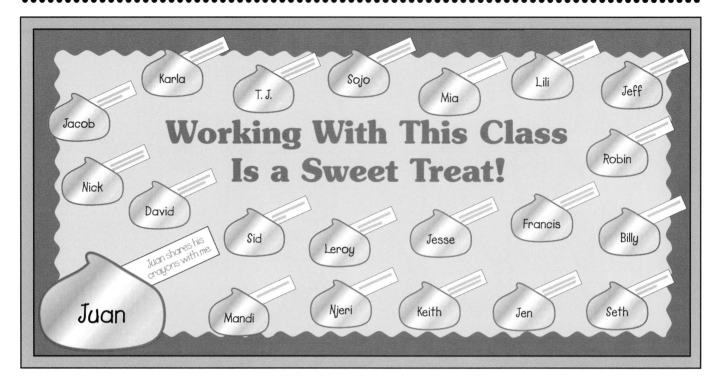

Give students' self-esteem a sweet boost! Have each child write on a paper strip a compliment about a different classmate. Tape each strip to a foil-wrapped candy kiss cutout (pattern on page 25) personalized for that child. Display the projects as shown. Each week ask students to submit compliments for different classmates, and then use them to update the display. February is sure to be a sweet month for all!

Jill Hamilton—Gr. 1, Schoeneck Elementary, Stevens, PA

A love for literature is in the air! Personalize a heart cutout for each child and then mount the hearts as shown. Have each child fold a half-sheet of paper in half, write on the front the title of a book she absolutely loves, write inside why she loves the book, and then illustrate her work. After each child tells the class about the book she loves, tape her project to her personalized heart. Now that's true love!

Sister Maribeth Theis—Gr. 2, Mary of Lourdes Elementary School, Little Falls, MN

When Has a Bit of Luck Come Your Way?

Sarah

I had a lot of luck on the day I found a lost puppy. My dad let me keep her and we are now best friends.

A wee bit of writing motivation quickly creates this eye-catching display! Mount a writing prompt and leprechaun character as shown. Ask each child to write and illustrate a story in response to the prompt. Then exhibit each child's work with a personalized shamrock cutout. And here's a bit of luck for you! Simply update the writing prompt and artwork each month and you have a year-round display.

Tiffany Gosseen—Gr. 1, North Nodaway R-VI Elementary, Hopkins, MO

Camera on the Community

Bea's Bakery
Bea's Bakery is a favorite place in our community. They have the best hot bread. They also sell cookies and cakes. Bea's Bakery has been open since 1966! I hope it never closes.

by Donna

Bring the community into focus at this informative display! Each child writes a brief report about a community landmark and mounts it on construction paper. Then she folds her project in half (keeping the writing inside), tapes a snapshot of the location on the front, and glues a camera cutout (pattern on page 25) over the photo so that the landmark is seen through the lens opening. Mount the picture-perfect projects as shown.

Kathleen Cowin—Gr. 2, Munson Primary School, Mulvane, KS

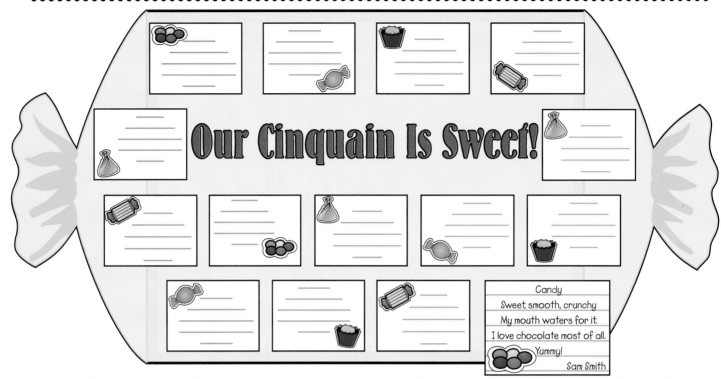

Our Cinquain Is Sweet!

Candy
Sweet, smooth, crunchy
My mouth waters for it.
I love chocolate most of all.
Yummy!
Sam Smith

April, National Poetry Month, is a perfect time to sweeten students' poetry-writing skills! To make the display, attach a paper cutout resembling the end of a wrapped candy to each side of a paper-covered board. Have each child write and publish a candy-related cinquain (or another form of poetry) and showcase the poems as shown. Attach a colorful candy sticker to each one, if desired. Now that's a delicious twist!

Tracy Welsch—Gr. 2, Camp Avenue Elementary School, North Merrick, NY

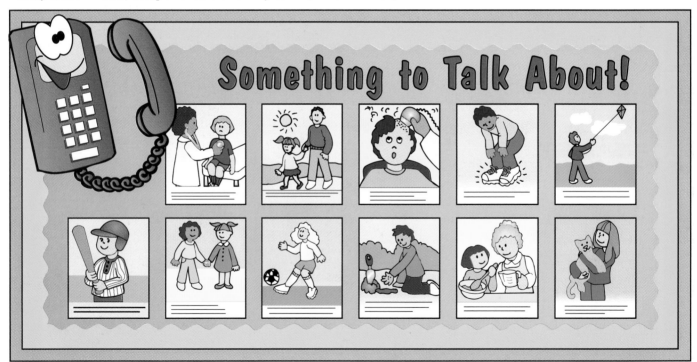

Something to Talk About!

Spotlight your youngsters' weekend experiences at this eye-catching display. Each Monday, every child who has a weekend experience that she'd like to share with the class creates an illustration and a caption about it. Showcase these projects and set aside time for each child to explain her work and provide added details about the pictured event.

Donna L. Hall—Grs. 1–2, Fairview Elementary, St. Louis, MO

16

Our Smiles Really Measure Up!

30 inches = 2 1/2 feet

Student smiles really add up at this math-related display! Working in pairs, each child uses a different piece of red yarn to measure the width of his partner's smile; then he trims the yarn to smile width and presents it to his partner. Next each child uses a ruler to measure his yarn. Total these measurements; then have each child make a self-portrait sporting his red-yarn smile! Display as shown. Cheese!

Cathy T. Howlett—Gr. 3, Franklin Elementary, Mt. Airy, NC

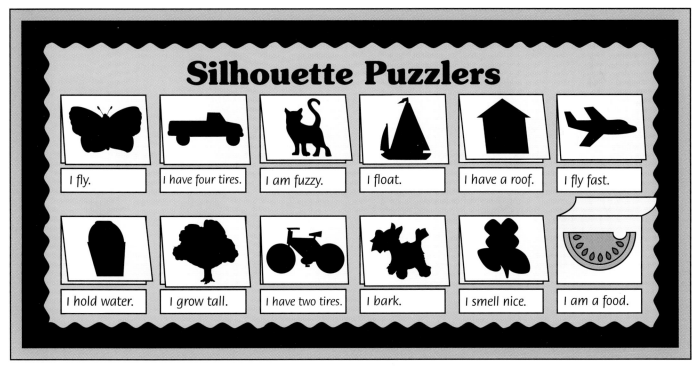

Silhouette Puzzlers

| I fly. | I have four tires. | I am fuzzy. | I float. | I have a roof. | I fly fast. |
| I hold water. | I grow tall. | I have two tires. | I bark. | I smell nice. | I am a food. |

Prompt plenty of creative thinking with shapely silhouettes! Each child cuts a different object from a discarded magazine, traces the cutout on black paper, cuts along the resulting outline, and glues her cutout on folded construction paper as shown. Then she writes a silhouette-related clue on provided paper. The resulting interactive display will be buzzing with creative thoughts!

Jill Hamilton—Gr. 1, Schoeneck Elementary, Stevens, PA

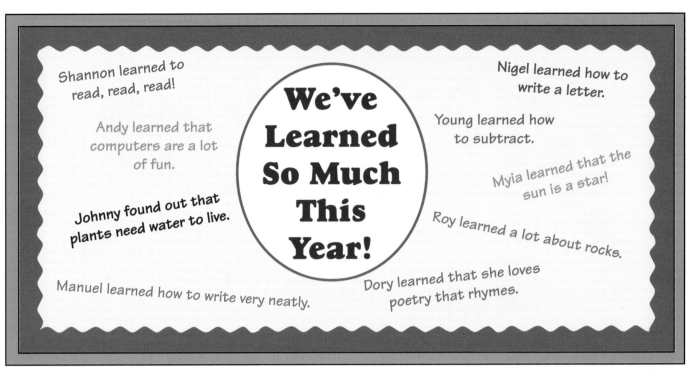

Shannon learned to read, read, read!

Andy learned that computers are a lot of fun.

Johnny found out that plants need water to live.

Manuel learned how to write very neatly.

We've Learned So Much This Year!

Nigel learned how to write a letter.

Young learned how to subtract.

Myia learned that the sun is a star!

Roy learned a lot about rocks.

Dory learned that she loves poetry that rhymes.

This end-of-the-year bulletin board is really smart! Mount the title on a recycled backdrop. Ask each child to tell one thing she learned during the past school year and use a colorful marker to write her comment on the paper. Students will be proud of their accomplishments, and you'll have a colorful display that's easy to remove on the final day of school.

Kari Mart—Gr. 1, LaMoure School, LaMoure, ND

Create a stir with this cool 3-D reading display! For every child, cover an empty tissue box with white paper. On each of three sides of his resulting ice cube, a student writes the title of a favorite book and illustrates a scene from it. Mount the projects as shown. Now that's a refreshing way for youngsters to share their favorite literature!

Julia Brown—Gr. 3
Forest City Elementary
Forest City, NC

READING IS COOL!

Splish, splash, summer's almost here! For this display a child describes on paper an activity she hopes to enjoy this summer. She trims her paper into a speech bubble. Then she colors a copy of the inner tube pattern on page 26 and cuts it out. Next, she uses art supplies to fashion a self-likeness from her waist up and glues it to the inner tube as shown. Showcase each child's projects together.

Catherine Broome—Gr. 1, Melbourne, FL

Keep the entire class on course by putting each student in the driver's seat! A child adds his name and self-likeness to a car pattern (page 26); then he colors the pattern and cuts it out. Next, he writes (on a precut construction paper shape) one thing he expects to learn in school the following year. Display the projects as shown. Vroom!

Trina Taylor—Gr. 2, High Point Elementary, Cedar Hill, TX

Patterns

Use the key pattern to use with "We Are the Key…" on page 6.

Use the car pattern with "Bumper-to-Bumper
Facts" on page 7.

Use the bone pattern with "Get Your Paws…" on page 7.

Title _____

Author _____

This book was   GREAT   GOOD   FAIR   OK

I think you SHOULD/SHOULD NOT read this book because _____

_____

_____

_____

Book reviewed by _____

Use the bee pattern with "Always 'Bee' a Friend!"
on page 8.

Friendship Honey

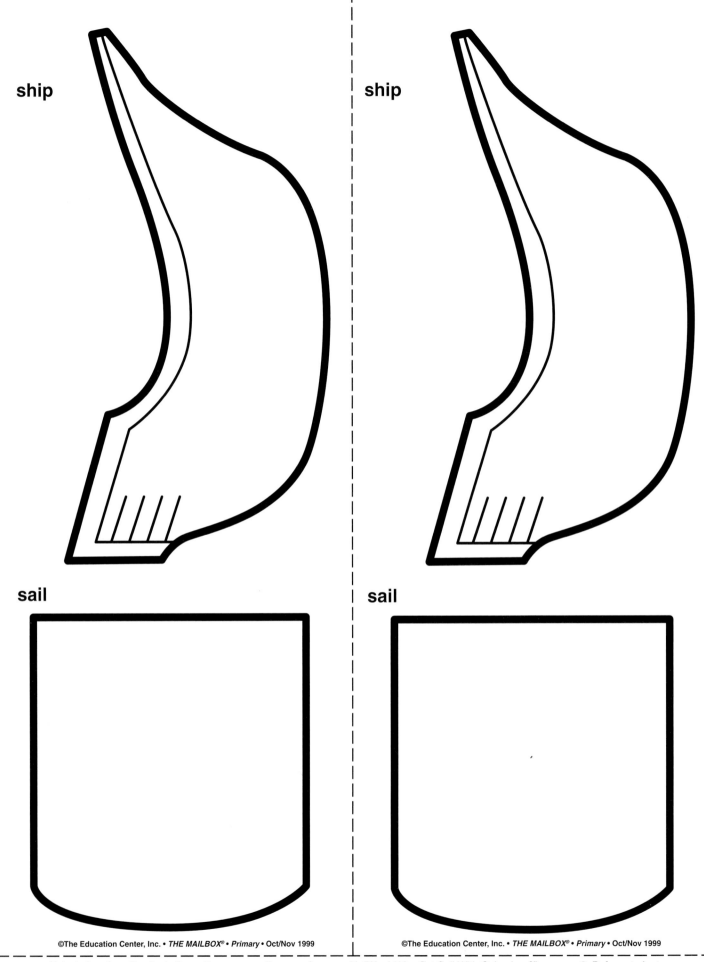

ship

ship

sail

sail

Note to teacher: Duplicate the patterns on manila paper for use with "Would You Set Sail With Columbus?" on page 9. Before students begin, tell them that during the time of Columbus, ship sails were brownish in color (because they were woven from flax) and often decorated with crosses and symbols. The parts of a ship above the waterline were usually painted bright colors.

Patterns

Use the holiday lightbulb with "Bright Wishes for the Holiday Season" on page 11.

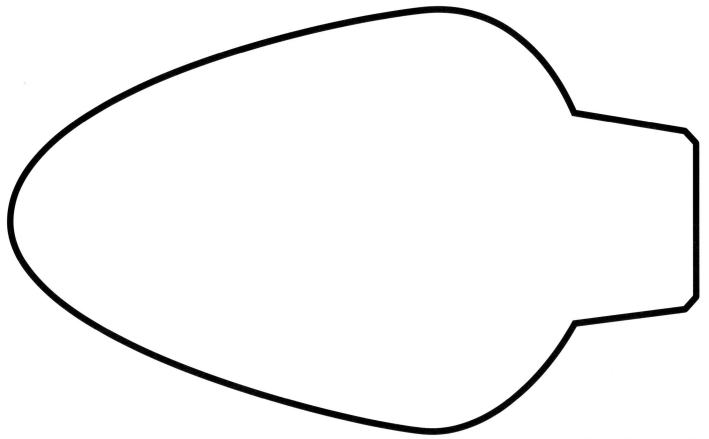

Use the penguin with "Our Winter WONDERland" on page 12.

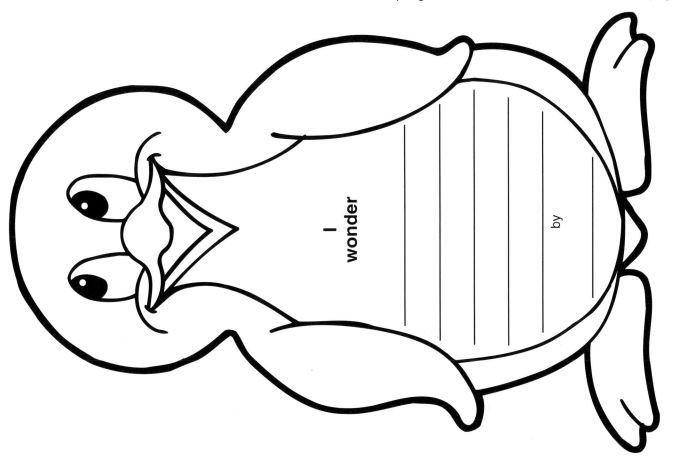

I wonder

by

Patterns

Use with "Learning Scores!"
on page 13.

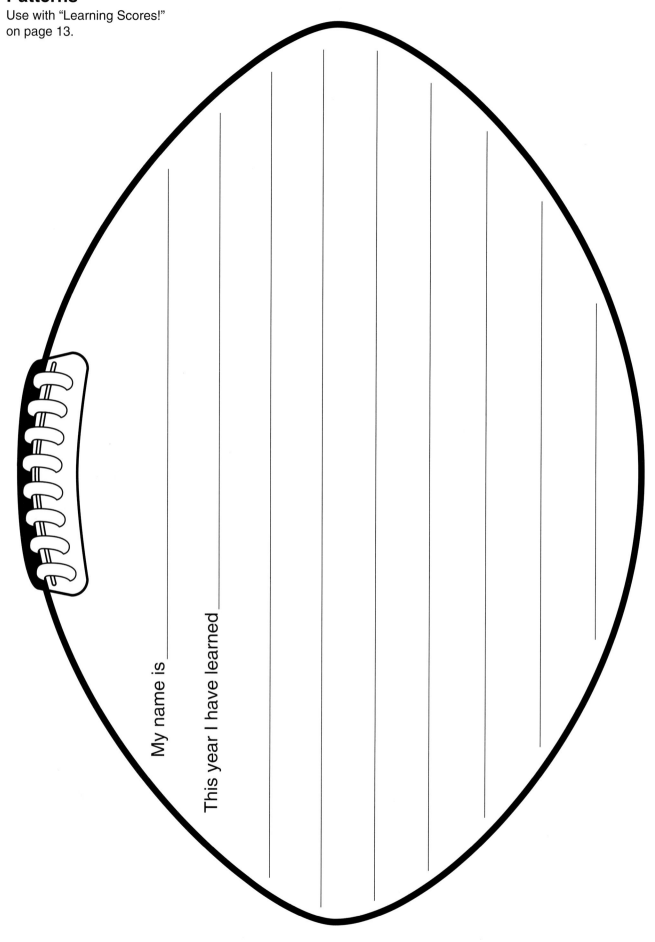

My name is _____

This year I have learned _____

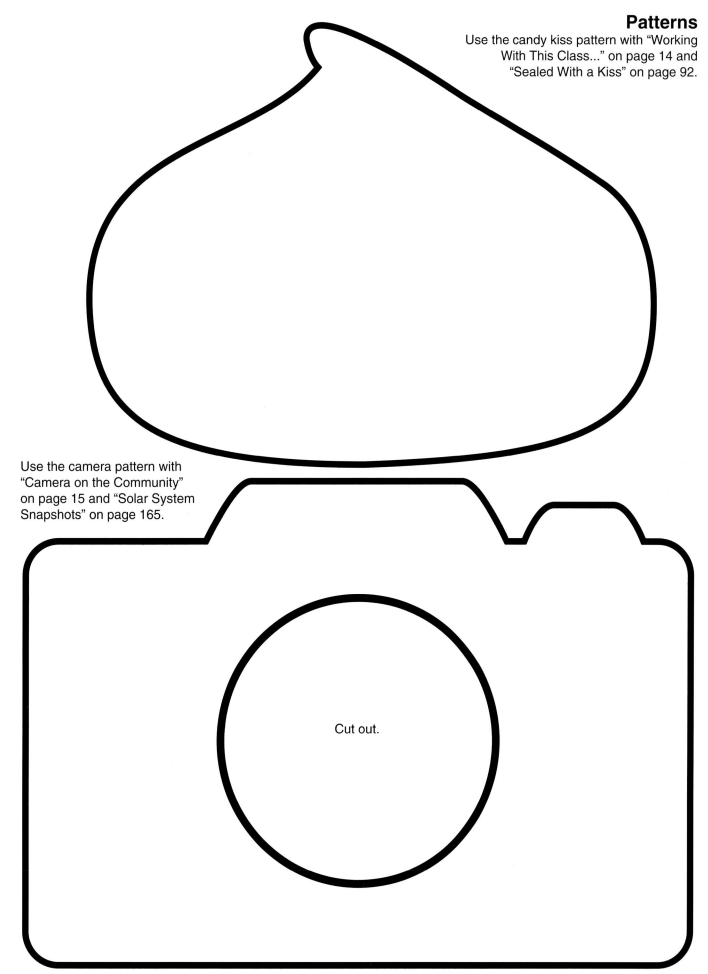

Patterns
Use the candy kiss pattern with "Working With This Class..." on page 14 and "Sealed With a Kiss" on page 92.

Use the camera pattern with "Camera on the Community" on page 15 and "Solar System Snapshots" on page 165.

Cut out.

Patterns

Use the inner tube pattern with " 'Water' We Doing This Summer?" on page 19.

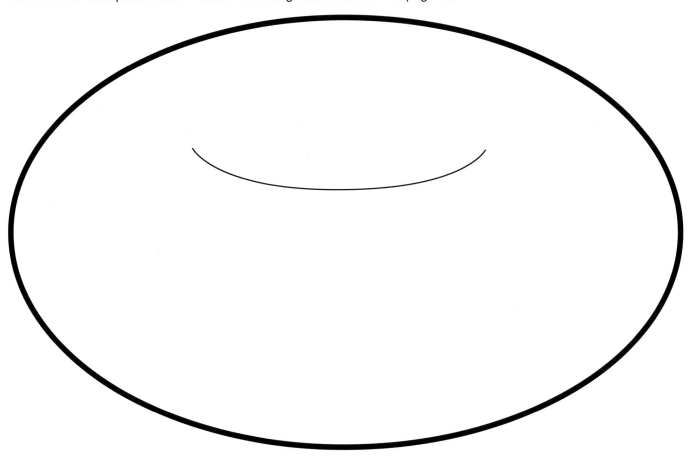

Use the car pattern with "On the Road to Third Grade!" on page 19.

LEARNING CENTERS

Learning Centers

Pipe Cleaner Spelling

Add a fun twist to spelling practice at this hands-on center! Cut a supply of pipe cleaners into half and quarter lengths. Store the pipe cleaner pieces in a resealable plastic bag. Place the bag and the spelling list for the week at a center. A student reads the first word on the list, turns the list over, and shapes pipe cleaner pieces into the letters needed to spell the word. Next he checks his spelling against the word list and makes any needed corrections. He then straightens the pipe cleaner pieces and repeats the activity for each of the remaining words on the list. When test time rolls around, students are sure to have a good feel for their spelling words!

Amy Ekmark—Gr. 1, Eastside Elementary, Lancaster, CA

Pocket Change

This versatile center activity is a great investment in your youngsters' money-counting skills. Glue several construction paper pocket cutouts onto a sheet of tagboard titled "Pocket Change." Number the pockets and then laminate the poster for durability. Use Sticky-Tac or tape to attach a desired combination of paper or punch-out coins to each pocket. Program an answer key and then place the poster, answer key, and a supply of blank paper at a center. A student numbers her paper and writes how much change is in the corresponding pocket.

To reprogram the activity, modify the coin combination on each pocket and provide a corresponding answer key. Now that's a "cent-sational" center!

Sherrie Rippy, Van Duyn Elementary, Clinton, IN

Top Ten Favorites

Here's a center that's sure to make your students' top ten list of writing activities! On each of several cards, write a different category, such as games, foods, books, and outdoor activities. Place the cards at a center along with pencils and a supply of writing paper. A student chooses a category card, titles his paper "[Student's name]'s Top Ten [category]," and lists his ten favorites for that category. Invite students to write top ten lists for as many categories as time allows. Later, sort the lists by categories and compile each collection into a class book for your youngsters' reading enjoyment.

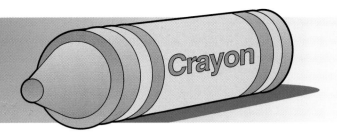

Word Family Houses

Students will feel right at home with this word family (rime) activity. To review three rimes, gather three empty cube-shaped tissue boxes. Cover the sides of each box with colorful paper, then decorate the box to resemble a house. Label each house with a different rime. Cut out pictures that represent the rimes from discarded workbooks and magazines. Glue each cutout onto a small card. On the back of each card, write the corresponding word with the rime underlined. Laminate the cards and store them in a resealable plastic bag. Place the bag and the houses at a center. A student sorts the cards into the houses by naming each picture and identifying its rime. To check her work, she removes the cards from the house and verifies that the rime underlined on the back of each card is on the house.

Patty Scranton, Tallahassee, FL

Caterpillar Count

Watch skip-counting skills grow right along with these cute caterpillars! To make a caterpillar for skip-counting, cut away the lid of an egg carton, then cut apart the individual egg cups. Turn each cup over. Decorate one to resemble a caterpillar head and program the remaining cups for skip counting. (Set aside or add extra egg cups as needed.) For self-checking, number the inside of the programmed cups in order (1, 2, 3, ...). Store the cups for each caterpillar in a labeled container or color-code each caterpillar. Working from left to right, a student arranges each set of cups in sequential order, starting with the caterpillar's head. To check his work, he inverts the caterpillar.

Nancy Y. Karpyk—Gr. 2, Broadview Elementary, Weirton, WV

An Orderly Lineup

Students who hang out at this center reinforce sequencing skills. Suspend a clothesline (heavy string or lightweight cord) in a convenient and safe classroom location. Cut out several clothing shapes from construction paper and laminate them for reprogramming. Use a wipe-off marker to label the cutouts for a sequencing activity like ABC order, number sequencing, or story order. Program the backs of the cutouts for self-checking. Store the cutouts in a laundry basket. Place this basket and a container of clothespins near the clothesline. A student clips the clothing items to the clothesline in sequential order, then checks the back of each cutout to verify her work. To reprogram the center, wash away the programming!

Ida Koll—Grs. 1–4 Resource Teacher, Shadycrest Elementary, Pearland, TX

Learning Centers

Odd or Even?

Sorting even and odd numbers at this center creates a spectacular display of fall foliage! Cut two large tree trunks with plenty of branches from brown tagboard. Label the cutouts "Even" and "Odd." Duplicate leaf patterns on red, orange, and yellow construction paper. Program each leaf with an even or odd number. Laminate and cut out the leaves. For self-checking, use a permanent marker to draw a triangle on the back of each odd-numbered leaf. Store the leaves in a resealable plastic bag. Place the bag and the trees at a center. A student sorts the leaves onto the trees and then he flips each set of leaves to check his work.

Katy Flesher, Chesterland, OH

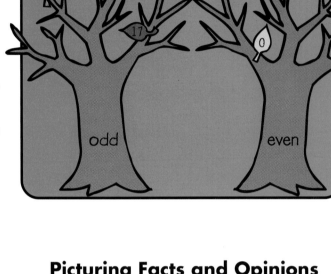

Picturing Facts and Opinions

Students report facts and opinions at this picture-perfect activity. Place scissors, a ruler, glue, pencils, discarded catalogs and magazines, and a supply of drawing paper at a center. A student cuts out a desired picture and glues it near the top of her paper. Below the picture she draws two columns and labels them "Facts" and "Opinions." Next she studies the picture and lists five facts and five opinions about it. If desired, ask each child to confirm with a classmate that her facts are facts and her opinions are opinions before she submits her work. The end result is a much clearer understanding of fact and opinion!

Joyce Hovanec, Glassport Elementary, Glassport, PA

Number Spin-Off

Here's a partner game that takes students' counting skills for a spin! Cut apart a duplicated hundreds chart and mount it on poster board as shown. Also visually divide a tagboard circle into five sections and number them 1 to 5. Laminate the resulting gameboard and spinner wheel. Snap a loose spinner in the center of the spinner wheel; then place the assembled spinner, the gameboard, and two game markers at a center. To play, the partners place their game markers on "1." Then, in turn, each child spins the spinner, moves (in numerical order) the corresponding number of spaces, and reads aloud the number he lands on. The first partner to reach 100 wins!

Kim Wachtel—Gr. 1, Sacandaga Elementary School, Scotia, NY

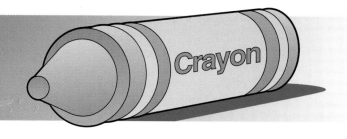

Sharon S.

An elequack is really cool because it has a long trunk like an elephant and it has feathers like a duck. It can quack, too! It also has wings. It can fly, swim, and run.

Invent an Animal

This creative-writing center is heads and tails above the rest! For each child, place a few Cheez-It® Heads and Tails™ Baked Cheese Crackers in a resealable plastic bag. Place the bags, story paper, pencils, and crayons or markers at a center. A student opens a bag of crackers and makes wacky animals by mismatching the head and tail crackers. She selects her favorite wacky critter and names it. Then she writes the critter's name on her paper and pens a story about the animal that describes several of its unique abilities. Finally she illustrates the animal in its natural habitat. When her work is done, she eats her crackers!

Leann Schwartz—Gr. 2, Ossian Elementary, Ossian, IN

Opposites Attract

Attract plenty of student interest at this antonym center! Cut out several construction paper bar- and horseshoe-shaped magnets. Add desired details to the cutouts and then glue them to a sheet of poster board titled "Opposites Attract." Attach a small piece of magnetic tape to each magnet pole and write one word of a different antonym pair near the tape. Write the remaining word in each pair on an individual card. Glue a paper clip to the back of each word card and create an answer key for self-checking. Store the cards, the poster, and the answer key at a center. A student attaches each card to its antonym. Then he uses the answer key to check his work.

Alice Fredley, Northumberland Elementary, Heathsville, VA

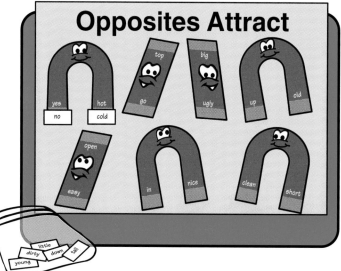

And the Time Is...

Time keeps on ticking at this math and writing center! Cut out a supply of individual comic strip frames that portray a variety of times. Store the frames at a center along with pencils, crayons, glue, 9" x 12" sheets of colorful construction paper, and student copies of page 40. A student chooses a comic strip frame and glues it in the center of a horizontally positioned sheet of construction paper. After she determines when the illustrated event might have occurred, she completes a copy of page 40. Then she glues her completed work to the back of her construction paper.

To make a kid-pleasing class book, stack the students' work so the comic strip frames are faceup. Bind the pages between tagboard covers and title it "And the Time Is…" Place the book in the class library for hours of reading enjoyment.

Rosetta M. Sanders—Gr. 2, Zervas School, Newton, MA

Learning Centers

Holiday Cookies

Create a taste for math fact practice with cookie cutouts! Use the patterns on page 41 to duplicate holiday cookie shapes on construction paper. Label each shape with a different math fact, laminate the shapes, and then cut them out. Use a permanent marker to program the backs of the cutouts for self-checking. Store the cookies in a holiday tin and place the tin and a cookie sheet at a center. A student arranges the cookies on the cookie sheet fact side up. Then she picks up each one, answers the fact, and turns it over to verify her answer. If her answer is correct, she puts the cookie in the tin. If it is not, she returns the cookie to the sheet. When all the cookies are in the tin, her work is complete!

Kathy Balzer, Potwin, KS

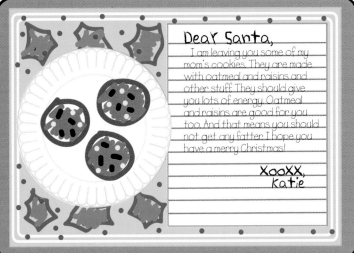

Snacks for Santa

Ho! Ho! Ho! This writing center is perfect for the holiday season! Stock a center with small paper plates, 5" x 8" rectangles of writing paper, 9" x 12" sheets of construction paper, pencils, crayons, and glue. In the middle of a paper plate, a student illustrates what she thinks is the perfect snack for Santa. Then she writes Santa a note that explains why she chose this snack for him. Next she decorates a sheet of construction paper to resemble a holiday placemat and glues her snack and note on it. Showcase the completed projects on a bulletin board titled "Snacks for Santa."

Amy Ekmark—Gr. 1, Eastside Elementary, Lancaster, CA

Stocking Stuffers

Students consult a dictionary to determine if the items named at this center are appropriate stocking stuffers. Number ten cards and label each one with the name of an object that appears in a student dictionary and may be unfamiliar to students. Create an answer key for self-checking and tuck it inside a holiday stocking. Suspend the stocking at a center and place the cards, writing paper, pencils, and a student dictionary there. A student numbers his paper and looks up each word in the dictionary. If the object will fit in the suspended stocking, he writes "yes" on his paper. If it will not, he writes "no." Then he checks his work against the answer key. To reprogram the center, replace the set of word cards and provide a corresponding answer key. Happy holidays!

adapted from an idea by Mary Jane Farrar—Gr. 1
Viscount Montgomery Public School
Hamilton, Ontario, Canada

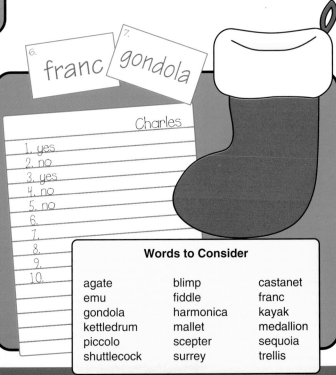

Words to Consider

agate	blimp	castanet
emu	fiddle	franc
gondola	harmonica	kayak
kettledrum	mallet	medallion
piccolo	scepter	sequoia
shuttlecock	surrey	trellis

New Year Headgear

At this seasonal center students fashion festive headgear suitable for any New Year's celebration! Make a class supply of the 2000 pattern on page 41 on white construction paper. Also cut a class supply of two-inch-wide tagboard strips to be used as headbands. Place the supplies at a center along with scissors, markers, and glue. A student colors a 2000 pattern, cuts it out, and glues it in the middle of a headband. After he decorates the headband, he flips the project over and writes his secret wish for the new year on the back. Size each child's project to his head and then staple the ends of the headband together. Now students can head into the new year in style!

Leslie C. Morin, West Hartford, CT

I wish to be a better soccer player.

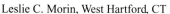

Mitten Matchup

Warm up your youngsters' matching skills with a handful of mittens! Use the small mitten patterns from page 240 to make an even number of colorful construction-paper mittens. Program every two mittens with a pair of rhyming words (antonyms, synonyms, etc.). Laminate the mitten patterns for durability and then cut them out. For self-checking, use a permanent marker to draw the same symbol on the back of each mitten in a matched pair. Store the cutouts and a supply of clothespins at a center. A student finds a match for each mitten and clips the pair together with a clothespin. To check her work, she flips the mitten pairs.

Amy Ekmark—Gr. 1, Eastside Elementary, Lancaster, CA

By the Number

Number order is key at this fact-finding center. Write each of five factual sentences on a different-colored sentence strip. Carefully cut each sentence strip into individual word cards, without changing the word order. Then turn over each set of cards and write a series of numbers ordered from smallest to largest. Store all the cards in a resealable plastic bag at a center. A student sorts the cards by color, number side up. To discover each fact, he sequences each set of numbers and then flips the cards. If a fact is not revealed, he rechecks the number order. Sequencing numbers can be very enlightening—and that's a fact!

Spring Bailey—Gr. 2, Gaston, SC

86	99	121	135	250	416
Polar	bear	cubs	are	born	blind.

33

Learning Centers

A.
5 + 3 = 8
3 + 5 = 8
8 − 5 = 3
8 − 3 = 5

B.
1 + 4 = 5
4 + 1 = 5
5 − 1 = 4
5 − 4 = 1

C.
6 + 2 = 8
2 + 6 = 8
8 − 2 = 6
8 − 6 = 2

D.
2 + 3 = 5
3 + 2 = 5
5 − 2 = 3
5 − 3 = 2

Fact-Family Fun

Now you can deliver fact-family practice at a moment's notice! Place a container of dominoes, drawing paper, and pencils at a center. A student folds a sheet of paper in half twice, unfolds the paper, and letters the four resulting boxes from A to D. To complete each box, he selects and illustrates a domino. He writes the two numbers from the domino as an addition fact and supplies the answer. Then he writes the three remaining number sentences in this fact family. Now that adds up to a whole lot of family fun!

Trudy White—Gr. 2
Mayflower Elementary
Mayflower, AR

Sweet Talk

This center gets to the heart of quotation marks! Stock a center with candy conversation hearts, heart-shaped writing paper, glue, pencils, scissors, pink construction paper, and red crayons. A student selects a candy heart and then she writes and punctuates a spoken sentence on her paper that incorporates the candy heart. After she carefully punctuates the sentence, she traces each punctuation mark with red crayon. Next she glues her work onto pink paper and trims the paper to create a narrow border. Students will ask to repeat this activity in a heartbeat!

Debra S. Sietsema—Gr. 2
Allendale Public Elementary School
Allendale, MI

Presidential Pie

Researching George Washington is as easy as pie at this center! Provide nonfiction books about Washington along with a two-inch circle template, glue, scissors, crayons or markers, and the following construction paper: 2" x 9" gray, 6" x 9" red, 9" x 12" yellow. A student traces five or more circles on red paper, writes a fact about Washington in each one, and then cuts out the shapes. He trims a strip of gray paper into a pie pan shape and colors a pie crust on it. Then he glues the cutouts on yellow paper as shown and adds desired details and a title. Or ask each child to contribute one cherry-shaped fact to a class pie pan that is displayed on a bulletin board at the center. Isn't research delicious?

Kristi Wood—Gr. 1
Woodridge Elementary
Stone Mountain, GA

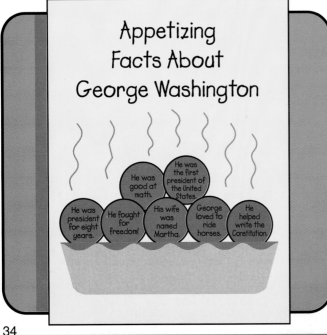

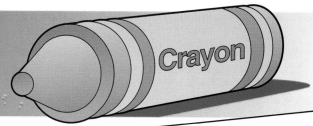

Grading the Teacher

Spark an interest in writing with a high-interest writing topic—*you!* Prepare several sentence starters that solicit opinions about your teaching. Place the writing prompts and a supply of writing paper at a center. A student copies and completes each sentence starter on his paper. Invite students to complete the center anonymously, if desired. You'll learn plenty about your youngsters' writing and your teaching!

Julie Simpson—Gr. 2
Cherry School
Toledo, OH

I like it when Miss Simpson...

I learn best when Miss Simpson...

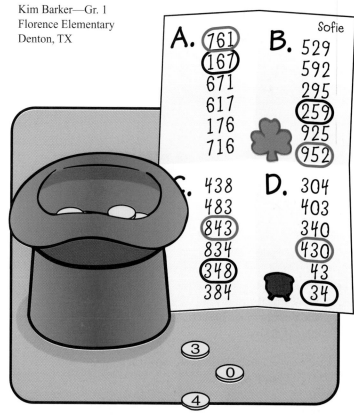

Compound

online   breakout   into

COUNTDOWN   overweight

Storytelling

notebook

OUTDOOR   within

everyday   Football

Collection

Word Collages

When it's time to assess your students' understanding of compound words, contractions, or specific parts of speech, try this! Stock a center with construction paper, scissors, glue, crayons, and discarded magazines and newspapers. Post a word hunt challenge such as "Can you collect ten or more compound words for a word collage?" To make his collage, a child cuts out examples of ten or more compound words and glues them on construction paper. Then he titles his work. Students enjoy the activity and you get a clear picture of each child's knowledge.

Kim Barker—Gr. 1
Florence Elementary
Denton, TX

Hats Off to Place Value

The luck of the Irish isn't needed at this math center, only a knowledge of numbers! Place ten coin-size tagboard circles numbered from 0 to 9 in an inverted leprechaun's hat. Display the container, blank paper, pencils, and crayons at a center. A student folds a sheet of paper in half two times, unfolds the paper, and letters the resulting boxes from A to D. To complete each box, she removes three coins from the container and uses them to make six different numbers. She writes each number in the box. Next she draws a green circle around the largest number and a black circle around the smallest number. Then she returns the coins to the container and draws three more. When her page is complete, she studies the numbers she's written before she draws a large green shamrock by the largest one and a black pot by the smallest one.

adapted from an idea by Christina Tschida
Greensboro, NC

Learning Centers

Egg Carton Multiplication

Do your students need "eggs-tra" practice with multiplication facts? Try this! Number 12 sticky dots with desired factors and press one sticky dot into each egg cup of an egg carton. Place the prepared carton, two pom-poms, paper, and pencils at a center. A student drops the pom-poms inside the egg carton, closes the lid, and gently shakes the carton. Then she opens the carton and on her paper writes (in the form of a multiplication problem) the factors where the pom-poms landed. Then she solves the fact, closes the carton, and repeats the activity until she's written and answered a designated number of facts.

adapted from an idea by Amy Barsanti—Gr. 3
Pines Elementary School
Plymouth, NC

ABC Egg Basket

Hatch plenty of alphabetical order practice at this seasonal center. Tuck cellophane grass and six different-colored plastic eggs in a basket. For each egg, label four color-coded construction paper cards (e.g., purple cards for a purple egg) with different words to alphabetize. Store each card set in its corresponding egg. Place the basket of eggs, paper, and pencils at a center. A student selects an egg and writes its color on her paper. Next she cracks open the egg, arranges the cards in ABC order, and copies the alphabetized words. Then she returns the cards to the egg, and the egg to the basket. Provide an answer key for self-checking, if desired.

adapted from an idea by Dawn Schroeder—Gr. 1
Kluckhohn Elementary
LeMars, IA

Hot off the Press

Publishing stories is in the cards at this writing center. Stock the center with index cards, markers, pencils, and clear tape. A student lays two index cards side by side, making sure the left-hand card shows lines and the right-hand card does not. Then he tapes the two cards together. Next he flips the left-hand card on top of the right-hand card and titles and decorates the resulting book cover. He opens the book, writes on the lined card, and illustrates the blank card. Then he flips the illustrated card, tapes a blank card to the right of the lined card, and continues writing and illustrating his tale. He continues in this manner until his tale is told!

Amy Emmons—Grs. K–3
Enon Elementary
Franklinton, LA

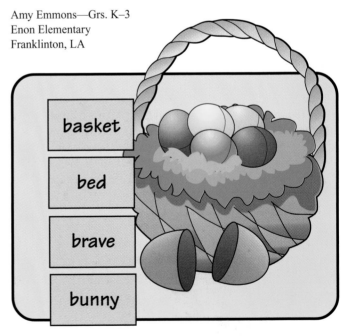

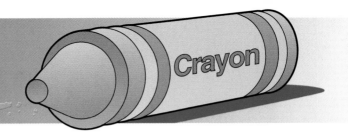

Right on the Money

Three little piggies can provide a wealth of money-counting practice! Use the pattern on page 42 to make three pink construction paper pigs. Write a different price on each pig; then cut out the patterns. Place the cutouts, a stamp pad, a set of coin stamps, pencils, and blank paper at a center. A student writes the price of one pig on his paper and then he stamps three (or more) different coin combinations that equal the price on the pig. He repeats the process for each remaining pig. Oink!

Jill Hamilton—Gr. 1
Schoeneck Elementary
Stevens, PA

Verb Garden

Sprout a review of verbs at this springtime center! Place colorful construction paper, green paper stems, markers or crayons, scissors, and glue at a center along with tagboard templates for a petal and a leaf (see page 42) and a seven-inch circle. Using the provided templates, a child traces one circle, two leaf shapes, and several petal shapes on construction paper. She cuts along the resulting outlines and then she uses the cutouts, a paper stem, and glue to make a flower. When the glue is dry, she writes a noun in the flower center. On each petal she writes a different action verb the noun can do. (Challenge older students to also label each leaf with an adverb that modifies a featured verb.) Post the students' work at the center. The following week have students use the resulting verb garden as inspiration for a writing activity.

Julie Decker—Gr. 3
Abbotsford Elementary
Abbotsford, WI

Picturing a Prefix

Students will want to return to this vocabulary center again and again! Label individual cards with different words containing the prefix *re*. Place the cards, a dictionary, paper, pencils, glue, and crayons or markers at a center. A student selects a word card and glues it to the top of a sheet of paper. On the paper he writes a brief definition of the word and then he writes and illustrates a sentence that features it. Display students' work at the center and the meaning of the prefix *re* is sure to become perfectly clear!

Sue Lorey
Arlington Heights, IL

Learning Centers

Picture-Perfect Memories

Use the photos you've taken during the school year at this writing center! Place the snapshots, pencils, crayons or markers, clear tape, a stapler, and half sheets of writing and construction paper at a center. A student selects a photo, describes her memory of the pictured event on writing paper, and staples her writing between two pieces of construction paper. Then she tapes the photo to the front cover and adds a title, her name, and other desired decorations. Now that's a picture-perfect memory!

Alyce Pearl Smith—Gr. 1
Butzbach Elementary
Butzbach, Germany

Fishing for Fractions

Reel in plenty of fraction practice at this tasty math center! In a clean container, mix a six-ounce package of cheddar fish-shaped crackers with similarly sized packages of pretzel and pizza fish-shaped crackers. Make a cracker code like the one shown. Then place the code, the container of crackers, napkins, a $\frac{1}{4}$-cup measurer, pencils, and student copies of page 43 at a center. A student places one-quarter cup of crackers on an unfolded napkin. Next he sorts the crackers and completes the reproducible activity. When his work is finished, he eats his catch!

Melanie J. Miller
Nashport, OH

Cracker Code
- Cheddar
- Pizza
- Pretzel

Sentence Structure Delivery

Here's a delivery that reviews sentence structure and rock-related facts! Cut 25 rock shapes from gray paper. Write "1" near the top of five cutouts and then write each word in Fact 1 (see "Rock Facts") on one of these cutouts. Prepare the remaining facts in a similar manner. Laminate the cutouts for durability; then cut them out and store them in a toy dump truck. Place the truck, writing paper, pencils, and an answer key at a center. A student unloads the paper rocks and sorts them by number. Next, she arranges the rocks in each set to make a fact sentence and copies the sentence on her paper. When she has written all five facts, she uses the answer key to check her work.

adapted from an idea by Sarah Mertz—Grs. 1–2, Owenton, KY

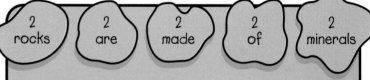

2 rocks 2 are 2 made 2 of 2 minerals

1. Rocks are everywhere on earth.
2. Rocks are

Rock Facts
1. Rocks are everywhere on earth.
2. Rocks are made of minerals.
3. A diamond is a very hard rock.
4. Some rocks are soft.
5. Many people collect rocks.

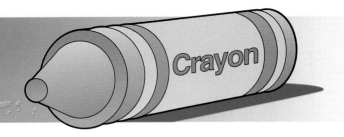

Lily Pad Problems

Careful computation is key at this froggie math center! Cut two large lily pad shapes from green paper and label them "Correct" and "Incorrect." Sequentially letter ten frog shapes (patterns on page 44); then write a different math problem on each one. Solve five of the problems correctly and five incorrectly. Create an answer key for the incorrect problems; then laminate all components for durability and cut them out. Store the frogs in a zipper bag. Place the bag, the lily pads, the answer key, a supply of paper, and pencils at a center. A student copies each problem on his paper, answers it, and sorts the corresponding frog onto the appropriate lily pad. Then he uses the answer key to check his work. Ribbit!

Patricia E. Moran
South Bend, IN

Pairs of Pears

Take this fresh approach to reviewing homophones! Use the patterns on page 44 to make ten pear shapes. Program every two pears with a pair of homophones. Laminate the shapes for durability and cut them out. Use a permanent marker to program each pair for self-checking. Store the cutouts at a center along with pencils, crayons, and a supply of paper. A student finds a match for each pear; then she flips the cutouts to verify her work. Next she copies each homophone pair on her paper and writes a sentence that includes the homophones (or forms of them).

Amy Barsanti—Gr. 3
Pines Elementary
Roper, NC

Keepsake Quilt Patches

The focus of this art center is favorite memories from the school year! Place 9-inch squares of drawing paper and 12-inch squares of colorful construction paper at a center along with crayons, a black marker, and glue. A student folds a square of drawing paper in half twice; then he unfolds the paper and draws and labels four favorite memories—one in each section. He mounts his artwork on construction paper and uses the black marker to write his name near the bottom of his resulting quilt patch. If desired, display the completed projects as a class quilt. Then send each child home with his keepsake on the last day of the school year.

adapted from an idea by Shirley Freeland—Gr. 3
Jefferson Parkway Elementary
Newnan, GA

40

Got the Time?

Think about the event pictured in the cartoon.
Write the time the event happened on the clock and in the speech bubble.
Write a story about the event.

Note to teacher: Use with "And the Time Is…" on page 31.

Patterns

Use seasonal shapes with
"Holiday Cookies" on page 32.

Use number pattern with "New Year
Headgear" on page 33.

Patterns   Use the pig pattern with "Saving Energy" on page 210 and "Right on the Money" on page 37.

Use the petal and leaf patterns with "Verb Garden" on page 37.

petal

leaf

Name ____________________

What a Catch!

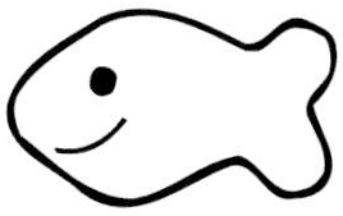

Sort your catch of fish crackers.
Write a number to answer each question.

1. How many crackers in your catch are pizza? ________
2. How many crackers in your catch are cheddar? ________
3. How many crackers in your catch are pretzel? ________
4. How many crackers did you catch in all? ________

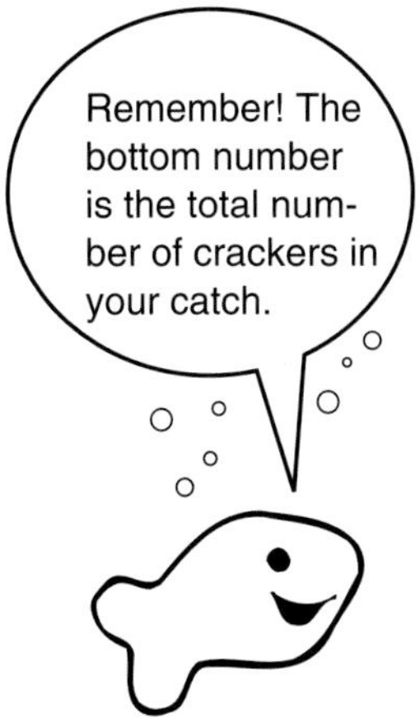

Remember! The bottom number is the total number of crackers in your catch.

Use the information above.
Write a fraction to answer each question.

5. What part of your catch is pizza?
6. What part of your catch is cheddar?
7. What part of your catch is pretzel?

The top number describes a part of the crackers.

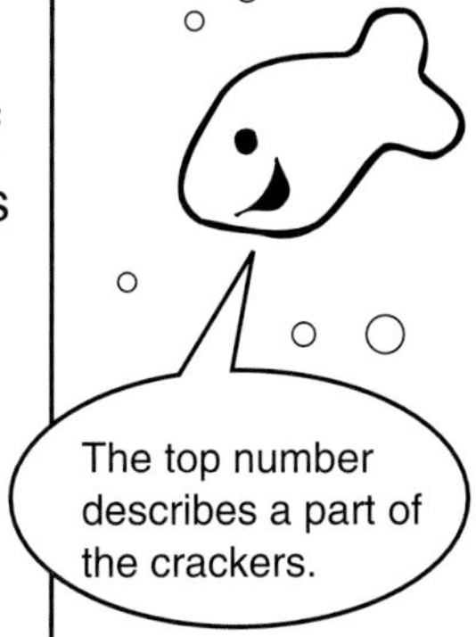

On the lines, write a comparative sentence about each cracker.
(For example: I have more pizza crackers than pretzel crackers.)

8. Pizza: ____________________
9. Cheddar: ____________________
10. Pretzel: ____________________

For Fraction Experts Only!

Write a fraction to answer each question.

11. What part of your catch is pizza and cheddar?
12. What part of your catch is pretzel and pizza?
13. What part of your catch is cheddar and pretzel?
14. What part of your catch is not cheddar?

Note to teacher: Use with “Fishing for Fractions” on page 38.

Patterns

Use the frog patterns with "Lily Pad Problems" on page 39.

Use the pear patterns with "Pairs of Pears" on page 39.

Arts & Crafts

Arts & Crafts

Me Monuments

With a pinch here and a pat there, students can create monuments spotlighting themselves. Give each child a sheet of waxed paper and two golf ball–sized portions of Crayola® Model Magic® (nontoxic, air-drying modeling compound). Or prepare your favorite paintable, air-drying dough recipe. Working atop his waxed paper, a child forms a shape from one ball of dough that represents a favorite interest or hobby. With the remaining ball of dough, he forms a base for his shape. Then he molds the shape to the base. When his resulting monument is dry, he paints it as desired. Lastly, he folds an index card in half and writes his name and a description of his monument on the front. Group your students' monuments and description cards together for a display that's sure to attract plenty of attention during open house!

Kathy Moore—Gr. 3
Stone Creek Elementary School
Rockford, IL

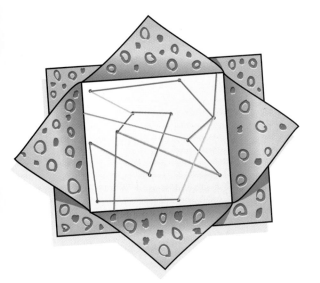

Abstract Artwork

Encourage oodles of creativity with this impressive project. Use a pencil to make several dots on an 8" x 10" sheet of white paper; then use a ruler and colorful markers or crayons to connect the dots. To make a frame for the design, center a 7" x 8" template atop a 9" x 12" sheet of colorful construction paper. Trace around the template; then draw two intersecting diagonal lines in the resulting rectangle. Carefully cut along the diagonal lines and fold back the flaps along the remaining lines. Tape the design to the back of the frame so the artwork is viewed through the opening and then decorate the frame as desired. Each piece of abstract artwork will be unique!

Rita Arnold—Grs. 2–5
Alden Hebron School
Hebron, IL

Sunny Pencil Boxes

Spread some sunshine and minimize messy desks with these eye-catching pencil holders!

Materials for one pencil box:

the bottom 2 1/2" of a cereal box
strips of green poster board, 2 1/2" wide
   (to cover the sides of the precut box)
one 7" yellow construction paper semicircle
one 2 1/2" x 6" strip of yellow construction
   paper
one 1 1/2" x 5" strip of construction paper
construction paper scraps
crayons or markers
glue
scissors

Steps:

1. Glue the green poster board strips to the four sides of the precut cereal box.
2. Cut out facial features from the construction paper scraps and glue them to the semicircle to make a cute sun character.
3. Glue the sun inside the back panel of the holder.
4. Cut the strip of yellow paper into short lengths. Glue the resulting sun rays around the edge of the sun.
5. Personalize the remaining construction paper strip and glue it to the front panel of the holder.

Elizabeth Searls Almy, Greensboro, NC

"Apple-tizing" Prints

Students can use this fun printing technique to decorate a bushel of school-related items like folders, nametags, notebooks, and more! Pour red and green tempera paints into individual shallow containers. Place the item to be decorated on a flat, newspaper-covered surface. To make an apple print, dip one end of a large marshmallow into the red paint and then press it onto the item. To make an apple leaf, insert a toothpick into one end of a small marshmallow (for a handle) and then dip the small marshmallow into the green paint and press it near the top of an apple print. When the paint is dry, use a black permanent marker to draw desired stems. "Apple-lutely" scrumptious!

Elizabeth Searls Almy
Greensboro, NC

Magnificent Macaws

Captivating and colorful, this fine-feathered project will brighten any classroom! Plan to use red, yellow, blue, and green construction paper—the vivid colors of the magnificent macaw.

Materials:
two 12" squares of different-colored construction paper
one 5" x 12" rectangle of construction paper
one copy of the head and bill patterns on page 272
glue   scissors
stapler   hole puncher
crayons or markers   monofilament line

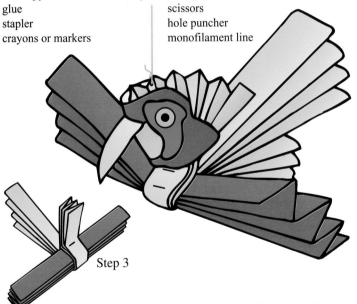

Step 3

Steps:
1. Accordion-fold the construction paper squares and rectangle at one-inch intervals.
2. To make the head and tail feathers, fold back approximately four inches of one accordion-folded square.
3. To make the wings, sandwich the second accordion-folded square between the head and tail feathers. Staple.
4. To make breast feathers, align the accordion-folded rectangle under the tail feathers and staple near the front of the wings.
5. Gently spread the head and tail feathers. Glue the bottom of the head feathers to the top of the tail feathers.
6. Color and cut out the head and bill patterns. Fold under the tab on the bill cutout and glue it to the head where indicated. Fold back the tabs on the head cutout. Position the head on the project and then glue the tabs to the head feathers.
7. To display the project, punch a hole in the head feathers and suspend it from a length of monofilament line.

Michelle McCormick—Gr. 1
Washington Elementary School
Holdrege, NE

Schoolwork Frame-Ups

Students and parents will agree that these fabulous frame-ups are perfect for displaying schoolwork. Glue the ends of four poster board strips (two 2" x 12" strips and two 2" x 14" strips) together to create a rectangle. When the resulting frame is dry, decorate it with stickers, construction paper scraps and glue, and/or markers. Next turn the frame over and center a gallon-size resealable plastic bag over the project. Securely tape the bottom and sides of the bag to the frame. Then open the bag, carefully insert the end of a stapler, and staple the bag (just below the zipper) to the frame. Lastly, press lengths of half-inch self adhesive magnetic tape around the perimeter of the back of the project. A student slips a work sample into his frame and then proudly displays his project on his family's refrigerator. Encourage students to replace their works samples one or more times a week!

Elizabeth Searls Almy

Arts & Crafts

"Hand-some" Leaves

When it comes to making these lovely leaves, students will be more than happy to lend a hand! To make a handprint leaf, paint the palm side of a hand using fall-colored tempera paint (orange, yellow, red, brown). Press the hand, with fingers spread, onto a sheet of white paper. When the painted paper has dried, draw a jagged outline around the handprint with a fall-colored crayon and then color the white areas inside the outline with a different fall-colored crayon. Cut out the leaf and the fall foliage is ready to display!

Sharon Hackley
Kingman, AZ

Bats in Flight

You'll generate plenty of enthusiasm right off the bat with these eerie nighttime scenes! Cut out a large construction paper moon and glue it on a 9" x 12" sheet of orange construction paper. To make the bat, cut two identical circles from black paper. Zigzag-cut one circle in half. Glue the two resulting wings to the remaining black circle. Next use construction paper scraps, glue, and a white crayon to add ears and facial features to the bat. Then glue the bat on the orange paper. Working atop a newspaper-covered surface, drip drops of thinned, black tempera paint onto the project. Spread the paint drops by blowing briskly through a drinking straw. Oh, spooky!

Lisa Von Hatten—Gr. 3
St. Paul Elementary
Highland, IL

Illuminating Cats

These wide-eyed kitties are "purrrrr-fect" for the holiday season or anytime! Begin with two construction paper copies of the pattern on page 58. Cut out each shape; then cut along the dotted lines to make eyeholes. (Assist students with this step as needed.) On one cutout, use a crayon to draw the nose, whiskers, mouth, and legs of the cat. On the remaining cutout, lay a flat lollipop over each eyehole and secure the lollipop sticks with tape. Next glue the two cutouts together, keeping the crayon features to the outside and the lollipops to the inside. Display the cute kitties in a window and watch their eyes glow!

Kristin Marple—Gr. 2
St. Nicholas School
Egg Harbor, NJ

Scarecrows From Spoons

Here's an art project that turns students' thoughts of harvest into spoonfuls of creative fun. Use craft glue to attach a wooden spoon (serving side up) to a 12" x 18" piece of light-colored tagboard. When dry, draw a scarecrow face on the spoon with a marker. Then use construction paper scraps, wallpaper scraps, yarn, glue, and other desired materials to embellish the spoon with scarecrow-like hair and clothing. Last, draw and color a background scene such as a pumpkin patch or a cornfield. Caw! Caw!

Ann Marie Stephens
George C. Round Elementary
Manassas, VA

Indian Corn Napkin Rings

Add the perfect touch to any Thanksgiving table with colorful Indian corn napkin rings. Cut a supply of empty toilet-tissue tubes and paper-towel tubes into two-inch sections or rings. To make a napkin ring, tear individual two-inch squares of brown, yellow, red, black, orange, blue, and purple construction paper into small pieces. Then, in a mosaic pattern, glue the torn paper pieces on a two-inch ring. When the glue dries, tuck a napkin inside. Happy Thanksgiving!

Elizabeth Searls Almy
Greensboro, NC

Gobbler Greetings

These gorgeous gobblers are the perfect place for students to pen thankful thoughts for their loved ones.

Materials for one card:

one 6" x 9" piece of yellow construction paper
one 6" x 9" piece of brown construction paper
one 3" brown construction paper circle
one 3" x 5" piece of white paper
two 1" x 5" orange construction paper strips
individual containers of red, green, and blue
   tempera paint

white, black, and orange
   paper scraps
3 cotton swabs
scissors
glue
pencil

Steps:

1. **For the tail feathers,** dip one end of a cotton swab in one paint color and repeatedly press it onto the yellow paper. Reload the swab as many times as desired. Then repeat the procedure for each remaining paint color, using a different cotton swab each time. When the painted paper is dry, cut several feather shapes from it.
2. **For the body,** fold the brown rectangle in half and round the corners. Keeping the fold at the top, glue the feathers to the back of the resulting body.
3. **For the head,** glue the brown circle to the body as shown. For facial features, cut two white eyes, two black pupils, and an orange diamond shape (for the beak) from paper scraps. Fold the diamond in half to create a beak. Glue the cutouts in place.
4. **For the legs and feet,** use a zigzag cut to trim one end of each orange paper strip. Then fold up the notched end of each paper strip to make a foot. Glue the legs to the body.
5. **To complete the card,** write a Thanksgiving message on the white paper. Unfold the body and glue the paper inside.

Elizabeth Searls Almy

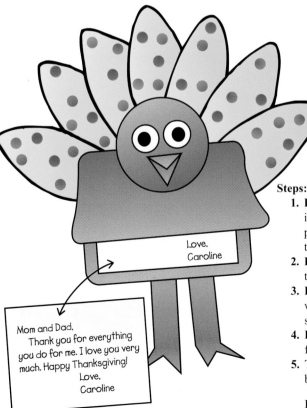

Arts & Crafts

Star of David

Brighten your Hanukkah festivities with the glow of this colorful Star of David. Prepare a tagboard tracer of the triangle pattern on page 59. Position the top point of the tracer near the top of an eight-inch square of yellow construction paper. Trace inside and outside the shape, and then flip the tracer so the top point is near the bottom of the yellow paper. Adjust the tracer as needed to make a six-pointed star; then trace inside and outside the tracer. Color each section of the resulting star a shade of blue or green. Then cut out the star, leaving a narrow border of yellow around the outer edge. Glue the cutout to dark blue paper. Cut out the shape again, this time leaving a narrow border of blue. Happy Hanukkah!

Elizabeth Searls Almy
Greensboro, NC

Torn-Paper Santa

Who's hiding behind that fluffy white beard? Why Santa, of course! To make a Santa, tear a beard shape from a 7" x 9" rectangle of white construction paper. Next tear the edges from a 3" x 6" rectangle of pink construction paper and glue the resulting face near the top of the beard as shown. Tear a hat shape from an eight-inch square of red construction paper and glue it above the pink face. Tear the edges from a 3" x 9" strip of white construction paper and glue the resulting hat band over the lower edge of the hat.

Next fold the top of the hat to one side and glue a cotton ball to the tip. Then cut two eyes and a nose from construction paper scraps and glue them on the face. Ho! Ho! Ho! Merry Christmas!

Lisa Strieker—Gr. 3
St. Paul Elementary
Highland, IL

Gingerbread Homes

These cozy cottages are deliciously fun to make! Partially fill a brown paper lunch bag with crumpled newspaper. Fold back the top of the bag and staple. Use construction paper scraps, crayons, glue, and a hole puncher (optional) to add a roof, windows, a front door, and an abundance of scrumptious-looking decorations. Now that's home sweet home!

Mara Bartusek—Gr. 3
Fairview Elementary
Mora, MN

Pretty Poinsettia Greetings

Pretty-as-can-be poinsettias are perfect for delivering heartfelt holiday greetings. To begin, make a tagboard tracer for each leaf and bracht pattern on page 59. Trace two A shapes on green felt. Trace the B and the C shapes on red felt. Cut out the four resulting shapes; then cut a slit in shape C as indicated on the tracer. Also cut three to five tiny circles from yellow felt or Fun Foam™.

To assemble the poinsettia carrier, fold the thin cutout (B) in half and carefully push its folded end through the slit in cutout C. When a small loop forms under the project (Figure 1), separate the two red brachts and glue the yellow dots to the center of the resulting bloom (Figure 2). Glue one end of each green leaf beneath the bloom as shown. Design a colorful and heartfelt greeting on a quarter page of blank paper; then roll the paper lengthwise into a tight tube and poke it through the loop of felt underneath the project. Seasons greetings!

Amy Barsanti—Gr. 3
Pines Elementary
Roper, NC

Figure 1

Figure 2

Kwanzaa Windsock

Herald the arrival of Kwanzaa with a striking windsock fashioned from traditional holiday colors.

Materials:
one 6" x 18" strip of black construction paper
one 2" x 18" strip of red construction paper
one 2" x 18" strip of green construction paper
six 16" strips of black crepe paper
one 36" length of black yarn
glue

Steps:
1. Glue the red and green strips to the black paper as shown.
2. When the glue has dried, roll the project into a cylinder and glue the overlapping edges together.
3. Glue one end of each crepe paper strip underneath the green rim.
4. Punch two holes opposite each other near the top of the black rim.
5. Thread each end of the yarn length through a different hole and securely tie.

More About Kwanzaa Colors
Black represents African-American people, *red* symbolizes the struggles of the people, and *green* stands for a happy future.

Arts & Crafts

Gift of Love

This handcrafted valentine keepsake is sure to win the heart of a loved one!

Materials for one frame:

6 tongue depressors
two 1" x 3" strips of red felt
one 5½" square of red felt
one 5½" square of
    white poster board
1 student photo
assorted colors of Fun Foam™
crayons
scissors
craft glue

Steps:

1. To make the wooden frame, lay two tongue depressors parallel to each other and about 4½ inches apart. Squeeze glue near the ends of each wooden stick and then connect the sticks with two more depressors. Allow to dry.

2. To make the frame stand, write, date, and sign a valentine greeting in the center of the poster board square. Glue a tongue depressor to the left edge and the right edge of the programmed square. Allow to dry.

3. Trim the photo as desired, and glue it in the center of the felt square. Then squeeze a trail of glue around the perimeter of the felt and press the wooden frame atop the glue. Allow to dry.

4. To connect the frame to the stand, glue the felt strips to the back of the frame and then to the frame stand as shown. Lay flat to dry.

5. Cut out desired decorations from the Fun Foam and glue them on the wooden frame.

Heather Graley—Gr. 3
Eaton, OH

Step 4

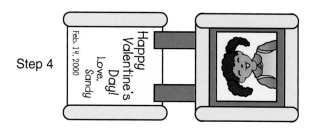

The Valentine Express

For speedy delivery of valentine wishes, "choo-choo-choose" the Valentine Express! Collect a class supply of clean and empty half-gallon milk cartons and then cut away the top and one side panel of each container. If desired, prewrap each child's container in red, pink, or white paper and brad four tagboard wheels in place. (Or assist students as they complete these steps.) Then set aside plenty of time for each child to personalize his boxcar to his heart's desire! Display the completed projects in alphabetical order (by student name) atop a bookshelf or table. It's full steam ahead for a happy Valentine's Day!

Karen Nelson—Gr. 2
Smith School, Helena, MT

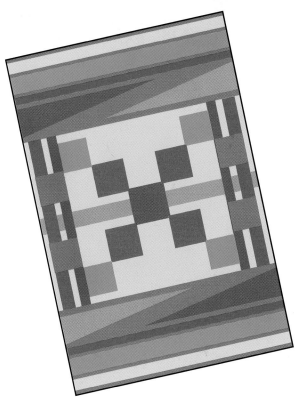

Colorful Kente Cloth

Spotlight the beauty and tradition of the kente cloth with this colorful project. (For an enjoyable and enlightening introduction to the bright and bold colors of the kente cloth, read aloud Debbi Chocolate's *Kente Colors* [Walker Publishing Company, Inc.; 1997].) Start with a 6" x 9" construction paper backdrop. Then cut out construction paper pieces and glue them on the paper to create an original kente cloth design. Mount the projects around the perimeter of a bulletin board for a breathtaking border.

Amy Barsanti—Gr. 3
Pines Elementary
Plymouth, NC

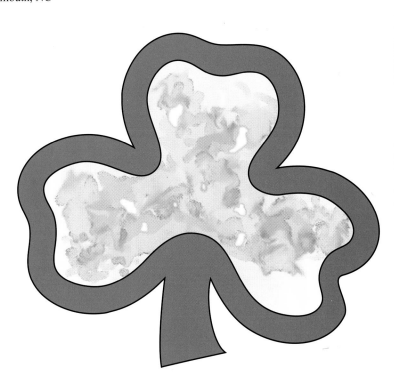

Striking Shamrocks

Your lads and lassies will be all smiles as these striking shamrocks take shape!

Materials for one shamrock:
iron, set on low
one 9" x 12" press cloth
one 18" x 12" length of waxed paper
handheld pencil sharpener
various shades of green crayons (wrappers removed)
a shamrock template like the one shown
two 9" x 12" sheets of green construction paper
scissors
glue

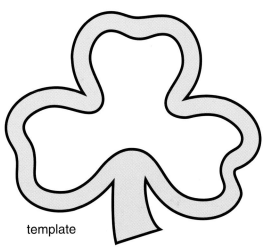

template

Steps:

1. Fold the waxed paper in half to 9" x 12" and unfold.
2. Sharpen the crayons and spread the shavings over one half of the waxed paper.
3. Refold the waxed paper and cover it with the press cloth.
4. Gently iron the press cloth and then carefully remove it. (This step must be supervised or completed by an adult.) Allow the waxed paper to cool.
5. Trace the shamrock template onto each sheet of green paper; then cut out the shapes.
6. Glue one shamrock cutout onto the waxed paper. When dry, trim away the excess waxed paper.
7. Flip the project over, align the second shamrock, and glue.
8. Tape the project on a window for a striking display.

adapted from an idea by Amy Ernst—Gr. 2
E. C. Miles Elementary
Miles, IA

Arts & Crafts

Fluffy Dandelions

These dandelion look-alikes confirm that spring has sprung! To begin, cut three stems and several leaves from green paper. Glue the cutouts to a 9" x 12" sheet of dark blue construction paper. Next glue a narrow strip of fringed, green paper to the lower edge of the project to resemble grass. To make the fluffy dandelion heads, dot a circle of glue at the top of each stem; then pull tiny tufts from a cotton ball and press them into the glue. If desired glue a few tufts blowing in the breeze. Aren't these dandelions just dandy?

Elizabeth Searls Almy
Greensboro, NC

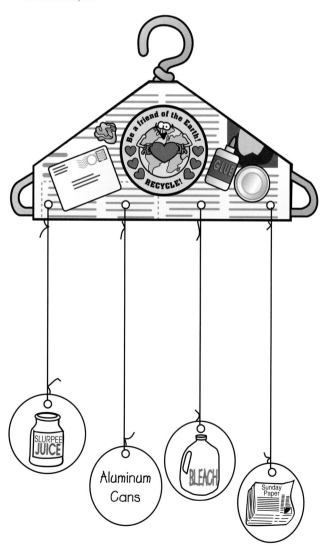

Earth-Friendly Mobile

Just in time for Earth Day—a mobile with important messages about recycling!

Materials for one mobile:

metal hanger
2-page spread of newspaper,
    folded twice
copy of patterns on page 60
four 4" white construction paper circles
four 1' lengths of string or twine

crayons or markers
scissors
glue
hole puncher
small recyclable items

Steps:

1. Lay the hanger on the folded newspaper with the neck extending off the paper. Fold down the top corners of the paper and bring the lower edge upward, folding the lower corners over the top of hanger (see below). Flip the hanger and glue.
2. Color the patterns on page 60 and cut them out. Glue one pattern on each side of the wrapped hanger.
3. Illustrate a different recyclable item on each circle. Hole-punch the top of the circle; then flip it over and describe the item on the back.
4. Punch four holes along the bottom of the wrapped hanger. Use the string lengths to attach the illustrated circles to the hanger.
5. Glue small recyclables to the newspaper-covered hanger as desired.

Jeri Daugherty
Mother Seton School
Emmitsburg, MD

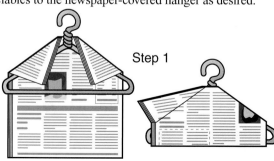

Step 1

Eggs Extraordinaire

Prepare pretty printed Easter eggs using pipe cleaners and paint! To begin, trace an egg shape onto construction paper. Bend pipe cleaner lengths into different shapes, fashioning a handle on each one. Dip one shape into a shallow container of paint and then repeatedly press it onto the paper. Reload as needed. Repeat the procedure with additional shapes and paint colors. (To use a pipe cleaner shape with more than one color of paint, rinse it clean and pat it dry with a paper towel.) When the prints are dry, cut out the egg shape and display it as desired. Very impressive!

Handmade for Mom

Delight moms and other significant women in your students' lives with handcrafted tokens of love! Paint the palm side of a child's hands a desired color. Keeping his thumbs aligned and his fingers spread, he presses his painted hands onto a 9" x 12" sheet of white construction paper. When the paint dries, he uses markers or crayons to draw and color the body and antennae of the resulting butterfly, and to write a desired greeting. Next he colors a copy of the poem on page 60, cuts it out, and glues it on the back of his project. He adds desired decorations with markers or crayons; then he writes the date and signs his name. If desired, laminate the projects for safekeeping before students deliver them to their loved ones.

Paula Stewart—Art, Grs. 1–5
Nathanael Greene Academy
Siloam, GA

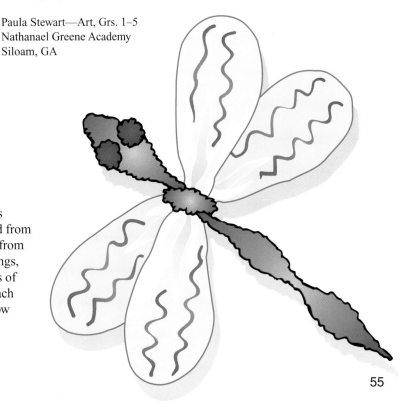

Dazzling Dragonfly

Sporting delicate wings like its real-life counterpart, this dragonfly impostor is made to dazzle. Snip one pointed end from a 12-inch chenille bump pipe cleaner. About one-half inch from the cut end, glue two small pom-pom eyes. To make the wings, draw dark, wavy crayon lines on each of two 3" x 12" strips of waxed paper. Round the corners and pinch the middle of each strip. Wrap the prepared pipe cleaner around the wings. Now that's a dapper dragonfly!

Darcy Brown
Elon College Elementary
Elon College, NC

Arts & Crafts

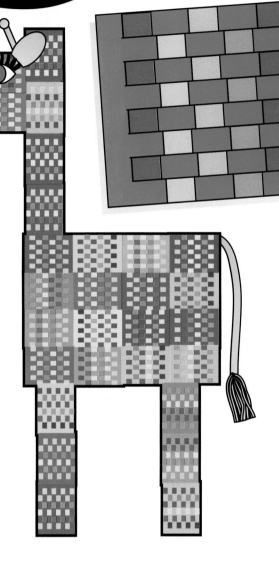

Woven Giraffe

There's more to this weaving project than meets the eye! To make a rectangular weaving, fold a 9" x 12" sheet of colorful construction paper in half (to 9" x 6"). Starting at the fold, cut a series of one-inch strips, stopping approximately one inch from the open ends. Unfold the resulting loom and weave six 1 1/2" x 9" colorful construction paper strips in the loom. Glue the ends of each woven strip in place. Assemble the projects into a giraffe shape like the one shown. Invite students to study the colorful critter and submit proposals for other critters to be woven. Then let the weaving continue!

Lisa Strieker—Gr. 3
St. Paul Elementary
Highland, IL

Bloomin' Bookmarks

Reading skills are sure to blossom over the summer with these colorful bookmarks! Use templates to trace four leaves on green paper and two tulip blooms on colorful magazine paper. Cut out the shapes. Also cut two 3" x 9" rectangles from clear Con-Tact® covering. Peel the backing from one rectangle. Arrange two leaves, one tulip bloom (facedown), and a 1/2" x 6" green paper stem on the adhesive. Next, carefully glue the remaining leaves and bloom (faceup) atop their like shapes. Then peel the backing from the second rectangle and align the rectangle, adhesive side down, atop the project. Trim the edges of the resulting bookmark, leaving space at the top to punch a hole and add a loop of yarn.

Elizabeth Almy
Greensboro, NC

Impressive Paintings

Anything goes with this hands-on approach to painting! Use tape to secure the top and bottom edges of a 9" x 12" sheet of art paper to a section of newspaper. Randomly drip colorful tempera paint onto the art paper and then cover the art paper with plastic wrap. Touching only the plastic, use your hands to smooth, smear, and swirl the paint colors. When a desired effect is achieved, remove the plastic and allow drying time. Next, peel away the tape and trim the painting into a desired shape. Mount the shape onto a complementary color of construction paper and then trim the paper to create an eye-catching border. Impressive!

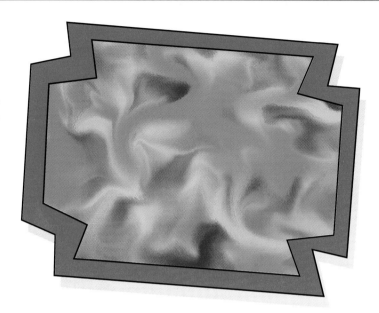

Just for Dad!

This gift-giving idea ties in perfectly with Father's Day!

Materials for one pencil holder:
clean, empty 12-oz. juice can
4¹/₂" x 9" rectangle of Con-Tact® paper (for shirt)
fine-tipped permanent marker
two ⁵/₈" x 9" lengths of craft ribbon (for tie)
1 decorative button (for tie tack)
two small buttons (for shirt)
tape
scissors
craft glue
pencils

Steps:
1. Use the marker to write a personalized message in the center of the Con-Tact® paper.
2. Peel the backing from the paper. Adhere the paper to the can, making sure the message is legible when the can is upright (opening at the top).
3. To make the tie, tape the ends of one ribbon length to a tabletop and loop the second ribbon length under the ribbon as shown in diagram A. Refer to the remaining diagrams to tie a necktie-type knot. (For best results, have parent volunteers provide assistance with this step.)
4. Remove the tape from the ribbon ends. Glue one ribbon end near the top rim of the can, above the written message. Wrap the ribbon around the can, overlap the ribbon ends, and glue.
5. Position the resulting tie over the paper seam at the front of the can. Trim and shape the ends of the tie as desired.
6. Glue the tie where the decorative button (tie tack) will be attached.
7. Glue the tie tack and small buttons in place as shown.
8. Place the pencils in the resulting holder.

Jane Manuel—Gr. 3
Wellington, TX

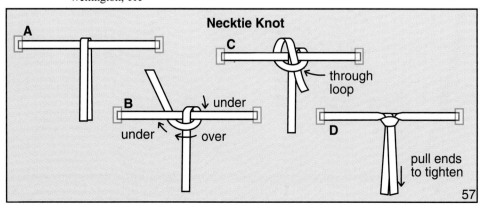

Necktie Knot

A

B
under   ↓ under
under ↙   ↑→ over

C
through
loop

D
pull ends
to tighten

57

Pattern

Use with "Illuminating Cats" on page 48.

Cut
out.

Cut
out.

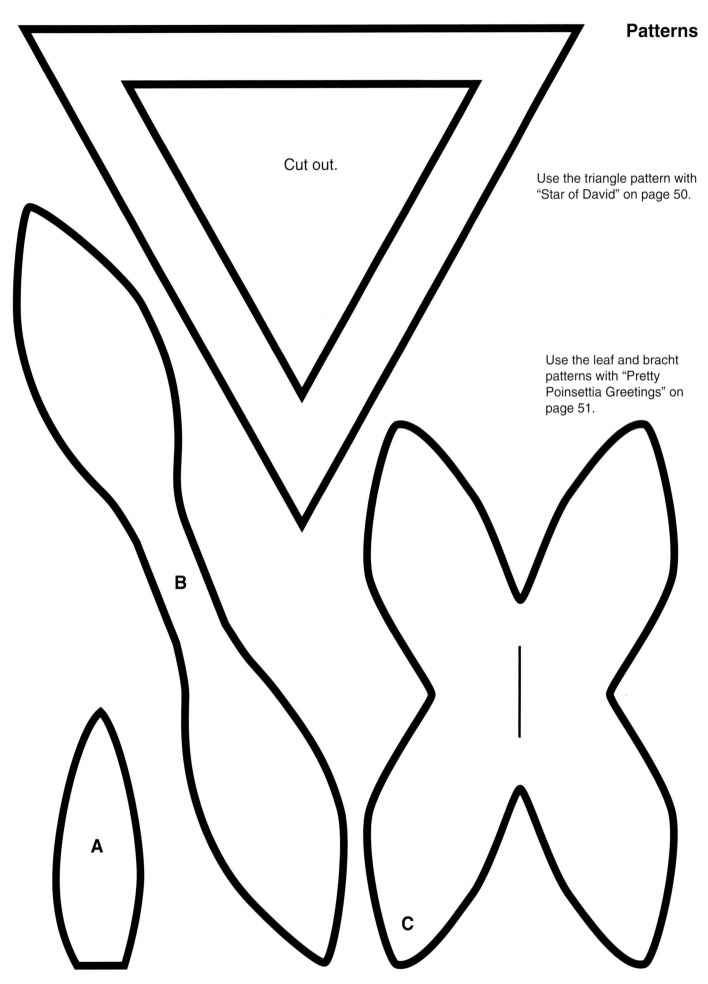

Patterns

Cut out.

Use the triangle pattern with "Star of David" on page 50.

Use the leaf and bracht patterns with "Pretty Poinsettia Greetings" on page 51.

B

A

C

Poem and Patterns

Use the poem with "Handmade for Mom" on page 55.

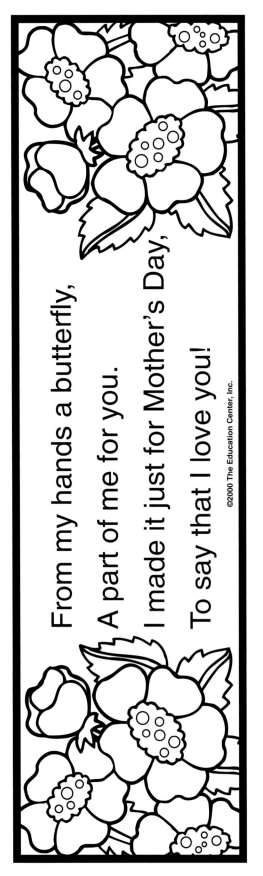

From my hands a butterfly,

A part of me for you.

I made it just for Mother's Day,

To say that I love you!

©2000 The Education Center, Inc.

Use the patterns with "Earth-Friendly Mobile" on page 54.

READING SKILLS
ROUNDUP

Reading Skills Roundup

• Phonics • Sight Words • And More!

For Beginning Readers

Final Feature

Give phonemic awareness a front-row seat with this version of Musical Chairs! Prepare a word list for each of several final consonant sounds. Intersperse the words on each list with words that have different ending sounds. Have youngsters form a circle of chairs with one less chair than students. To play a round, announce a final sound. Then slowly read the corresponding list as students walk around the circle. When a youngster hears a word that does not end with the featured sound, he quickly tries to sit in a chair. The student who is unable to find an empty chair repeats the last word called and identifies its ending sound. Then play resumes. When all of the words on the list have been called, continue the activity with a different word list. For older students, spotlight vowels, blends, or digraphs.

hen
pin
happen
begin
pet
again
even
children
make

LaDawn Rhodes, Shelton Park Elementary, Virginia Beach, VA

Phonics Show-and-Tell

Youngsters love show-and-tell, so why not put a twist on this favorite to review phonics? Ask each student to bring to school a small item with a name that includes a particular phonics element. Give her an opportunity to show the item to the class. Enlist her help to write its name on the chalkboard and to point out the phonics element. After each youngster's item has been listed, review the words and use them to write a class story on chart paper. Read the story with youngsters; then ask each student to find and circle a listed word. What a great way to reinforce phonics in context!

Julie Davenport—Gr. 1, W. A. Wright Elementary, Mt. Juliet, TN

Word-Go-Round

This lively word family activity will have students walking in circles! Visually divide chart paper into five columns and label each column with one of the following: -at, -et, -in, -op, and -ug. Divide students into two equal groups. Give each student in one group a card labeled with a word family (rime) shown on the chart. Give each child in the other group a card bearing a different initial consonant or blend (onset). Ask one group to form a circle and then have the remaining group form a circle around it.

Instruct one group to walk clockwise and the other counterclockwise when music is playing. Start the music and then stop it after a few moments. Ask each student to show his card to the classmate nearest him in the other circle. Have each pair, in turn, tell whether its cards make a word. If a word is formed, write it on the chart paper in the corresponding column. Then resume play by restarting the music. Continue the activity as described for as long as desired. The resulting chart makes a handy classroom reference. For younger students, decrease the number of onsets and rimes.

Cynthia House—Gr. 2
East Goshen Elementary School, Westchester, PA

Spotlight on Sight Words

Here's a star-studded idea for practicing sight words! In advance, cut out a construction paper star for each student. Also cut out and label one star for each sight word that you want to reinforce. Display the programmed stars in a prominent classroom location and put the remaining stars aside. To practice the words, a student shines a flashlight on each star and reads aloud its word. After a youngster successfully reads the entire galaxy of stars, recognize her stellar achievement by programming a blank star with a positive phrase, such as "Star Reader." Then present it to her along with plenty of praise. No doubt students will take a shine to this "star-ific" reading activity!

Sue Nagel—Grs. 1–2
Reading Resource Teacher
St. Hugo of the Hills School
Bloomfield Hills, MI

because   does   have

Farmyard Phonics

Everyone knows that Old MacDonald had animals on his farm, but do your students know that he had vowels, too? Teach youngsters short-vowel sounds with this toe-tapping tune. With students' help, modify the verse shown to highlight each vowel. For added fun, ask students to make posters to illustrate the song. Or change the setting of the song to another familiar place, such as a zoo or grocery store; then change the verses accordingly.

Ann R. Colvin
Louisville, KY

Old MacDonald Had Some Vowels
Old MacDonald had a farm, A-E-I-O-U.
And on his farm he had a [short a word], A-E-I-O-U.
With an [a, a] here and an [a, a] there,
Here an [a], there an [a],
Everywhere an [a, a].
Old MacDonald had a farm, A-E-I-O-U.

Blend Relay

On your mark, get set, search for blends! For this fast-paced team game, choose two initial blends to reinforce and write each one on a card. Gather small objects (or pictures of objects) that depict these initial blends. You need one or more objects per student. Then, making sure that each blend is equally represented, divide the items among four paper grocery bags. Also add a few items to each bag that have initial letters other than those being reinforced.

To play, have students sit single file in four parallel lines, and give a prepared bag to the last child in each line. Hold up a blend card. The last student in each line searches his team's bag for an item beginning with this blend. Then he and his teammates quickly pass the item to the first child in line. This student names the item and identifies its blend. The first team to correctly complete this task earns a point. When all four teams are finished, the last child in each line moves to the front of the line. To begin the next round of play, hold up a blend card. Continue in this manner until every child has chosen an item from the team bag. The team with the most points wins. For an added challenge, increase the number of blends featured and prepare team bags to match.

Dianne Neumann—Gr. 2, Frank C. Whiteley School, Hoffman Estates, IL

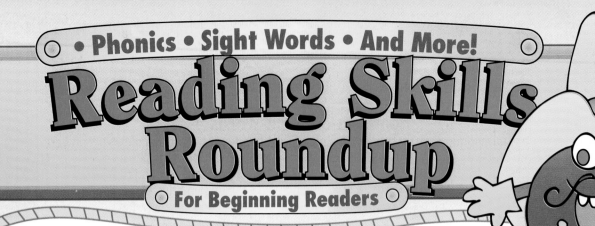

Flock of Phonics

-EEP

Introduce a flock of word-family fun with the woolly characters in Nancy Shaw's *Sheep in a Jeep* (Houghton Mifflin Company, 1988). After an initial reading, reread the story, asking each youngster to raise his hand every time he hears a word that has the *-eep* sound. Then ask students to name these words as you list them on the chalkboard. Lead students to note that the *-eep* and *-eap* word families (rimes) sound the same but are spelled differently.

Next have each student make an *-eep* word-family critter. To do so, he draws a large sheep on a sheet of white construction paper. He writes as many *-eep* words on his sheep as he can, carefully referring to the listed words as needed. The student uses a black crayon to outline his sheep and add details; then he glues bits of cotton onto the outline of the sheep's body. To extend the activity, have each student use his woolly words to write a new adventure for Shaw's amusing sheep. What "shear" delight!

Amy

sheep deep
jeep keep
peep sweep
sleep

Dixie Brooker—Gr. 2
Rosewood Elementary, Vero Beach, FL

Funny Faces

LONG A

This grin-inducing partner game will have students clowning around with vowels! Program a full-page grid of 20 boxes with 10 long *a* words and 10 short *a* words. Give each student a copy of the resulting game cards and the game pieces on page 74 (for larger cards and pieces, duplicate the pages at 125 percent onto 11" x 17" paper). To make her game, a student colors the game pieces; then she cuts out the pieces and cards. She stores her game in a large resealable plastic bag.

To play, one student in each pair shuffles her cards and stacks them facedown on a playing surface. Each student, in turn, draws a card and reads the word. If it has a long *a* sound, she selects one facial feature and places it on her clown face. Then she places the card in a discard pile. If the word has a short *a* sound, she places the card in the discard pile and her turn is over. The first player to complete a clown face that consists of two eyebrows, two eyes, one nose, and one mouth wins. (Have students shuffle the discarded game cards and restack them as needed.) Vowel practice has never been so much fun!

Sara Harris—Gr. 2
West View Elementary
Knoxville, TN

race

Word Wall Worm

SIGHT WORDS

When it comes to sight words, this wriggly worm is a letter-perfect resource! For each letter of the alphabet, cut out an 8 1/2-inch colored construction paper circle. Cut out 13 more circles, cutting each one in half. Staple each half to a matching whole circle to create a pocket. Then label each pocket with a different letter. Place a blank 4" x 6" card in each pocket and add facial features to the circle labeled "A." To assemble the worm, mount the circles on a classroom wall in alphabetical order and within easy student reach. Each time you introduce a sight word, write it on the corresponding card. Encourage youngsters to use this unique display for a reading and writing reference. No doubt lots of words will inch right into their sight vocabularies!

Stephany Ezekiel
Marion, IL

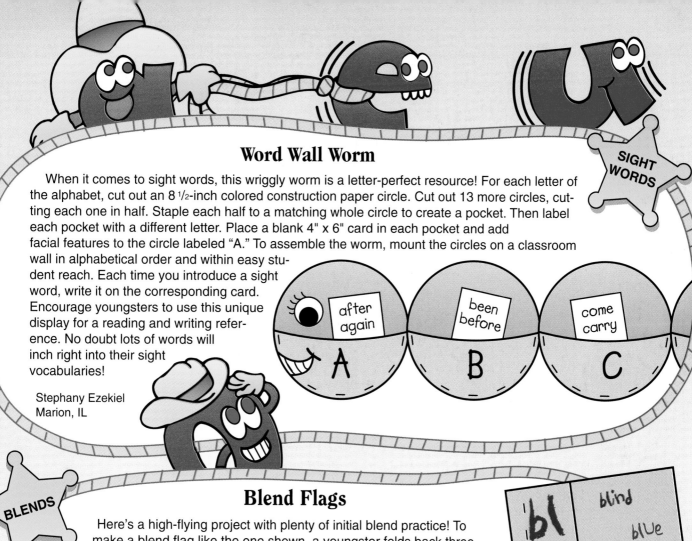

Blend Flags

BLENDS

Here's a high-flying project with plenty of initial blend practice! To make a blend flag like the one shown, a youngster folds back three inches of a 12" x 18" sheet of construction paper to create a 12" x 15" rectangle. Keeping the fold on the left edge of her paper, she uses a marker or crayon to write an assigned blend in the upper left-hand corner and then she draws a large rectangle around it. In the remaining space she writes words that begin with this blend. Next the student folds a sentence strip in half, slides the resulting flagpole into the fold of her paper, and staples it in place. To create a handy reference of blends, showcase the completed projects in your classroom. Now that's a great way to flag blend skills!

Cynthia Holcomb—Gr. 2
Irion County Independent School District
Mertzon, TX

Digraph Drawings

DIGRAPHS

In this game, a picture isn't worth a *thousand* words—it's worth one with a digraph! Select a digraph to reinforce and then program each of several blank cards with a different word that contains this digraph. To play the game, announce the featured digraph, choose one student to come to the chalkboard, and hand him a card. The student reads the word on the card to himself; then he draws a representation of it on the chalkboard. As he works, the rest of the class tries to guess the word. The student who identifies the word becomes the next drawer. If this student has already drawn, he chooses a classmate who has not. Play continues in this manner until game time is over. Whether you choose to reinforce letter or vowel sounds, digraphs, or blends, this game is sure to *draw* your youngsters into reading!

Kelly A. Lu—Gr. 2, Berlyn School, Ontario, CA

• Phonics • Sight Words • And More!

Reading Skills Roundup

For Beginning Readers

Consonant Catch

Transform a game of catch into a phonics-boosting activity! Stand with students in a large circle. Toss a foam ball to one youngster; then announce a consonant. Challenge the youngster to name a word that begins (or ends) with the consonant and then toss the ball back to you. If the student is unable to name a word, he passes the ball to the classmate on his right. If this student names a word, he tosses the ball to you. If he does not, he passes the ball to the right, and so on, until one youngster successfully names a word or the ball reaches you. Continue play with different consonants until each student has provided at least one word. For more advanced students, focus on word families (rimes) or vowels.

adapted from an idea by Diana Riley—Gr. 1
Seneca Grade School
Seneca, KS

CONSONANTS

Mystery Words

BLENDS

Here's a case for your young word detectives to crack—the case of the mystery blend words. Give each student a card bearing a different noun that has a beginning blend, cautioning her not to reveal the word to her classmates. Ask her to write at least three clues for the word. Then have each student, in turn, read aloud her clues. After each clue, she invites her classmates to identify the mystery blend word. The first classmate who correctly identifies it takes the next turn (or, if she has already taken a turn, she selects another youngster who has not). What a nifty way to get students hot on the trail of blends!

adapted from an idea by Cindy Ward
Yellow Branch School
Rustburg, VA

glitter

1. It is shiny.
2. It comes in different colors.
3. It is used to decorate things.

Sort and List

LONG VOWELS

This small-group activity provides all sorts of practice with long-vowel words! Prepare a class set of long-vowel word cards, being sure to include words with vowel teams as well as words with vowel patterns. Visually divide a poster-sized piece of paper into five columns, label the columns as shown, and display the resulting chart.

To begin, divide the students into small groups, and give each child a card. Ask each group to sort its words by long-vowel sounds. After verifying each group's work, ask each child to list her original word on the chart. Next, have each student, in turn, read aloud a different word on the chart and underline the letters that make its long-vowel sound.

Annetta Ward—Gr. 1
Springfield School
Columbia Cross Roads, PA

ā	ē	ī	ō	ū
way	meet	ice	rope	cube
train	treat	five	coat	tune

Oodles of Fun

What better way to reinforce the vowel digraph $\overline{oo}$ than with the beloved Bear and moon books? Read aloud Frank Asch's *Moondance* (Scholastic Inc., 1994) or *Happy Birthday, Moon* (Aladdin Paperbacks, 1985). Then have students brainstorm $\overline{oo}$ words. List their responses on a poster-sized moon cutout. Next ask each youngster to choose one or more words from the list. Near the top of a sheet of drawing paper, have the student use the word(s) in an original sentence about Bear. Then revisit several of Asch's illustrations and discuss their style (simple figures with bold colors). Have each student imitate Asch's style to illustrate his sentence. Display students' work on a bulletin board titled "Oodles of Fun With Bear."

Kelly McCalla—Gifted and Talented
Oakland Elementary
Greenwood, SC

Order books online.
www.themailbox.com

food   moon
tooth   cool
school rooster
spoon   loose

Bear wiggled his loose tooth.

Dandy Dictionaries

These sight word dictionaries are a real find! Give each student a 6" x 9" booklet with a construction paper cover and 14 pages (seven sheets of white paper). Have the youngster draw a line across the center of the each page except the last one. Working in alphabetical order, have the student label half a page for each letter.

To enter words in her dictionary, a student cuts words that she can read from discarded newspapers and magazines. Then she glues each word in her dictionary on the appropriate page. Invite each youngster to use her dictionary for a writing reference. For extra reading reinforcement, encourage her to take the dictionary home regularly and read it to a family member. Have the family member sign and date the dictionary on the last page each time the youngster reads it at home.

adapted from an idea by Erika DeVita—Grs. K–2
The Primary School
Newburgh, NY

about
again   A
Board
Brown   B

Wipeout!

Students are sure to flip over this sight word game! Prepare two identical class sets of sight word cards. Divide students into small groups of equal size. Give each youngster a word card from the first set and have him place it faceup in front of himself. Place the second set of cards in a large bag.

To play, remove a card from the bag and read it aloud. The child who has the word flips over his card. Play continues in this manner. When all members of a group have turned their cards facedown, they stand and call "Wipeout!" To win the round, each child in the group reads aloud his word for verification. Next, have the students exchange word cards as you return your set of cards to the bag. Play as many additional rounds as desired. Out-of-sight!

Kathryn Levy—Gr. 1, Jacksonwald Elementary School, Reading, PA

Reading Skills Roundup

RHYMES

Creature Feature

It's rhyme time! And what better way to develop rhyming skills than with a Dr. Seuss book? Read aloud "Yertle the Turtle" from *Yertle the Turtle and Other Stories* by Dr. Seuss (Random House, Inc.; 1988). Point out that *Yertle* and *turtle* rhyme; then, as a class, brainstorm rhyming names for several animals. Next, have each student write a rhyming name for an animal at the top of a 12" x 18" sheet of drawing paper and then illustrate her critter using crayons, markers, or watercolor paints. Display the students' work on a bulletin board titled "Creature Feature." For a fun creative-writing extension, have each youngster pen a rhyming story about the animal she has illustrated.

Betsy Crosson—Gr. 1, Pleasant Elementary, Tulare, CA

Grabbit the Rabbit

Josie

Hats Off to Word Families!

WORD FAMILIES

Cap off a study of the *-at* word family with this booklet idea! Give each student one booklet base, one cover, and seven pages (page 75). To assemble his booklet, a student colors and cuts out the base and cover. He cuts out the pages and stacks them on the left side of the base. Then he places the cover atop the stack and staples the entire stack where indicated. On each page, he writes a different consonant letter, blend, or digraph to make an *-at* word. Invite each youngster to read his booklet to a classmate before taking it home to share with his family. Now that's a phonics idea that you can hang your hat on!

Sue M. Cross, Little Valley, NY

SIGHT WORDS

Directions on Sight

Energize your reading lessons with this lively sight word activity! Ask each student to stand behind her chair with her back to the chalkboard. On the board, write a one- or two-sentence direction that includes at least one sight word. Then announce "One, two, three—look and see!" On this signal, each student turns to face the board, silently reads the message, and follows the direction. Ask a student volunteer to read aloud the message. Then erase the board and continue with additional directions. What a great way to get students reading (and thinking) on their feet!

Amber Linley—Gr. 1, Tularosa Elementary, Tularosa, NM

Cookie Clues

Double up on phonics and snacktime with these tempting vowel digraphs! Give each student two small round cookies, a set of manipulative letters, and a paper towel for a workmat. Explain that each student's cookies represent double *o*'s as in *cookie.* Lead youngsters in using their cookies and letters to spell several words that have the *oo* digraph. Then pair students. Have each youngster, in turn, use his cookies and letters to spell an *oo* word for his partner to read. After each youngster has formed and read a desired number of words, invite students to munch on their tasty cookie vowels. Now when a student reads an *oo* word, he is sure to remember the cookie clues, and decoding will be a snap!

Amy T. Ekmark—Gr. 1
Eastside Elementary School
Lancaster, CA

Vowel Review

What's in the cards? A quick and easy short-vowel review for the whole class! Give each student five cards and have her label each one with a different short vowel. Call out a word that has a short-vowel sound. Have each youngster silently identify the vowel sound and then hold up her corresponding vowel card. Quickly scan the raised cards to determine the youngsters' accuracy. Ask a student who is holding the correct card to announce the vowel. Continue in a like manner with a desired number of other short-vowel words.

Dianne Neumann—Gr. 2
Frank C. Whiteley School
Hoffman Estates, IL

Wanted: *Your* Ideas for Teaching Reading

We're on the lookout for more rip-roarin' reading ideas! So rustle up your favorite activities and strategies for the following:
- teaching phonics skills
- building sight words and high-frequency word vocabularies
- using literature to reinforce beginning reading skills

Submit the ideas following the directions in "How to Submit Ideas" on page 2 of your most recent issue of The Primary *Mailbox*® magazine. We'll be mighty glad to hear from you!

Order books online.
www.themailbox.com

69

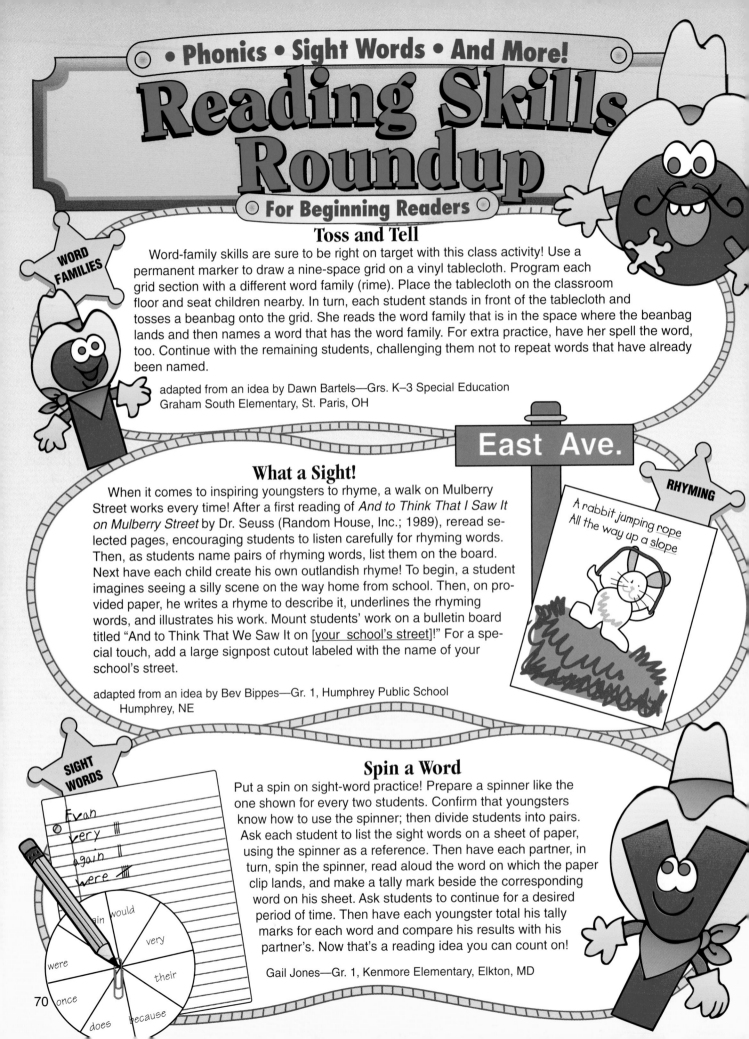

• Phonics • Sight Words • And More!
Reading Skills Roundup
For Beginning Readers

WORD FAMILIES

Toss and Tell

Word-family skills are sure to be right on target with this class activity! Use a permanent marker to draw a nine-space grid on a vinyl tablecloth. Program each grid section with a different word family (rime). Place the tablecloth on the classroom floor and seat children nearby. In turn, each student stands in front of the tablecloth and tosses a beanbag onto the grid. She reads the word family that is in the space where the beanbag lands and then names a word that has the word family. For extra practice, have her spell the word, too. Continue with the remaining students, challenging them not to repeat words that have already been named.

adapted from an idea by Dawn Bartels—Grs. K–3 Special Education
Graham South Elementary, St. Paris, OH

What a Sight!

When it comes to inspiring youngsters to rhyme, a walk on Mulberry Street works every time! After a first reading of *And to Think That I Saw It on Mulberry Street* by Dr. Seuss (Random House, Inc.; 1989), reread selected pages, encouraging students to listen carefully for rhyming words. Then, as students name pairs of rhyming words, list them on the board. Next have each child create his own outlandish rhyme! To begin, a student imagines seeing a silly scene on the way home from school. Then, on provided paper, he writes a rhyme to describe it, underlines the rhyming words, and illustrates his work. Mount students' work on a bulletin board titled "And to Think That We Saw It on [your school's street]!" For a special touch, add a large signpost cutout labeled with the name of your school's street.

adapted from an idea by Bev Bippes—Gr. 1, Humphrey Public School
Humphrey, NE

East Ave.

RHYMING

A rabbit jumping rope
All the way up a slope

SIGHT WORDS

Spin a Word

Put a spin on sight-word practice! Prepare a spinner like the one shown for every two students. Confirm that youngsters know how to use the spinner; then divide students into pairs. Ask each student to list the sight words on a sheet of paper, using the spinner as a reference. Then have each partner, in turn, spin the spinner, read aloud the word on which the paper clip lands, and make a tally mark beside the corresponding word on his sheet. Ask students to continue for a desired period of time. Then have each youngster total his tally marks for each word and compare his results with his partner's. Now that's a reading idea you can count on!

Gail Jones—Gr. 1, Kenmore Elementary, Elkton, MD

Evan
very |||
again |||
were |||

again / would / very / their / because / does / once / were

Reading Ribbons

What's a surefire way to reinforce sight words? Why, with lots of opportunities to read them, of course! Program a class supply of award ribbon cutouts with sight words. Have each student adhere a cutout to her clothing with a loop of tape. Then try these blue-ribbon reading suggestions:

- Have groups of students line up in ABC order by their words. Then ask the students in each group to chorally read their words.
- Gather youngsters in a circle for a game of sight-word catch. To take a turn, a youngster reads a classmate's word aloud and then tosses a foam ball to her.
- Form a circle with students. Have each youngster, in turn, read aloud the word that the student to her right is wearing. Then go around the circle in reverse order, asking each student to read the word on her left.

Cynthia Holcomb—Gr. 2
Irion County Independent School District, Mertzon, TX

before

Pick the Pairs

Here's a center idea that pockets plenty of short-vowel fun! On poster board, glue 15 library card pockets in five columns of three. Title the board "Pick the Pairs" and add a decorative border. Duplicate, color, and cut out the pictures on page 76. Glue each picture on a 3" x 5" card as shown and label the back of the card with the corresponding short-vowel sound and word. Insert a picture card in each pocket, being sure that exactly two pictures in each column represent the same vowel sound. Display the board and a supply of writing paper at a center. A youngster determines which two pictures in the first column represent the same vowel sound and writes the word for each one on his paper. Then he checks the back of each card to verify his answer. The student continues with the remaining columns in a like manner. To vary the task, rearrange the cards to result in different pairs.

Stephanie Shelton—Gr. 1, Virginia Smith Elementary
Harrah, OK

ĕ
tent

Blend Express

All aboard the Blend Express! Program each of a number of cards with a different blend. Divide students into small groups of equal size. Then have each group line up its chairs one behind the other to represent a train. In turn, show a card to the first student in each train (the engineer) and ask her to name a word that begins with the blend. Next make a train whistle sound. At this signal, have each engineer move to her train's last chair (the caboose) as each of the other students moves to the chair in front of her. Present a different blend card to the new engineers. Continue with the activity until each youngster has been an engineer at least once. What a nifty way to keep blend skills on track!

Judy Wetzel—Gr. 2, Woodburn Elementary, Falls Church, VA

Reading Skills Roundup

For Beginning Readers

Thumbs Up!

/ŭ/

Combine vowel practice and literature for a royally fun listening activity! Read aloud *King Bidgood's in the Bathtub* by Audrey Wood (Harcourt Brace & Company, 1985), a humorous tale about a king who refuses to leave his bathtub. As you reread the book, ask each student to listen for words with the short *u* sound and give a thumbs-up sign each time he hears one. Next, display a jumbo tub cutout. As students recall words from the story that have the featured sound, write them on the cutout. Then encourage youngsters to brainstorm additional words that have this sound and add them to the list. Display the tubful of words for a handy reading reference.

Marilyn Campbell—Gr. 2, North Wales Elementary School, North Wales, PA

Blends by the Bunch!

GR

When it's time to review blends, go grape! Write a student-generated list of words that begin with *gr* on the chalkboard; then assign each student a word. Have him use a purple crayon to write his word on a card and then use a pencil to write a sentence that features the word. Next, have him glue his card on a purple paper plate (or construction paper circle). After each student reads his word and sentence aloud, mount the plates on a bulletin board to resemble a bunch of grapes. Embellish the display to resemble the one shown.

Kim Costanza—Gr. 1, Andy Woods Elementary, Tyler, TX

A Bunch of Blends

Read a Mat

SIGHT WORDS

Dinner is served—along with a hearty helping of sight-word practice! Program a grid with sight words. Give each student a copy of the grid and a large tagboard oval. After a review of the sight words, each child decorates her oval with colorful markers. Next, she cuts along the grid lines to make separate word cards, and then she glues the cards on the oval in a pleasing arrangement. Laminate each youngster's resulting placemat, and have her take it home for daily servings of summer sight-word practice!

Teresa Swenson—Grs. 1–2
Shimek Elementary, Iowa City, IA

about   does   done   only   very   because   kind   goes   their   own

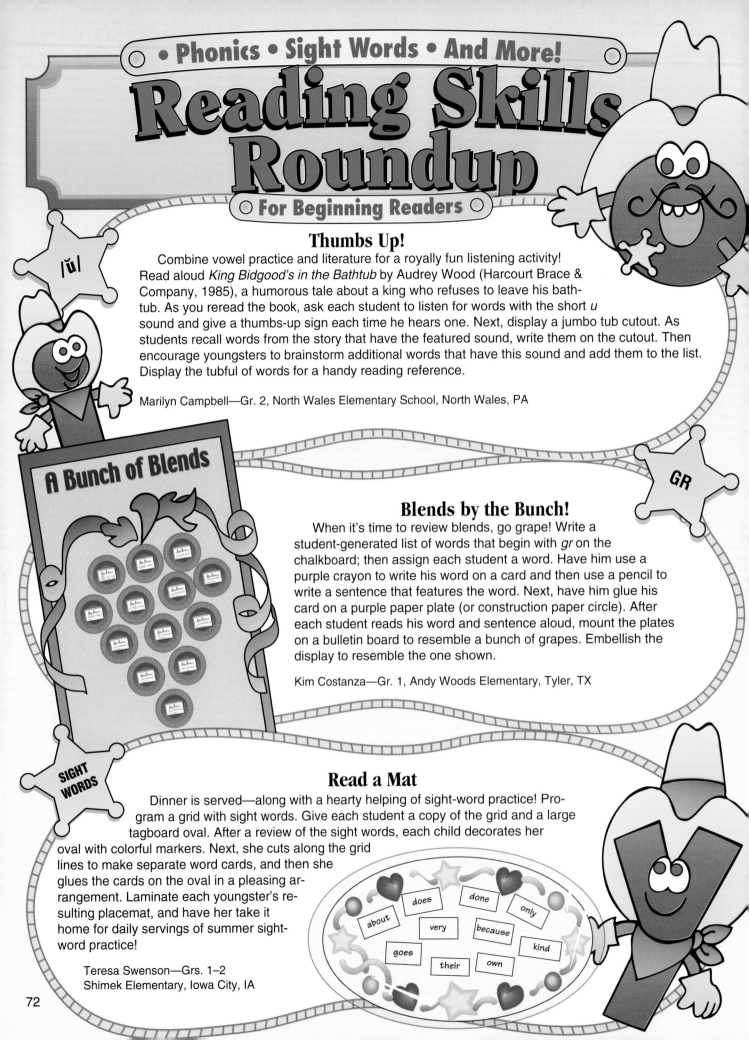

Who Lives Here?

Students are sure to feel right at home with this word-family review! A student brainstorms words from an assigned word family (rime) and lists them on scrap paper. Next, he folds a 12" x 18" sheet of drawing paper in half and cuts away the top two corners as shown. On the front of the resulting house (near the top), he writes "Who lives here?" Then he draws a door, two windows, and other desired decorations. In each window he illustrates one word from his list. Inside the house he completes a phrase like the one shown and writes clues for other words from his list. To share his work, a student shows a partner his window illustrations and challenges him to identify the corresponding word family. After his partner correctly names the rime, he reads each clue and asks his partner to name the corresponding word.

Mendy Bull—Special Education, Grs. 1–2
R. F. Woodall Primary School, White House, TN

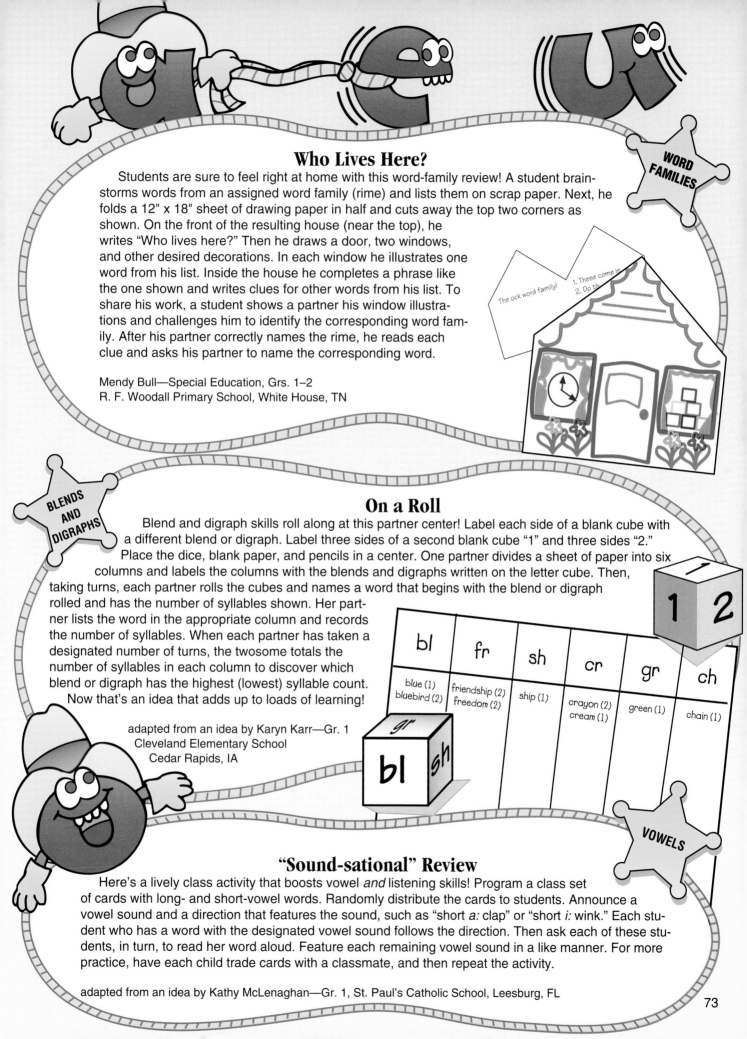

The ock word family!

1. These come in
2. Do th

WORD FAMILIES

On a Roll

BLENDS AND DIGRAPHS

Blend and digraph skills roll along at this partner center! Label each side of a blank cube with a different blend or digraph. Label three sides of a second blank cube "1" and three sides "2." Place the dice, blank paper, and pencils in a center. One partner divides a sheet of paper into six columns and labels the columns with the blends and digraphs written on the letter cube. Then, taking turns, each partner rolls the cubes and names a word that begins with the blend or digraph rolled and has the number of syllables shown. Her partner lists the word in the appropriate column and records the number of syllables. When each partner has taken a designated number of turns, the twosome totals the number of syllables in each column to discover which blend or digraph has the highest (lowest) syllable count.

Now that's an idea that adds up to loads of learning!

adapted from an idea by Karyn Karr—Gr. 1
Cleveland Elementary School
Cedar Rapids, IA

bl	fr	sh	cr	gr	ch
blue (1) bluebird (2)	friendship (2) freedom (2)	ship (1)	crayon (2) cream (1)	green (1)	chain (1)

"Sound-sational" Review

VOWELS

Here's a lively class activity that boosts vowel *and* listening skills! Program a class set of cards with long- and short-vowel words. Randomly distribute the cards to students. Announce a vowel sound and a direction that features the sound, such as "short *a:* clap" or "short *i:* wink." Each student who has a word with the designated vowel sound follows the direction. Then ask each of these students, in turn, to read her word aloud. Feature each remaining vowel sound in a like manner. For more practice, have each child trade cards with a classmate, and then repeat the activity.

adapted from an idea by Kathy McLenaghan—Gr. 1, St. Paul's Catholic School, Leesburg, FL

73

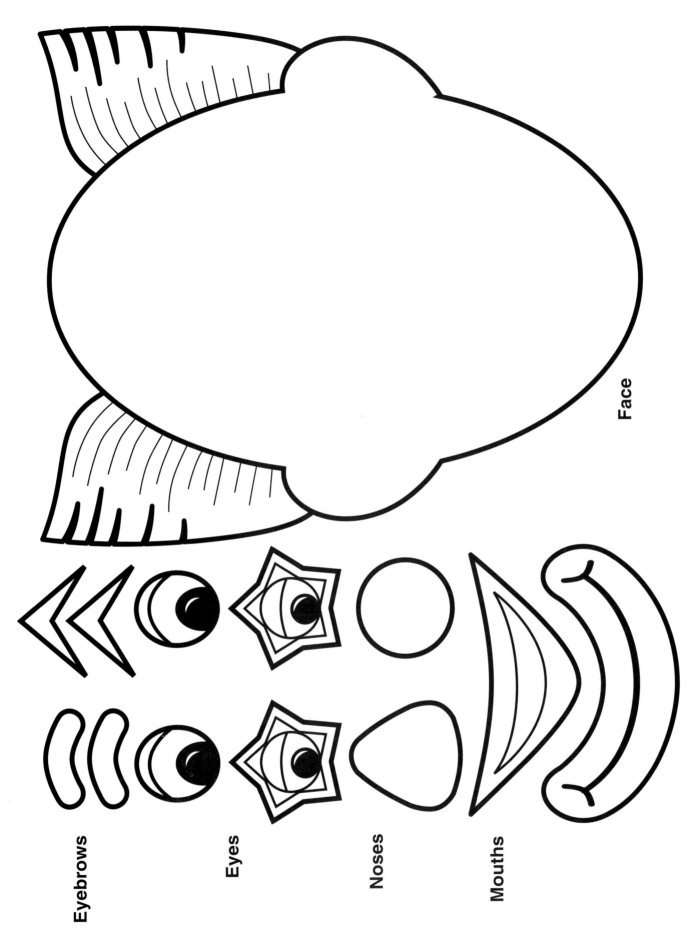

Face

Eyebrows

Eyes

Noses

Mouths

©The Education Center, Inc. • *THE MAILBOX*® • *Primary* • Oct/Nov 1999

74 **Note to teacher:** Use with "Funny Faces" on page 64.

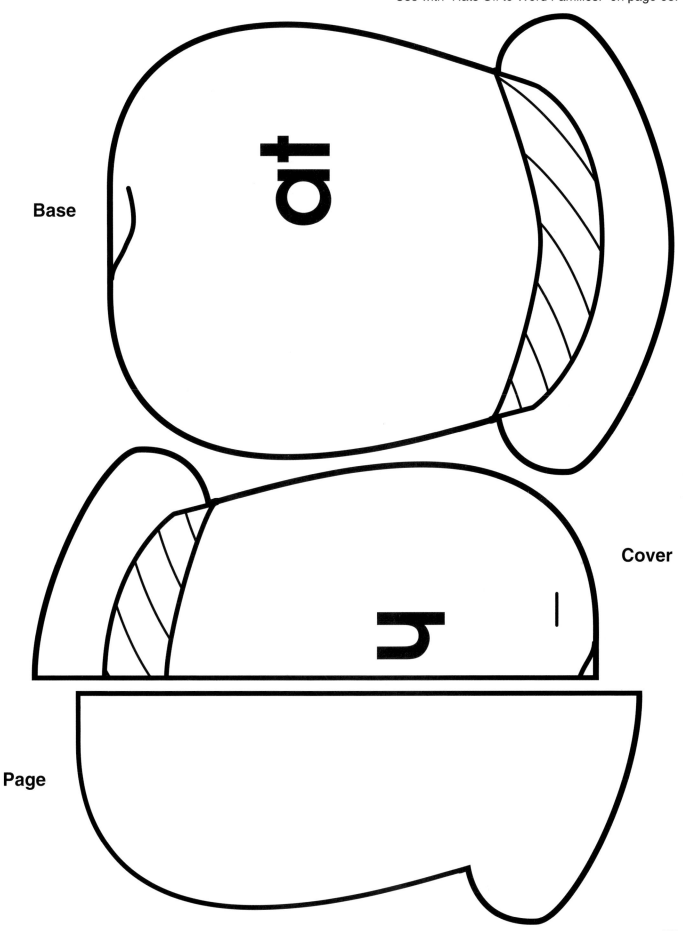

Base

at

Cover

in

Page

Short-Vowel Picture Cards
Use with "Pick the Pairs" on page 71.

LITERATURE UNITS

The Flunking of Joshua T. Bates

by Susan Shreve
Illustrated by Diane de Groat
Alfred A. Knopf, Inc.; 1995

Joshua is devastated! His mother has just informed him that when school starts tomorrow, he'll return to third grade. How will he ever endure the taunts of his former classmates *or* survive his new teacher, who in his eyes resembles a military tank? His solution is simple—he'll move to East Africa. This humorous and touching tale is perfect for promoting perseverance and fostering an understanding of individual differences.

ideas contributed by Stacie Stone Davis

The Joy Of Reading: 3

Setting the Stage

Before you introduce the story, prompt a discussion of individual differences. To do this, pair students and ask each child to trace the outline of his partner's shoe-clad foot on a sheet of white construction paper. Then have each child personalize and cut out the shape that represents his shoe. Tape the completed cutouts to the chalkboard and ask the students why no two shapes are the same. Lead the class to conclude that each child is unique: the shape of the shoes he wears, his likes and dislikes, the way that he learns. Then show the class the cover of *The Flunking of Joshua T. Bates*. Explain that this story tells about a third-grade boy who learned at a different pace from his classmates.

Agree or Disagree

Joshua's life becomes a nightmare when he learns he must repeat third grade. At the conclusion of the first chapter, have students share their opinions about the following statements. If desired, poll the class to see if they agree or disagree with each statement, recording the results. Then repoll the students at the conclusion of the book to find out if their opinions have changed.

- Joshua's idea to move to East Africa is a smart solution to his problem.
- Joshua's parents are doing what is best for him.
- Joshua's sister is a snob.
- A teacher who looks like a military tank can't be any good.
- The first week in third grade will be the toughest for Joshua.
- If Joshua had tried really hard last year, he would not be repeating third grade.

A Good Teacher Must...

be helpful
⭐ be smart
⭐ care about kids
be fair
like children
work hard
⭐ be funny
be nice

The Military Tank

It's clear from the start that Joshua has misgivings about his new teacher, Mrs. Goodwin. Before beginning chapter 2, post a length of bulletin board paper that you've titled "A Good Teacher Must..." Ask students to name the qualities of a good teacher and list their ideas on the paper. When the list is complete, invite students to predict how many of these traits Mrs. Goodwin will have. Then, at the conclusion of chapter 2, have students review the list. Draw a colorful star in front of any trait that the class agrees Mrs. Goodwin displayed. Repeat the activity several times throughout the story, each time offering to add additional qualities to the list if the class so desires. Students will quickly realize, right along with Joshua, that Mrs. Goodwin is a gem of a teacher.

Best Friends

By the conclusion of chapter 6, students will be abuzz about the special friendship that Joshua and Andrew share. Have them recall how the boys maintain their special friendship, even when the going gets tough. Then give each child a copy of the booklet project on page 80. Ask each student to write her name on the front cover of the booklet and complete the sentence on each booklet page. Next have her color the artwork on the front and back booklet covers. To assemble her project, she cuts out each circle along the bold lines, stacks her booklet pages in sequential order, and places the front cover on top of the stack. Then she places the back cover on the bottom of the stack (keeping the artwork to the outside) and staples the project at the top. Now that's a project that encourages students to "bee" best friends!

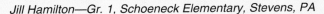

Star Students

In chapter 8, Joshua receives his first-quarter report card. When he finally musters up the nerve to open it, he is astonished by his good grades! To review the progress that Joshua has shown, use your students' ideas to complete a Venn diagram labeled like the one shown. Ask students to study the diagram and then help them conclude that in addition to learning how to read, Joshua has learned to believe in himself! For a stellar follow-up project, have each child trace a large star template onto a 12-inch square of yellow construction paper. Have each child illustrate and label Joshua in the center of the star, and then on each star point describe a different trait that contributes to Joshua's star-student status. After each child has cut out his project, have him turn it over, draw and label a likeness of himself in the center of the blank star, and program each star point with a characteristic that contributes to *his* star-student status! Help each child hole-punch the top of his project and tie a loop of yarn through the hole. Suggest that he suspend his project at home from a desired doorknob so that he will be reminded of his stellar traits.

Story Highlights

At the conclusion of this feel-good book, write a student-generated list of story highlights. To begin, write the numerals 1 through 10 on the chalkboard to represent the ten book chapters. As students recall different story events, list each one below its corresponding chapter. Continue in this manner until two or more events are listed per chapter. Then, working individually or with partners, have the students describe and illustrate the events on provided paper. Enlist the students' help in sequencing the projects on a bulletin board titled "Story Snapshots" and decorated like the display shown. (For a year-round display, have students complete this activity at the conclusion of each chapter book that you read aloud.)

Jill Hamilton—Gr. 1, Schoeneck Elementary, Stevens, PA

More About Joshua

If your youngsters enjoyed *The Flunking of Joshua T. Bates,* they'll also enjoy these two sequels!

Joshua T. Bates in Trouble Again
Now that Joshua's been promoted to fourth grade, everything should be wonderful, right? Not so. Joshua quickly discovers that fitting into fourth grade comes with plenty of challenges.

Joshua T. Bates Takes Charge
As a fifth grader, Joshua still remembers how it felt being the class outcast of third grade. But does he dare stand up for the nerdy new kid that the other fifth-grade boys are teasing?

2.

Two things I think
a best friend should
always do are

1.

Joshua and
Andrew are best friends
because

4.

Joshua and
Andrew's special
friendship taught me

On the
Ball About
Best
Friends

by

3.

Two things I think
a best friend should
never do are

©The Education Center, Inc. • *THE MAILBOX® • Primary* • Aug/Sept 1999

Note to teacher: Use with "Best Friends" on page 79.

Literature From the Black Lagoon
Using Mike Thaler's Books in the Classroom

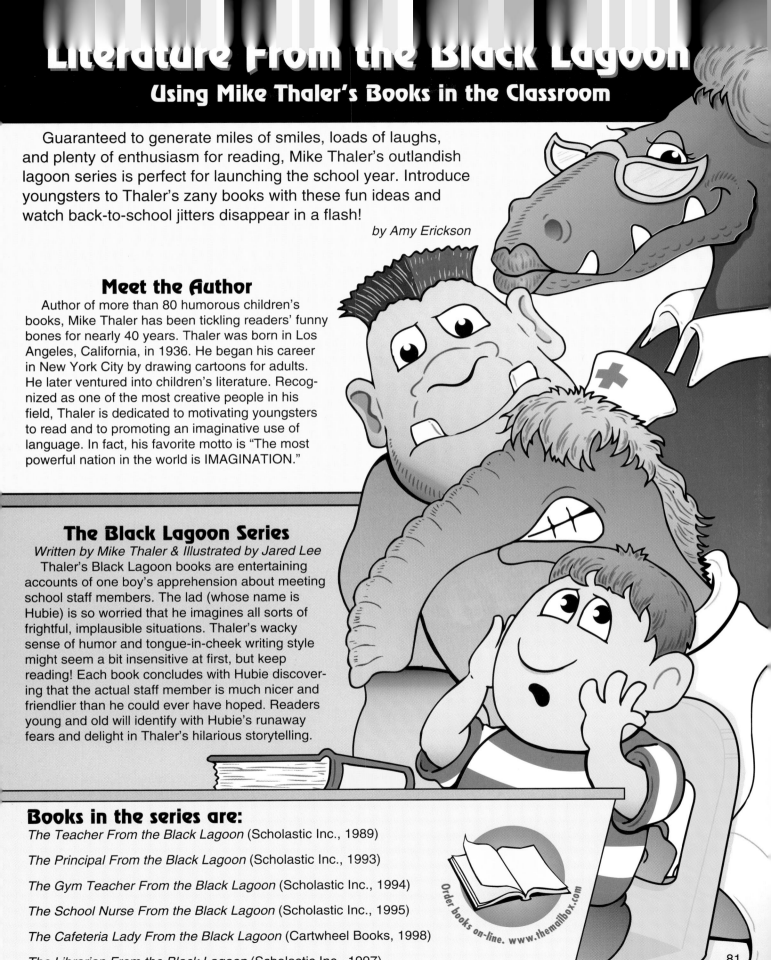

Guaranteed to generate miles of smiles, loads of laughs, and plenty of enthusiasm for reading, Mike Thaler's outlandish lagoon series is perfect for launching the school year. Introduce youngsters to Thaler's zany books with these fun ideas and watch back-to-school jitters disappear in a flash!

by Amy Erickson

Meet the Author

Author of more than 80 humorous children's books, Mike Thaler has been tickling readers' funny bones for nearly 40 years. Thaler was born in Los Angeles, California, in 1936. He began his career in New York City by drawing cartoons for adults. He later ventured into children's literature. Recognized as one of the most creative people in his field, Thaler is dedicated to motivating youngsters to read and to promoting an imaginative use of language. In fact, his favorite motto is "The most powerful nation in the world is IMAGINATION."

The Black Lagoon Series

Written by Mike Thaler & Illustrated by Jared Lee
Thaler's Black Lagoon books are entertaining accounts of one boy's apprehension about meeting school staff members. The lad (whose name is Hubie) is so worried that he imagines all sorts of frightful, implausible situations. Thaler's wacky sense of humor and tongue-in-cheek writing style might seem a bit insensitive at first, but keep reading! Each book concludes with Hubie discovering that the actual staff member is much nicer and friendlier than he could ever have hoped. Readers young and old will identify with Hubie's runaway fears and delight in Thaler's hilarious storytelling.

Books in the series are:

The Teacher From the Black Lagoon (Scholastic Inc., 1989)

The Principal From the Black Lagoon (Scholastic Inc., 1993)

The Gym Teacher From the Black Lagoon (Scholastic Inc., 1994)

The School Nurse From the Black Lagoon (Scholastic Inc., 1995)

The Cafeteria Lady From the Black Lagoon (Cartwheel Books, 1998)

The Librarian From the Black Lagoon (Scholastic Inc., 1997)

Order books on-line. www.themailbox.com

First-Day Introductions

No doubt youngsters will arrive on the first day of school with plenty of questions about you and their new classmates. Get introductions rolling and set minds at ease with this follow-up activity to *The Teacher From the Black Lagoon.* To prepare, cover an empty cube-shaped box with colorful paper. Label each side with a different topic, such as hobbies or favorite food. For younger students, add a corresponding picture for each topic.

Inform students that in *The Teacher From the Black Lagoon,* a young boy named Hubie has so many questions about his new teacher that he imagines all kinds of frightful things about her. At this point, poll the students to find out how many of them have questions about you! Then read aloud this amusing book about first-day jitters. At the book's conclusion, gather students in a circle on the floor. Tell them that instead of having their imaginations get the best of them (like Hubie!), you've planned an activity that will help them get to know you, and each other, better. Then roll the prepared cube and respond to the topic that you roll. Have each student take a turn in a similar manner. Repeat as desired. Conclude the activity with a short question-and-answer session to address any remaining concerns.

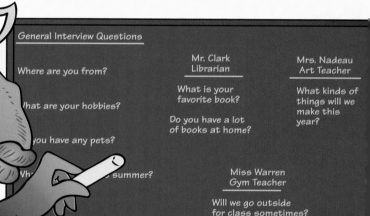

Pleased to Meet You!

Tell students that not only does Thaler's wary main character fear that his teacher comes from the Black Lagoon, he suspects that other staff members do too! To establish this, read aloud another title or two from the series. Then ask youngsters how suspicions like Hubie's could be put to rest. Lead them to conclude that the best way to alleviate fears about staff members is to get to know them! Have students identify general questions that would help them get acquainted with the school staff. Write these questions on the chalkboard. Also write the name and position of each staff member who has agreed to visit your classroom and be interviewed. Invite the class to brainstorm additional questions for each of these people. Next, group students and assign each group a staff member to interview. Instruct each group to compile a list of interview questions and decide which group member will ask each one. Require that all members be involved.

Conclude each interview by photographing the visitor. Then ask students to dictate what they learned about this staff member as you write the information on chart paper. Later copy the information onto booklet-size paper. Compile the student-generated paragraphs and the corresponding staff photographs into a class book. The resulting who's who of staff members is sure to be a favorite!

I Heard That...

From the nurse who vaccinates students kebab-style to the gym teacher who has youngsters running laps around the world, the Black Lagoon series is filled with rumors of absurd situations and comical exaggerations. After students have heard a few of Thaler's tales, they'll be ready to conjure up (and resolve) their own amusing and implausible rumors.

To begin, a child draws a line five inches from each end of a 4 1/2" x 12" strip of white construction paper. Then she chooses a staff member and writes this person's name and title between the two lines. Next she aligns the left end of the paper with the line on the left, flattens the paper, creases the fold, and writes "I heard that…" on the resulting flap. She opens the flap, completes the sentence with an outlandish rumor, and adds an illustration, being careful to stay to the left of the line. In a similar manner, she makes a flap on the right end of her paper. She labels this flap "I found out that…" Then she opens the flap and completes and illustrates a truthful sentence about the featured staff member. Showcase the youngsters' grin-inducing work on a bulletin board titled "Really Ridiculous Rumors!"

The Staff From the Black Lagoon

So just exactly what is a lagoon? Gather your youngsters' ideas, then reveal that it is a shallow body of water similar to a pond. Ask students why they think Thaler chose to have the school staff come from a *black* lagoon. Lead them to realize that a black lagoon creates a creepy and mysterious mood. Then invite youngsters to name locations that would set a silly mood for staff-related stories. Write their ideas on the chalkboard, and have each child write and illustrate a silly tale about an imaginary staff member from one of these locations.

To create a cover for his story, a student folds in half a 12" x 18" sheet of white construction paper. Next he colors a copy of the schoolhouse pattern on page 85 and cuts it out. Then he carefully cuts along the dotted lines and folds back the resulting doors along the fine lines. Keeping the doors of the schoolhouse open, the student glues the cutout to the front of his folded paper as shown. He illustrates his character in the open doorway, and adds a title, his name, and other desired decorations to the cover before stapling his story inside. No doubt this creative-writing activity will receive high marks from your young authors!

Who Else Lurks There?

Are there other mysterious characters lurking around in the black lagoon? Sure! Ask students to name school-related staff whom Thaler has not yet featured in his Black Lagoon series. Write their suggestions on the chalkboard. Ideas might include a custodian, substitute teacher, vice-principal, teacher assistant, secretary, and school bus driver. Then have each child write and illustrate a story about one of these people. To do this, give each child a copy of the booklet project on page 86 (for a larger booklet, photocopy the page at 125% onto 11" x 17" paper). Have each child complete the cover by writing the title of her main character on the line and then drawing and coloring a picture inside the box. For best results, suggest that students study the covers of the books in the Black Lagoon series before they complete their illustrations. Then have each child finish and illustrate the sentence on each booklet page. To assemble her booklet, she cuts on the bold lines, stacks the pages in sequential order, places the cover on top, and staples along the left edge. The Black Lagoon will definitely be teeming with activity!

Hi! I'm Mrs. Beamster, the librarian. May I help you find a book?

A Fun Follow-up for Each Story in the Series

The Teacher From the Black Lagoon *Hubie sets out for his first day of school with bone-chilling preconceptions of his new teacher.*

Hubie's dream about his new teacher is downright scary! Have students ponder what Hubie could dream if his thoughts were safe and sweet. Then ask each child to share one of her sweet dreams (or hopes) for the school year. List the responses on a large cloud-shaped cutout labeled "Our Sweet Dreams for the School Year." Be sure to add a hope of your own before you showcase the dreamy project in a prominent classroom location.

The Principal From the Black Lagoon *Will Hubie survive his visit to the dreaded principal's office?*

Word has it that Principal Green's experiments leave Freddy with chicken feet and Eric with hamster hands! For a dose of fun, ask each child to imagine that he has gained one or more animal parts as a result of Principal Green's experiments. Have him draw a picture to show what he imagines. Then ask him to write about the benefits and drawbacks of his new body part(s). Now that's an idea that's "tail-or-made" for rib-tickling fun!

The Gym Teacher From the Black Lagoon *Yikes! Big, mean Coach Kong is in charge of gym class!*

Baseball with live bats and parachute games high above the ground—it must be Coach Kong's gym class! Brainstorm traditional gym activities with the students. Then have each child choose one activity and make a poster that shows how it would be done in Coach Kong's class.

The School Nurse From the Black Lagoon *Rumor has it that Miss Hearse the Nurse has a fondness for ghoulish cures and a tongue depressor as long as a surfboard!*

Hubie is so overjoyed when Nurse Hearse miraculously cures his mysterious ailment that he eagerly sets out to write her a thank-you letter. After reviewing the parts of a friendly letter, have each youngster pen a note to the nurse on Hubie's behalf.

The Cafeteria Lady From the Black Lagoon *Hubie braces himself to meet Wanda Belch, the much-talked-about cafeteria lady.*

What's on the menu? A generous helping of wordplay and a dash of descriptive writing! After serving up this tale about Wanda Belch's rumored culinary specialties, have each child create his own frightful lunch menu. Seconds, anyone?

The Librarian From the Black Lagoon *Watch out for Mrs. Beamster, a.k.a. The Laminator. It's rumored that she'll laminate anyone who talks in the library!*

The imagined Mrs. Beamster takes her job of protecting library books very seriously—a little too seriously if you ask Hubie! Try this bookmark-making project after a visit to *your* school's library. To make her bookmark, a youngster writes and illustrates one fact about the imagined Mrs. Beamster on one side of a white construction paper strip and one fact about your school's librarian on the other side. Laminate the bookmarks before students put them to use. Or have students present the laminated projects to the school librarian for a nifty back-to-school gift.

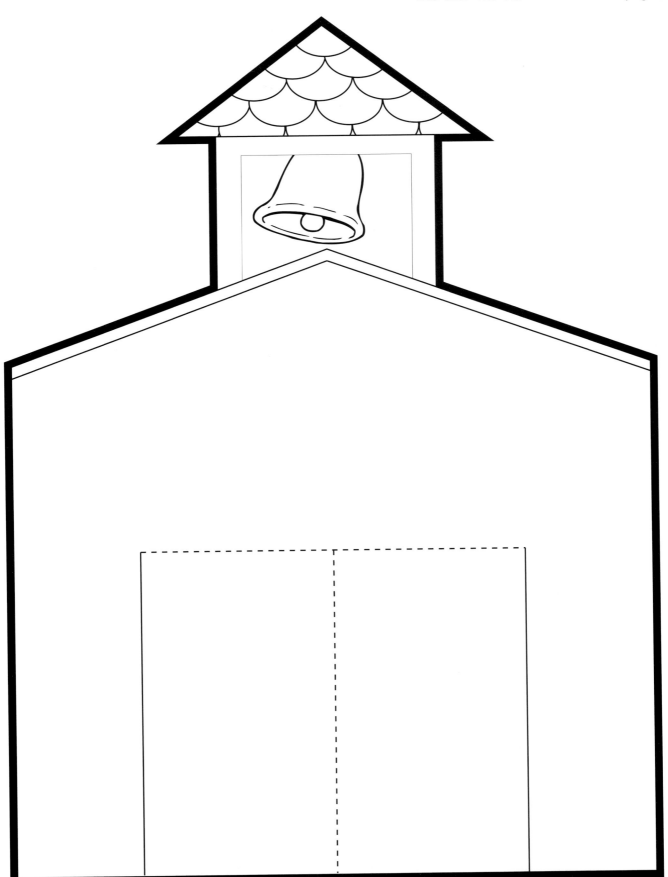

Booklet Project

The _____
from the
Black Lagoon

by _____

I heard _____

1

I thought _____

2

I saw _____

3

I believe _____

4

I now know _____

5

Note to teacher: Use with "Who Else Lurks There?" on page 83.

Catwings

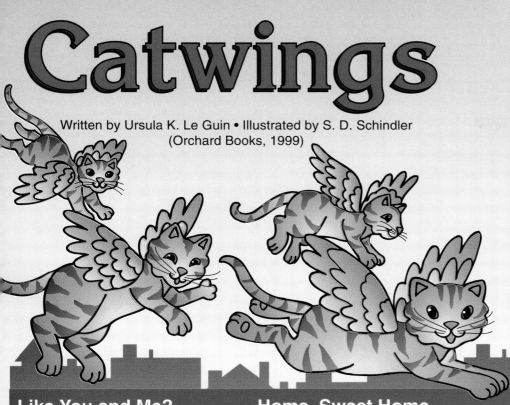

Written by Ursula K. Le Guin • Illustrated by S. D. Schindler
(Orchard Books, 1999)

Like most cats, Thelma, Harriet, Roger, and James Tabby have a fondness for milk and a strong distrust of dogs. But one thing sets these siblings apart from all other cats—wings! This first installment of the popular Catwings series describes the adventures of the four winged felines as they search for a safe home. Use the following activities to enhance your presentation of this award-winning and "paws-itively" irresistible chapter book.

*ideas contributed by
Stacie Stone Davis*

Like You and Me?

Mrs. Tabby seems to have a lot in common with human mothers, at first. She cares deeply for her offspring and does her best to raise them well. However, when she asks her young cats to leave home, her behavior is not at all humanlike. At the conclusion of chapter 1, draw a large two-circle Venn diagram on the chalkboard and label it "Cats" and "People." As students name characteristics and behaviors of the two, write their responses on the diagram in the appropriate spaces. Then have students analyze the information you've recorded.

Home, Sweet Home

At the conclusion of chapter 1, the young Tabbys set out to find a home that is far away from ferocious dogs and life-threatening traffic. Before reading chapter 2 aloud, set aside time for students to ponder the perfect home for the kittens. Give each child two 4" x 8" pieces of white paper that are folded in half. Have her illustrate the cat's city home on the front of one folded paper and then describe it inside. Have her illustrate and describe her prediction of the cat's new home on the second paper. Next have each child title a 6" x 18" strip of construction paper "Home, Sweet Home" and then glue her two projects on the paper and label them as shown. Invite interested students to share their new home ideas before collecting the projects. After the last chapter in the book is read, have each student illustrate and describe the kittens' new home on a third piece of folded paper. Then return the construction paper projects so students can add their final illustrations to them.

Home, Sweet Home

on the streets. It is never quiet. Fierce rats and dogs live here. It is a dangerous place for the cats to live.

Old Home

will have plenty to eat at their home in the country.

Prediction

New Home

Fearful Firsts

There's no doubt about it—the Tabbys are a bit apprehensive when it's time to leave home. By sticking with each other and keeping a good sense of humor, the cats cope with their fear. This picture-perfect idea increases your youngsters' awareness of their own success in conquering fear. Review the situations from chapters 1 and 2 that are frightening to the Tabbys and have students recall how the cats face these fears. Next ask each child to think of a situation that was once fearful for him, but that no longer seems frightening. Then have him copy, complete, and illustrate the sentence stems shown. Invite each youngster to share his work in a small group or with the entire class for a pride-boosting reminder of how he overcame a fear!

At first I was afraid to go swimming.
But then I took swimming lessons.
Now I am on the swim team.

Dear Mom,

It has been hard work, but we are all getting better at flying. We flew west today and found a quiet little spot with a creek. I caught some fish in the creek for dinner. They were delicious! We miss you and hope you and Tom are okay.

Love,
Roger

October 6

Roger Tabby
4 Country Lane
Small Town, IL

Mrs. Jane Tabby
22 Busy Street
Big City, IL

Dear Mom,

Mrs. Tabby would surely love to know how her kitties fare in their search for a new home. So why not invite students to keep her posted? For each student, staple three half sheets of writing paper between two white construction paper covers. On the front cover of his booklet, have each child write a mailing address for Mrs. Tabby and a return address for the kitty of his choice. Then have him draw and color a stamp in the upper right-hand corner. At the conclusion of chapter 2, review the main chapter events with the class. Then have each child pen a letter in his booklet to Mrs. Tabby, writing from the point of view of the young cat he has named in his return address. Repeat the activity after each of the two remaining chapters. Now that's an activity that delivers first-class letter-writing practice!

Peaceful Solutions

The forest critters are frightened and outraged when the flying Tabbys move into their habitat, so Owl decides to take the matter into her own talons. After reading chapter 3, discuss the results of Owl's behavior, leading students to conclude that her unfriendly actions are not a good solution. Then challenge youngsters to brainstorm peaceful solutions that would satisfy the forest animals *and* the Tabbys. Invite students to apply the practices they use in resolving conflicts and in getting along with others. To further extend the activity, divide students into small groups and secretly assign each group a different made-up situation that needs to be resolved. Have each group, in turn, role-play its situation and act out a peaceful resolution for it. Count on this activity to increase positive (and peaceful) student interactions!

"Cat-chy" Expressions

Introduce youngsters to cat-related idioms with this fun feline project! Follow up chapter 2 by writing "sitting in the catbird seat" on the chalkboard. Ask students what they think the expression means. Then read aloud the corresponding passage from page 12 and help students use context clues to determine that from Harriet's perch, she has a fantastic view! Write several more cat-related idioms on the chalkboard and have students interpret each one literally before you reveal its figurative meaning. Then have each child fold a 6" x 18" strip of white construction paper in half two times and unfold the paper to reveal four equal-size sections. Instruct each student to copy a cat-related idiom from the list and illustrate its literal meaning in the second section of her paper. In the third section of her paper, have her use the idiom correctly in a sentence and illustrate her work. Lastly have her color the first and fourth sections of her paper to resemble cat fur.

To make her feline booklet, a student accordion-folds her project. Next she trims the bottom two corners from a 4" x 5" construction paper rectangle, cuts two ears from the paper scraps, and glues them to the larger cutout to create a cat head. She glues this cutout to the front of her folded project; then she uses construction paper scraps, glue, and crayons to add desired facial features and feet. Lastly she cuts a cat's tail from construction paper and glues it to the back of the closed booklet as shown. Meow!

Let the cat out of the bag.

When she mentioned her birthday, he let the cat out of the bag.

We're having a surprise party!

Cat-Related Idioms

Cat got your tongue?   Rain cats and dogs.
Let the cat out of the bag.   Look what the cat dragged in.
Play cat and mouse.   When the cat's away, the mice will play.

Kind Hands

Promote compassion for pets with this handy project! On page 29, Thelma recalls, " 'Mother always said...that if you found the right kind of Hands, you'd never have to hunt again. But if you found the wrong kind, it would be worse than dogs.' " Revisit this passage at the conclusion of chapter 3 and ask students what it means. Then have each child describe on a 3" x 6" piece of writing paper how kind hands treat pets. To create the project shown, she uses a seven-inch construction paper circle, crayons, construction paper scraps, and glue to create her self-likeness. She glues her self-likeness and her writing to a 6" x 18" strip of colored construction paper. After she adds desired details to the resulting shirt, she traces her hands on construction paper. She cuts out the tracings, glues one cutout to the end of each shirt sleeve, and carefully folds over the hands and sleeves as shown. For a display that's sure to be a hands-down favorite, showcase the students' completed projects on a bulletin board titled "Kind Hands!"

What Characters!

Students will be on a roll with this character analysis activity! To make a character cube, cover a square box with colorful paper. Label each side of the box with a different character's name. (Or to reuse the box, write each name on a cutout and then use Velcro® or tape to attach the cutouts to the box.) Seat students in a circle on the floor. Have each student in turn roll the cube, announce the character she rolls, and then (without repeating previous responses) name an adjective that describes the character or make a statement about him or her. Roll on!

Kind hands gently pet a cat and brush its fur.

What's Next?

The Catwings crew may have found a new home, but that doesn't mean the kitties won't continue to have many more adventures! At the conclusion of this delightful tale, have students brainstorm ideas for follow-up stories and then write them. To publish his tale in a barn-shaped booklet, a student cuts away the top two corners of a 9" x 12" sheet of red construction paper. Behind this paper he staples a supply of writing paper and a 9" x 12" sheet of red paper. He trims all the paper to match the front cover before he writes his edited story inside the resulting booklet. Then he uses crayons to add his name, his story's title, and any other desired details to the booklet covers. Invite each child to share his story with the class. For more Catwing adventures by Le Guin, read aloud these "purr-fectly" delightful sequels:
- *Catwings Return*
- *Wonderful Alexander and the Catwings*
- *Jane on Her Own: A Catwings Tale*

The Catwings Go to School

by Adam

Order books on-line. www.themailbox.com

90

Name _____

Homeward Bound

Cut out the story events below.
Glue the events on the path in the order that they happen.

What do the kitties find besides a home?
To find out, match the letters in the boxes to the numbered lines below.

| 1 | 2 | 3 | 4 | | 5 | 6 | 3 | | 4 | 7 | | 5 | 6 | 3 | | 4 | 7 | | 1 | 2 | 3 | 4 | ! |

James escapes from Owl.	A dog chases Harriet.		The cats visit Overhill Farm.	Harriet meets a nice girl.	Owl thinks about the cats.	Mrs. Tabby tells the cats to leave.	The birds get upset about the cats.
H	K	S		A	D	I	N

The Chocolate Touch

Written by Patrick Skene Catling • Illustrated by Margot Apple
(Bantam Doubleday Dell Books for Young Readers, 1996)

John Midas is a young boy who is so crazy about chocolate that he isn't interested in eating other foods. He knows his eating habits worry his parents, but he really doesn't understand what all the fuss is about—at least not yet! This highly entertaining tale satisfies young readers and teaches them a memorable lesson about selfishness.

ideas contributed by Stacie Stone Davis

Too Much of a Good Thing?

John quickly dismisses the concerns his parents and doctor have about his candy-eating habits. But do your students think he should be worried? At the conclusion of chapter 2 give each child a quarter-size circle of gray construction paper to represent the coin that John finds. Ask him to write his initials on one side of the cutout and then tape it on a bar graph labeled like the one pictured. Discuss the resulting graph and invite students to share their opinions and the reasoning behind them. Plan to repeat the activity after chapters 6 and 10, each time investigating why students' opinions about John's chocolate-eating habits do or do not change. If desired, give each child a foil-wrapped chocolate coin to eat at the conclusion of each discussion!

Should John be worried about eating too much candy?

Yes	T.M.	P.C.	A.R.	B.B.	C.E.			
No	N.G.	E.S.	C.H.	J.D.	K.M.	N.B.	R.G.	D.F.

Chocolatey Changes

When his toothpaste and breakfast taste like chocolate, John is convinced something strange and wonderful has happened! Before beginning chapter 4, invite students to describe what they think has happened to John and predict how the chocolatey change might affect his school day. At the end of chapter 4, have students recall the chocolate-related events that have occurred in the story. Then ask a different child to illustrate each one on provided paper. Display the illustrations side by side in chronological order. Conclude each remaining chapter by selecting different students to illustrate the chocolate-related events from the chapter and then display the pictures as described. At the end of the story students will have a clear picture of John's chocolate touch.

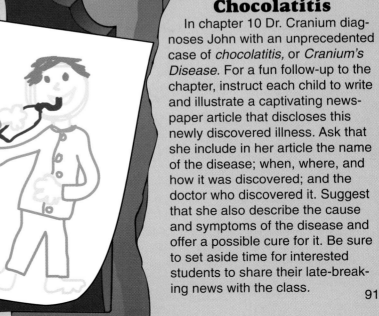

A Case of Chocolatitis

In chapter 10 Dr. Cranium diagnoses John with an unprecedented case of *chocolatitis,* or *Cranium's Disease.* For a fun follow-up to the chapter, instruct each child to write and illustrate a captivating newspaper article that discloses this newly discovered illness. Ask that she include in her article the name of the disease; when, where, and how it was discovered; and the doctor who discovered it. Suggest that she also describe the cause and symptoms of the disease and offer a possible cure for it. Be sure to set aside time for interested students to share their late-breaking news with the class.

Sealed With a Kiss

It isn't until John's mother turns into a lifeless chocolate statue (chapter 11) that he stops thinking only of himself. Help students understand that John's selfish chocolate-eating habits end up hurting the people he loves the most. Then have them name things their parents routinely remind them to do, such as pick up their clothes, wash their hands, brush their teeth, and so on. List their ideas and discuss why having to be reminded to do each action is selfish.

Next have each child make a selfless pledge and seal it with a kiss—a candy kiss, that is! To do this a child chooses a selfless act and describes it on a white candy kiss pattern (page 25). Then he cuts out the pattern, glues it on brown paper, and trims the brown paper to create an eye-catching border. On a paper strip he writes to whom his pledge is dedicated and glues one end of it to the back of his project. Students will be proud to present these sweet pledges of selflessness, and others will be pleased to receive them.

I pledge to make my bed each morning without a reminder from you. Love, Billy

My favorite character in The Chocolate Touch is John Midas. I like this character because I love chocolate, too! I thought he was funny. He taught me something.

Candy Bar Book Reports

What's the perfect way for students to wrap up this irresistible chapter book? A candy bar book report, of course! To make a report, a child completes a copy of page 93 by finishing and illustrating the sentences. Then she cuts along the bold lines, stacks the resulting rectangles in sequential order, and staples the left-hand edge of the stack. Next she wraps a 7" x 9" length of foil around her project and folds the foil ends toward the center. To make the outer wrapper, she centers her project atop a 6" x 7" construction paper rectangle, folds the top and bottom edges of the paper toward the center of the project, and secures the overlapping edges with tape. Then she temporarily removes the foil-wrapped pages while she decorates and personalizes the resulting candy bar wrapper. How sweet!

Thoughtful Touches

This follow-up activity puts students in touch with their thinking skills! If possible read aloud *King Midas and the Golden Touch* as told by Charlotte Craft (Morrow Junior Books, 1999), and discuss with students the similarities and differences between the two tales. Remind students that John's last name is Midas and invite them to speculate why the author did this. Then challenge each child to write and illustrate a story in which the main character is given a magic touch. What's the catch? The magic touch must be one that will help—not hurt—other people! Publish these one-of-a-kind tales in a class book titled "Thoughtful Touches."

Order books online. www.themailbox.com

My favorite character in *The Chocolate Touch* is

_____. I like this character

because_____

_____

_____

1

In this story the problem that needs to be solved is

_____

_____

_____

_____

2

The problem is solved when _____

_____

_____

_____

_____

3

My favorite part of *The Chocolate Touch* is _____

_____

_____

_____

_____

4

©The Education Center, Inc. • THE MAILBOX® • Primary • Feb/Mar 2000

Note to teacher: Use with "Candy Bar Book Reports" on page 92.

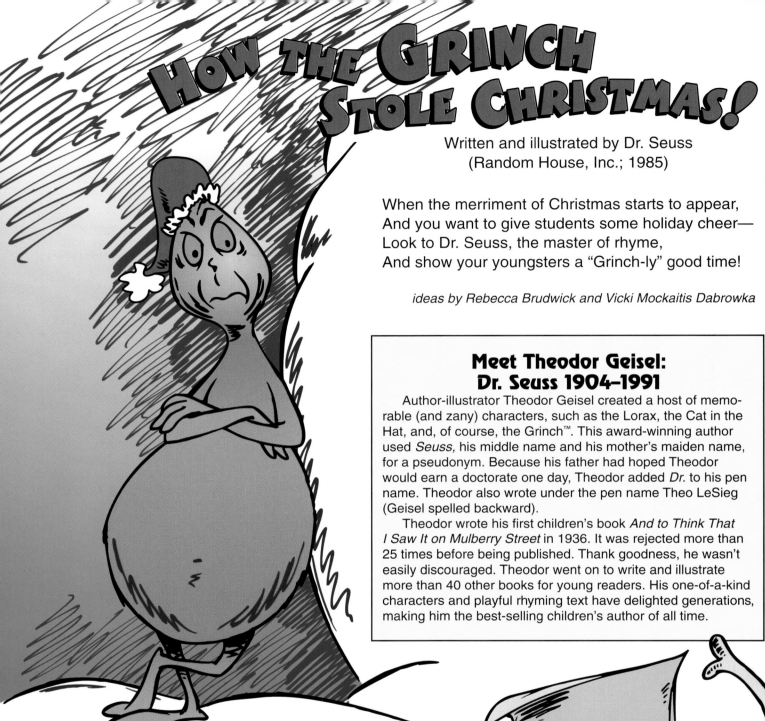

HOW THE GRINCH STOLE CHRISTMAS!

Written and illustrated by Dr. Seuss
(Random House, Inc.; 1985)

When the merriment of Christmas starts to appear,
And you want to give students some holiday cheer—
Look to Dr. Seuss, the master of rhyme,
And show your youngsters a "Grinch-ly" good time!

ideas by Rebecca Brudwick and Vicki Mockaitis Dabrowka

Meet Theodor Geisel: Dr. Seuss 1904–1991

Author-illustrator Theodor Geisel created a host of memorable (and zany) characters, such as the Lorax, the Cat in the Hat, and, of course, the Grinch™. This award-winning author used *Seuss,* his middle name and his mother's maiden name, for a pseudonym. Because his father had hoped Theodor would earn a doctorate one day, Theodor added *Dr.* to his pen name. Theodor also wrote under the pen name Theo LeSieg (Geisel spelled backward).

Theodor wrote his first children's book *And to Think That I Saw It on Mulberry Street* in 1936. It was rejected more than 25 times before being published. Thank goodness, he wasn't easily discouraged. Theodor went on to write and illustrate more than 40 other books for young readers. His one-of-a-kind characters and playful rhyming text have delighted generations, making him the best-selling children's author of all time.

A Stolen Season?

Originally published in 1957, *How the Grinch Stole Christmas!* conveys a timeless message about the true meaning of Yuletide. To set the stage for this book, ask students if they think it is possible to steal Christmas. After students share their opinions, read aloud the story. Next ask students to recall Christmas-related objects and feelings from the story. List their responses on a sheet of chart paper. Then, with students' input, make a check mark beside each thing that the Grinch took and a star beside each thing he did not take. Ask youngsters to analyze the coded list and share their observations. Lead them to conclude that the Grinch only took things that he could see and touch. Ask students again if they believe Christmas can be stolen, this time encouraging plenty of discussion. Students are sure to agree that many things can be stolen—but not the holiday spirit!

✓ stockings
✓ wreath
☆ happiness
✓ tree
☆ singing
☆ love
✓ presents

Something to Sing About

After snatching every Christmas box, bag, and gift from the Whos' homes, the Grinch is astonished the next morning to hear singing in Who-ville. Explore possible reasons for the Whos' joyfulness with this bulletin board project. Revisit with the class the illustration that shows the Whos singing. Ask students why they think the Whos are happy and thankful. After a bit of discussion, have each child write on a heart cutout one reason he thinks the Whos are singing. Next have him make a Who character with outstretched arms (like in Seuss's illustration). Provide a variety of arts-and-crafts materials for this project. To create the display, mount the student projects, music note cutouts, and a title as shown. What a great way to tune in to the story's theme!

Very Merry Thoughts

The Whos have plenty of reasons to be thankful and happy, and there's no doubt your youngsters do, too. Invite students to showcase their merry thoughts with this "heart-y" wreath project. In advance, cut out the center of a thin, white paper plate for each student. To make his wreath, a youngster sponge-paints the bottom of his prepared plate green. Next he cuts out five hearts, each from a three-inch square of red or pink construction paper. On each heart he writes a different reason he is happy or thankful. When his painted wreath is dry, he glues the hearts he labeled and a ribbon bow on the wreath. Encourage each youngster to share his cheery holiday decoration with the class before taking it home.

Seuss-Style Stockings

When it comes to creating rhymes, there's no better inspiration than Dr. Seuss's humorous stories! To begin this rhyme-related activity, read aloud the scene in which the Grinch takes the Whos' Christmas stockings and gifts. Then have students recall rhyming word pairs from the scene as you list them on the chalkboard. When you write "chimbley," explain that Dr. Seuss sometimes made up a new word to create a rhyme, which makes his books even more fun to read. Next give each student a white construction paper copy of page 97. Ask each child to write pairs of rhyming words (real or nonsense) on the cuff of the stocking. Then have him sign his name, color the rest of the stocking as desired, and cut it out. Set aside time for student pairs to create original (and silly!) rhymes using the words on their cutouts. Invite students to orally present their favorite rhymes to the class or have them write and illustrate the rhymes on provided paper. To extend the fun, display the stockings throughout the holiday season so students can continue composing Seuss-style rhymes!

Problems in Whoville

Put your youngsters' brains, or, as Dr. Seuss might have said, puzzlers, to work with this problem-solving idea! At a center, place a basket filled with green and red pom-poms, a lidded container, and a supply of paper slips. Each morning write on the chalkboard a different story-related math problem (see "Sample Problems"). Each youngster visits the center and solves the problem, using the pom-poms as needed. Then he writes his name and answer on a paper slip and deposits it in the lidded container.

At the end of the day, take two or more slips from the container. Ask the owner of each slip to demonstrate how he solved the problem. (Remind youngsters that often there is more than one correct way to solve a problem.) Later, read the remaining slips and give appropriate feedback.

Sample Problems

The Grinch put 3 checkerboards, 2 dolls, and 5 drums in his sack.
How many objects in all did he put in the sack? *(10)*

One recipe of Who pudding serves 7 Whos.
How many recipes are needed to serve 21 Whos? *(3)*

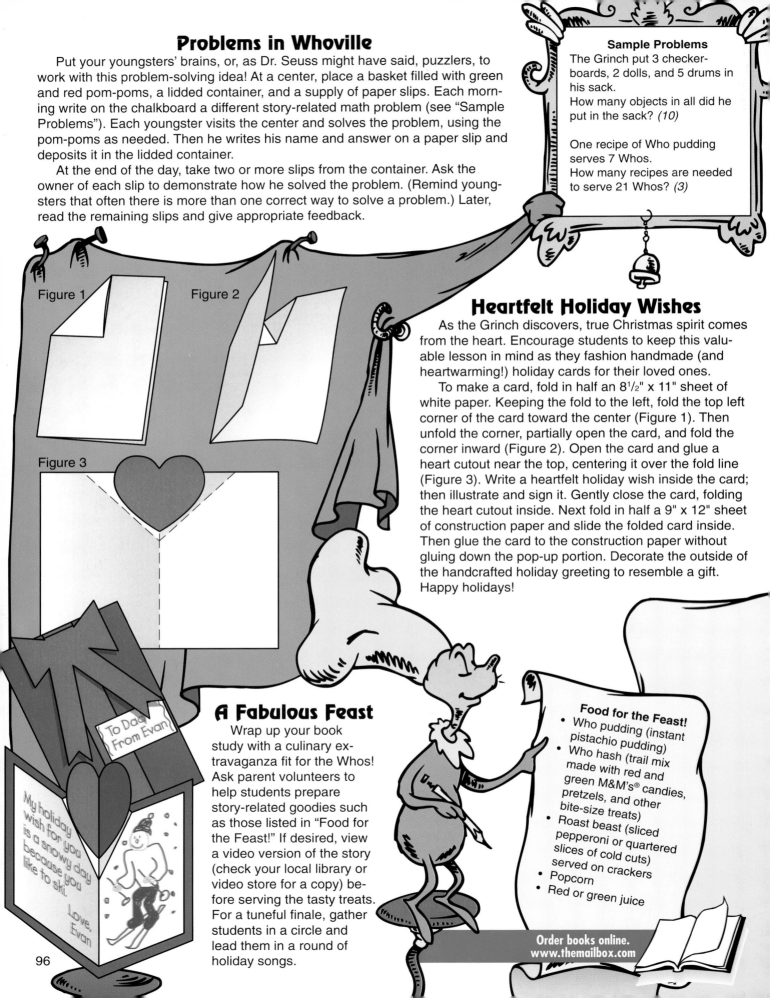

Figure 1

Figure 2

Figure 3

Heartfelt Holiday Wishes

As the Grinch discovers, true Christmas spirit comes from the heart. Encourage students to keep this valuable lesson in mind as they fashion handmade (and heartwarming!) holiday cards for their loved ones.

To make a card, fold in half an 8½" x 11" sheet of white paper. Keeping the fold to the left, fold the top left corner of the card toward the center (Figure 1). Then unfold the corner, partially open the card, and fold the corner inward (Figure 2). Open the card and glue a heart cutout near the top, centering it over the fold line (Figure 3). Write a heartfelt holiday wish inside the card; then illustrate and sign it. Gently close the card, folding the heart cutout inside. Next fold in half a 9" x 12" sheet of construction paper and slide the folded card inside. Then glue the card to the construction paper without gluing down the pop-up portion. Decorate the outside of the handcrafted holiday greeting to resemble a gift. Happy holidays!

A Fabulous Feast

Wrap up your book study with a culinary extravaganza fit for the Whos! Ask parent volunteers to help students prepare story-related goodies such as those listed in "Food for the Feast!" If desired, view a video version of the story (check your local library or video store for a copy) before serving the tasty treats. For a tuneful finale, gather students in a circle and lead them in a round of holiday songs.

Food for the Feast!
- Who pudding (instant pistachio pudding)
- Who hash (trail mix made with red and green M&M's® candies, pretzels, and other bite-size treats)
- Roast beast (sliced pepperoni or quartered slices of cold cuts) served on crackers
- Popcorn
- Red or green juice

To Dad
From Evan

My holiday wish for you is a snowy day because you like to ski.

Love,
Evan

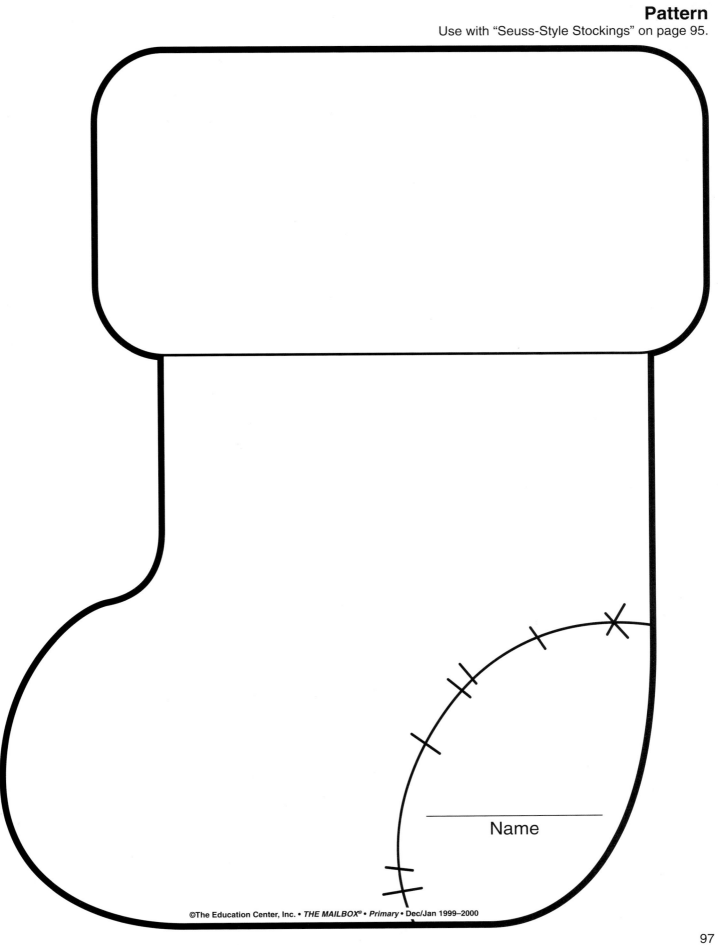

Name

The Magic Tree House Series

Written by Mary Pope Osborne & Illustrated by Sal Murdocca • Random House, Inc.

Reading enthusiasm will reach the treetops when you introduce students to this delightful series of beginning chapter books! Whether you read the books aloud or ask students to read them independently, one thing is certain—no one can read just one! Enrich your students' reading experiences with the activities and reproducibles found in this teacher-contributed collection!

About the Series

Eight-and-a-half-year-old Jack and his seven-year-old sister Annie discover a mysterious tree house library at the top of a tall oak tree. The pair quickly learns that the books in the tree house can take them on journeys through time and to locations around the world.

Personal Passports

Passports are the perfect place for youngsters to record the adventures they experience within the pages of the Magic Tree House books! For each student, staple a supply of blank passport pages (from page 102) between a folded piece of 5½" x 8" construction paper. Next, ask each child to color a copy of the cover pattern from page 102, draw himself in the box, and write his name on the line. Then have him glue the cover on the front of his passport.

To complete a page in his passport, a student writes the title of the book that was read on the line. Then he describes his favorite part of the book and ranks the book by checking the appropriate box. Next, he colors a passport stamp, cuts it out, and glues it in the provided circle. (See page 102 for stamps. If an appropriate stamp is not provided, program a copy of the blank stamp and copy it for student use.) Collecting stamps for this passport is educational, inexpensive, and fun!

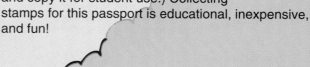

Title: Dinosaurs Before Dark
My favorite part of the story was when Annie fed her magnolias to the antosaurus.

This book was:
X Great!
☐ Good
☐ Okay

Editor's note: *Our staff enthusiastically reviewed books 1–17 of this series for use in the primary classroom. It was brought to my attention that the content of book 3,* Mummies in the Morning, *is quite graphic—unlike any other title in the series. Please preread the book and use only at your own discretion.*

Tree House Happenings

You can sprout plenty of reading enthusiasm at this tree house display! Cover a bulletin board with sky blue paper; then use twisted brown paper, tape, and a stapler to make a tree that *grows* from the floor to the top of the bulletin board. Add a tree house cutout, green paper foliage, and the title "News From the Magic Tree House!" Keep a supply of blank paper and pushpins near the display. Invite students to post at the display opinions, illustrations, summaries, and other work that relates to the books in the Magic Tree House series. No doubt this tree house will be buzzing with excitement, too!

Take Note!

In each story Jack carefully notes the interesting facts he learns in a small notebook. Have students make these nifty notebooks and they'll have the perfect place to write the facts that they learn! To make a notebook, a child folds one 9" x 4" sheet of construction paper in half. Next, she stacks and aligns several 8" x 4" pieces of white paper, folds the stack in half, and tucks the stack inside the folded construction paper so that the folds meet. Near the fold of the resulting booklet, she punches two holes. Then she threads a ten-inch length of yarn through the holes, ties the yarn ends, and adds her name and desired decorations to the front cover. To begin her note taking, she writes the title of the book being read near the top of the first page; then she enters each fact she learns. Write on!

#12 Polar Bears Past Bedtime
– The Arctic Tundra is treeless.
– In summer, the sun shines 24 hours a day.

Story Souvenirs

Since trips and souvenirs go hand in hand, it makes perfect sense for students to fashion souvenirs from their Magic Tree House travels! At the conclusion of a book, provide an assortment of arts-and-crafts materials from which souvenirs can be made. For example, after reading *Dinosaurs Before Dark* (#1), a child might use yellow paper and glitter paint to make a medallion like the one Jack found in the tall grass. Or she might fashion a cowboy boot from brown paper and paint markers at the conclusion of *Ghost Town at Sundown* (#10). Invite each student to share the souvenir she makes and explain its significance in the story. If desired, showcase these items at the display described in "Tree House Happenings" on this page.

99

What's Cookin'?

This recipe for writing Magic Tree House book reports suits students to a tee—a teaspoon, that is! To complete a report, a student copies the book title on a copy of page 103, provides details about the story (as prompted by the text), signs her name, and colors the artwork. Next, she illustrates her favorite event from the story on another sheet of paper. To publish the projects, slip each child's report and illustration into a plastic page protector (keeping the blank sides together) and exhibit the pages in a three-ring binder. Place the binder in the class library for all to read. Keep a supply of blank paper, report forms, and plastic protectors near the binder so students can continue to publish reports about the Magic Tree House books they read.

Where in the World?

Turning Magic Tree House adventures into geography lessons is a snap! Post a large world map on a bulletin board. Place a yellow pushpin on Pennsylvania, Jack and Annie's home state. Each time the siblings travel to a location shown on the map, gather students at the display. When the siblings' location is found, ask a student to insert a red pushpin there. Then ask several geography-related questions for students to answer, such as the following: What continent are the siblings on? What direction did they travel to get there? What direction will they travel to get home? For added fun, indicate the class's location with a green pushpin and ask students questions that relate to this location, too!

"Tree-rrific" Triaramas

What part of this follow-up project is most difficult for students? Choosing *just one* favorite story event to showcase in a triarama! To begin, a student positions a ten-inch square of tagboard on his desk. He folds the square in half vertically and unfolds. He folds the square in half horizontally and unfolds. Using construction paper scraps, glue, and crayons or markers, he creates a backdrop for his chosen event on the top half of the square. To make the bottom of his triarama, he cuts a straight line from the bottom of the square to its center (using the fold line as a guide), overlaps the two pieces, and glues them in place. He uses the supplies on hand to complete his scene. Then he describes his featured event on a lined index card. If possible, showcase the students' projects in the school library for all to see!

Midnight on the Moon
Book Title

Add one magic tree house traveling to __the moon in the future__

Mix with one reason for Jack and Annie to go: __to find one more M__
__thing to free Morgan from her spell.__

Sprinkle with some danger for Jack and Annie: __they both fall down__
__and can't get up! The moon man finds them!__

Fold gently with an exciting ending: __Peanut the mouse turns into__
__Morgan le Fay. The fourth M thing was a mouse!__

And you end up with a book that is __exciting and teaches you__
__about the moon.__

Prepared by Chef __Sherry Simpson__

Afternoon on the Amazon
I liked it when Peanut the mouse leads Jack and Annie to the tree house. Then the monkey gives Annie the red fruit. The monkey claps and laughs!

A Hometown Visit

Jack and Annie find adventure everywhere they go, and a visit to your students' hometown would be no exception! For this large-group writing project, have students name different sites within the community that the twosome could visit. List the sites on the chalkboard along with one or more reasons why Jack and Annie might visit each place. Next, help the group identify a setting, a mission to accomplish, and several community-related facts for its Magic Tree House adventure. Then write the class-created tale on chart paper. Post the completed story for all to see, and assign each child a different sentence or two to copy and illustrate on story paper. Sequence the students' work into a class book titled "Adventure to [name of your town]!" Then arrange for different small groups of students to read the book aloud to other classes in your school!

Original Adventures

When student interest is firmly rooted in the Magic Tree House series, challenge students to write original adventures for Jack and Annie! On the chalkboard write a student-generated list of possible story settings. Ask each child to prepare a story outline that includes where her story will take place, the mission Jack and Annie will accomplish, and several facts that can be incorporated into her tale. Next, pair students and have the partners work together to improve their individual story outlines. Then have each child write and illustrate her story, using her edited outline as a guide. After each child shares her tree house tale, bind the projects into a class book titled "More Tree House Tales!"

The Magic Tree House Online

To learn more about the Magic Tree House series, go online to http://www.randomhouse.com/kids/magictreehouse today! At this kid-pleasing site, students can vote on book ideas, ask the author questions, and participate in contests. There's also a special class club for teachers to join! It's one more adventure just waiting to be taken!

Our thanks to the following teachers whose ideas appear in this unit: **Laura Bassitt**—*Gr. 3, St. Charles Elementary, Lima, OH;* **Mary Gardner**—*Title I, Rahn Elementary School, Mt. Morris, IL;* **Patty Henderson**—*Gr. 2, Evergreen Elementary School, San Jose, CA;* **Kristin McBride**—*Gr. 2, A. G. Elder Elementary School, Joshua, TX;* **Lisa Nicklow,** *Genoa Elementary School, Houston, TX;* **Ashley Rebman**—*Gr. 2, Cresset Christian Academy, Durham, NC;* **Manuel Silva**—*Grs. 2–3, Sacré-Coeur School, Winnipeg, MB, Canada;* **Beth Taylor**—*Special Education, Rahn Elementary School, Mt. Morris, IL*

Passport Patterns

Use with "Personal Passports" on page 98.

Cover

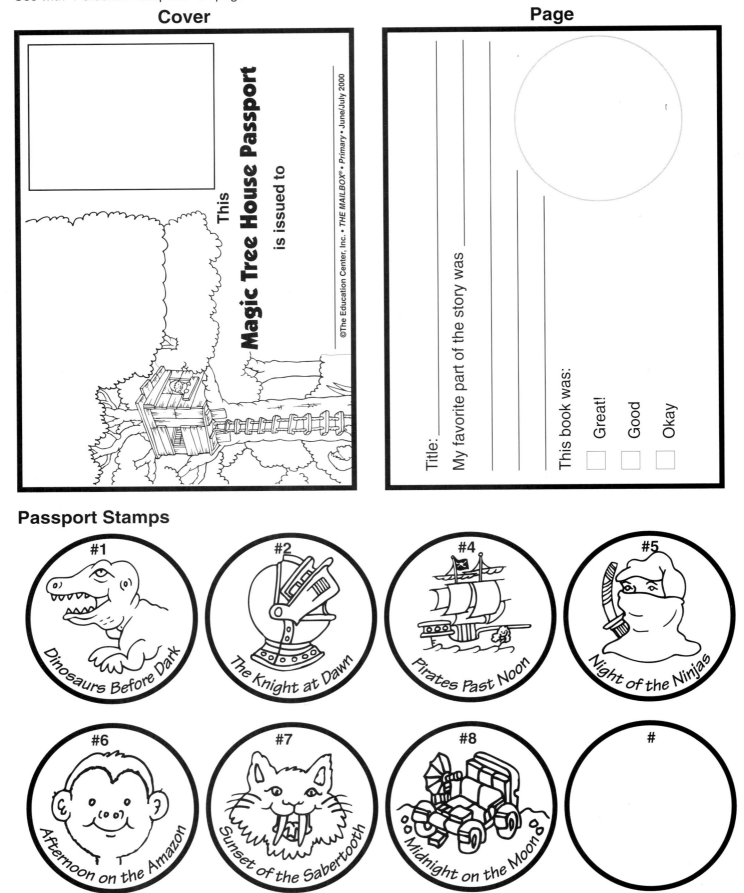

This

Magic Tree House Passport

is issued to

©The Education Center, Inc. • THE MAILBOX® • Primary • June/July 2000

Page

Title:

My favorite part of the story was

This book was:

☐ Great!

☐ Good

☐ Okay

Passport Stamps

#1 Dinosaurs Before Dark

#2 The Knight at Dawn

#4 Pirates Past Noon

#5 Night of the Ninjas

#6 Afternoon on the Amazon

#7 Sunset of the Sabertooth

#8 Midnight on the Moon

#

_____
Book Title

Add one magic tree house traveling to _____

Mix with one reason for Jack and Annie to go: _____

Sprinkle with some danger for Jack and Annie: _____

Fold gently with an exciting ending: _____

And you end up with a book that is _____

Prepared by Chef _____

©The Education Center, Inc. • THE MAILBOX® • Primary • June/July 2000

Note to teacher: Use with "What's Cookin'?" on page 100.

Helen Keller
Crusader for the Blind and Deaf

Written by Stewart and Polly Anne Graff
Illustrated by Wayne Alfano
(Bantam Doubleday Dell Books for Young Readers, 1991)

An illness at the age of 1½ left Helen Keller unable to see or hear. With the help of a loyal teacher named Annie Sullivan and others, Helen learned to read, write, and even speak! Forever grateful to those who helped her conquer the odds against her, Helen devoted her adult life to informing others about the special needs of deaf and blind children. This inspirational biography teaches young readers the true meaning of courage and perseverance.

ideas contributed by Laura Wagner

Seeing Without Sight

In chapters 1 and 2, students discover that Helen relies on her senses of touch and smell to learn about her surroundings. This partner activity helps youngsters gain a better understanding of the challenges she faced. Sequentially number one paper lunch bag for every two students. In each bag place two different items that are similarly shaped, for example, a gum ball and a marble, a penny and a button, a tennis ball and an orange. Pair students and give each twosome a bag. In turn, each child closes her eyes and reaches inside the bag. She feels the items and notes any smells coming from the bag. Then she writes on her paper the number on the bag and what she thinks is in it. On a signal from you, each pair passes its bag to the next pair along a prearranged route. After each pair has investigated every bag, invite students to share what they think is in each bag before you reveal the mystery items.

Front-Page News

Helen was only eight years old when newspapers began featuring articles about her amazing accomplishments. At the conclusion of chapter 5, have each student create a newspaper story that spotlights Helen's achievements. Give each child a two-page spread from a discarded newspaper. Keeping the spread folded, she glues two sheets of 12" x 18" newsprint to the front and trims away the excess newsprint. Next she cuts letters from additional sheets of discarded newspaper to spell a newspaper name and a captivating headline about Helen. She glues these letters on her newsprint. Then she dates her newspaper and writes and illustrates her article. Family members are sure to be impressed when students deliver these newsworthy projects!

The Daily News

Wednesday, October 4, 1894

15 cents

People Come to Visit Helen

Reported by
Njeri Legrand

Helen Keller had more visitors this week. Everyone wants to meet this amazing little girl! Helen is deaf and blind. She has learned to read, write, and speak. Her latest accomplishment was building a snowman with the other students at Perkins Institute in Boston.

Choosing a Career

At the conclusion of chapter 6 Helen graduates from college. Reveal the title of chapter 7 and have students contemplate different careers Helen might choose. At the end of the chapter, discuss why Helen chose the career she did, making sure students understand that it was her desire to help others that led her to a career of writing and lecturing. Next ask students to brainstorm ways they can help those who face greater challenges than themselves. List their ideas on colorful paper titled "Making a Difference." Display the resulting poster in the classroom as a positive reminder of the difference they can make in the lives of others.

The Gift of Sight

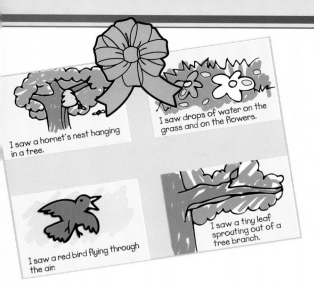

I saw a hornet's nest hanging in a tree.

I saw drops of water on the grass and on the flowers.

I saw a red bird flying through the air.

I saw a tiny leaf sprouting out of a tree branch.

Remind students how amazed Helen is in chapter 9 to hear a friend say she saw nothing of interest during a walk outdoors. As a class talk about how easy it is to take sight for granted. To encourage students to appreciate the gift of sight, take them on a walk around the school grounds. Challenge them to really look at their surroundings and notice things they normally overlook. As a follow-up, give each child four 4" x 6" rectangles of yellow construction paper. Instruct each child to describe and illustrate one unique observation from the walk on each rectangle. Next have him glue each rectangle in a different corner of a 9" x 12" sheet of construction paper. To complete his project he cuts out a construction paper bow (pattern on page 106) and glues it to the top of his project. The resulting present is a poignant reminder that sight is a special gift.

Opening Doors for Others

As a *crusader* for the blind and deaf, Helen worked enthusiastically to inform others of their special needs. Ask students to recall how her efforts *opened doors* (created opportunities) for those who could not see and hear. List their ideas on the chalkboard. Then have each student complete the project shown as a symbol of Helen's accomplishments.

To begin, a child folds in half a 9" x 12" sheet of brown construction paper. Keeping the fold to the left, she draws and colors a large door on the front. Then, starting at the bottom of the door and cutting through both thicknesses, she cuts along one side and across the top. Next she turns the folded paper over and decorates the resulting back flap to resemble a second door. She then opens the folded paper and dots glue over the entire surface of the paper, except for the doors. She positions a 6" x 9" piece of white construction paper on one side of the fold line; then she refolds the paper. When the glue is dry, she opens each door and writes and illustrates one way the blind and deaf benefited from Helen's efforts.

Helen Keller helped start schools for blind and deaf students.

Remembering Helen

Wrap up this moving biography with a thought-provoking booklet project. Distribute white construction paper copies of page 107. Have each student color the cover and complete and illustrate each sentence starter. Then have him cut along the bold lines, stack the pages in sequential order, place the cover on top of the stack, and staple his booklet together. To complete his project, he signs his name inside the front cover.

Remembering

Helen Keller

(1880–1968)

I think the most important thing Helen did was

1

I think the most difficult thing Helen did was

2

I think the happiest moment for Helen was

3

I think the saddest moment for Helen was

4

I think one way I am like Helen is

5

Note to teacher: Use with "Remembering Helen" on page 105.

Name _____

A Courageous Woman

Read each pair of sentences.
If the **cause** is underlined, draw an X over the letter in the cause box.
If the **effect** is underlined, draw an X over the letter in the effect box.

Cause	Effect	
F	O	1. Helen was lonely. <u>Helen could not understand others</u>.
R	J	2. Annie taught Helen braille. <u>Helen learned to read</u>.
T	L	3. <u>Helen and Annie had a party to raise money</u>. Tommy Stringer had no money for school.
G	M	4. Helen learned to speak. <u>Helen copied the way Miss Fuller moved her mouth</u>.
I	H	5. <u>Helen wanted people to learn about the blind and deaf</u>. Helen spoke to people about the blind and deaf.
D	N	6. <u>President Taft opened a library for the blind</u>. Helen asked the government for help.
P	K	7. Helen made a movie about her life. <u>Helen needed money to do her work</u>.
V	C	8. <u>Annie was very ill</u>. Helen and Polly nursed Annie.
A	Q	9. Helen was asked to help the blind and deaf in Japan. <u>Helen traveled across the Pacific Ocean</u>.
E	U	10. Many soldiers were blinded during the war. <u>Helen visited hospitals around the country</u>.

What did
Helen
Keller do
her entire
life?

Find out
below!

For each number, write the letter that is not crossed out.

S __ __   W __ __ __ __ __   __ __   __ __ __ __

 5 10   1 2 7 10 6   3 1   4 9 7 10

__ __ __   __ __ __ __ S __   __ __ __ __   __ __ __ U __!

 5 10 2   6 2 10 9 4   8 1 4 10   3 2   10

Note to teacher: Use this activity after completing the book.

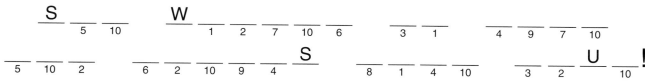

Language Arts Units

Brushing Up on Adjectives

Use this colorful collection of activities to teach the long and short of adjectives. In no time at all, your youngsters' descriptive writing will be picture perfect!

Lovely Leaves

For a memorable adjective activity, take students outdoors when fall leaves are in full color. Provide plenty of time for youngsters to investigate the various colors, sizes, shapes, and textures of the fall foliage. Then return to the classroom and ask them to use adjectives to describe what they saw. For a creative follow-up project, challenge each child to create a unique leaf for a class tree. To do this, she decorates a leaf cutout and then she labels a small card with the adjective that best describes it. Encourage students to be creative! Display the projects for all to admire.

Julie Evans—Gr. 2, Spring Hill Elementary
McLean, VA

Perfect

Rich

By the Handfuls

At the conclusion of this activity students are convinced that adjectives go hand in hand with nouns! Ask each child to trace the outline of his hand onto a sheet of skin-tone paper, write a noun in the palm of his outline, and write a different adjective that describes the noun in each finger. Then, on provided paper, have him write and illustrate a descriptive sentence or two that supports his handiwork. Next have him cut out the hand shape, mount it on a slightly larger sheet of construction paper, trim the construction paper to create an eye-catching border, and then glue the cutout onto the corner of his paper. Display the completed projects on a bulletin board titled "Adjectives by the Handful!"

Jacqueline Acevedo—Grs. 3 & 4 ESL
Cupey María Montessori School, Río Piedras, Puerto Rico

Here Tiger! Kitty, Kitty!

fat
fluffy
big
cat
orange
striped

I have a big fat fluffy cat named Tiger. He is orange with lots of stripes.

Adjective Upmanship

The next time you have five minutes to spare, play a few rounds of Adjective Upmanship. To begin play, state a simple sentence like "I have a dog." The first student to play adds an adjective when he repeats the sentence for the class. The next player adds a second adjective to the sentence, and so on, until a student either omits an adjective from the sentence or forgets to add one of his own. To restart the game, provide another simple sentence. Students have a ball one-upping each other, and they're practicing using adjectives all the while!

Heather Disharoon—Grs. 1–2
Dawson County Primary School
Dawsonville, GA

Noun for the Night

Create enthusiasm for adjectives with this homework assignment! Name a noun and ask students to brainstorm with their families adjectives that describe the noun. The following day, write the noun on a length of bulletin board paper and list the students' compiled suggestions. Write the total number of adjectives reported on the paper, and then mount the resulting poster. Repeat the activity as often as desired, using a different noun each time. Vocabularies will be on the rise as students try to exceed the number of adjectives reported for all previous homework assignments.

Heather Disharoon—Grs. 1–2

Theresa Lewis

Best of Buddies

Friendly handshakes remind students that adjectives and nouns are buddies. For this large-group activity, have students stand in two straight lines facing each other. Name the lines "Nouns" and "Adjectives." To begin, the first player in the Nouns line steps forward and names a noun. Then the first player in the Adjectives line steps forward and names an adjective that adds meaning to the stated noun. Next the two buddies exchange a handshake and step back to their places in line. Play continues down the two lines in this manner until every player has taken a turn. Then rename the lines so that the Nouns line becomes the Adjectives line and vice versa, and repeat the activity.

Nancy Lujan—Gr. 3, C.I. Waggoner Elementary School, Tempe, AZ

Hat Extravaganza

Any shape of hat will do for this large-group activity! First a student traces a hat-shaped template onto tagboard, cuts out the shape, and decorates the cutout using a variety of arts-and-crafts supplies. Next she writes a description of her hat. Encourage students to work carefully, explaining that the descriptions they write will later be used for identification purposes. On another day, gather students in a large circle on the floor and display the hat projects inside. Read aloud each student-written description and challenge the group to identify the matching hat (without the help of the student who created it). When an identification is made, find out what parts of the written description were most helpful in making the positive hat identification.

Heather Disharoon—Grs. 1–2
Dawson County Primary School
Dawsonville, GA

For Sale!

This drawing activity gives students a quick lesson on the value of adjectives! From catalogs that feature student-appealing merchandise, cut out a class supply of pictured items and their corresponding descriptions. Code each picture to its description. Store the pictures for later use. Have each student glue a description to the bottom of a sheet of drawing paper and then carefully read the description and illustrate the item that's for sale. When the illustrations are finished, give each student the catalog picture that corresponds to the description he illustrated. After they compare their illustrations to the catalog pictures, invite students to share their work and tell how the written descriptions helped them create accurate illustrations.

Leigh Ann Newsom—Gr. 3
Greenbrier Intermediate, Chesapeake, VA

Descriptive Doodles

Looking for a unique way to reinforce adjectives? Try this! Write the adjective *blue* on the chalkboard twice—once with white chalk and once with blue chalk. Ask students which word best conveys the meaning of the adjective. Next write the adjective *tiny* on the chalkboard. Challenge students to write (or doodle) this word on scrap paper so its meaning is more effectively conveyed. Repeat the activity for the adjectives *loud, thin, huge, scary,* and *fast.* Invite students to share their descriptive doodles with their classmates and then encourage them to track down additional adjectives to doodle! Totally cool!

Darcy Gruber
Greenfield, WI

Vocabulary Stretchers

Get vocabulary skills in tip-top shape with this word workout! Whether you choose a few ideas for vocabulary warm-ups or try them all for more well-rounded practice, your language arts routine is sure to be energized!

Whopping Words

Most youngsters love to use big words and no doubt your students are no exception. So why not start each morning with a written message that contains a colossal word! Choose a word that relates to a topic students will study that day. For example, if they will be learning about insects, pen a message such as "Today we will be <u>entomologists</u>. We will talk about animals that have six legs. These animals do not have noses. They smell with feelers instead!" Read the message with students and lead them to conclude the meaning of the underlined word. Then display the word on a card to promote further use.

Janice Keer—Grs. 1–2, Irvin Pertzsch School, Onalaska, WI

Make a Guess!

It's no surprise that this idea motivates students to learn new words! A few days before a spelling test, secretly choose a bonus word that is not an assigned spelling word. Give the class a few clues about the word, such as its topic, syllable count, and part of speech. On test day, administer the scheduled spelling test before inviting youngsters to share their bonus word guesses. Then reveal the secret bonus word for students to spell. Award extra spelling points to each child who correctly spells the surprise word!

Phyllis Bowling—Gr. 2, Smithville Elementary, Smithville, MS

"Word-o"

This lotto game has vocabulary covered! Post a list of theme-related words. Distribute game markers and individual blank lotto boards to students. Ask each child to draw a theme-related picture in one board space (to create a free space) and then write words from the posted list in the remaining spaces. While students work, write each word on an individual card and shuffle the resulting deck.

To begin play, draw a card from the deck. Without revealing the word, announce its meaning (or provide a related clue). When a volunteer correctly identifies the word, each player checks his lotto board. If he finds the word, he covers it with a game marker. Continue play in this manner until a player calls "Word-o!", signaling that he has covered a horizontal, vertical, or diagonal row. After verifying the player's covered words, declare him the winner. Then have youngsters clear their boards for another round of play.

Marilyn Webb—Gr. 1, Brookhouse School
Dartmouth, Nova Scotia, Canada

	flippers	mammal	oce
migrate	b er	fin	breach
pla kton	krill	blowhole	sonar
calf	fluke	baleen	squid

Writing With Word Wear

These nifty necklaces add pizzazz to students' writing! On the chalkboard, write a sentence with a word students overuse. Underline the word. Then have students brainstorm words that can replace it without changing the meaning of the sentence. Repeat the activity with other frequently overused words. Next, give each child three paper cards and a length of yarn. A child chooses a word he frequently overuses and writes a substitute for it on both sides of each card. He hole-punches his cards, threads them onto the yarn, ties the yarn ends together, and slips on the resulting necklace. Now, when he writes, he has a string of interesting words right at his fingertips!

Dawn Renta—Gr. 3
District 30 P.S. 149 Annex, Queens, NY

Growing Vocabularies

Cultivate rich vocabularies with a synonym garden! Divide students into small groups. Give each group a construction paper circle bearing a word that has a number of possible synonyms. The group members brainstorm synonyms for the word on provided paper, using thesauruses as needed. Then each group member uses a template to make a construction paper petal, glues her petal to the circle, and labels it with a synonym. To complete the flower, group members add a construction paper stem and leaves. Mount the flowers on a bulletin board titled "Growing Vocabularies." What a "plant-astic" writing reference!

adapted from an idea by Cherie Rodriguez—Gr. 2
Hay Branch Elementary
Killeen, TX

Vocabulary With Character

This vocabulary-building idea is one for the books! Post a chart like the one shown and label it with the title of a class read-aloud. After sharing the book with students, enlist their help to complete the chart with the name of each main character and the corresponding information. Make and complete additional charts for other books in a like manner. Then ask students to compare and contrast characters from different books. Not only will students increase their reading vocabularies, they'll boost their critical-thinking skills, too!

Pam Seymour—Gr. 2
Heritage Elementary
Murrysville, PA

Charlotte's Web

Character	Trait	How the character shows the trait	Synonyms
Wilbur	lonely	-complains about having no friends -cries	friend
Charlotte	kind	-offers to be Wilbur's friend -tries to save	-ca -unsel
Templeton	unfriendly	-refuses to play with Wilbur -only thinks about himself	

113

Leading Questions

When it comes to reinforcing vocabulary in context, this activity is a real find! To prepare, program a class set of cards as shown (with nouns underlined) so that the question at the bottom of each card is addressed at the top of another card (the last question is for the phrase at the top of the first card). Give each student a card. Ask one student to read his question aloud. The child who has the corresponding response phrase reads it aloud and completes it. Then she reads the question on her card aloud. Continue in this manner until every question is read and answered. This activity is sure to become a class favorite, so collect the cards and redistribute them later for more question-and-answer fun!

Bonnie Lanterman—Gr. 1, Armstrong Elementary, Hazelwood, MO

The colt is . . .

Where is the shore?

The shore is . . .

Where is the mansion?

The mansion is . . .

Where is the arachnid?

Sorting Beyond Words

What's in the cards? All sorts of vocabulary practice! Choose a desired number of vocabulary categories from a recent read-aloud, science unit, etc. Prepare a class set of word cards so that there are several cards for each category. Use yarn to visually divide a bulletin board into as many columns as categories, and then title the columns. Randomly distribute the cards to students. Each student, in turn, reads her word aloud, identifies its corresponding category, and explains her reasoning. Then she tacks the card in the appropriate column. When all cards are displayed, invite each student to use a pointer to indicate a different word. Ask the child to read the word aloud, use it in a sentence, and if desired, provide additional information about it, such as whether it has a prefix or suffix.

adapted from ideas by Kelli DeVore—Gr. 2
Mirror Lakes Elementary, Lehigh, FL and
Julie Plowman—Gr. 3, Adair-Casey Elementary, Adair, IA

KITTIE'S ATHLETIC CLUB

Zap!

The element of chance adds excitement to this small-group vocabulary game! Fold several paper cards in half. Write a different vocabulary word inside each card and write its definition on the outside. To make one of a few distracter cards, write "Zap" on the front of a folded card. Inside, write "Return your vocabulary cards and discard this one." Store all cards in an unlidded container.

To play, each student, in turn, removes a folded card from the box and reads the outside of the card aloud. If he reads a definition, he names the word he thinks is defined. Then he opens the card to check his answer. If he is correct, he keeps the card. If not, he refolds the card and returns it to the box. If he reads aloud "Zap!", he unfolds the card and follows the provided directions. Play continues until no cards remain in the box. The student with the most cards wins.

Susan Pickardt—Special Education
Lee Hamilton School
Ferguson, MO

ZAP!

ZAP!

amphibian

a person who lives close to another person

114

Vocabulary Puzzlers

A picture is worth 1,000 words—vocabulary words, that is! To prepare a picture-perfect center, mount a discarded calendar picture on tagboard and then cut it into a desired number of puzzle pieces. On the back of each piece, write a different word that relates to the picture. Prepare a second puzzle in a similar manner; then mix and place all of the pieces in one container. A student removes the pieces, silently reads the words, and sorts them into two topic-related piles. Next, he lists each group of words on provided paper. To check his work, he assembles the puzzles picture-side up. Then, if desired, have the youngster write a paragraph that includes several words from one list.

Sheri Saner—Grs. 2–3
South Hutchinson Grade School
South Hutchinson, KS

"Word-ercise"

This versatile partner activity stretches minds *and* vocabularies! Give each twosome one copy of page 116. Have the two students write a word in each box that begins with the corresponding letter and fits the category. Challenge them to write words that they think no one else will think of. Next, announce each letter and category combination in turn. Ask each student pair to announce its corresponding word. If no other twosome wrote the word and the word fits the criteria (beginning letter and category), one youngster in the twosome writes "2" in the corner box. If one or more student pairs wrote it, she writes "1." Then have each twosome total its points, write the resulting score where indicated, and color the corresponding cats. For more vocabulary practice, white-out the letters and/or categories on a copy of page 116 and reprogram the sheet for another mind-stretching exercise.

Take Your Pick!

Here's a vocabulary game that scores big! Label each of three containers with a different point value. For each value, program cards with words of a corresponding level of difficulty to make a class set of cards. Label each card set with the appropriate value and drop it in the corresponding container. Divide students into equal-size teams and ask one player on each team to be scorekeeper. Explain that the container with the lowest number holds the easiest words and the container with the highest number holds the most challenging words.

To play, each team lines up single file. The first player on each team, in turn, removes a card from a container of her choice. She reads the word aloud and defines it. If her definition is correct, her team receives the corresponding number of points, and she places the card in a discard pile. If not, she returns the card to the container and no points are awarded. Each first-round player goes to the end of the line and a new round of play begins. Continue until each child has taken one turn. The team with the most points wins.

adapted from an idea by Kimberly D. Nunes-Bufford—Grs. K–2
Jeter Primary School, Opelika, AL

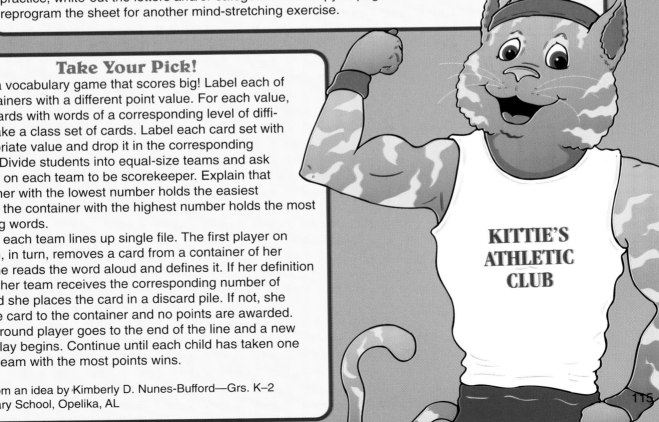

KITTIE'S ATHLETIC CLUB

Names _____

"Word-ercise"

Follow your teacher's directions.

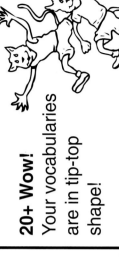

Category	S	T	R	O	N	G
Food						
Place						
Animal						

Word Fitness Score	0–9 Yikes! It's time to tone up your vocabularies!	10–19 Great! Keep stretching those vocabulary muscles!	20+ Wow! Your vocabularies are in tip-top shape!
_____			

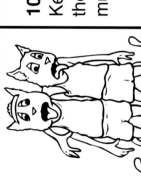

Note to teacher: Use with "Word-ercise" on page 115.

Laugh and Learn With Poetry

We've packed a gaggle of giggles and endless learning opportunities into this one-of-a-kind poetry unit! Activities to use with any poem are featured below. Three grin-inducing poems and activities to use with each one are the focus of the following pages. Could there be any better way to celebrate National Poetry Month this April?

poems and activities by Geoff Mihalenko—Gr. 3
Frank Defino Central School, Marlboro, NJ

Pick Your Poem

Use these "verse-atile" activities with any poem and reinforce the featured language arts skills.

- **Context Clues:** Young detectives must rely on context clues to crack the case of the mystery words! Copy an entire poem, or selected stanzas from it, on chart paper. Use a sticky note to either partially or completely cover one word in each of several lines. Lead students in reading the poem aloud, pausing at each mystery word. Ask youngsters to predict the word by using context clues. Then, with great fanfare, remove the sticky note and reveal the mystery word.

- **Sequencing:** Create a poetic mix-up and reinforce sequencing skills in short order! Select a short poem or choose a stanza from a longer one. Use a wipe-off marker to write each line on a laminated sentence strip. Display the strips in order on a pocket chart. Point to every word as you read aloud each line with the students. Then scramble the strips and have the class direct you in sequencing them correctly.

- **Choral Reading:** Why not make oral-reading practice a group effort? Copy each stanza of a poem on poster-sized paper and then sequentially number the backs of the resulting posters. Divide students into the corresponding number of groups. Give each group a poster and provide time for reading practice. Then collect the posters and stack them in order on an easel, with the first stanza on top. The group who practiced the first stanza reads it aloud. Then move this poster to the back of the stack and continue with the remaining posters in a like manner. For more reading practice, redistribute the posters to different groups and repeat the activity as described.

The Birthday Surprise
(page 119)

When Pamela Drake tries her hand at baking a cake, she learns a BIG lesson about yeast! Use the prereading activity on this page to introduce students to this unique baking ingredient. Then, after students are familiar with the grin-inducing poem, extend their learning with the remaining mouthwatering ideas.

Prereading Activity
Rising to the Occasion

Sharpen your youngsters' observation skills with this yeast-related investigation. The knowledge students gain about yeast will help them better understand Pamela's baking catastrophe!

Materials:
- 1/3 cup warm water in a bowl
- 1 package dried yeast
- 1 tablespoon sugar
- 1 clean 20-ounce plastic soda bottle
- 1 spoon
- 1 funnel
- 1 balloon
- 1 rubber band

Directions:
1. Stir the yeast into the water until it dissolves.
2. Add the sugar and stir.
3. Insert the funnel into the bottle and pour the mixture inside.
4. Remove the funnel. Slip the open end of the balloon over the neck of the bottle.
5. Secure the balloon with the rubber band.
6. Place the project in a warm area.

Ask students to predict what will happen and list their ideas on the chalkboard. Then, during the next 30–45 minutes, have each of several small groups observe the experiment and share their findings with the class. (The yeast mixture bubbles and swells as it eats the sugar. This process releases carbon dioxide, which causes the balloon to inflate.) Ask students why they think yeast is often used when baking bread. Lead them to conclude that the gas bubbles formed by yeast make bread dough rise.

Sweet Details

Students will be eager to sink their teeth into this main-idea activity! To make the project shown, each child writes the main idea of "The Birthday Surprise" on a 6" x 9" piece of construction paper. Then she writes a different supporting detail on each of four 1" x 3 1/2" construction paper strips and glues a yellow paper flame to the top of each one. To assemble her project, she glues the candles to the top of the paper rectangle; then she decorates the resulting cake. If desired, display the projects with the title "Main Idea Is a Piece of Cake!"

Food for Thought

Could Pamela have fared better if instead of randomly combining ingredients she had used a cake mix? Most likely. However, as students learn during this lesson, a baker must follow directions and apply math skills even when he uses a cake mix! Give each child a copy of the back panel of a cake mix box. Read the baking directions with students. Then have each child use a crayon to circle each number in the baking directions. To emphasize the importance of these numbers, have students contemplate the effects of inadvertently increasing or decreasing the circled numbers. For example, what could happen if a baker adds too much or too little water, cooks his cake at too high or too low a temperature, or uses a baking pan unlike those listed on the cake mix panel? For a tasty conclusion, serve each child a small piece of cake!

The Birthday Surprise

Pamela Drake wanted to bake
A birthday surprise for her dad.
It seemed a small matter
To make the cake batter
By mixing the things that she had.

Pamela's cake began to bake,
And it quickly started to rise.
Then she wandered away
To her bedroom to play—
An act that was very unwise.

Suddenly Pam heard a loud BOOM,
So she ran down the stairs to look.
Putting yeast in the cake
Was her fatal mistake.
Next time she will use a cookbook!

by Geoff Mihalenko

Note to teacher: Give each student a copy of this page. After reading the poem for enjoyment, have her circle each two-syllable word for skill reinforcement.

Buddy's Blunder
(page 121)

Even a builder as experienced as a beaver can make a construction mistake, and that's exactly what happens in this comical poem! Use the prereading activity on this page to give students hands-on experience with the challenges of building construction. Then use the remaining activities to make curricular connections after the poem has been enjoyed by the class.

Prereading Activity
Building Creativity

Take teamwork, creativity, and an appreciation for building to new heights! Divide students into small groups. Give each group an identical assortment of building materials (such as blocks, straws, and empty film canisters) and a different building task like constructing a tall building, a U-shaped building, a house with three windows, etc. Allow 10–15 minutes' construction time. Then have the groups share their projects with the class. Ask each group to reveal its building task and describe its favorite and least favorite building materials. Guide students to understand that each group's preference of building materials was influenced by its building task.

Country or City?

Here's a blueprint for critical-thinking success! Challenge students to use clues within "Buddy's Blunder" to determine whether the beaver lives in the city or the country. Suggest that students listen carefully for the types of structures Buddy has built as you reread the poem. Then ask students to recall the buildings that were named. Write each name on a light-colored card. Next have students brainstorm additional types of buildings. Write these names on individual white cards. Then draw a large Venn diagram on the chalkboard and label it "Country" and "City." Have different youngsters tape the labeled cards on the diagram. Help students conclude that several kinds of buildings are found in both the city and the country, and that, unlike most beavers, Buddy is a city slicker!

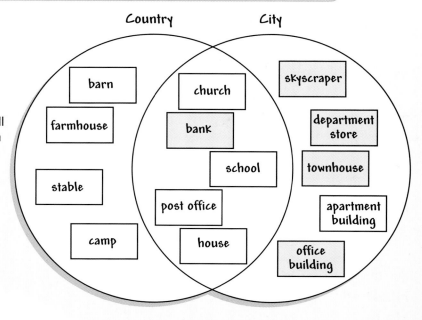

Word Family House

Provide word family (rime) practice by inviting students to put the finishing touches on Buddy's next building project! Give each child a copy of page 124 and review the listed word families. On each roof, a student writes three words that have the featured word family. Then he writes one word from the roof in a rhyming sentence at the bottom of the house. He also adds an illustration. After he signs and colors the booklet cover, he cuts along the bold lines, sequences the pages behind the cover, and staples the stack where indicated. This building project is complete!

Buddy's Blunder

Buddy Beaver was a builder,
One worthy of respect.
He went to college to become
A master architect.

He built offices, townhouses,
And two department stores.
He even built a skyscraper
With 97 floors!

One day a wealthy banker asked
The beaver if he could
Construct a thief-proof bank within
The local neighborhood.

So Buddy quickly went to work
And chomped down many trees.
He used the wood to build the bank
And finished it with ease.

As Buddy viewed the finished bank,
His heart was filled with pride.
He built the bank secure and safe.
No thief could get inside.

The banker saw the bank and said,
"You should have planned some more.
No one will ever get inside—
You didn't build a door!"

by Geoff Mihalenko

Note to teacher: Give each student a copy of this page. Read the poem as a class. Then secretly select words in the poem that may be unfamiliar to students. One by one, provide the meaning of each word. Challenge each child to use context clues to find the corresponding word; then ask him to circle it.

Easy Answers
(page 123)

In this humorous poem, homework teaches a youngster an unexpected lesson. Use the pre-reading activity on this page to familiarize students *with a variety of timesaving inventions. Then, after several readings of the poem, follow up with the remaining activities.*

(page 123)

Prereading Activity
Timesaving Inventions

Since saving time is at the heart of "Easy Answers," a quick investigation of various timesaving machines in use today is in order. Provide a variety of discarded magazines, catalogs, and sales circulars. Have each child cut out a picture of a timesaving invention and glue it near the top of a sheet of writing paper. Below the picture have her write how this invention saves time and how life would be different without it. After each child shares her work with the class, introduce the poem.

Simple-Machine Search

The inventive student in the poem understands that a machine is designed to make life easier. What he hasn't figured out is how to build one! Explain that all machines are based on one or more simple machines. List the six types of simple machines and provide an example of each one. Next give each student a checklist like the one shown. Ask him to find at home or at school at least one example for each type of machine and then list the examples on his paper. To display the students' findings, use yarn to visually divide a bulletin board into six sections. Label one section for each type of simple machine. Give each child six white construction paper squares and have him label and illustrate each square with an example of a different simple machine that he found. Then have him mount his cards in the corresponding bulletin board sections. Now that's a simple-machine reference that really works!

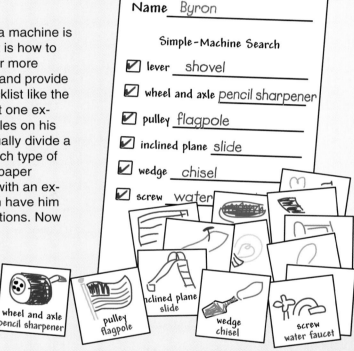

Marvelous Motivation Machine

The machine in this poem doesn't help the youngster finish his homework, but this incentive program is sure to motivate your students to complete theirs! Decorate a box and lid to resemble a machine and label it "Homework Machine." Display the box near a poster titled "Homework Points." When a youngster completes her homework, she places it inside the Homework Machine and makes a tally mark on the poster. When you remove the homework from the box, add another tally mark for each paper that is completed neatly and accurately. After the class accumulates a predetermined number of points, award each student with a pass for a homework-free night or plan a special class activity. There's no doubt about it—doing homework pays!

Easy Answers

I thought homework might be more fun
If I could quickly get it done.
So I made a speedy machine—
The neatest thing you've ever seen.

I built it using copper wire,
Some metal gears, a rubber tire.
It has a bell that rings on top
And flashing lights that never stop.

The next day when I went to school,
I acted very, very cool.
"My machine can do all my work,"
I thought to myself with a smirk.

When I got home, I took the stack
Of homework out of my backpack.
The most homework I'd ever seen—
I put it into my machine.

The lights began to blink and shine.
All systems seemed to work just fine.
The answers magically appeared.
I jumped for joy and then I cheered!

When morning came I wore a grin
As I handed my homework in.
I waited for my teacher's praise.
Instead I saw her eyebrows raise.

My new machine was fast, you see,
But it did not work carefully.
It made some mistakes in its haste,
And everyone knows: haste makes waste.

So thanks to my special device,
I had to do my homework twice.
Now I know it will always pay
To do it the old-fashioned way.

by Geoff Mihalenko

Note to teacher: Give each student a copy of this page. Read the poem for enjoyment. Then challenge each student to circle the pairs of rhyming words on the page. Next have her draw a star beside each circle that contains a pair of words that end with the same spelling.

Booklet Patterns

Use with "Word Family House" on page 120.

At Home
With Word Families

by _____

1

-ice

_____

_____   _____

Buddy built a house for
five fine m<u>ice</u>.

_____

_____

2

-eat

_____

_____

Inside there is a
yummy tr<u>eat</u>.

_____

_____

3

-at

_____

_____   _____

Outside there is a
big welcome m<u>at</u>.

_____

_____

MATH UNITS

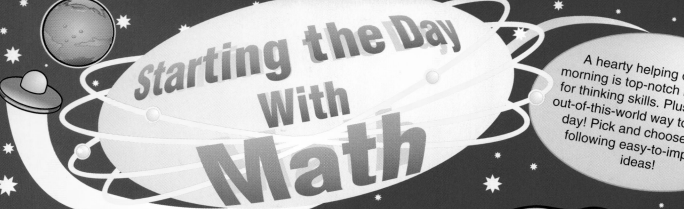

Starting the Day With Math

A hearty helping of math each morning is top-notch nourishment for thinking skills. Plus it's just an out-of-this-world way to start every day! Pick and choose from the following easy-to-implement ideas!

Money Matters

Cash in on money skills with these calendar-related activities!

- Have students brainstorm coin combinations that equal the current date. For example, for September 20, possible combinations include 2 dimes, 20 pennies, 1 dime and 2 nickels, and so on.
- At the beginning of each month place one coin in a designated container for each day in that month. Vary the value of the coins. Then, every day, have a student take coins from the container to represent the current date (e.g., two coins on the second, ten coins on the tenth). Lead the class in calculating the cash value of the day and then return the coins to the container.

Mental Math

Get each morning rolling with some thought-provoking computation! Near the class calendar, mount three laminated squares, one laminated circle, and an equal sign in the order shown. To begin, have one student roll a die. Use a wipe-off marker to write the number he rolls in the first laminated square. Ask another student to roll the die and write the number he rolls in the third laminated square. Give the class ample time to mentally solve the equation. Then ask a volunteer to name the missing operation and number as you add them to the math sentence. Next have the volunteer explain for his classmates how he solved the equation. You'll quickly discover that the students' verbal explanations are invaluable for promoting their classmates' problem-solving skills. For a more difficult activity, provide two dice for students to roll and then write the numbers each child rolls as a two-digit number. Roll on!

Trisha Owen—Gr. 3, Libbey Elementary School, Wheatland, WY

Hundreds Board

You can count on this activity to liven up the group. Position a laminated hundreds chart near your class calendar. Each morning, after the calendar is updated, use the chart to lead the students in rousing counts—by ones, by twos, by fives, and by tens. For extra fun, vary the beat of the count and add accompanying movements.

Lisa Strieker—Gr. 3
St. Paul Elementary School
Highland, IL

clap clap clap

2, 4, 6, 8, 10...

Welcome To Mrs. Squid's Second Grade!

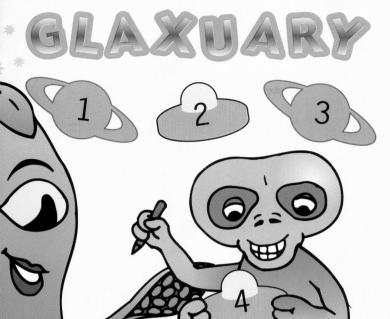

GLAXUARY

Patterning Possibilities

If one picture is worth a thousand words, imagine the chatter your classroom calendar will create when you use it to reinforce patterning skills! Each month prepare calendar pieces that reveal a different pattern relating to the month, season, or a current theme or topic of study. Keep the pieces in a container near the calendar. At the beginning of the month ask each child on daily calendar duty to state the current date before finding and posting the corresponding cutout. As soon as the monthly pattern is established, each child on calendar duty states the day's date and identifies the shape and/or color of the corresponding cutout before he adds it to the calendar. Increase the difficulty of the pattern each month and by the end of the year your youngsters will be pros at identifying patterns!

Sherrie L. Scott
Warnsdorfer School
East Brunswick, NJ

Weather conditions indicate moderate cloudiness....

MONTHLY WEATHER DATA

10					
9					
8					
7					
6					
5					

Weather Graph

Collecting, displaying, and discussing weather-related data reinforces a variety of math concepts. Display a bar graph, like the one shown, near your classroom calendar. Each morning the daily weather reporter graphs the current weather condition and then asks the class two or three graph-related questions. On the last day of each month, remove all the data that's been collected. The outlook for this morning math activity is sunny and bright!

Lisa Strieker—Gr. 3
St. Paul Elementary School
Highland, IL

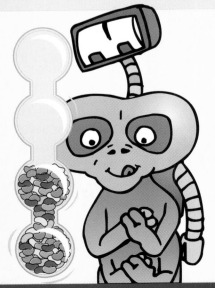

Enticing Estimation

Take a daily approach to estimation and your students' accuracy is sure to increase! Each week provide a different snack item to be estimated. Before the students arrive on Monday morning, count out several snack items into a clear, airtight container. When a student arrives, she studies the contents of the container and records her estimate in her math journal or at a display provided for this purpose. Later in the day, reveal the exact number of snack items in the container. For each remaining day of the week, add or delete items from the container, always keeping an accurate count, and always revealing this count to the students after their estimates are made. Encourage students to utilize the count(s) from the previous day(s) when making new estimates. Then, on Friday, invite the student with the most accurate estimate to evenly distribute the snack items to her classmates, keeping any remainders for herself. Fine-tuning estimation skills is a very tasty experience!

adapted from an idea by Christine Joyner—Gr. 1, Lincoln Heights GT Magnet School
Fuquay–Varina, NC

Blue-Ribbon Recipes
for Math Reinforcement

When we asked our trusty subscribers for their favorite math activities, we received a full-course menu of prizewinning suggestions! In this delicious assortment, you'll find ideas for strengthening assorted skills, from basic facts to expanded notation. Serve up these appetizing activities and watch students develop an undeniable taste for math!

On-Target Fact Review
Skill: Basic facts

This large-group game is right on target when it comes to reinforcing basic math facts! Draw a dartboard on the chalkboard. For a review of addition facts, label each section of the dartboard with a different sum. Group students into two teams and have each team stand single file facing the chalkboard. The first player in each line takes a turn choosing a sum from the dartboard and stating a corresponding addition fact. If a correct fact is given, the player scores team points equal to the sum. (To avoid repetition of facts, write the sums on the chalkboard and list each correct fact under its answer.) If an incorrect fact is given, no points are scored. Both players then move to the end of their respective lines. Continue play as described until all students have participated at least once. The team with the most points wins!

Heather Fischer—Gr. 2, Prairie Heights Elementary, Dwight, KS

Flash Card Tic-Fact-Toe!
Skill: Basic facts

Add a mathematical twist to tic-tac-toe with this large-group game. For a review of subtraction facts, have each child label 15 to 20 construction paper cards with provided subtraction facts and write the corresponding answers on the backs. To make her gameboard, a child chooses nine cards from her set and arranges them, fact side up, in three rows of three cards each. To begin play, call the answer to one of the provided subtraction facts.

10–7	5	4–2
11–4	8–2	0
9–8	3–0	10–6

Each child checks her array of cards for a matching subtraction fact. If she finds one, she turns the card over to confirm her selection. If the answer matches, she leaves the answer showing. If it does not, she flips the card over so that the fact shows. (Only one fact card may be turned over for each stated answer.) The first student to show three answers in a vertical, horizontal, or diagonal row on her gameboard declares, "Tic-fact-toe!" As soon as a game winner is confirmed, each child creates a new nine-card gameboard. At the end of game time have each child store her cards in a plastic sandwich bag for future games.

Ron Derr—Gr. 3, Brecknock Elementary School Shillington, PA

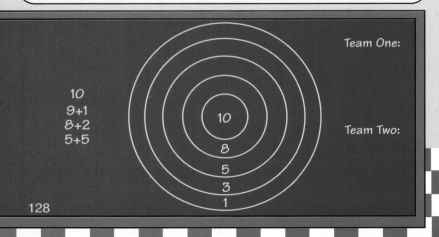

10
9+1
8+2
5+5

Team One:

Team Two:

10
8
5
3
1

Addition Facts to 7 by Samantha

0 + 7 = 7   7 + 0 = 7
1 + 6 = 7   6 + 1 = 7
2 + 5 = 7   5 + 2 = 7
3 + 4 = 7   4 + 3 = 7

Buried Treasure
Skill: Basic addition facts

If you're searching for a way to reinforce basic addition facts, you'll find this treasure chest project as precious as gold! Select a sum on which students need extra reinforcement, such as sums to 7. Or for an individualized project, help each child select a sum that she finds especially challenging. Then have each child list and solve basic addition facts that total the spotlighted sum. After verifying the students' work for accuracy, help them make treasure chests in which to record their precious problems. To make a chest, a student folds up the bottom of an 8" x 18" strip of light-colored construction paper to make a seven-inch flap. Next she folds the top four inches of the strip forward. She rounds the top corners of the folded shape, unfolds the shape, and then copies her problems inside. Instruct each student to refold her shape. If desired, also have her round one end of a 1" x 5" paper strip and glue it to the top flap of the folded shape as shown. Then invite her to title and decorate her resulting treasure chest as desired. Finally, encourage each child to refer to her treasure chest as she works on memorizing the facts that she's stored there.

adapted from an idea by VaReane Gray Heese—Gr. 2, Springfield Elementary
Springfield, NE

Odd and Even
Skill: Odd and even numbers to ten

Get youngsters in tune with odd and even numbers with the little ditty shown! As soon as students are familiar with the song, try this follow-up activity. Give each child ten animal crackers. Announce a number from one to ten. A student counts out the corresponding number of crackers and groups them by twos to determine if the number is odd or even. If the number is even, she oinks. If the number is odd, she moos! Repeat the activity several times, announcing a different number each time. Then serve milk or juice and invite students to eat their crackers!

Gale Gervais Yost—Gr. 1, Whiting Lane Elementary
West Hartford, CT

Odd and Even
(sung to the tune of "B-I-N-G-O")

There was a farmer who had a pig,
And Even was his name-o.
0, 2, 4, 6, 8; 0, 2, 4, 6, 8; 0, 2, 4, 6, 8;
And Even was his name-o.

There was a farmer who had a cow,
And Odd was her name-o.
1, 3, 5, 7, 9; 1, 3, 5, 7, 9; 1, 3, 5, 7, 9;
And Odd was her name-o.

Add It!
Skill: 2-digit addition with regrouping

You can sum up this partner game in one word—FUN! Each child needs a pencil, a sheet of paper, and a die. For each round of play, a partner rolls his die twice and writes the two numbers he rolls as a two-digit number. Then he makes a second two-digit number in the manner described and uses it to create a two-digit addition problem on his paper. He solves the addition problem and then he asks his partner to check his work. Next the partners compare sums. The partner with the higher sum scores a point for the round. If the sums are equal, both partners earn a point. Students continue playing in this same manner until time is called. The partner with the most points at the end of game time wins! Add 'em!

Jodi Moll—Gr. 3, Fairfax Elementary, Valley, AL

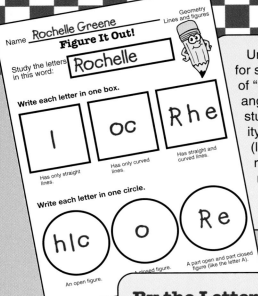

Name Rochelle Greene

Geometry
Lines and figures

Figure It Out!

Study the letters in this word: Rochelle

Write each letter in one box.

l	oc	Rhe
Has only straight lines.	Has only curved lines.	Has straight and curved lines.

Write each letter in one circle.

hlc	o	Re
An open figure.	A closed figure.	A part open and part closed figure (like the letter A).

What's in a Name?
Skill: Geometry

Understanding curved and straight lines and open and closed figures is a cinch for students when they take this personalized approach. Distribute student copies of "Figure It Out!" from page 133. Have each child write his first name in the rectangle at the top of the page and then complete the activity as described. Next pair students and have each child confirm his partner's answers. To extend the activity, enlist the students' help in identifying the student names that have the most (least) letters in each category presented. Then invite interested students to repeat the activity using their middle names, last names, nicknames, family members' names, pets' names, or other desired word choices.

Shelly Lanier, Reeds Elementary, Lexington, NC

By the Letter
Skill: Patterns

Students take a personal interest in this patterning activity! Writing from left to right, have each child continuously write his name on a sheet of one-inch graph paper—one letter per square—until each square is written in. To make his pattern, he assigns a different color to each letter in his name and then he colors the one-inch squares accordingly. Encourage students to study the patterns they make and compare them to the patterns their classmates make. Mount the students' projects on a bulletin board titled "Name Patterns—Unique Just Like Us!"

Diane Wiss—Gr. 2, Fox Meadow School, South Elgin, IL

Searching for Solid Shapes
Skill: Geometry

Send students on a search for solid shapes with this homework activity! Give each child a copy of "Solid Shape Hunt" from page 133. Have him write a search location such as "kitchen" or "bedroom" in the first blank at the top of the page and a due date in the second blank. When the homework papers are returned, compile the students' research on individual solid-shape posters and then use the information gathered to create a class graph (see the illustration). Pose a variety of graph-related questions for students to answer. Wow! Solid shapes are everywhere!

Marjorie Crawford, Herndon, VA

Cylinders We Found

soup can	dog food can
potato chip can	cat food can
coffee can	vegetable can
biscuit can	salt container
soda can	oatmeal container
tuna fish can	

Searching the Kitchen for Solid Shapes

Shapes	Items Found											
cube												
box												
cone												
sphere												
cylinder												
	1	2	3	4	5	6	7	8	9	10	11	12

Measure It!

1 2 3 4 5 6 7 8 9 10 11 12

3 inches long by 2 inches wide

How long? How wide?

For Good Measure
Skill: Linear measurement

Keep students' measurement skills in tip-top shape and create a class book with this fun-to-repeat activity! Have each child copy the two questions "How long?" and "How wide?" near the bottom of a 4½" x 12" rectangle of white construction paper. Next she draws and colors a picture of a desired item on the remainder of her paper, measures the length and width of the illustrated item at its longest and widest points, and records the resulting measurements on the back of her paper. Ask students to trade their completed papers with another classmate and confirm the measurements written on the back. As students work, decorate two 4½" x 12" rectangles of yellow construction paper to resemble rulers. Then collect the students' work and compile the pages between the resulting yellow covers. Title the book "Measure It!" and place the book and a ruler in your math center. A student measures the length and width of each illustrated item and then she turns the page to check her work. Now that's a project that really measures up!

Leigh Anne Newsom—Gr. 3, Greenbrier Intermediate, Chesapeake, VA

Lunch Money
Skill: Money

Create an appetite for money-counting skills with this whole-group activity. Sequentially number a class set of resealable plastic bags, seal a different combination of real coins inside each bag, and prepare a corresponding answer key. Place the bags and answer key in a lunchbox for safekeeping. Prepare a math journal for each child that contains one blank page for each prepared coin set. Distribute the math journals and have students number the pages. Every morning place a different coin set on each child's desk. A student counts the lunch money without opening the bag. On the corresponding page in his journal, he writes the total money amount and then he draws and colors the matching coin set. Collect the bags and store them in the lunchbox. Repeat the activity daily until every student has counted each bag of lunch money. Periodically collect the students' journals and use the answer key to check their work.

Kathie Jamieson—Gr. 1, Fulton Grammar School, Fulton, MS

17¢

4

5

1 + 5 8 ÷

Got the Time?
Skill: Time

This large-group game provides timely feedback on time-telling skills! To make the game cards, use a clock stamp and an ink pad to stamp a clock face on a class supply of blank cards. Program each clock with a different time. If desired, use a red fine-point marker to draw the hour hands and a blue fine-point marker to draw the minute hands. Keep a record of the times shown on the cards. Laminate the cards for durability. To play, distribute the cards and quickly announce each recorded time. The child with the corresponding card holds it up for your approval. When all the times are called, collect the cards, shuffle them, and play another game!

Sandy Shaw
Jeannette McKee Elementary
Jeannette, PA

"McMarvelous" Math
Skill: Place value

Beginning place-value skills are in the bag when you take this kid-pleasing approach! Ask a local fast-food restaurant for a donation of two paper french fry bags per student. Cut 12" x 18" sheets of yellow construction paper into 1/2" x 5" strips (cut two sheets for every five students) and sequentially number a class supply of paper plates. Give each child a paper plate with a batch of yellow paper fries (no more than 29), two french fry bags, and a sheet of paper. Have each child number his paper to match the paper plate count; then have him bag his fries. Explain that each bag holds ten fries—no more, no less. Any unbaggable fries are to be placed on the paper plate. When his fries are bagged, he writes on his paper (beside the corresponding number) how many fries are in the batch. Then he pours all the fries on the paper plate, and on a signal from you, passes the plate of fries to the next person along a predetermined route. After bagging several batches of fries, students begin to clearly understand the concept of tens and ones! To increase the difficulty of the activity, have students work in pairs. Give each pair four french fry bags and up to 49 fries to bag. "McMarvelous"!

Patricia Onofrio—Gr. 1, C. T. O'Connell School, Bristol, CT

Stump the Principal
Skill: Word problems

Increase the appeal of word problems with this unique plan. Each child writes three or more word problems for the school principal to solve and then she makes a corresponding answer key. Arrange a time for each child to deliver her problems to the principal. The principal solves the problems and returns the paper to the child to grade. The child grades the principal's paper and writes a positive comment on it. Before she returns the paper to the principal, she tells her classmates about her experience and what she plans to tell the principal about his or her work. Word problems will become so appealing that students will be eager to prepare them for family members, friends, and you to solve!

Maria Smith—Gr. 2, Bess Race Elementary, Crowley, TX

Expand It!
Skill: Expanded form

These handy manipulatives are ideal for reinforcing expanded form. Cut a supply of sentence strips into one-foot lengths. To make the manipulative shown, write the expanded form of a three-digit number on a one-foot strip. Then fold the strip to reveal the standard form. To do this, reverse-fold the right end of the strip so that the ones digit of the second number is covered. Then make a second reverse fold, this time covering the ones and tens digits of the third number. When folded, the strip shows the standard form of the number. When unfolded, it shows the expanded form. Program your supply of strips with different numbers and place them at a center for students to use. Or have each child contribute one manipulative to the center!

Patti Hirsh—Gr. 3, Casis School, Austin, TX

Name

Solid Shape Hunt

Search a _____ for _____
solid shapes.
List the items you find in the boxes below.
Return this paper to school by _____.

sphere	cone
cube	box
	cylinder

©The Education Center, Inc. • THE MAILBOX® • Primary • Oct/Nov 1999

Name

Figure It Out!

Study the letters
in this word:

Write each letter in one box.

Has only straight lines.   Has only curved lines.   Has straight and curved lines.

Write each letter in one circle.

An open figure.   A closed figure.   A part open and part closed figure (like the letter A).

©The Education Center, Inc. • THE MAILBOX® • Primary • Oct/Nov 1999

Note to teacher: Use "Figure It Out!" with "What's in a Name?" on page 130. Use "Solid Shape Hunt" with "Searching for Solid Shapes" on page 130.

133

Now Serving: Fractions!

DELICIOUS!

WHOLESOME!

Served fresh daily!

After sampling these appetizing math activities, students are sure to agree that fractions are as easy as pie!

Pie Problems

When two friends have one scrumptious pie, what do they do? They share it equally, of course! That's exactly what two alligators do in *Gator Pie* by Louise Mathews (Sundance Publications, 1995). After reading this book aloud, give each student two identical white circles, a 12" x 18" sheet of white construction paper, and a card labeled with a group of animals like "5 squirrels" or "8 giraffes." A student colors one circle to resemble a pie the animals might enjoy; then she colors the second circle to match. Next she glues one pie on the left half of her paper. She cuts the other pie into equal-sized pieces for the animals and glues the pieces on the right half of her paper. Then she labels her paper in a manner similar to what is shown. Students quickly see that equal shares are only fair!

A banana pie for eight monkeys.

Each monkey gets $\frac{1}{8}$ of the pie.

Take Part

Any way you slice it, this hands-on fraction activity is guaranteed to please! Working on waxed paper, have each student shape a small portion of play dough into a square. Next have him use a plastic knife to cut the square into two equal-sized parts, pointing out that there is more than one way to do this. Invite several students to the chalkboard to draw how they divided their squares. Add to these illustrations as needed to provide a variety of solutions. Then choose a halved square and explain that each part of the square is one half of its shape. Demonstrate how to write "$\frac{1}{2}$" and ask each child to use a toothpick to write the fraction on each half of his square. Then have him smooth and reshape his dough to explore thirds and fourths in a similar manner. Now that's an idea that's a cut above the rest!

Carol Newland—Gr. 2, Banner County School, Harrisburg, NE

Sorting Fractions

The fraction cards on page 138 provide students with all sorts of practice identifying parts of a figure!

- **For an individual activity,** give each child a 12" x 18" sheet of construction paper and a copy of page 138. A student folds the construction paper in half twice, then unfolds it to reveal four boxes. She cuts out the four labels from her copy of page 138 and glues each one in a different box. Then she cuts out the fraction cards, sorts them into the labeled boxes, and glues them in place. Challenge students to write a fraction for each card in the "Other" box.
- **For a center activity,** laminate a construction paper copy of page 138 and cut along the bold lines. Use a permanent marker to code the backs of the cards for self-checking. Store the cutouts in a zippered bag and place the bag at a math center. A student sorts the cards into the four designated groups and then flips them to check his work.

Spill the Beans

At this center, spills create fractions—not messes! Spray-paint one side of a supply of dried kidney beans. When the paint is dry, place varying numbers of the beans in several empty film containers. Store the containers in a shoebox at the center. Also provide crayons and a supply of paper. A child removes the lid from the shoebox, chooses a container, and carefully spills the beans from it into the lid. She illustrates the spilled beans on her paper and writes a fraction for each set of sprayed and unsprayed beans shown. Then she returns the beans to the container and repeats the process with the remaining containers. To increase the difficulty of the center, use two different colors of spray paint to paint the beans.

Cindy Wann—Gr. 3
Westside Elementary
Jonesboro, AR

$\frac{7}{10}$ brown $\frac{3}{10}$ orange

Fraction "Stamp-ede"

Count on students to give this partner activity their stamp of approval! Have each student fold a large sheet of drawing paper in half three times and then unfold his paper to reveal eight equal-sized sections. After he traces the fold lines, he uses a stamper to make several images in each section. Then he circles a desired number of images in each group. Next he trades papers with a classmate. In each section of his classmate's paper, he writes what fraction of the stamps in that group are circled. When he finishes, he returns the paper to his partner for verification, and he verifies the activity he created and his partner completed.

If you have a computer and a program that has stamp tools such as Kid Pix Studio® or Fine Artist, have students prepare (and complete) computer-generated activities.

Nancy Hyrczyk—Grs. 1–2
Eisenhower School
Prospect Heights, IL

Family-Style Fractions

Fraction skills are all in the family with this nifty idea! To begin, ask a few boys and girls to stand at the front of the room. With input from the rest of the class, identify the fraction that names the male part of the group and the fraction that names the female part of the group. Write these fractions on the chalkboard. Repeat the process with several different groups of students. Then explore fractional parts of a different type of group—the family. To do this, each child chooses an attribute such as hair or eye color by which to describe herself and her family members. On provided paper, she draws her family in two or more sets by the chosen attribute. Then she labels each set with the corresponding fraction. Display students' completed work on a bulletin board titled "Fractions Are All in the Family!"

$\frac{2}{5}$ of my family has blonde hair $\frac{3}{5}$ of my family has brown hair

I have $\frac{1}{2}$ dozen eggs.

Fabulous Fraction Diary

A fraction a day builds skills in a fun way! Have each student staple four sheets of blank paper inside construction paper covers. Ask her to label the front cover "Fraction Diary" and personalize it as desired. Then have her label one blank page for each day of the week. Every day the student describes and illustrates at least one fraction she encounters (at home, at school, or in the community). After seven days, invite each student to share her favorite or most unique entry with the class.

adapted from an idea by
MaryMargaret Clement
Cohoes, NY

Real-World Fractions

$\frac{1}{3}$: 1 wheel of a tricycle

$\frac{1}{8}$: 1 stick of gum from a package

$\frac{1}{12}$: 1 month of the year

$\frac{2}{12}$: 2 eggs from a dozen

$\frac{3}{4}$: 3 sections of a cracker

$\frac{2}{6}$:

On the Lookout

This activity reminds students that fractions aren't just in math class—they're everywhere! Show a few examples of real-world fractions, such as an orange cut into quarters or one-half of a pair of shoes. Then ask students to brainstorm additional examples and list their ideas on chart paper. Next give each student a large index card bearing a fraction. For homework have him find an example of the fraction at home and then illustrate it on the back of the card. Or invite students to bring examples of their assigned fractions to school on a predetermined date. With this engaging approach to math, your youngsters will be keeping their eyes peeled for fractions for a long time to come!

Leigh Anne Newsom—Gr. 3
Greenbrier Intermediate School
Chesapeake, VA

My dad made pancakes this morning. He used $1\frac{1}{4}$ cups of flour and $\frac{1}{2}$ teaspoon of salt.

For Good Measure

Fractions really measure up with this tasty classroom recipe! On a copy of page 139, list three snack mix ingredients in the "Ingredient List" box at the bottom of the page. (The third ingredient will make up most of the recipe.) Then distribute a class supply of the page. Explain to students that they will be writing a recipe for snack mix. Guide students through the activity, providing assistance as needed. When the recipe is written, ask each child to bring one-quarter cup of a designated ingredient to school the following day. Use the class-created recipe to make a batch of snack mix for your students' eating pleasure. Periodically repeat the activity, varying the ingredients used and the number of people eating the snack mix. Students quickly discover that fractions are not only handy, they're downright delicious!

Dolores Joiner—Gr. 1
Furry Elementary
Sandusky, OH

136

In a Word

What's in a word? Plenty of fraction practice! Prepare a form like the one shown and give each student a copy. Dictate six words and ask each student to write each one on the appropriate line. Then instruct the youngster to write one fraction for the part of the word that is vowels and one for the part that is consonants. After each child has completed her work, describe each dictated word by announcing its corresponding fractions. Challenge students to identify the word you have described. To extend older students' learning, ask them what they notice about the *numerators* and *denominators* for each word's fractions. Lead them to conclude that the sum of the numerators equals the denominator.

Melanie J. Miller
Nashport, OH

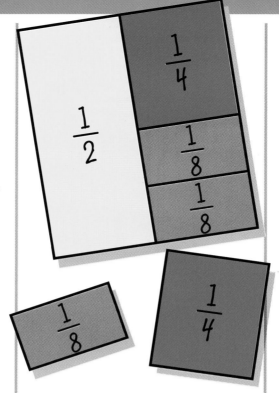

Colorful Equivalents

The concept of equivalent fractions takes shape with these student-made manipulatives! Give each student four 9-inch construction paper squares, each a different color. To prepare a set of manipulatives, a student writes "1" on one square to represent a whole. He folds another square in half, opens it, cuts along the fold line to make two equal parts, and labels each resulting half "$1/2$." He uses a similar process with the two remaining squares to make and label four quarters and eight eighths. Then ask each student to determine different ways to completely cover the whole square with assorted manipulatives without overlapping any pieces. Invite students to share their solutions.

For more exploration with equivalents, have each youngster use his manipulatives to determine how many eighths are needed to cover one fourth and how many fourths are needed to cover one half. To reuse the manipulatives, have each child store his set in a large resealable zippered bag.

adapted from an idea by
Phil Forsythe—Gr. 3
Northeastern Elementary
Bellefontaine, OH

A Menu of Fraction Books

If your students are hungry to learn more about fractions, whet their appetites with these terrific titles!

Fraction Fun
Written by David A. Adler
Illustrated by Nancy Tobin
Holiday House, Inc.; 1997

Jump, Kangaroo, Jump!
Written by Stuart J. Murphy
Illustrated by Kevin O'Malley
HarperCollins Children's Books, 1999

Fraction Action
By Loreen Leedy
Holiday House, Inc.; 1996

Give Me Half!
Written by Stuart J. Murphy
Illustrated by G. Brian Karas
HarperCollins Publishers, Inc.; 1996

Name **Anna**

Spelling Word	Consonants	Vowels
1. hot	$\frac{2}{3}$	$\frac{1}{3}$
2. spot	$\frac{3}{4}$	$\frac{1}{4}$
3. hottest	$\frac{5}{7}$	$\frac{2}{7}$
4. cotton	—	—
5. forgot	—	—
6. spotlight	—	—

Order books on-line. www.themailbox.com

137

$\frac{1}{2}$	$\frac{1}{3}$	$\frac{1}{4}$	other

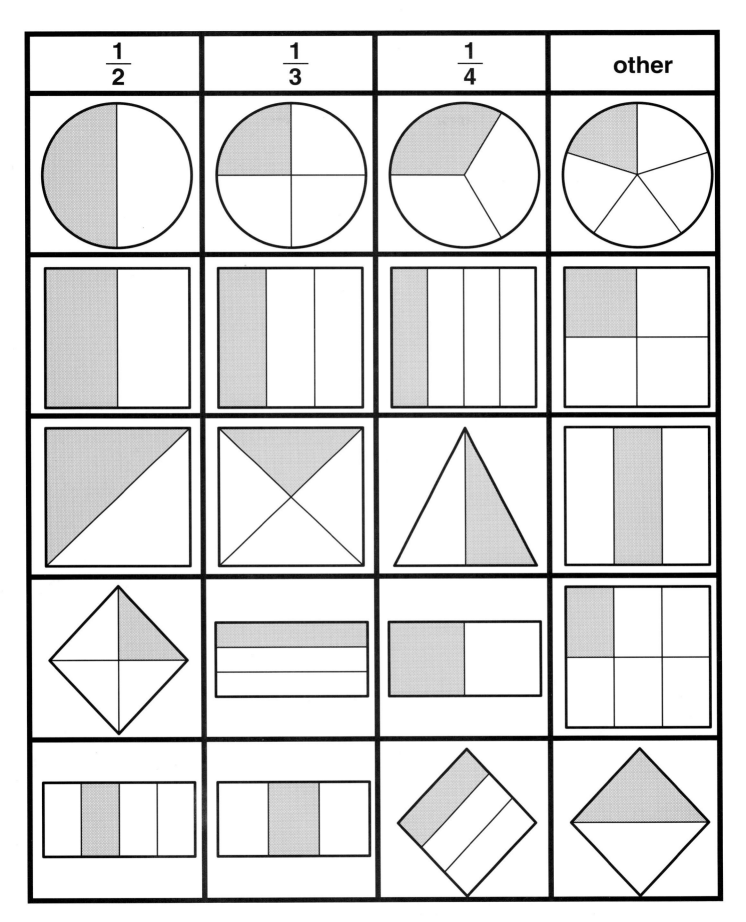

©The Education Center, Inc. • *THE MAILBOX*® • *Primary* • April/May 2000

138   **Note to teacher:** Use with "Sorting Fractions" on page 134.

Super Snack Mix

Write a snack mix recipe!

1. How many people will eat snack mix? _____

2. Color ¼ of a measuring cup for each person who is eating snack mix. Start with the first cup.

3. Study the measuring cups. How much snack mix do you need? _____

4. Write an ingredient below each cup you colored. Use the ingredient list.

5. Finish the recipe below.

 A. _____

 B. _____

 C. _____

 C. _____

 C. _____

 C. _____

C. _____

 C. _____

 C. _____

 C. _____

Super Snack Mix
(Serves _____ people)

_____ of ingredient **A.**

_____ of ingredient **B.**

_____ of ingredient **C.**

Mix well. Serve each person ¼ cup.

Ingredient List

A. _____

B. _____

C. _____

Note to teacher: Use with "For Good Measure" on page 136.

March Math

Look what the March winds blew in—a seasonal collection of skill-based math ideas just right for your students!

ADDITION

Up, Up, and Away!

Addition skills are sure to take flight with this high-flying game! Divide students into pairs. Give each youngster a copy of page 142 and two dice. Each player, in turn, rolls the dice. He colors the space on his kite that corresponds with the sum of the numbers rolled. If this space has already been colored, his turn is over. If he rolls a double, he may color in either the corresponding space for the sum or one kite tail. The first player to color in all 12 spaces and the kite tails or the player who colors the most spaces within the allotted game time wins.

LOGICAL REASONING

Go for the Gold!

Here's a golden opportunity to reinforce logical reasoning. Divide students into pairs. Give each twosome ten gold foil–covered chocolate coins. To play one game round, the students in each pair sit across from each other. They lay the coins in a line on the playing surface between them. In turn, each player removes either one or two coins from either end of the line. The student who takes the last coin wins the round and goes first in the next round. After each twosome has played a desired number of rounds, ask students to share their game strategies. Next invite each child to keep one coin for snacking; then collect the remaining coins to use as incentives during the remainder of March.

PLACE VALUE

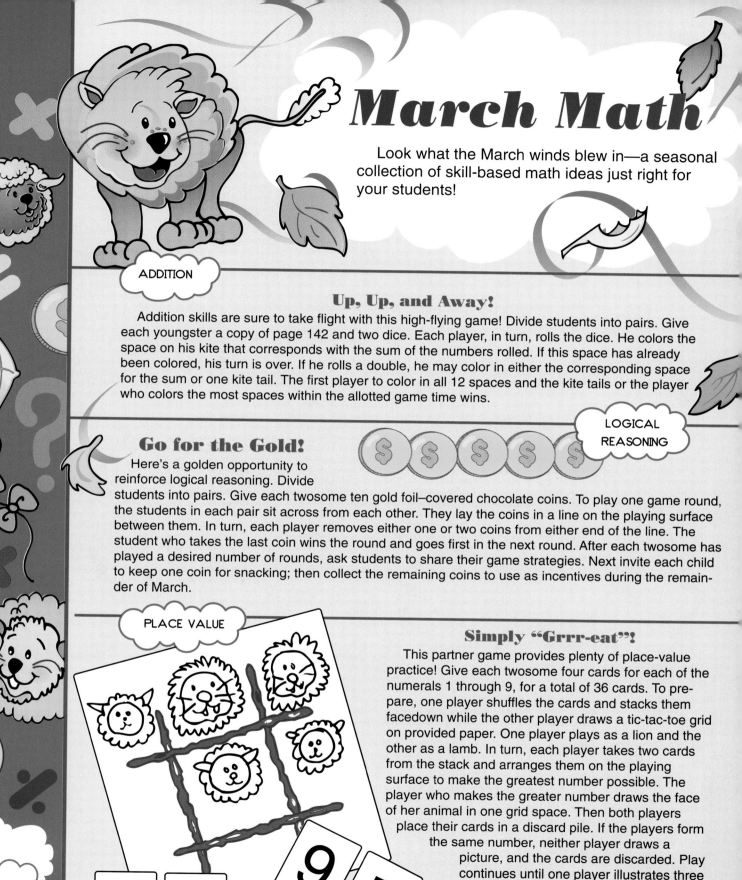

Simply "Grrr-eat"!

This partner game provides plenty of place-value practice! Give each twosome four cards for each of the numerals 1 through 9, for a total of 36 cards. To prepare, one player shuffles the cards and stacks them facedown while the other player draws a tic-tac-toe grid on provided paper. One player plays as a lion and the other as a lamb. In turn, each player takes two cards from the stack and arranges them on the playing surface to make the greatest number possible. The player who makes the greater number draws the face of her animal in one grid space. Then both players place their cards in a discard pile. If the players form the same number, neither player draws a picture, and the cards are discarded. Play continues until one player illustrates three spaces in a horizontal, vertical, or diagonal row and wins the game, or until the grid is completely illustrated and a tie is declared. (Have students shuffle the discarded cards and restack them as needed). Invite youngsters to play a desired number of additional rounds.

Likely Lions and Lambs

Put a spin on probability with this wild and woolly activity! Pair students and give each child a paper clip and a copy of the spinner wheel, lion, and lamb patterns from page 143. Ask one partner to connect the Xs on her spinner wheel. Ask the other partner to connect the two dots on her spinner wheel and then connect the center dot to an X. Next have each student color and cut out her animal patterns and glue one in each section of her spinner wheel.

To begin, have each child study the equally divided spinner wheel and predict if she will spin more lions or more lambs in 15 spins. Then have each student test her prediction while her partner records the results. Invite students to share their findings. Next have students predict how their results will differ when they use the unequally divided spinner wheels. After these predictions are tested, have students evaluate their findings from the two types of spinners. Lead them to conclude that the larger the space on a spinner wheel, the greater the chance that a spinner will land there. Now that's a probability idea worth roaring about!

Jumbled Hats

Hats off to problem solving! Read aloud *The Wind Blew* by Pat Hutchins (Aladdin Paperbacks, 1993), a humorous tale about the confusion caused one day by the wind. Then ask students to imagine that three people are wearing hats: one hat is green, one blue, and one yellow. The wind blows the hats off these people and onto three others. Challenge youngsters to determine all of the possible hat-landing combinations. *(There are six combinations.)* To solve the problem, have each student draw pictures, write an organized list, or use another strategy of his choice. After each youngster is satisfied with his solution, ask student volunteers to share their strategies with the class. Students are sure to see that there is more than one way to find a solution—you can hang your hat on it!

Golden Puzzler

You can bank on this wee display to reinforce money skills. Color, cut out, and laminate an enlargement of the leprechaun pattern on page 143. Then mount the cutout on a bulletin board titled "What Is in the Leprechaun's Pot?" Decorate a container with St. Patrick's Day art, and store a supply of coin manipulatives inside. Place the container, a set of coin stamps, and a supply of paper near the display. Each day, use a wipe-off marker to program the leprechaun's pot with a different value and number of coins. Arrange for each youngster to visit the display area, use the manipulatives to determine the coin combination that fits the programmed criteria, and then use the stamps to record his answer on the provided paper. Ask students to share their solutions at the end of the day. Now that's an idea rich with problem-solving potential!

Theresa Lewis

141

Up, Up, and Away!

©The Education Center, Inc. • THE MAILBOX® • Primary • Feb/Mar 2000

142 **Note to teacher:** Use with "Up, Up, and Away!" on page 140.

Use spinner wheel, lion, and lamb patterns with "Likely Lions and Lambs" on page 141.

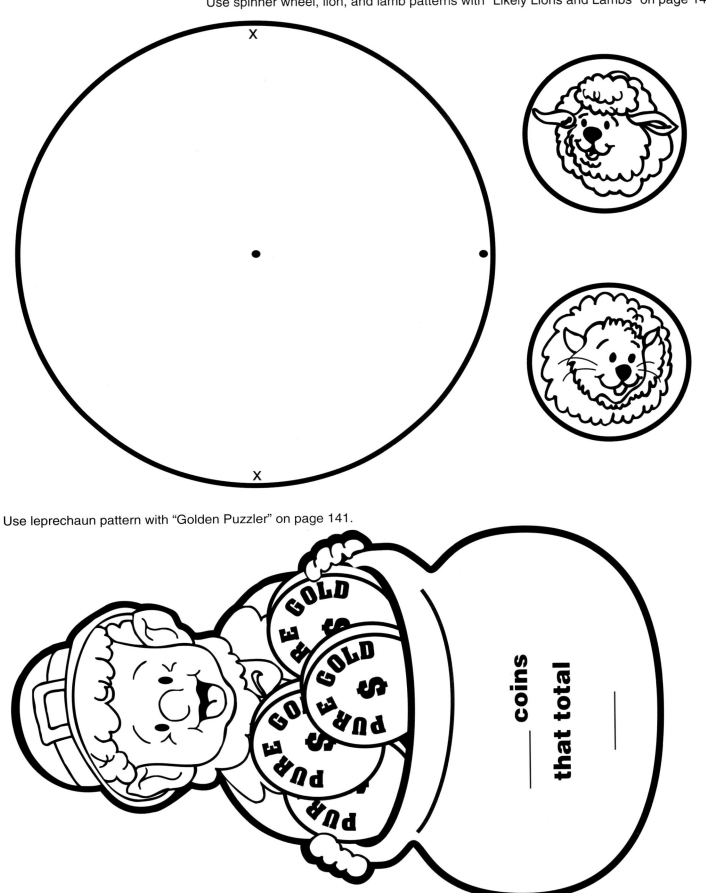

X

X

Use leprechaun pattern with "Golden Puzzler" on page 141.

coins

that total

Exploring Math in the Great Outdoors

Give your end-of-the-year math review a creative twist by heading outdoors! A healthy dose of fresh air and sunshine is the perfect way to rejuvenate and reinforce a variety of math skills!

ideas contributed by Monica Cavender

Warming Up to Math

Set the stage for outdoor math adventures by gathering students around an imaginary campfire. Explain that math is all around, even in the great outdoors! Invite youngsters to share examples of math in their everyday environments. Then, if possible, read aloud *Math Curse* by Jon Scieszka (Viking Children's Books, 1995). This experience around the campfire is sure to spark an interest in outdoor math!

Gearing Up

Take a few minutes to gear up your math scouts for outdoor adventure! Explain that in addition to her math expertise, each scout can use a pair of math-spotting binoculars and a scouting journal. Then refer to the following directions to lead students in making their supplies. (*To incorporate math skills, have students measure and cut these items.)

Math-Spotting Binoculars
Supplies to make one pair:
two 9-oz. Dixie® cold cups
clear tape
18" length of yarn*
pencil
access to a hole puncher

Directions:
1. Use the point of the pencil to pierce the bottom of each cup; then carefully tear away the bottom of each cup.
2. Hold the cups side by side. Tape the top rims together.
3. Tape the bottom rims of the cups together; then hole-punch the outside edges of each bottom rim as shown.
4. Securely tie one end of the yarn length in each punched hole.
5. Wear (and use) your math-spotting binoculars during outdoor math adventures!

Scouting Journal
Supplies to make one:
1 copy of the cover pattern from page 148
four 6" x 18" sheets of drawing paper*
14" length of raffia (or twine)*
scissors
access to a hole puncher
crayons or markers
glue

Directions:
1. Stack and align the drawing paper; then fold the stack in half.
2. Punch two holes at the top of the stack, near the fold. (Provide assistance as needed.)
3. Thread the raffia through the holes, tie, and fashion a bow from the ends.
4. Color and personalize the cover pattern. Cut it out and glue it to the front of the journal.
5. Complete outdoor math activities in your journal as directed by your teacher.

Estimating the Distance

An outdoor hike is just what your scouts need to sharpen their estimation skills! Before heading outdoors, ask each child to sketch a chart in his journal like the one shown. Then gather students at a designated class campsite near the edge of the playground and divide them into five groups. Select five playground objects that are comparable distances from the class campsite and assign one to each group. Each scout estimates how many steps it will take him to walk from the class campsite to his group's object and writes his estimate on his chart. Next, he counts his steps as he hikes to the object. He records this number on his chart and returns to the class campsite.

Instruct students to complete their charts in a like manner, by first estimating the number of movements needed to reach the object, counting the movements, and then recording the actual count. Encourage them to evaluate the data they've recorded before they make a new estimate, as this can help them sharpen their estimation skills. In conclusion, have the students in each group compare their findings, discuss which methods of movement were easiest (most difficult) to estimate, and propose reasons why actual counts may differ among group members.

Shape Spotters

Watch your scouts' geometry skills take shape during this outdoor expedition! In advance, review the names and attributes of the basic shapes introduced during the school year. Then lead the class around the school grounds. Ask each scout to search for objects that represent the shapes reviewed and record his findings in his journal. After you return to the classroom, list on the chalkboard the different sightings of each shape. Accept all reasonable answers. Next, have each scout choose a different item from the chalkboard to illustrate on provided paper. While students work, label a sheet of poster board for each shape being reviewed. Then have each child glue his illustration to the appropriate poster. Display the shapely projects around the classroom for all to see. Invite students to add illustrations to the posters as they spot additional shapes in the great outdoors!

Pattern Trails

The great outdoors is the perfect place to find manipulatives for patterning practice. Have each child collect small loose items—such as fallen leaves and twigs, pieces of grass, and stones—in a paper lunch bag. Then have each child use the items she collects to create one or more patterns. Ask each child to illustrate her favorite pattern in her journal. For an added challenge, have students keep a tally of how many different patterns they can make using the items they've collected.

Searching for Sums

Reinforce addition skills with an outdoor sum search! To prepare, list on the chalkboard ten different basic fact sums. Ask each scout to copy the sums near the top of a journal page. Then take the scouts outdoors to search for items that add up to each sum. When a student finds a sum, he writes and solves a number sentence in his journal (see illustration). Then he marks out the sum on his original list. Challenge students to find each listed sum within an allotted amount of time! Now that's "sum" fun!

Kellie Henry—Gr. 3
St. Joseph Grade School
St. Joseph, IL

Outdoor Ordinals

Polish ordinal skills with this outdoor challenge! Label half of a class set of cards with ordinal numbers through "tenth." Label the remaining cards to match. Shuffle each resulting deck. Have an adult helper arrange a line of ten plastic cones in a grassy outdoor area, leaving ample space between them. Have the adult helper take half of the students, a deck of cards, and scorekeeping materials to one end of the cones. Take the remaining students and similar supplies to the opposite end.

To play, each adult simultaneously announces the first ordinal number in her deck. The first player in line jogs to the corresponding cone and touches it. Then he jogs back to the team and asks, "Did I touch the correct cone?" If the team responds "yes," he earns two points and goes to the end of the line. If the team responds "Choose a friend," he selects a teammate and the pair repeats his turn, making sure the correct cone is touched. When the twosome returns, one point is added to the team score. The friend returns to her place in line and the original player goes to the end of the line. The adult then announces the next ordinal number in the deck. Play continues in a like manner until all cards have been played. The team with more points wins. When both teams score equal points, both teams win!

adapted from an idea by Sammie Hardy—Grs. 1–5
Goodrich Elementary
Goodrich, TX

Lively Skip-Counting

This mathematical version of hopscotch hones skip-counting skills! On a paved outdoor surface, use chalk to draw a gameboard like the one shown. Divide students into two groups and have one group line up at each end of the gameboard. Call out a desired multiple and point to Line 1. The first person in Line 1 hops through the gameboard as her classmates skip-count by the number called. When she reaches the end of the gameboard, she proceeds to the end of Line 2 as the first person in Line 2 hops back through the pattern to his classmates' counting. When he reaches the end of the gameboard, the round is over. He walks to the end of Line 1, a different multiple is announced, and another round of hopping and counting begins.

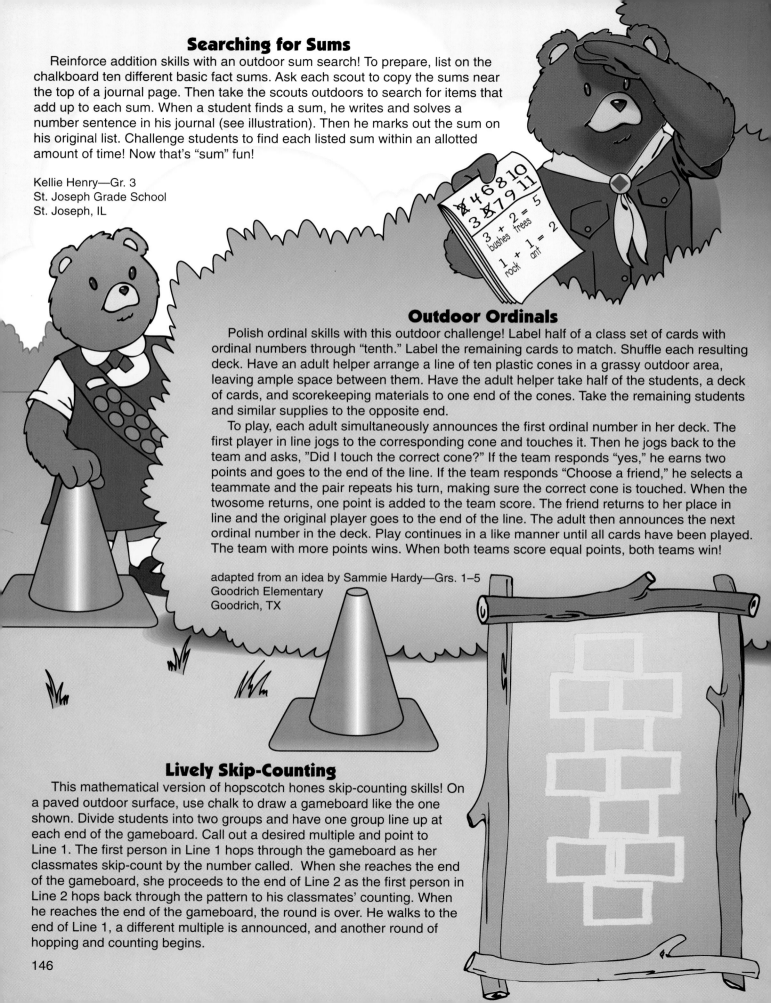

Fractional Finds

A review of fractions is just a step away! If desired, read aloud *Fraction Action* by Loreen Leedy (Holiday House, Inc.; 1996) to review fractional parts of sets. Then head outdoors and arrange your scouts in a horizontal line. Ask each of four scouts to take a giant step forward and then turn to face the class. Lead the remainder of the class in counting the number of classmates in this set. Next, ask individual students to use fractions to describe how many boys (girls) are in the set, how many students in the set are wearing sneakers, and so on. Then have the set of four return to the class line. Repeat the activity a number of times, choosing different students and varying the size of the sets. Continue until each scout has been a part of a set one or more times. When the class is back in the classroom, ask each scout to illustrate and label a favorite fraction from this outdoor experience.

Colors in the Great Outdoors

15
14
13
12
11
10
9
8
7
6
5
4
3
2
1

data collected by _Nicole_

Colorful Data

Colorful bar graphs result from this outdoor math adventure! To begin, have each child draw lines to divide two journal pages into four sections each. Then have her label the eight resulting sections with the following color words: red, orange, yellow, green, blue, purple, black, and brown. Next, lead your scouts to an outdoor area where they can sit comfortably. Instruct them to quietly observe their surroundings for colors that appear in nature. Then, in their journals, have them list the objects they see by color. Return to the classroom at a predetermined time and give each child a bar graph like the one shown. Ask each child to organize the data she collected on the graph. Set aside time for students to compare the results of their work; then, as a class, discuss why the results of this graphing experience differ.

Bloomin' Calculations

Computation skills are sure to blossom with this thought-provoking activity! If possible, take your scouts outdoors to observe real flowers. Then have each child illustrate in his journal a flower with several individual petals. Next ask him to count the petals on the flower he drew, write this number on the page, and circle it. Finally, challenge each scout to write multiple math equations in his journal that equal the circled number. Encourage students to be creative! After a predetermined amount of time, pair students and have each child check his partner's work. Now that's a creative approach to computation practice!

Exploring Math in the
Great Outdoors

Data Collected by

Math Scout _____

Math Scout

Merit Badge

Math Scout

Merit Badge

Note to teacher: Use the cover pattern with "Gearing Up: Scouting Journal" on page 144. Copy one merit badge on construction paper for each child. Upon completion of a desired number of outdoor math activities, award each math scout a merit badge to color and cut out.

SCIENCE & HEALTH
UNITS

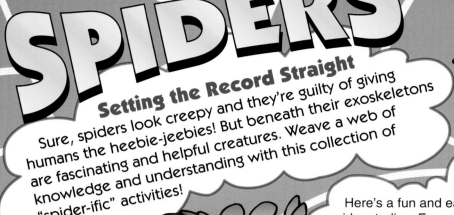

SPIDERS

Setting the Record Straight

Sure, spiders look creepy and they're guilty of giving humans the heebie-jeebies! But beneath their exoskeletons are fascinating and helpful creatures. Weave a web of knowledge and understanding with this collection of "spider-ific" activities!

Getting Started

Here's a fun and easy way to spin some assessment into your spider studies. For your first activity, ask each child to illustrate a spider on drawing paper and then flip her paper over and write (or dictate for you to write) a sentence that describes her feelings about spiders. Also invite her to share any spider facts that she knows. Collect and store the papers. Repeat the activity at the conclusion of your spider unit. When each youngster compares her two projects, she'll surely see that she's become a skillful spinner of spider information. And there's a decent chance that her feelings about spiders will have changed as well!

Insect or Arachnid?

Why isn't a spider an insect? After this hands-on activity, students will know the answer! Pair students and give each twosome a blank sheet of paper, a pencil, a plastic ant (or another plastic insect), and a plastic spider. Be sure the critters are anatomically correct. (To purchase plastic spiders and ants, call Oriental Trading Company, Inc., at 1-800-228-2269.) To complete the activity, one partner divides the paper in half and labels the resulting columns "Ant" and "Spider." Then the twosome studies each critter and lists its features on the paper. Invite students to name the features they've noted and then assist them in identifying the similarities and differences between the critters. Finally inform students that you wish to collect the insects first, then the arachnids. If necessary, alert students that an insect has *three* body parts and *six* legs. Students will quickly surmise (and remember!) that a spider is not an insect. They'll also conclude that an arachnid has *two* body parts and *eight* legs.

Faye Fowler Haney—Gr. 2, Valley View Elementary, Jonesboro, AR

Ant	Spider
6 legs	8 legs
3 body parts	2 body parts
legs attached to middle	legs on front part
sort of ugly	really ugly
	legs are longer

Eight-Legged Wonders

Dangle this project in front of students and they'll learn the different parts of a spider's body! Give each child a white construction paper copy of page 154. Each child colors up to eight eyes on the cephalothorax of the unprogrammed pattern, colors both patterns, and cuts them out. (Remind students that spiders come in a variety of colors.) Next he folds a 4½" x 12" rectangle of colorful construction paper in half and cuts out four pairs of spider legs. He glues the leg cutouts to the back of one pattern, making sure they're attached to the cephalothorax. He also glues or tapes one end of a foot-long length of yarn to the back of one pattern near the spinnerets. Last, he glues the two patterns together, keeping the colored surfaces to the outside. Refer to the information at the bottom of page 151 to lead a discussion about the spider body parts. Then use tape to suspend each child's project from his desk.

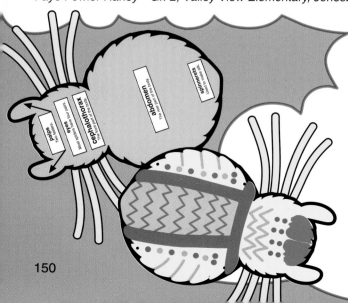

Arachnid Sing-Along

Invite students to sing out their spider knowledge!

Hanging Out With Spiders
(adapt to the tune of "Head, Shoulders, Knees, and Toes")

Cephalothorax, abdomen, abdomen.
Cephalothorax, abdomen, abdomen.
Spiders have two main body parts.
Cephalothorax, abdomen, abdomen!

Eight strong legs are attached, are attached.
Eight strong legs are attached, are attached,
Near the head, NOT on the abdomen.
Eight strong legs are attached, are attached!

Arachnid is the group where they belong, they belong.
Arachnid is the group where they belong, they belong.
Can't call them insects in this little song,
'Cause that's not the group where they belong, they belong.

Faye Fowler Haney—Gr. 2, Valley View Elementary, Jonesboro, AR

From Egg to Adult

Investigating the spider's life cycle is a breeze with this spiffy project. Make a copy of the unprogrammed pattern on page 154. Using a pencil, a ruler, and the four small dots on the pattern, divide the abdomen into four equal sections. Then draw a small circle where the lines intersect and label the quadrants as shown. Duplicate two copies of the pattern on manila drawing paper for each child. After discussing the spider's life cycle with the class, have each child illustrate the four life cycle stages on one pattern. To complete this pattern, she colors the cephalothorax (making sure to add eight or fewer eyes), cuts out the pattern, and then glues eight construction paper legs to the underside of the cephalothorax. Next she cuts out her remaining pattern, cutting away the egg quadrant and leaving the small circle intact. She flips the pattern over, colors it, and then uses a brad to attach it atop her programmed cutout. To review the spider's life cycle, she turns the top cutout clockwise.

Spider Life Cycle

Egg: A mother spider lays her eggs and then bundles them in a strong silk egg sac.

Spiderlings: In a few days baby spiders hatch, but they stay inside the egg sac for several weeks. When the light-colored spiderlings emerge, they eat food provided by their mother. As they grow and molt, their skin becomes darker. They are soon making silk and are ready to leave the nest.

Young Spider: A young web-making spider spins its own web in a new location. Its first web is small. As the young spider grows, its webs get bigger.

Adult: The spider is now full-grown. The length of a spider's life varies. Most can live up to one year, though some live much longer!

Spider Vocabulary

abdomen: The rear section of the spider where the heart, liver, lungs, and silk-producing glands are found.

arachnid: Any animal that has eight legs; two body parts; and no backbone, wings, or antennae. Spiders, scorpions, ticks, and mites are members of this group.

cephalothorax *(sef • ah • low • THOR • ax):* The front section of the spider that has the eyes, brain, and jaws. The legs are attached here.

exoskeleton: All spiders have this hard outer shell that covers and protects their bodies. It does not grow.

eyes: Most spiders have four pairs of eyes (one main pair and three smaller pairs); however, some species have fewer. Few spiders see well.

legs: All spiders have four pairs of legs: two pairs facing front and two pairs facing back. The hairs on a spider's legs pick up vibrations and smells from the air. At the end of each leg are two or more tiny claws.

molt: As a spiderling grows, its exoskeleton becomes tight and eventually cracks open. When the young spider sheds this outer layer, it has molted.

palps: These leglike limbs at the sides of the spider's jaws serve as feelers. Spiders also use them to hold, taste, and crush their prey.

spinnerets: Openings on the underside of a spider's abdomen (at the rear) where silk is released.

Silk Spinners

Do all spiders weave webs? No, only about half of them do. Do all spiders spin silk? Yes! All spiders spin one kind of silk and some spin as many as six different kinds! Share this fascinating information with students; then have them name different ways spiders might use their silk (to build homes, protect eggs, trap prey, escape danger). Next ask students if they've ever seen a spider with a thread of silk behind it. Explain that this silk thread is called a *dragline.* The other end of the silk is attached to a stationary object. As the spider travels, it lets out more silk. If the spider senses danger, it quickly drops or jumps away and hangs on its dragline until the danger disappears. For a fun wrap-up, have each child write and illustrate an adventure story in which a spider's silk saves the day. After each child has shared her story, bind the projects into a class book titled "Saved by the Silk!"

A Close Encounter!

One day Spuds the spider was investigating a new corner in his house. He had hooked his dragline to the light fixture where he often hung out. All of a sudden he heard a shriek and a long yellow monster came at him. He jumped away and hung by his dragline. That was a close call!

Weaving Webs

Put your students' web-weaving skills into practice with this booklet activity. To make his booklet, a student stacks three 4¼" x 11" sheets of manila drawing paper and holds the pages vertically. He slides the top sheet upward approximately one inch and the bottom sheet downward approximately one inch. Next he folds his paper forward to create six graduated layers and then staples the resulting booklet close to the fold. He writes the title "Spiderwebs Woven by [student's name]" on the cover, adds cover art, and then labels the bottoms of the booklet pages as shown.

Each day spotlight one kind of spiderweb. Supplement the provided web information as desired and show students one or more pictures of the web type. (Each web featured in the booklet is pictured in *Spiders* by Gail Gibbons [Holiday House, Inc.; 1994].) Then have each student illustrate a scene that features the web on the corresponding booklet page. As students are working, remind them that no two spiderwebs are exactly the same!

Types of Webs

The sheet web often looks like a hammock with a series of threads above it. A spider hangs upside down beneath the sheet. An insect hits the series of threads and falls onto the sheet. Then the spider quickly pulls it through the silk.

The tangled web is a tangled mass of threads. When an insect is trapped in the web, the spider runs out to get it.

The funnel web looks something like a sheet web, except it is shaped like a funnel. It has a big top and a narrow bottom. The spider sits in the narrow mouth of the funnel and waits for an insect to enter its web.

The triangle web is anchored at three different points, which creates a triangle shape. Inside the web are smaller triangles, each woven with horizontal lines.

The orb web is a pattern of many circles. When an insect lands on the web, the web shakes. Quickly the spider pounces on the insect and wraps it in silk. When an orb weaver wishes to move its web, it rolls the web into a ball and eats it. The spider then recycles the silk and uses it to weave its next web!

What's for Dinner?

What do spiders eat? Spiders are *carnivores,* or meat eaters. However, their eating habits are unique because they do not chew their food—they drink it! For a tasty simulation of this process, give each child an individual pouch of CapriSun® juice drink. After students have finished the drinks, have them examine the collapsed containers. Explain that spiders drink their dinner in much the same way. First they inject a fluid into their prey that liquefies its insides. Then they suck up the juice and leave behind the empty shell of the body. Now that's a spider fact students are sure to remember!

Mingling With Spiders

Spiders help humans by preying on insects and other animals that are harmful to plants and people. They are also interesting to watch! However, there are a few spiders, like the black widow and the brown recluse, that are poisonous to humans. For this reason, enlist your youngsters' help in weaving a web of responsible spider-related behavior like the one shown. Post the web in a classroom corner or another location where a spider might like to hang out.

Do not tear down webs outside.

Leave spiders alone.

To move a spider, capture it in a jar.

SPIDERS

Do not touch.

Do not kill.

Remember that spiders help us.

Never tease a spider.

Motel Spider
Stay a Day With Us!

Reported by: Aaron

Registration

Type of spider Water Spider

Description (please give details) Eight legs, two body parts. Brown all over. About one-half inch long. Not sure how many eyes.

Habitat Underwater. Lives only in Europe and parts of Asia.

Web Weaver? (YES) NO

If yes, type of web woven bell shaped

Please list five interesting facts about this spider.

1. This spider lives, eats, and lays its eggs underwater.
2. It traps bubbles of air and takes them down to its nest so it has air to breathe!
3. It's the only spider that lives most of its life underwater.
4. The only time it leaves its bell-shaped web is to catch prey or go get air bubbles.
5. It holds air bubbles close to its body.

Spider Investigation

With more than 34,000 different species of spiders to choose from, students are sure to find one in the bunch that they'd like to investigate! Or label a class supply of individual cards with the names of spiders that you'd like students to study, and have each youngster select one. Give each child two jar patterns, one titled "Motel Spider: Stay a Day With Us!" and one programmed as a registration form (see illustration). Each child illustrates his spider on the first pattern and then completes the registration form about it. Then he cuts out both patterns and staples the cutouts together so his illustration is on top. Set aside time for each child to share his findings with the class.

For a social studies connection, have each child illustrate and name his spider on a small card. Then help each student tape his card to a world map in an area where the spider lives.

Wait a Minute, Miss Muffet!

For a fun review of spider facts, position a rag doll so that it faces the students and hold a plastic spider attached to a length of monofilament line in your hand. Then use the props as you enact the familiar nursery rhyme, "Little Miss Muffet." Tell students that you think if Miss Muffet had known all that they now know about spiders, she would not have run away! Then invite students to take turns sharing facts about spiders that will convince Miss Muffet to stay put. At the end of this fact-sharing session, enlist your students' help in rewriting and then choral-reading an updated version of "Little Miss Muffet." In conclusion, thank the students for helping to set the record straight about spiders. If desired, serve each child a cup of apple cider and a cupcake decorated with icing to resemble a spiderweb!

Faye Fowler Haney—Gr. 2, Valley View Elementary, Jonesboro, AR

Patterns

Use both patterns with "Eight-Legged Wonders" on page 150.
Use the unprogrammed pattern with "From Egg to Adult" on page 151.

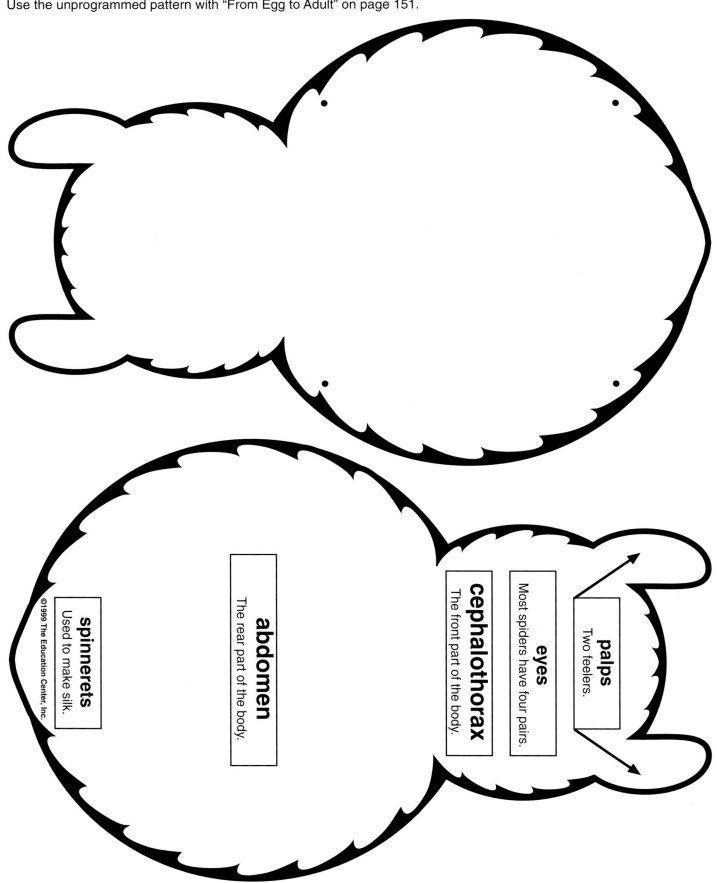

spinnerets
Used to make silk.

abdomen
The rear part of the body.

cephalothorax
The front part of the body.

eyes
Most spiders have four pairs.

palps
Two feelers.

©1999 The Education Center, Inc.

Science With A Song
MAGNETS

Use this collection of activities to explore the fascinating forces of magnetism through music, hands-on experiences, literature, and a whole lot more!

ideas contributed by Michele Converse Baerns and Charles J. Wohl

Sing a Song

Keep students tuned in to major magnet concepts with this little ditty. It's fun to sing and it teaches, too!

What's a Magnet?
(adapt to the tune of "Ten Little Indians")

A magnet is a stone or piece of metal,
North or south pole on each end.
Like poles repel or push apart.
Opposites attract like friends.

Magnets attract things made of iron,
Also cobalt, steel, and nickel;
But not aluminum, brass, or copper,
Paper, glass, or a pickle!

by Faye Fowler Haney—Gr. 2, Valley View Elementary, Jonesboro, AR

Sort the Soup

What does a bowl of soup have to do with a study of magnets? Plenty, when the soup recipe calls for marbles, screws, buttons, scrap paper, rubber bands, washers, coins, toothpicks, paper clips, cotton balls, and craft bells! For this science experience, give each pair of students a nonbreakable bowl of magnetic and nonmagnetic soup items, a sorting sheet like the one shown, and a pencil. Ask each twosome to sort the items in its bowl onto the sorting sheet, placing the items that it predicts will be attracted by a magnet under "Yes" and all others under "No." Then give each pair a magnet and have the partners take turns testing their predictions.

To extend the activity, ask each pair to write a recipe for either Magnetic Soup or Nonmagnetic Soup. Encourage students to move around the classroom using their magnets to test and verify possible soup ingredients. Be sure to set aside time for students to read aloud their one-of-a-kind recipes!

Magnets Everywhere!

Realizing how often magnets impact day-to-day activities is an important discovery for students to make and remember. Title a paper-covered bulletin board "Magnets Are Everywhere!" Near the display, place a supply of discarded magazines and a receptacle for collecting cutouts. As students discover items that utilize magnets, invite them to cut out the corresponding pictures and place them in the container. Later, staple the cutouts to the board, overlapping them slightly to create a colorful and informative collage. (Items include electrical appliances, video games, televisions, telephones, radios, vacuum cleaners, computer monitors, floppy disks, audio and video equipment, and airplanes!)

155

A Field of Force

Every magnet has a field of force called a *magnetic field*. Here's a quick and easy way for students to investigate and feel the force of a magnetic field. As an introduction, hold a magnet high above a collection of paper clips. Ask students why the paper clips are not pulled to the magnet. Then gradually lower the magnet until it pulls the clips to it. Explain that around every magnet there is a field (or area) of magnetic force. When the paper clips are within the magnet's magnetic field, they are pulled to the magnet. Then give each pair of students a magnet to share and a handful of paper clips or other magnetic objects. Allow plenty of time for the partners to investigate the magnetic field of their magnet and feel its force. If the twosomes are using magnets of different shapes and sizes, encourage the pairs to trade magnets for additional investigation.

Seeing the Invisible

This hands-on activity gives students a detailed look at magnetic fields.

In advance:
For every three students, place one teaspoon of iron filings and one-half cup of mineral or baby oil inside a resealable plastic bag. Carefully release any air captured in the bag; then secure the bag's seal with clear packaging tape to prevent all possible spills.

What each trio needs:
1 prepared bag of iron filings   1 lab sheet (page 158)
a variety of magnets   3 pencils
8 1/2" x 11" sheet of white paper

What to do:
Have each child write her name and the question "What does a magnetic field look like?" on her lab sheet. Then have her draw or list the materials that have been provided for this science experience. Next instruct each trio to place one magnet under its white paper, gently tip and tilt its bag to evenly disperse the iron filings inside, lay the bag on the paper directly on top of the magnet, and observe what happens. Have the trios repeat this activity for each of their magnets. Also provide plenty of time for open investigation. Finally, have each student complete numbers 3 and 4 on her lab sheet and then invite students to talk about what they saw and learned.

This is why:
The iron filings are attracted to each magnet along invisible lines of force. Because the filings are so small, the lines of force are clearly illustrated. These lines of force make up the magnetic field. A magnet has a field of force all around it; however, it is always strongest near the ends of the magnet.

Tiny Bits of Matter

While an investigation of iron atoms is most likely beyond the grasp of your youngsters, they will surely be fascinated by how these tiny bits of matter line up in magnetic items. Give each trio of students a sheet of white paper, a strip of magnetic tape (or something similar) and a prepared bag of iron filings from "Seeing the Invisible" on this page. Ask each trio to slide its magnetic tape under the paper so the magnetized side is up and then lay its bag of evenly dispersed iron filings on the paper directly on top of the magnetic tape. Students will see how the bits of iron in their magnetic objects line up. Explain that the atoms in nonmagnetic items do not line up. Allow time for students to repeat the activity using a variety of objects and, if desired, complete individual copies of the lab sheet on page 158.

Making Magnets

Can magnets be made? Believe it or not, yes! To demonstrate *induced magnetism* (a temporary form of magnetism), give each student pair a magnet, a handful of paper clips, and two copies of the lab sheet on page 158. Have each student write his name and the question "Can a magnet be made?" on his paper. Then have him draw or list the provided materials. Next instruct each pair to experiment with its magnet and paper clips before completing the written portion of the activity. Students will discover that when a paper clip is attached to the magnet (or another magnetized paper clip), the magnetic force of the magnet is transferred to it. However, each paper clip immediately loses its magnetism when it is isolated.

Pam
Crane

A Delicious Discovery

These cookies are not magnets, but they will—without a doubt—attract plenty of student interest!

North-South Bars
(makes approximately 28 cookies)

Ingredients:
tube of prepared sugar cookie dough
red-tinted icing
blue-tinted icing

Directions:
1. Remove the packaging and then cut the tube of dough in half.
2. Slice the dough lengthwise into 1/4-inch thick slices. Slice each resulting rectangle in half to create two bars.
3. Bake the bar-shaped cookies according to the package directions.
4. When the cookies are cool, have each child decorate a cookie by applying red and blue icing to indicate its north and south poles.

Books About Magnets

Further investigate the force of magnetism with the information and hands-on experiences in these books.

What Makes a Magnet?
Written by Franklyn M. Branley
Illustrated by True Kelley
HarperTrophy®, 1996

Janice VanCleave's Magnets:
Mind-Boggling Experiments You Can Turn Into
Science Fair Projects
By Janice Pratt VanCleave
John Wiley & Sons, Inc.; 1993

Science With Magnets
Written by Helen Edom
Illustrated by Simone Abel
EDC Publishing, 1992

The Science Book of Magnets
Written by Neil Ardley
Photographs by Dave King
Harcourt Brace Jovanovich, Publishers; 1991

Order books online. www.themailbox.com

Name_____

  # Investigating Magnets

1. Write the question you are trying to answer. _____

_____

_____

2. Draw or list the materials you will use during your investigation.

3. Draw what happened and then write about it.

_____

_____

_____

_____

_____

_____

_____

_____

4. Explain what you learned. _____

_____

_____

_____

Note to teacher: Use this lab sheet with activities suggested on pages 156 and 157. To use the lab sheet with another science topic, make a copy of the page. Mask out the title and magnet art and then add a desired title and corresponding clip art.

Science With A Song
MATTER

Help students make sense of matter with these easy-to-implement ideas.

ideas contributed by Valerie Wood Smith

Sing a Song
Use this catchy tune to reinforce basic matter concepts.

What Is Matter?
(adapt to the tune of "Three Blind Mice")
What is matter?
What is matter?
A solid, liquid, or gas.
A solid, liquid, or gas.
It takes up space and it weighs something, too.
It's everywhere—that includes me and you.
Did you ever think such a thing could be true?
That is matter.
That is matter.

inspired by Pam Dillie—Gr. 2
Baker Elementary
Pittsburgh, PA

Bag It!
Investigate the three states of matter with a large-group demonstration. On bulletin board paper draw a chart like the one shown. List the questions, but do not list the three states of matter. Also gather three resealable quart-size plastic bags. Blow air into the first bag and quickly seal it. Seal a colorful block in the second bag and seal tinted water in the third bag. Show students the three bags and ask them to identify the type of matter represented in each one. Write each answer in a different column of the chart. Next use the bags to help students discover the answer to each question on the chart. When all the answers are recorded, lead your budding scientists to the following conclusions: All matter takes up space and has weight. Solids and (most) liquids are visible, but most gases are not. Liquids and gases change shapes easily, but solids do not. Then display the chart for future reference.

Matter	Solid	Liquid	Gas
Does it take up space?	Yes	Yes	Yes
Does it have weight?	Yes	Yes	Yes
Is it visible?	Yes	Yes	No
Can it change shape easily?	No	Yes	Yes

Showcasing Matter

These eye-catching collages keep students on the lookout for matter! Mount three sheets of poster board on a bulletin board and title each one for a different state of matter. Throughout your study, invite students to cut out samples of matter from discarded magazines and glue the cutouts on the appropriate posters. When your investigation of matter is complete, laminate each poster, cut it into large puzzle pieces, and store the pieces of all three puzzles at a science center. Invite students to sort the puzzle pieces by state of matter and then assemble each puzzle.

Denise Tinucci Farrell
Sharon Hill, PA

Physical Properties

Keep students guessing with an investigation of physical properties! Inform youngsters that scientists use physical properties to describe matter. Explain that the most common properties are weight, color, hardness, shape, and size, but that taste and smell are also used when they apply. List all seven properties on the chalkboard and hand out index cards. Each child looks around the classroom and secretly selects an example of matter. He writes the name of the item and his name near the bottom of his card. Then he lists four or more physical properties of the item. Collect the cards. Each day read aloud several sets of clues. If an object is not identified after three or four guesses, ask the child who programmed the card to identify it. Challenge the class to brainstorm additional properties for each identified item.

More Property Practice

This partner activity provides more practice with physical properties. Give every two students a paper lunch sack. Ask each pair to collect four or more classroom items that collectively fit inside the sack and share a common physical property. Next have each pair team with another pair and trade sacks. Each twosome removes its new collection and looks for the items' common property. When both pairs have made correct identifications, the collections are returned to the sacks. Then each pair trades sacks with a different duo. Continue in this manner until time runs out or each pair has investigated every sack.

Molecules and Matter

All matter contains tiny particles called *molecules*. So why isn't all matter the same? Entertain your youngsters' answers to this question. Then lay two student jump ropes on the floor so that a circle is formed. Choose three students to quickly move around inside the circle. Invite the class to speculate which state of matter the student molecules are demonstrating and accept all answers. Next instruct half of the student audience to join these molecules. Ask this group of molecules to move slowly and cautiously within the circle. Again ask the class to speculate which state of matter is being simulated. Finally have the remainder of the audience step inside the circle and ask all molecules to march in place. After students return to their seats, reveal that a gas was simulated first, then a liquid, and then a solid. Use the information from "Molecules in Motion" for further explanation and page 162 as an assessment tool.

Molecules in Motion

In a gas, molecules are very far apart and they move about quickly in all directions.

In a liquid, the molecules are closer together. They move about in all directions, but they do not move very far because they keep colliding.

In a solid, the molecules fit together very tightly. Because of this, the molecules move together as one unit like a marching band.

Paper

Tear it.
Cut it.
Fold it.
Wad it up.
Color it one color.
Draw on it with a pencil.
Change its shape.
Make it very hard.
Make it all wrinkly.
Color it many colors.

Changes in Matter

Matter can change in two ways. A *chemical change* occurs when the composition of matter changes, such as when a piece of paper burns to ashes. A *physical change* alters physical properties (see page 160), but there is no change in the matter's composition.

Explore physical change with this small-group activity. Divide students into five groups. Give each group five half sheets of blank paper, a pencil, and a different sample of solid matter, such as a sheet of drawing paper, a crayon, an apple, a ball of clay, and a piece of chalk. Provide two minutes for each group to brainstorm possible physical changes for its matter sample. Have one child in each group write the name of the matter on a half sheet of blank paper and then list the ideas generated by the group. Repeat the activity four more times, each time rotating the matter samples and, if possible, selecting a different student recorder in each group. Then, for each type of matter explored, compile the groups' suggestions into one list of possible physical changes. The final result is a much clearer understanding of physical change for all!

Books About Matter

Further investigate matter with the information and hands-on experiences in these books.

What Is the World Made Of?
All About Solids, Liquids, and Gases
Written by Kathleen Weidner Zoehfeld
Illustrated by Paul Meisel
HarperCollins Publishers, Inc.; 1998

Solids, Liquids, and Gases
Written by The Ontario Science Centre
Photographs by Ray Boudreau
Kids Can Press Ltd., 1998

Solid, Liquid, or Gas?
Written by Fay Robinson
Includes photographs
Children's Press, 1995

Name _____

Molecules in Matter

Label the pictures.
Write **solid**, **liquid**, or **gas** on each line.
Show the molecules in each state of matter.

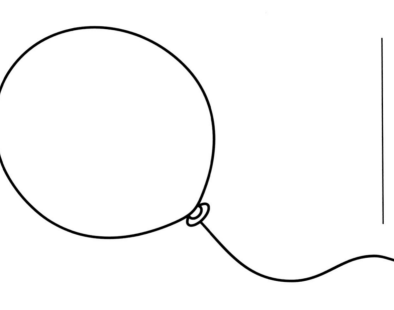

_____

_____

162

©The Education Center, Inc. • *THE MAILBOX*® *Primary* • Dec/Jan 1999–2000

Note to teacher: Use this activity with "Molecules and Matter" on page 161. Have students use pencils or crayons to draw molecules on each object. Or have each child hole-punch a scrap of dark-colored construction paper and glue the resulting molecules in place.

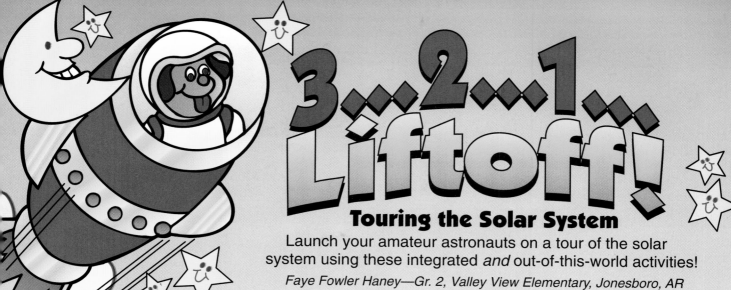

3...2...1... Liftoff!

Touring the Solar System

Launch your amateur astronauts on a tour of the solar system using these integrated *and* out-of-this-world activities!

Faye Fowler Haney—Gr. 2, Valley View Elementary, Jonesboro, AR

Shuttle Preparations

Making mini space shuttles is sure to spark enthusiasm for a class tour of the solar system! Before you begin the project, explain that the names of NASA's four space shuttles (*Columbia, Discovery, Atlantis, Endeavour*) were also names of famous ships. Invite students to find similarities between a large ship and a space shuttle *(big, powerful, explore unknown territory, etc.)*. Then have them contemplate animals that share similarities with a space shuttle. Next give each child a white construction paper copy of the space shuttle pattern on page 169, a white 4½" x 6" rectangle, and an empty toilet tissue tube. A student chooses an animal for which to name his shuttle, and illustrates it in the center of his pattern. Then he writes why he chose this animal on his paper rectangle. He glues the paper rectangle around the cardboard tube, keeping the writing to the outside. Next he cuts out the pattern and glues it to the tube along the paper seam. Invite students to share their projects with their classmates. Keep the space shuttles on display throughout your solar system tour.

My space shuttle is called Polar Bear because a polar bear is big and white like a space shuttle. It also likes cold places and it gets really cold in space!

Astronaut Assessment

Track your youngsters' understanding of solar system concepts with these adorable astronaut look-alikes! To make an astronaut likeness, a child cuts out the spacesuit and glove patterns from a white construction paper copy of page 168. She glues each glove to the space suit where indicated. Then she cuts her face from a school photo (or another snapshot) and glues it to the pattern. Collect the projects and staple an opened snack-size resealable plastic bag near the waist of each astronaut, keeping the gloves free to overlap the bag. Then staple the projects along the bottom of a solar system display. Set aside a few minutes at the end of each solar system lesson for every student to summarize what she learned that day on a 3" x 5" index card. Then have her slip the card into her astronaut's bag. A quick read by you reveals how well the students understood the day's lesson. A quick read by students provides an instant review of the concept(s) covered!

Pam Crane   February 15, 2000

Today I learned that the Sun is at the center of the solar system.

163

Alien Alert!

Could there be aliens in the solar system? Before blastoff, find out how your amateur astronauts feel about life beyond Earth. Ask volunteers to define alien, extraterrestrial, and U.F.O. Or read aloud *Arthur's First Sleepover* by Marc Brown (Little, Brown and Company; 1996), which describes Arthur's uncertainty about his sister's claim that there are space aliens in the neighborhood. After plenty of discussion, post a bar graph like the one shown. Have each child personalize a small sticky note and attach it to the graph to show his feelings. Then pose several graph-related questions for students to answer. Plan to repeat the graphing activity after students have studied the solar system. Who knows? The knowledge they gain may make them change their minds about aliens!

Do You Believe?

Yes | No

3...2...1...Liftoff!

Signal the start of your students' space tour with an uplifting demonstration that won't soon be forgotten!

Materials needed:
copy of space shuttle pattern from page 169, reduced to 60%
1 empty Fuji® film canister (must have inner seal)
1 Alka-Seltzer® tablet (known only as "magic fuel")
length of double-sided tape   1 long jump rope
sandwich bag   water
large plastic trash bag   scissors
empty trash can

In advance:
Remove the canister top and invert the canister. Cut out the space shuttle pattern and tape it to the inverted canister. Store the canister top, the decorated canister, and the magic fuel in the sandwich bag. Choose an outdoor location for the launch and set up the launch pad. To do this, invert the trash can and cover it with the plastic bag. About 10 to 15 feet away from the launch pad, extend the rope.

Procedure:
Lead students outside to the launch pad (take the sandwich bag and some water with you). Ask students to stand behind the rope in the spectator viewing area. (Remind students that during an actual space shuttle launch, observers are always a safe distance from the launch site.) At the launch pad, pour water into the canister until it is about one-third full. Drop the magic fuel inside the canister. *Very quickly* snap the canister lid in place, shake the canister once, and place it on the launch pad so the shuttle is sitting upright. Quickly step away from the launch pad as you begin counting down from 10 with your students. The shuttle will launch when gas pressure inside the canister (from the magic fuel) causes the canister lid to pop off. Blast off!

USA

First Stop, the Moon!

After a successful launch (see "3…2…1…Liftoff!" on page 164), the class will be eager to begin touring space! Make your first stop the Moon. Ask students what they know about the Moon's surface. Then confirm that it is dry and dusty and covered with craters that were formed long ago when meteoroids crashed into the Moon. To show students how this happened, prepare a Moon surface by placing a two-inch layer of flour in the bottom of a large baking dish; then use a flour sifter to cover the flour with a dusting of gray powdered tempera paint. Place the dish on the floor atop newspaper and assemble students around it. Distribute several different-sized spheres like marbles, plastic beads, and dried peas. One at a time, ask each child holding a sphere to drop it into the prepared surface. Then, using tweezers, remove the sphere so students can examine the resulting crater. Ask questions that lead students to discover that the size and weight of a sphere, and the distance from which it is dropped, directly affects the size and depth of the crater it forms. Imagine your students' surprise when you tell them that one known Moon crater measures 180 miles across!

More Than Craters

In addition to craters, the Moon's surface is covered with ridges, mountains, and valleys. Because of this, when the moon is full, its color is uneven. Some people think the dark spots on the Moon look like a face or an animal. Whatever a person sees, it never changes because the same side of the Moon always faces Earth! Wrap up your stop at the Moon by serving each child a banana-flavored Moon Pie® marshmallow sandwich. For added fun, provide chocolate icing and plastic knives and invite each child to decorate the top of his pie to show a face, an animal, or whatever *he* sees when he views a full moon!

Solar System Snapshots

During your tour of the solar system, have students keep snapshot journals. Prepare a 6" x 9" booklet of blank pages for each child. Then have her cut out a construction paper copy of the camera pattern on page 25, glue it to the front cover of her booklet, and write "Snapshots of the Solar System by [student's name]" in the lens area. Encourage each student to add snapshots (illustrations) and descriptive captions to her journal as she learns new and exciting things about the solar system. Why not make the first journal entry a snapshot of the Moon?

Snapshots of the Solar System by Astro Pup

Solar System Sing-Along

Students will have a blast singing their way through the solar system, and they'll learn plenty, too! Plan to sing this little ditty each time you transition into your study of space and youngsters will have the solar system sized up in no time at all!

Sing a Song of Solar System

(sung to the tune of "Sing a Song of Sixpence")

Sing a song of solar system,
Nine planets in all,
Orbiting around the Sun,
Each shaped like a ball.

The Sun is in the middle.
It's a hot, burning star.
Next come the inner planets,
Mercury, Venus, Earth, and Mars.

Sing a song of solar system.
Be sure to avoid
All those rocks in the belt
Known as asteroids.

Next Jupiter and Saturn,
They're gassy as you know;
Then Uranus and Neptune,
And don't forget Pluto!

Pam Crane

The Solar System

The solar system is the Sun and everything in space that travels around it.

The Sun is the only star in the solar system. It is also the biggest and hottest object.

The Sun controls all of the bodies around it. This includes nine known planets.

Planetary Fact Cards

Present a wealth of planetary knowledge using the solar system fact cards from pages 169 and 170. Have each child cut out a set of cards (ten in all) and glue each fact card onto a small index card for durability. Next have him hole-punch the top of each index card and then thread his card collection onto a two-inch loose-leaf ring, in order, beginning with the solar system card and ending with the Pluto card. During your tour of the solar system, have students refer to the cards to discover facts about each planet visited. Encourage them to list additional facts about the planets on the backs of the corresponding cards. Also keep a stack of blank cards and a hole puncher handy so interested explorers can program additional cards and add them to their collections. With these planetary fact cards on hand, students will never be lost in space!

Fact Card Challenges

Each day send students into orbit by posting a fact card challenge for them to solve using their planetary fact cards. Add to the fun by uniquely rewarding students who find the answers. For example, have each student who finds the answer write it in the top left-hand corner of her math assignment for that day. Reward each correct answer with an extra-credit point, a smelly sticker, or five minutes of free time! The possibilities are endless!

Fact card challenges to consider:
What are the two smallest planets?
Which two planets do not have moons?
Which two planets have one moon?
Which planet has the most moons?
Which planet will orbit the Sun twice in 168 years?

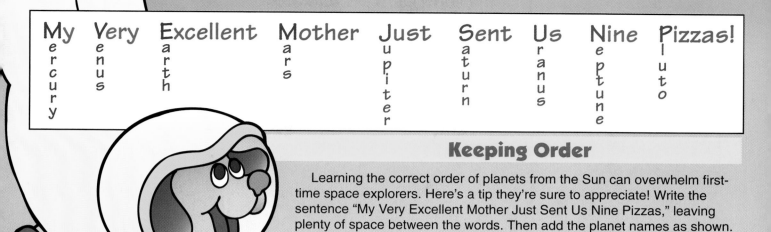

My	Very	Excellent	Mother	Just	Sent	Us	Nine	Pizzas!
Mercury	Venus	Earth	Mars	Jupiter	Saturn	Uranus	Neptune	Pluto

Keeping Order

Learning the correct order of planets from the Sun can overwhelm first-time space explorers. Here's a tip they're sure to appreciate! Write the sentence "My Very Excellent Mother Just Sent Us Nine Pizzas," leaving plenty of space between the words. Then add the planet names as shown. Encourage students to use this sentence to help them remember planet order. When a student can recite the planet names in correct order, give him a large foil star to attach to the spacesuit of his astronaut look-alike (see "Astronaut Assessment" on page 163).

Beyond the Solar System

With the exception of the Sun, all stars are far beyond Pluto. Remind students that stars are huge hot balls of gas, and even though many are much larger than the Sun, they look smaller because they are so far away. Review important solar system concepts with this stellar display. Laminate seven large star cutouts and display them in the shape of the Big Dipper. Then use a wipe-off pen to program each star with a different review question. Gather students around the display and engage them in orally answering the questions. Encourage plenty of discussion among the students. If the class answers a question correctly, award one class point and wipe away the question. If an incorrect answer is given, leave the question on display. At a later time, reprogram each blank star with a new question and repeat the activity. When the class earns a predetermined number of points, reward them with a special privilege or tasty snack.

Which planet is almost the same size as Earth?

Cool Comets

When it's time to conclude your class tour of the solar system, have students chase a comet during their return trip to Earth! Explain that a comet is a ball of cosmic snow, ice, and dust that comes from the icy cold edges of the solar system and orbits the Sun. As a comet's orbit brings it closer to the Sun, the Sun's heat turns some of its snow into gas, which forms the comet's tail. As the comet moves away from the Sun, its tail gradually disappears.

Students are sure to enjoy making and showing off these flashy comets! Have each child cut out a white construction paper copy of the pattern on page 207 and tape several lengths of iridescent curling ribbon at the pointed end of the pattern. Then, keeping the taped ribbon ends to the inside, the student overlaps the straight edges of the pattern to form a cone and pokes a two-inch Styrofoam® ball into the open end. Next she adjusts the size of the cone until it fits snugly around the ball. Then she tapes the overlapped edges of the pattern. Last she glues the ball inside the cone. Very cool!

Patterns

Use with "Astronaut Assessment" on page 163.

Glove A

Glove B

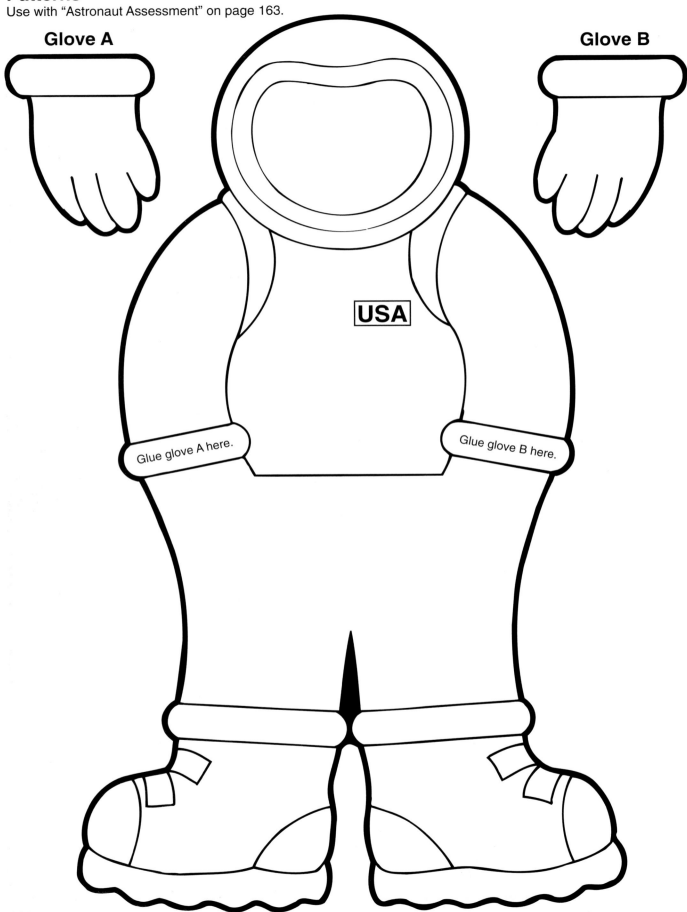

USA

Glue glove A here.

Glue glove B here.

Use space shuttle pattern with "Shuttle Preparations" on page 163 and "3…2…1… Liftoff!" on page 164.

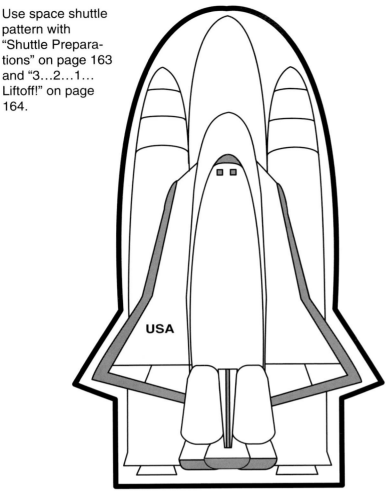

USA

Use cards with "Planetary Fact Cards" on page 166.

Pattern and Fact Cards

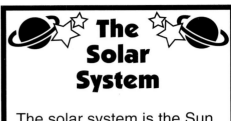

The Solar System

The solar system is the Sun and everything in space that travels around it.

The Sun is the only star in the solar system. It is also the biggest and hottest object.

The Sun controls all of the bodies around it. This includes nine known planets.

Mercury

First planet from the Sun

Surface: craters, smooth plains, no water

Orbit Time: 88 days

Diameter: 3,030 miles

Planet Power Points: Of the planets, it has the greatest range of temperatures. The days are very hot and the nights are very cold. It has no moon.

Venus

Second planet from the Sun

Surface: rocky plains of lava, clouds

Orbit Time: 225 days

Diameter: 7,520 miles

Planet Power Points: It rotates in the opposite direction of the earth. It has no moon. Except for the earth's moon, it is the brightest object in the night sky!

Earth

Third planet from the Sun

Surface: about 70% water and 30% land

Orbit Time: 1 year or approximately 365 days

Diameter: 7,930 miles

Planet Power Points: It is the only planet known to have life. Its surface is always changing. It has one moon.

Fact Cards

Use cards with "Planetary Fact Cards" on page 166.

Mars

Fourth planet from the Sun

Surface: dusty and rocky, looks reddish

Orbit Time: 687 days

Diameter: 4,220 miles

Planet Power Points: It has two moons. It also has polar ice caps. It has a canyon ten times longer than the Grand Canyon!

Jupiter

Fifth planet from the Sun

Surface: mainly gas and liquid, thick clouds

Orbit Time: 11.9 years

Diameter: 89,000 miles

Planet Power Points: It has 16 moons. It is the largest planet. The Great Red Spot is a huge storm in its clouds.

Saturn

Sixth planet from the Sun

Surface: mostly gas and liquid, thick clouds

Orbit Time: 29.5 years

Diameter: 75,000 miles

Planet Power Points: It weighs the least of any planet. More than 20 moons have been counted! It has spectacular rings made of icy rock.

Uranus

Seventh planet from the Sun

Surface: mostly gas and liquid, blue-green clouds

Orbit Time: 84 years

Diameter: 32,000 miles

Planet Power Points: It rolls around its orbit instead of spinning like a top. It has 17 moons and narrow dark rings.

Neptune

Eighth planet from the Sun

Surface: gas, blue and white clouds

Orbit Time: 164 years

Diameter: 30,800 miles

Planet Power Points: It has the strongest winds of any planet. It has eight moons and thin rings. It has a large storm spot like Jupiter.

Pluto

Ninth planet from the Sun

Surface: types of ice

Orbit Time: 248 years

Diameter: 1,430 miles

Planet Power Points: It is the smallest planet. It has one moon. At times its orbit and Neptune's cross, and it is the eighth planet from the Sun!

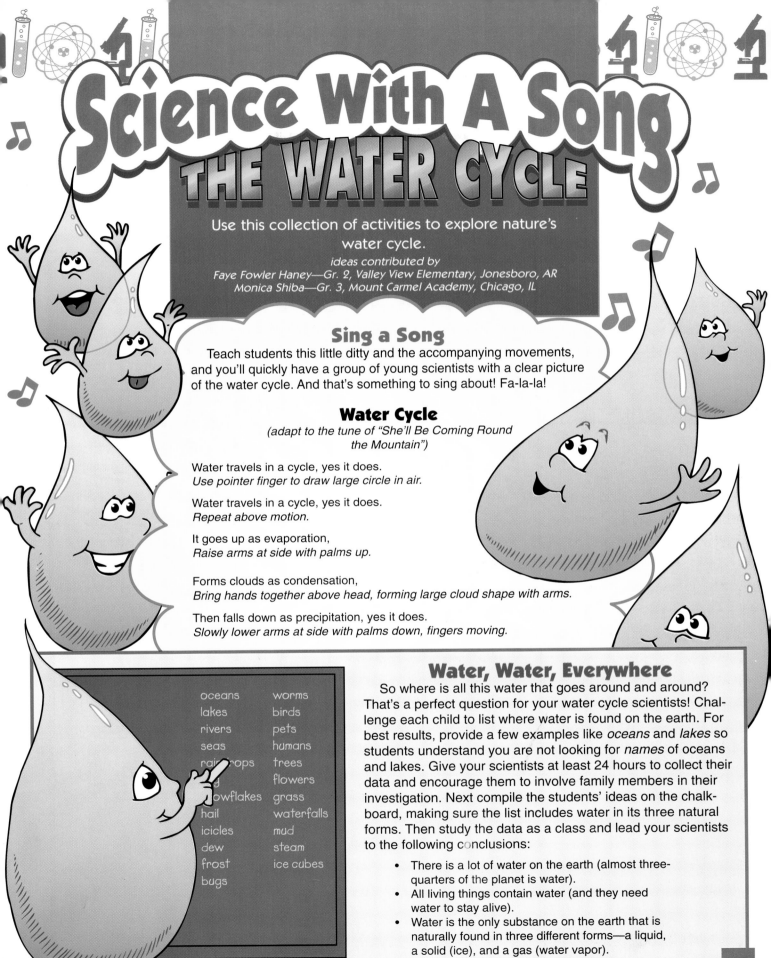

Science With A Song
THE WATER CYCLE

Use this collection of activities to explore nature's water cycle.

ideas contributed by
Faye Fowler Haney—Gr. 2, Valley View Elementary, Jonesboro, AR
Monica Shiba—Gr. 3, Mount Carmel Academy, Chicago, IL

Sing a Song

Teach students this little ditty and the accompanying movements, and you'll quickly have a group of young scientists with a clear picture of the water cycle. And that's something to sing about! Fa-la-la!

Water Cycle
(adapt to the tune of "She'll Be Coming Round the Mountain")

Water travels in a cycle, yes it does.
Use pointer finger to draw large circle in air.

Water travels in a cycle, yes it does.
Repeat above motion.

It goes up as evaporation,
Raise arms at side with palms up.

Forms clouds as condensation,
Bring hands together above head, forming large cloud shape with arms.

Then falls down as precipitation, yes it does.
Slowly lower arms at side with palms down, fingers moving.

Water, Water, Everywhere

So where is all this water that goes around and around? That's a perfect question for your water cycle scientists! Challenge each child to list where water is found on the earth. For best results, provide a few examples like *oceans* and *lakes* so students understand you are not looking for *names* of oceans and lakes. Give your scientists at least 24 hours to collect their data and encourage them to involve family members in their investigation. Next compile the students' ideas on the chalkboard, making sure the list includes water in its three natural forms. Then study the data as a class and lead your scientists to the following conclusions:

oceans	worms
lakes	birds
rivers	pets
seas	humans
raindrops	trees
	flowers
snowflakes	grass
hail	waterfalls
icicles	mud
dew	steam
frost	ice cubes
bugs	

- There is a lot of water on the earth (almost three-quarters of the planet is water).
- All living things contain water (and they need water to stay alive).
- Water is the only substance on the earth that is naturally found in three different forms—a liquid, a solid (ice), and a gas (water vapor).

Observing the Cycle

What's the sum of *evaporation, condensation,* and *precipitation?* The water cycle! Use this large-group demonstration to show students the ins and outs of this fascinating natural phenomenon.

Materials needed:
electric skillet
water
oven mitts
pie pan filled with ice cubes

What to do:
Pour water into the skillet and heat it. From a safe distance, have students watch as the heated water turns into steam and disappears.

Question to ask:
1. Why is the water heated?
2. What happens to the steam?

Next:
Wearing the oven mitts, hold the pan of ice cubes about six inches above the steaming water and direct students to watch the bottom of the pie pan.

Questions to ask:
1. What part of the water cycle do the ice cubes represent?
2. Why do drops of water fall back into the skillet?

This is why:
The water in the skillet is heated because it is heat from the sun that causes water to evaporate. Water evaporates in the form of water vapor. As the vapor rises, it cools along with the air around it. Eventually the air cools off so much that it can no longer hold the water vapor. At this point the water vapor changes or condenses into water droplets. In this demonstration the pan of ice cubes is used to quickly cool the water vapor and the air. In nature, the water droplets that form on the bottom of the pan would be seen as clouds. As the droplets continue to gather moisture, they increase in weight. Eventually they become so heavy that they fall back to the skillet (earth) as precipitation. Then the cycle begins again.

Step-by-Step Bracelets

Not only are these beaded bracelets fashionable, they make remembering the steps of the water cycle a cinch! Give each child an eight-inch length of beading cord elastic and four plastic beads—one yellow, one clear, one white, and one blue. To make his bracelet, a student threads his beads onto his elastic in the following order, working from right to left: yellow for the sun, because it is heat from the sun that begins the cycle; clear for evaporation, because water vapor is an invisible gas; white for condensation, because condensed water vapor forms clouds; and blue for precipitation, because blue represents water. Once the beads are in place, help each child securely tie the ends of his elastic cord and snip off any excess. The bracelets are ready to wear!

Recycling at Its Best

Revealing that the water cycle is a natural recycling process will lead students to make a startling discovery—the water on the earth today is the same water that was on the earth billions of years ago! This means that the water students are drinking may have been drunk by a *Tyrannosaurus rex!* For a fun writing follow-up, serve each child a paper cup of water and invite him to drink the water as he writes and illustrates a story about all the different places the water could have been. Bind the tales into a class book titled "The Water in My Cup."

If desired, read aloud *The Drop in My Drink: The Story of Water on Our Planet* written by Meredith Hooper and illustrated by Chris Coady (Viking Children's Books, 1998) for writing inspiration. This beautifully illustrated book provides an intriguing look at water and its role throughout life on the earth.

The Water in My Cup
The water in my cup has been in some really cool places. It has been inside the belly of a dinosaur. It was part of the iceberg that sank the Titanic. It even went to the moon with Neil Armstrong! Then it rained on Michael Jordan! Now it is in my cup.
by Clevell

A Watery Wheel

The conclusion is clear—the earth's water is constantly moving and changing! Use this nifty project to review water's never-ending journey. Give each child a copy of page 174, a 9" x 12" sheet of colorful construction paper, and a brad. A student colors the artwork on his paper and cuts along the bold lines. He mounts the wheel and spinner patterns on the construction paper and then he cuts out the patterns again, leaving an eye-catching border around the wheel. To assemble his project, he uses his brad to connect the spinner to the wheel as shown. Last he glues the vocabulary words to the back of his project, positioning each one directly behind the process it represents. Encourage students to use these handheld props to explain the water cycle to friends and family members.

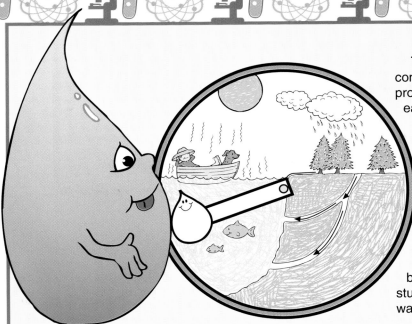

Caring for Water

Wrap up your study of the water cycle by reminding students of the preciousness of water. Ask youngsters to describe how water affects their daily lives. Remind them that all life on the earth depends on water. Then ask students to ponder the effect that pollution has on the earth's water. If possible, read aloud the picture book *A River Ran Wild* by Lynne Cherry, a true story that conveys a powerful message about water pollution. Then have each child trim a sheet of light blue construction paper into a raindrop shape, and write and illustrate a message on the cutout that encourages others to look after the earth's water. Display the resulting posters around the school.

No water=No life

Please Protect Earth's Water

Do not waste water!

Do not pollute water!

Thank you!

Water Cycle Reading

Make a splash with these informative and engaging books about the water cycle.

Water Dance
Written & Illustrated by Thomas Locker
Harcourt Brace & Company, 1997

A Drop Around the World
Written by Barbara Shaw McKinney
Illustrated by Michael S. Maydak
Dawn Publications, 1998

Down Comes the Rain
Written by Franklyn M. Branley
Illustrated by James Graham Hale
HarperTrophy, 1997

The Magic School Bus®: Wet All Over
A Book About the Water Cycle
TV script adaptation by Pat Relf
Illustrated by Carolyn Bracken
Scholastic Inc., 1996

The Magic School Bus® : At the Waterworks
Written by Joanna Cole
Illustrated by Bruce Degen
Scholastic Inc., 1988

Order books online. www.themailbox.com

173

Water Cycle Project

Use with "A Watery Wheel" on page 173.

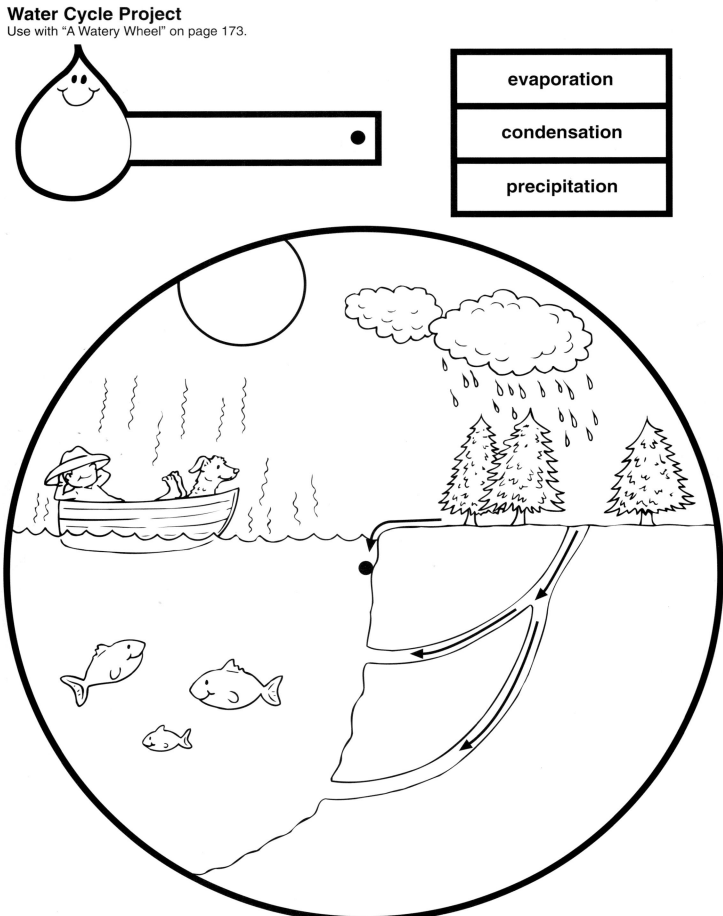

evaporation

condensation

precipitation

Science With A Song
ROCKS

Unearth an avalanche of rock-related learning by incorporating these educational experiences into your rock study!

ideas by Monica Shiba—Gr. 3, Mount Carmel Academy, Chicago, IL

Sing a Song

What's the best way to dig into your rock studies? With some *rock* music, of course! In addition to introducing the three main rock groups, this song teaches rookie rock hounds that rocks change.

Changing Rocks
(adapt to the tune of "Are You Sleeping?")

Igneous rocks, igneous rocks
Form when magma
Cools and hardens.
When magma cools quickly
Basalt and pumice are made.
Changing rocks, changing rocks.

Sedimentary, sedimentary
Rocks formed in layers,
Limestone and shale.
Broken pieces of matter
Are squeezed and pressed together.
Changing rocks, changing rocks.

Metamorphic, metamorphic
Rocks that were
Another kind before.
Changed by heat or pressure
Limestone becomes marble.
Changing rocks, changing rocks.

Digging Into Properties

For a hands-on investigation of rock properties, ask each child to bring five to ten small rocks to school. Display the rocks in the center of a large paper-covered table. Program individual cards with rock properties such as rough and smooth, dull and shiny, large and small, colorful and not colorful, and speckled and not speckled.

Tell students that, like geologists, they can learn a lot about rocks by studying their *properties,* or characteristics. At each end of the rock table, tape one card from a pair of opposite properties, such as dull and shiny. Then have each child sort a designated number of rocks. When every child has taken at least one turn and all the rocks are sorted, ask students what they learned. Then return the rocks to the middle of the table, replace the cards with another pair of opposing properties, and repeat the activity. Continue in the manner described until the rocks have been sorted by desired properties. Students will never again look at rocks in quite the same way!

A Trio of Types

All rocks belong to one of three main rock groups: *igneous, sedimentary,* and *metamorphic.* Use the following information and activities to introduce your rookie rock hounds to these three groups.

Meltdown

Igneous rock forms when hot, liquid rock cools and hardens. Volcanoes spew liquid rock onto the earth's surface where it cools and hardens. Other liquid rock remains underground where it slowly cools and hardens into igneous rock.

To demonstrate how igneous rock forms above the earth's surface, melt approximately 12 ounces of peanut butter or milk chocolate chips. For each child, spoon a dollop of the resulting liquid rock onto a small square of waxed paper. Have students observe the liquid rock as it cools and hardens. When the candy solidifies, invite each child to eat his igneous treat!

Layer It On

Sedimentary rock forms when small particles of shell, rock, sand, and other like matter are carried by wind, water, or ice to different locations. In time layers of particles (or *sediment*) result. Over time the layers compress and join together, forming a new type of rock.

To demonstrate this process, press a tube of prepared sugar cookie dough into the bottom of a greased nine-inch-square pan. Explain to students that this layer represents the earth. Then enlist your youngsters' help in sprinkling several layers of sediment (mini baking chips, shredded coconut, raisins, chopped nuts, etc.) atop the dough. Next, lay a length of waxed paper atop the layers and select volunteers to press the layers of sediment together. Explain that even though it takes layers of sedimentary rock thousands of years to bond, this experiment will be ready the following day. Later in the day remove the waxed paper and cook the concoction at 350° for approximately 25 minutes. The following day, serve each child a slice of sedimentary bar. As a class, discuss how the layers of sediment compressed and joined. Then let the youngsters eat their sedimentary treats!

A New Look

Metamorphic rock forms when heat or pressure changes the appearance of any igneous or sedimentary rock while it remains in a solid state. (If rock *melts* and rehardens, it is igneous.)

To demonstrate this process, quarter a supply of brown and white bread slices and gather several rolling pins. Give each child a folded length of waxed paper, two quarters of one bread type, and one of the other. Instruct each child to stack his pieces of bread atop his waxed paper, alternating the types. Then have him use his palm to gently flatten the stack. Ask students what kind of rock they have formed. Clarify that by pressing the layers together without changing the structure (or appearance) of the rock, they formed sedimentary rock. Then distribute the rolling pins while the students place their rocks inside their folded waxed paper. Provide time for each child to take a turn using a rolling pin to completely flatten his rock. Lead students to conclude that these rocks are metamorphic because they have a whole new look!

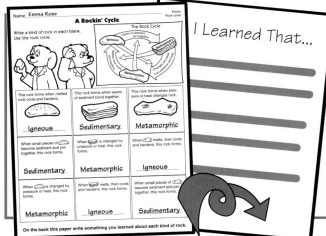

I Learned That...

A Rockin' Cycle

Now that students have learned how the three different types of rocks are made, ask them to hypothesize whether the amount of rock on earth is increasing. Accept all answers. Then lead them to conclude that because rock is made from rock, the amount of rock on earth doesn't change much. Explain that the never-ending process by which rocks change from one type to another is called the *rock cycle*. Next, give each child a copy of page 178 to complete. Soon your rock hounds will realize any type of rock can change into any other type of rock. Rock on!

Remarkable Rock Reports

Wrap up your rock studies by asking each rock hound to use the knowledge she's learned to investigate a mystery rock! Select distinctive rocks from the class collection and place them in a designated container. You will need one rock per child. Ask each rock hound to remove one rock from the container without looking inside it, carefully observe the rock, and then write a report about it. After each child shares her report with the class, showcase each rock and its related report at a display titled "Remarkable Rock Reports."

A Remarkable Mystery Rock
by Sofie B.
My rock is dull and rough. It has lots of speckles. It is medium size. It is either igneous or metamorphic, I think.

Books About Rocks
These rock-related books are real gems!

Rocks and Minerals
Written by Neil Morris
Includes illustrations and photographs
Crabtree Publishing Company, 1998

Let's Go Rock Collecting
Written by Roma Gans
Illustrated by Holly Keller
HarperCollins Children's Books, 1997

The Magic School Bus® Inside the Earth
Written by Joanna Cole
Illustrated by Bruce Degen
Scholastic Inc., 1989

Rocks and Minerals (Spotlights)
Written by Neil Curtis
Illustrated by Debra Woodward
Oxford University Press, 1998

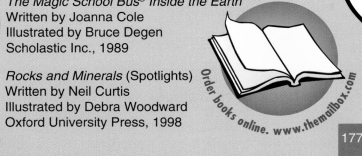

Order books online. www.themailbox.com

A Rockin' Cycle

Write a kind of rock in each blank.
Use the rock cycle.

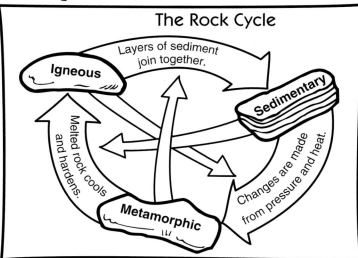

The Rock Cycle

Igneous

Layers of sediment join together.

Sedimentary

Melted rock cools and hardens.

Changes are made from pressure and heat.

Metamorphic

This rock forms when melted rock cools and hardens. _____	This rock forms when layers of sediment bond together. _____	This rock forms when pressure or heat changes rock. _____
When small pieces of  become sediment and join together, this rock forms. _____	When  is changed by pressure or heat, this rock forms. _____	When  melts, then cools and hardens, this rock forms. _____
When ⬭ is changed by pressure or heat, this rock forms. _____	When 🪨 melts, then cools and hardens, this rock forms. _____	When small pieces of 🪨 become sediment and join together, this rock forms. _____

On the back of this paper write something you learned about each kind of rock.

©The Education Center, Inc. • THE MAILBOX® • Primary • June/July 2000

SOCIAL STUDIES UNITS

Getting to Know A Classroom Pet

If your classroom is home to a pint-size pet, such as a gerbil, guinea pig, or goldfish, or you're considering welcoming such a pet, implement the following kid-pleasing projects and literature suggestions into your back-to-school plans. Or save the ideas and incorporate them into an upcoming pet unit. Either way, you'll be teaching valuable lessons about caring for and respecting pets.

ideas contributed by Mary Lester

Pondering a Pet

The benefits of having a classroom pet are plentiful. It's a wonderful way to promote compassion for animals, teach proper pet care, and nurture students' observation skills. However, the decision to welcome a critter into your classroom is one that must be carefully considered. It is no secret that having a classroom pet results in added responsibility and expense for the teacher. A brochure from the National Association for Humane and Environmental Education outlines the pros and cons of keeping animals in the classroom. It also provides guidelines for choosing an appropriate pet and activities that promote respect and appreciation for animals, even if a classroom pet is not in the picture. To order, send $.50 to NAHEE, P.O. Box 362, East Haddam, CT 06423-0362.

Gerbils are very good jumpers. They can leap away from danger.

A Pet Investigation

What is a hamster? How big is a gerbil? Is a guinea pig part pig? A pet investigation will answer many of your students' questions. If you already have a class pet, make it the focus of your investigation. If you're undecided about which type of pet to adopt, enlist your students' help in locating facts about the different animals you're considering.

To begin your investigation, read aloud a nonfiction book or two (see page 182 for suggestions). Then, on a length of colorful paper, write a student-generated list of the facts learned. On each of several days, set aside time for students to share additional facts they've uncovered. Add these facts to the list. When the number of listed facts equals or exceeds your student enrollment, have each child copy a different fact from the list onto provided paper and then illustrate his work. Compile the students' work into a nonfiction class book called "Learning About _____." Display the informative book near the class pet's habitat or in the class library.

Caring for a Pet

A pet, like any animal, is a living being with special needs. Explain that wild animals live in natural habitats where they find food, water, and shelter. Pets, however, are dependent on their owners to meet their special needs. Use the critter-friendly project on page 183 to spotlight the needs of a class pet or any pet in which a youngster is interested. Have each student illustrate a pet in the "Love a Pet" frame, color the front and back of the frame as desired, and write her name on the provided line. She then completes each sentence, using the word bank as needed. Next she illustrates the sentences, showing how they apply to her featured pet. To assemble her project, she cuts along the bold lines and the dotted line. After she stacks her pages in sequential order, she folds the frame along the thin line, unfolds it, and staples the stack just below the crease. To display her project, she folds the tab along each thin line. Then she inserts the end of the tab in the slit at the back of the frame.

MADE WITH LOVE

by Shawanna

Observation Is Key

Observing a pet is a wonderful way to learn about and better understand its behavior. This idea fine-tunes your youngsters' observation skills and provides your pet with plenty of attention! Display a chart tablet and a container of markers near your pet's home. Each day, on a blank page of the tablet, write the title "We Keep an Eye on Our [pet(s)]!" At first, oversee small group observations. On the paper, write student-generated comments followed by the initials of the corresponding students. Eventually invite individual students to write and initial observations on the provided paper. Every few days set aside class time to review the most recent entries. Urge students who made the observations to elaborate upon them. Also challenge the class to look for patterns of behavior and then make (and follow up on) behavior-related predictions.

We Keep an Eye on Our Goldfish.

Spotto swims fast! LM

Goldie swishes her tail a lot. SV

MARKO

Interesting fact about hamsters

What a hamster likes to eat

dry hamster food · tomatoes
sunflowers · carrots · corn
grapes · apples · water
NEVER!
potato chips
chocolate

Is there more than one kind of hamster?

How long does a

Pet Pointers

Students will be in a spin over this freewheeling project! Give each child a white construction paper copy of page 184 and have him select a pet he'd like to learn more about. If the pet is pictured, he colors it. If it is not, he illustrates the pet in the blank circle. Then he cuts out the wheel, the handle, and his pet artwork along the bold lines. After he glues his artwork to the handle, he hole-punches the dot at the opposite end of the handle. He pokes a brad through the center of the large circle and then through the hole in the handle before he secures it. Next he writes a research question or guide-line at the top of each circle quadrant (these may be student generated or provided by you). The student writes the results of his research in the corresponding quadrants. To share his work with the class, he rotates his pet artwork around the circle as he shares the information he's gathered. For transport or storage, have each youngster paper-clip the handle to the wheel of the project.

From a Pet's Perspective

Attempting to view the class surroundings through a pet's eyes is enlightening, and it fosters compassion for the pint-size pal. For this writing activity, ask students to imagine how the classroom and everything in it looks to the class pet. Stir up interest by having students consider how a pencil may look to a guinea pig or what a hamster may think of a chalkboard eraser! Or read aloud *Cinnamon's Day Out: A Gerbil Adventure* (see page 182). Then have every child choose an object and illustrate how it might look to the class pet. Post each picture, along with a student-dictated (or -written) caption, on a bulletin board titled "From Our Pet's Perspective."

It looks like a flying snake!
It has a blue head!

Books About Pint-Size Pets

Gerbils, guinea pigs, and hamsters take center stage in this "pet-tacular" literature collection!

Picture Books

John Willy and Freddy McGee
Written & Illustrated by Holly Meade
Marshall Cavendish Corporation, 1998

Two guinea pigs, John Willy and Freddy McGee, have cage fever—but not for long! When the door to their safe but oh-so-boring habitat is accidentally left ajar, the two furry friends scurry out and find their way into the tunnels of the family pool table. Mixed-media illustrations add to the charm of this engaging escapade.

Cinnamon's Day Out: A Gerbil Adventure
Written & Illustrated by Susan L. Roth
Dial Books for Young Readers, 1998

Bright collages created from wood chips, wallpaper, cardboard, cut paper, and other assorted materials deliver a delightful tale told from a gerbil's point of view. When Cinnamon is rescued and reunited with her cagemate, Snowball, she describes from a gerbil's perspective the things she has seen during her daylong adventure.

Beginning Chapter Books

Godzilla Ate My Homework
Written by Marcia Thornton Jones
Illustrated by Robert Krogle
Scholastic Inc., 1997

Parker, an enthusiastic second grader, discovers that being a pet owner is more challenging than he could ever have imagined! Of course, how is he to know that the multicolored guinea pig he picks as his pet likes to eat paper? This humorous story is sure to make the grade with your students!

Jenius: The Amazing Guinea Pig
Written by Dick King-Smith
Illustrated by Brian Floca
Hyperion Books for Children, 1996

Eight-year-old Judy is the proud owner and trainer of a smarter-than-average guinea pig, named Jenius. How she convinces others of her pet's astute talents makes for a very entertaining story.

Nonfiction Books

I Love Guinea Pigs
Written by Dick King-Smith
Illustrated by Anita Jeram
Candlewick Press, 1997

Irresistible watercolor illustrations adorn the pages of this affectionate and informative introduction to guinea pigs. One of several Read and Wonder Books, this slim paperback may even win over those who don't like guinea pigs.

First Pets: Gerbils
Written by Kate Petty
Includes Illustrations and Photographs
Barron's Educational Series, Inc.; 1995

Brief, easy-to-read text gives basic information about the varieties, characteristics, and life cycles of gerbils. Other books in the First Pet series include *Hamsters, Guinea Pigs,* and *Rabbits.*

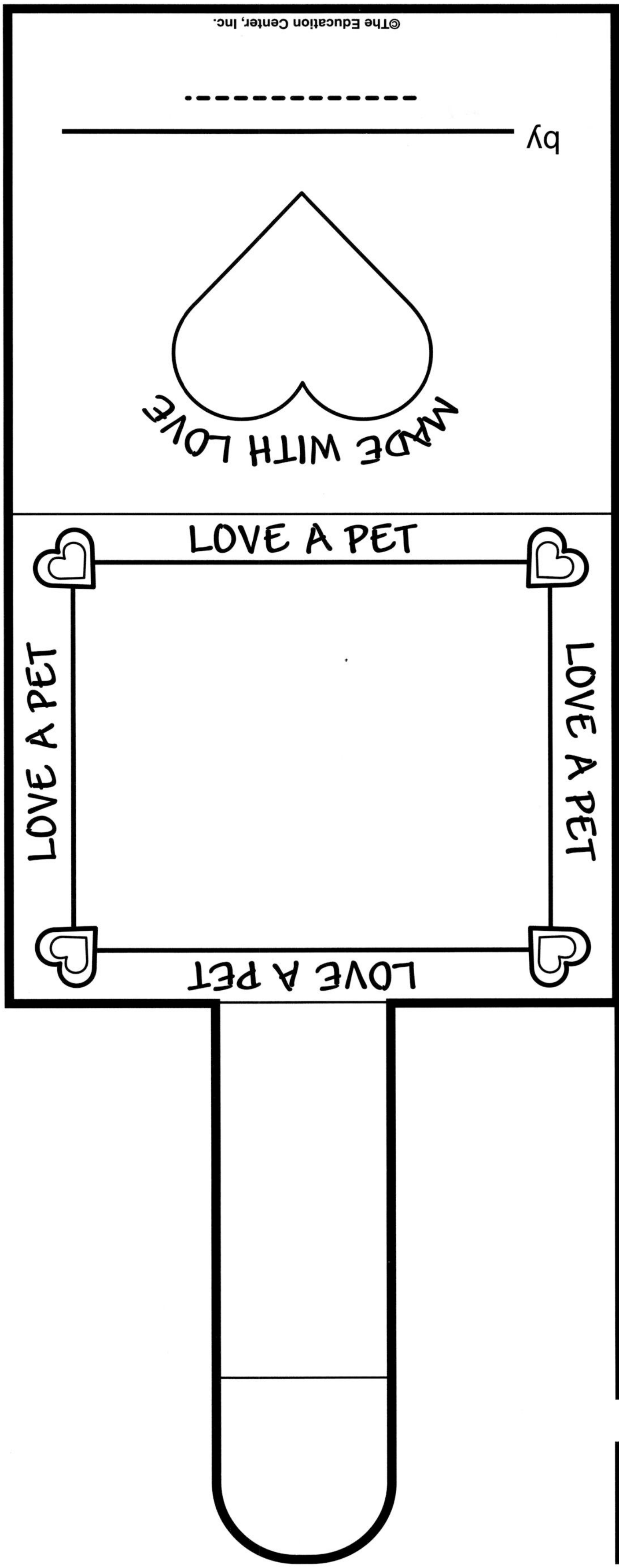

by _____

MADE WITH LOVE

LOVE A PET

LOVE A PET

LOVE A PET

LOVE A PET

A pet needs a safe __ __ __ __ __ __ and fresh __ __ __ __ __ and __ __ __ __.

1

A pet needs to get plenty of
__ __ __ __ __ __ __ __.

2

And you can never give a pet too much __ __ __ __!

3

Word Bank

exercise   food   love   shelter   water

Patterns
Use with "Pet Pointers" on page 181.

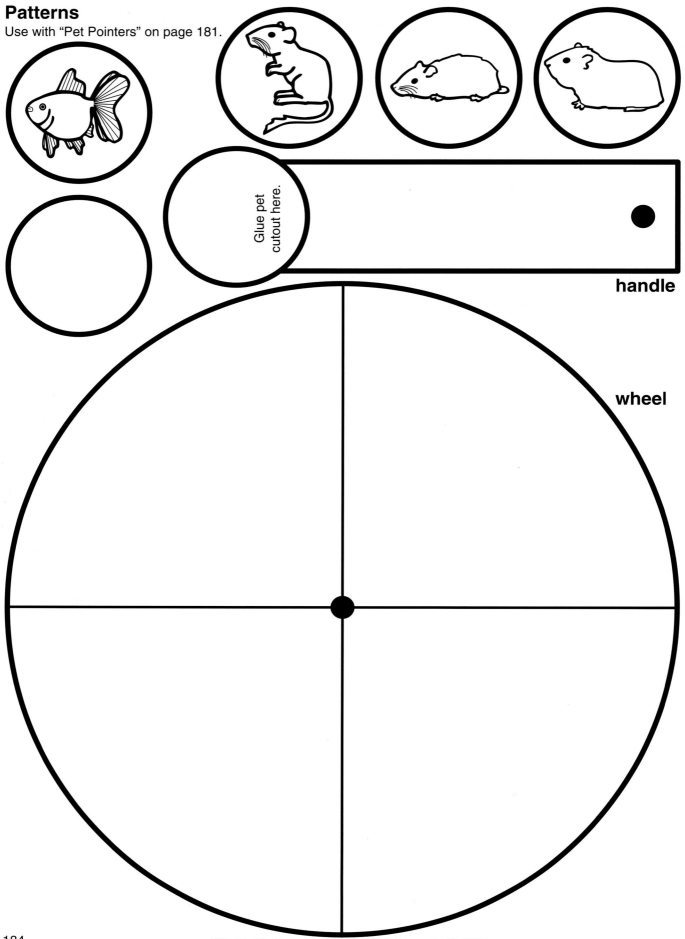

Glue pet cutout here.

handle

wheel

Courageous Characters

When it comes to courage, there are no better models than the lionhearted characters in these books. Promote courageous behavior among your students with these literature suggestions and the related activities.

by Vicki Mockaitis Dabrowka and Amy Erickson

Storm in the Night
Written by Mary Stolz • Illustrated by Pat Cummings
HarperTrophy, 1990
As a thunderstorm rages, Grandfather tells Thomas about a storm that occurred long ago, revealing a noteworthy truth—everyone becomes frightened at times. Grandfather's candid tale of how he bravely faced a fear gives Thomas the courage to admit his own anxiety about the storm.

As Thomas learns, being afraid doesn't necessarily mean being a coward. In fact, admitting a fear takes courage! This writing project helps students realize that talking about a fear is a step toward conquering it. In advance have each child ask a family member to tell him about a time that he or she was afraid. Ask that he tell the family member about one of his own fears, too. Then, on provided paper, the student writes about the two fears and glues his writing inside a construction paper folder as shown. On the front folder he glues two slightly overlapped paper-doll cutouts (pattern on page 189) and decorates them to resemble himself and his family member. Provide assorted arts-and-crafts supplies for this purpose. Display the projects with the title "Facing Fear Together." If desired, follow up with a reading of *Thunder Cake* by Patricia Polacco (PaperStar, 1997), another heartwarming story about facing a frightening storm with the help of a loved one.

Maybe if I learn more about snakes, I won't be so scared of them.

A person shows **courage** if he or she
- confronts a fear bravely
- faces a difficult task instead of avoiding it
- stands up for what he or she believes

as clever as a fox

Emily's Web of Courage

Brave As a Mountain Lion
Written by Ann Herbert Scott • Illustrated by Glo Coalson
Clarion Books, 1996
Spider is terrified at the thought of participating in a spelling bee! With the support of his family and the guidance of his spirit, this Native American boy conquers his fear, and in doing so, becomes a true winner.

Spider tackles his fear by reminding himself of qualities he wants to emulate. These nifty courage-boosting reminders can help your students muster up courage, too. To make a reminder, a child folds two 9-inch circles into quarters, unfolds them, and traces along the resulting fold lines. Next she cuts away one quadrant of one circle, titles the resulting shape "[Student name]'s Web of Courage," and adds spiderweb details. Then she uses a brad to fasten the personalized cutout atop the remaining circle. Last she turns the circle and writes and illustrates a courage-boosting simile in each blank quadrant. Suggest that a student turn to her web of courage when she needs additional confidence to confront a fear.

185

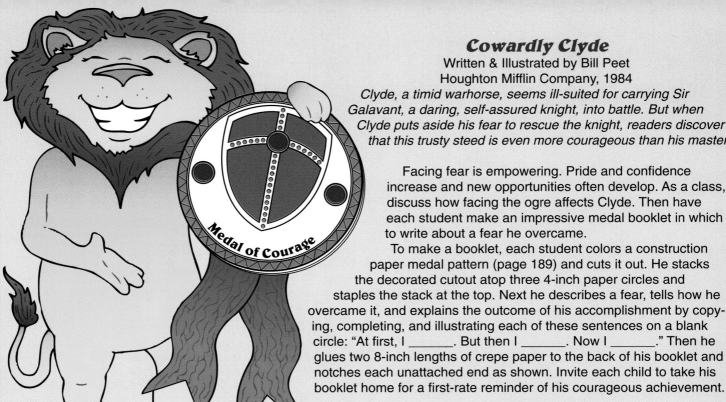

Cowardly Clyde
Written & Illustrated by Bill Peet
Houghton Mifflin Company, 1984

Clyde, a timid warhorse, seems ill-suited for carrying Sir Galavant, a daring, self-assured knight, into battle. But when Clyde puts aside his fear to rescue the knight, readers discover that this trusty steed is even more courageous than his master.

Facing fear is empowering. Pride and confidence increase and new opportunities often develop. As a class, discuss how facing the ogre affects Clyde. Then have each student make an impressive medal booklet in which to write about a fear he overcame.

To make a booklet, each student colors a construction paper medal pattern (page 189) and cuts it out. He stacks the decorated cutout atop three 4-inch paper circles and staples the stack at the top. Next he describes a fear, tells how he overcame it, and explains the outcome of his accomplishment by copying, completing, and illustrating each of these sentences on a blank circle: "At first, I _____. But then I _____. Now I _____." Then he glues two 8-inch lengths of crepe paper to the back of his booklet and notches each unattached end as shown. Invite each child to take his booklet home for a first-rate reminder of his courageous achievement.

Knots on a Counting Rope
Written by Bill Martin Jr. & John Archambault
Illustrated by Ted Rand
Owlet Books for Young Readers, 1997

Born sickly and blind, Boy-Strength-of-Blue-Horses faces great physical challenges. But by participating in a much-celebrated horse race, he proves that the challenges are not insurmountable. As this tender story unfolds, it captures the undying love of this determined, courageous boy and his caring grandfather.

As they enjoy each other's company by a campfire, Grandfather and Boy-Strength-of-Blue-Horses recount a heroic tale of courage. Bring that campfire atmosphere of camaraderie into your classroom with this speaking activity. Gather students in a circle on the floor. Explain that courage takes many forms, such as pushing oneself to achieve a difficult physical goal and standing up for one's beliefs. Hold a length of rope as you tell students about a brave deed (one of your own or someone else's). Then tie a knot in the rope and pass the rope to a student seated beside you. Invite the student to tell about another act of courage, knot the rope, and then pass it to the person beside her. Continue in a like manner until each youngster has made a knot.

To extend the activity, have each student tape a length of rope to the side of her desk. On a slip of paper, she writes a personal goal that requires courage to achieve. Then she tapes the paper to the end of the rope. Each time the youngster works toward the goal, she ties a knot in the rope to mark her progress.

Courage

Last year, I was so afraid to dive in a pool that I didn't want to go to a swimming party. I was disappointed to miss the party.

I went on the ride with a friend. It turned out to be fun.

Kate Shelley and the Midnight Express
Written by Margaret K. Wetterer • Illustrated by Karen Ritz
First Avenue Editions, 1991
Battling a fierce storm, 15-year-old Kate selflessly risks her own life to save 200 people on a train bound for disaster. This easy-to-read true story of the 1881 rescue is a perfect choice for young readers who have a taste for suspense.

Have students showcase a trainload of courage with this display! Lead students in a discussion about how Kate encounters many obstacles, including fear, and how she triumphs over each of them. Ask each student to think about a time when a fear was a hindrance for him. Have him describe the fearful situation on a half sheet of writing paper. On another half sheet of paper, have him write and illustrate how he overcame his fear. To make his train car, he glues his first writing inside a 6" x 9" construction paper folder so that the fold is at the top. Then he glues his second writing to the front of the project. Next he adds two construction paper wheels. Label a train engine cutout "Courage" and post it on a classroom wall. Display the students' train cars linked to the engine with strips of paper. All aboard the Courage Express!

Birdie's Lighthouse
Written by Deborah Hopkinson
Illustrated by Kimberly Bulcken Root
Atheneum Books for Young Readers, 1997
The solitary and sometimes dangerous life of a Maine lighthouse keeper in the 1850s comes to life in the diary of ten-year-old Birdie. Based on the true-life experiences of several women, this exquisitely illustrated picture book describes how Birdie bravely takes over the lighthouse keeper's duties when her father becomes ill.

At first, Papa is unsure that a girl can be an assistant keeper, but he later realizes that Birdie has the skills and courage for the job. Emphasize that anyone can be courageous regardless of his or her age. Next have students brainstorm other jobs that require bravery. List their ideas on the chalkboard. Ask each child to choose a different job from the list and then write and illustrate a diary entry from the perspective of a person performing that job. Bind the students' writing between covers titled "It Takes Courage!" and place the resulting class book in your classroom library. What a great way to provide positive role models *and* reinforce writing skills!

Courageous Workers
police officers
firefighters
doctors
stuntpeople
race car drivers
volunteers
animal trainers
pilots
astronauts
rodeo riders
ambulance drivers
roofers
rescue workers
bank tellers
trapeze artists
rodeo clowns
military

More Books of Bravery
If your students can't get enough of these two heroic tales, they're sure to enjoy these titles:

Kate Shelley: Bound for Legend
Written by Robert D. San Souci
Illustrated by Max Ginsburg
Dial Books for Young Readers, 1995

Keep the Lights Burning, Abbie
Written by Peter and Connie Roop
Illustrated by Peter E. Hanson
Carolrhoda Books, 1987

187

The Story of Ruby Bridges
Written by Robert Coles • Illustrated by George Ford
Scholastic Inc., 1995

Prejudice is difficult to face at any age, but that's exactly what first-grader Ruby Bridges does. Ruby resolutely takes a stand for what she believes and becomes the first Black American student to attend Frantz Elementary School. Watercolor and ink illustrations capture the intense emotions expressed during this tumultuous time in United States history.

Ruby shows tremendous courage by attending school. But she is not the only character in this story who faces the issue of integration with bravery. Use this project to help students realize that courage can be shown in many ways. First discuss how Ruby, Ruby's parents, Miss Hurley, and the people in the crowd all show courage. Then, have each student fold a large sheet of drawing paper in half lengthwise and make three equally spaced cuts in the top layer to create four flaps. To complete his project he labels and illustrates one flap for each of the four parties mentioned; then, under each flap, he writes about the story events from that party's perspective. Set aside time for each student to share his work with a classmate and explain how he feels the characters showed bravery.

Ruby

We were so proud of Ruby! We were scared for her though because so many people seemed angry at her.

Miss Hurley

The Crowd

Your Move
Written by Eve Bunting • Illustrated by James Ransome
Harcourt Brace & Company, 1998

James sets out to prove himself to the members of a gang. Even though he passes their frightening test with flying colors, it's not until James decides against joining the gang that he truly shows courage. This boldly illustrated picture book sets the stage for thought-provoking discussions with older students about peer pressure.

It not only takes courage to resist peer pressure, it takes wise decision-making skills, too. James shows both of these qualities. This role-playing activity gives students an opportunity to follow James's example by practicing good decision-making skills. In advance, label individual paper strips with different scenes involving peer pressure. Fold the strips and place them in a container. Then divide students into small groups. For each group, draw a strip and read it aloud. Instruct the group to role-play the described scene for their classmates, demonstrating good decision making. Then, as a class, discuss how courage was displayed.

To follow up, write "Courage Club" and the provided poem on tagboard. Display the resulting poster and lead students in reciting the poem. Then provide colorful markers and invite each child to sign the poster to show her intent to make wise choices—even if her decisions are not popular with all of her peers. Keep the poster on display as a visual reminder of your students' pledge.

COURAGE CLUB

When it is time to make a choice,

We know just what we will do.

We will stand by what is right,

And to ourselves be true.

Mary Libby Lisa
J.T. Shayne Nina
Monique Jermaine
Lauren Leo

When you go out to recess, you see two friends teasing a student.

Your class is taking a test. Your friend asks you to show him your answers.

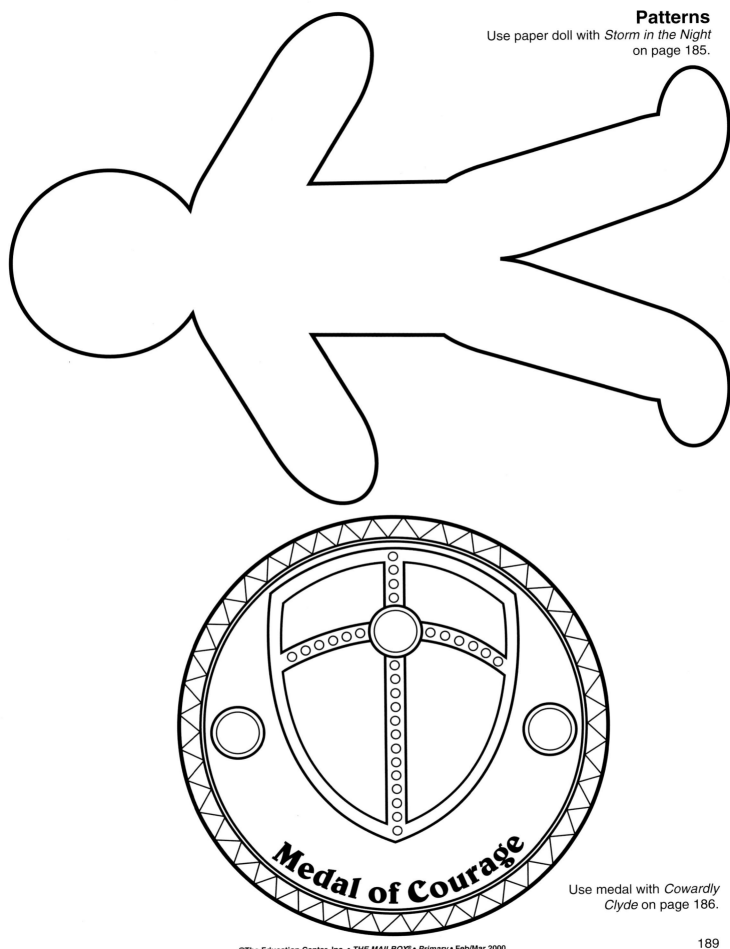

Medal of Courage

Use medal with *Cowardly Clyde* on page 186.

A World-Class Tour
Learning About Oceans and Continents

With the help of these suggestions from our subscribers, you can take your students to the seven continents and four oceans of the world—without stepping outside the classroom! Now that's having your ducks in a row!

Start With a Song

Begin your world tour with this little ditty, and there's a good chance you'll hear students singing it throughout the trip!

Earth Song
(adapt to the tune of "My Bonnie Lies Over the Ocean")
Earth is the name of our planet.
It's shaped like a ball or a sphere.
It's covered with land and water.
A globe makes this picture quite clear.

(Chorus)
Seven continents, four oceans, on our planet Earth…
Seven continents, four oceans, on our planet Earth!

On Earth there are seven continents.
A continent's a large mass of land.
Four large bodies of water are oceans.
In fact, there's more water than land!

(Repeat Chorus)

Kaye Williams—Gr. 3
Chilhowee Intermediate School, Knoxville, TN

Travel Preparations

These nifty student-made backpack folders are perfect for storing important travel papers like a passport, an itinerary, and other paperwork completed during the world tour. To make a folder, stack two 9" x 12" sheets of construction paper and then lay a 6" x 9" sheet of construction paper on top of the stack. Align the bottom edges and round the two bottom corners of all three papers. Staple around the bottom of the project; then fold down one inch of the top full sheet of paper before stapling the sides of the project as shown. Tape two 1" x 18" strips of construction paper to the back of the folder for backpack straps, and then loop and staple a 1" x 5" paper strip to the back of the folder near the top. Have each child personalize his backpack folder and store paperwork related to his world tour inside.

To add to the fun, duplicate a class set of the continent cards on page 194. During your study of a continent, give each child a corresponding card to color. Have him trim around the continent and glue the shape to his backpack folder. During an ocean study, have each child write the name of the ocean on a blue paper card, trim the card so that it resembles a body of water, and glue the cutout to his folder. When the trip is over, these folders will be packed with mementos from the trip—inside and out!

190   adapted from an idea by Sue Majors—Gr. 2, Palmer Lake Elementary, Monument, CO

Where in the World?

Keep your youngsters' mapping skills on course with this eye-catching and informative bulletin board. To make a simple world map, back a bulletin board with blue paper. Enlarge the continent patterns from page 194 to bulletin board size, cut them out, and staple them to the display in the appropriate locations (trimming Antarctica as needed). If desired, add a yarn equator and a compass rose cutout. Next write the names of the continents and oceans on individual cards. As each location is studied, staple the appropriate card to the display. Also invite interested students to draw and color pictures on small paper squares that represent the location. Display these illustrations on the map. If desired, cut a supply of arrow shapes from red paper and use them to mark the class's path of travel on the map. By the conclusion of your study, the bulletin board will contain a wealth of information and be a king-size souvenir of your trip!

Sue Majors—Gr. 2, Palmer Lake Elementary, Monument, CO

Musical Map Time

Put your students' knowledge of continents and oceans on the map with this upbeat sing-along! Gather students in front of a large world map. Point to a continent or an ocean and have students sing a corresponding rendition of the continents and oceans song. Continue in the manner described until the names and locations of several oceans and continents have been musically reviewed. You can count on plenty of requests for musical map time!

Continents and Oceans

(adapt to the tune of "He's Got the Whole World in His Hands")

We've got [name of continent or ocean]
On our map.

We've got [same as above]
On our map.

We've got [same as above]
On our map.

We've found [a continent/an ocean]
On our map!

Jill Erickson—Gr. 3
McMillan Elementary , Las Vegas, NV

X Marks the Spot

This world-class center activity provides unlimited mapping practice! To prepare the center, color a copy of page 195 and draw an X on each continent and ocean. Trim off the name and skill lines at the top of the page and then cut along the top dotted line. Glue the map near the top of a 9" x 12" sheet of construction paper. Laminate the map project and the continent and ocean names. Cut out the laminated names and use a pinch of Sticky-Tac to attach each one below the map. Place the project and a globe at a center. A student peels off each name (with the Sticky-Tac affixed) and repositions it on the X that marks its corresponding location. Then he uses the globe to check his work. Before he leaves the center he returns the name cutouts to the bottom of the project.

For an individual activity, make a copy of page 195 and draw an X on each continent and ocean. Duplicate a class supply of the page. A child cuts along the dotted lines on her copy of the page and glues each ocean and continent name atop an appropriately placed X.

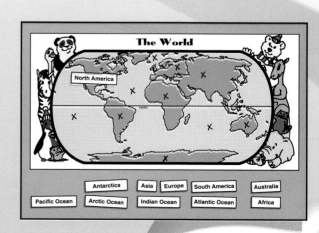

Sherrie Rippy, Van Duyn Elementary, Clinton, IN

Pumpkin Globes

Harvest a crop of colorful hands-on learning with this globe-making project. Enlist the help of a local grocer or your school's parent group in gathering a class supply of basketball–size pumpkins. Use a fine point permanent marker to draw an equator (and a prime meridian, if desired) on each pumpkin. Each student studies a simple world map. Then she imagines her pumpkin as a globe and outlines the seven continents, using the map and the lines on her pumpkin as guides. Working atop a newspaper-covered surface, she tips her pumpkin over and paints Antarctica and the area surrounding it, using green acrylic paint to represent land and blue acrylic paint to represent water. When Antarctica is dry, she turns her pumpkin upright and continues painting in the manner previously described. After the paint dries, she uses a fine point permanent marker to outline her work and label the continents and oceans of the world. Impressive!

Marcia Roth—Gr. 3, Waco Elementary, Crawsfordsville, IA

Name That Continent

Students are sure to think the world of this review game! Divide the class into groups of three and give each trio a set of seven continent cards (see page 194). One player stacks the cards facedown and draws the top card. The two other players ask this student questions to find out which continent is on his card. To avoid questions like "Is it Asia?" or "What continent is it?" post a list of suggested questions. When the continent is identified, the card is placed at the bottom of the stack and play continues with a different student drawing the top card in the stack. At the end of game time, place the card sets at a free time center for additional review. Now that's a continental review that really stacks up!

Jodi Fedoruk—Gr. 3, St. Eugene School, Chicago, IL

Continent Quest

This poetic quest for continents creates a colorful keepsake booklet. Start by giving each student a 9" x 12" sheet of construction paper and a copy of page 195. Ask each child to label the oceans and continents on his map, referring to the names at the bottom of the page as needed. Then have him color his map, instructing him to color each continent a different color. Next have him cut along the top dotted line (cutting away the words below the map) and glue his map near the top of his construction paper. Distribute student copies of page 196. Read aloud the poem as students follow along. Then re-read the poem, stopping after every two-line stanza. Ask each child to find the corresponding continent on his map, color the circle that follows the stanza to match the continent, and color the boxed artwork. (Have each child illustrate himself in the empty box that accompanies the stanza about North America.) To complete his project, the student cuts along the bold lines, stacks the stanzas in sequential order behind the title, and staples the left edge of the stack. Then he staples the stack below his map as shown.

To extend the fun, copy the poem from page 196 onto chart paper and display it in the classroom. Periodically, take students on a quest for continents. As students chorally read the poem, have a student volunteer or two point to the corresponding land masses on a world map.

poem by Sheri Beersman—Gr. 2, Pleasant Hope Elementary, Morrisville, MO

Worldly Pitas

For this tasty review, pair students and have each twosome work together to show the world on a pita bread! To do this, the partners spread pizza sauce on their slice of pita bread and place shredded cheese on the bread to show where the seven continents are located. Then the twosome places a slice of pepperoni or another desired topping in each ocean of the world. Bake the projects until they are thoroughly heated and the cheese melts; then carefully slice each twosome's project into two hemispheres and serve!

Amy Kallelis—Gr. 3, Sanders Elementary, Smyrna, GA

By the Book!

Enrich your study of the world's continents and oceans by visiting each location through literature! Enlist the help of your school's media specialist in collecting books that are set around the world. Select one or two books to read aloud during each tour stop. Display the remaining books for your students' reading enjoyment.

There are numerous books that take readers all over the world. For a well-versed collection, include fiction, nonfiction, and folklore titles, making sure that students understand that folklore consists of stories that have been shared throughout history and do not reflect current lifestyles. If desired, use the picture book titles that follow as a starting point.

Vicki Good—Library Assistant, Second Avenue Elementary, Columbus, Ohio
Bonnie Keyser—Library Media Specialist, East Bradford Elementary, West Chester, PA
Christine Reid—Gr. 2, Marcus Hook Elementary, Boothwyn, PA

Book List

Africa
Bringing the Rain to Kapiti Plain
The Day of Ahmed's Secret
Jamela's Dress

Antarctica
Solo
Antarctica
A for Antarctica

Asia
Cherry Tree (India)
Weighing the Elephant (China)
The Walking Stick (Vietnam)
A Carp for Kimiko (Japan)

Australia
Possum Magic
The Singing Snake
The Gift Stone

Europe
Percy to the Rescue (England)
Gabriella's Song (Italy)
Mama's Perfect Present (France)
Dog (Ireland)

North America
A Prairie Alphabet (Canada)
Tulip Sees America (United States)
Saturday Market (Mexico)
Abuela's Weave (Guatemala)

South America
Tonight Is Carnaval
Saturday Sancocho
Necklace of Stars

Oceans
Otter on His Own
Annushka's Voyage
Okino and the Whales
Nilo and the Tortoise
Ice Bear and Little Fox

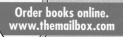

Continent Cards

Use with "Travel Preparations" on page 190,
"Where in the World?" on page 191, and
"Name That Continent" on page 192.

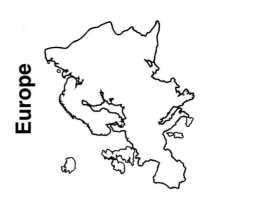

Europe

Australia

Asia

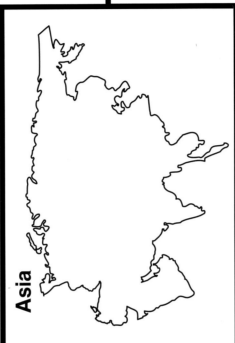

Antarctica

North America

Africa

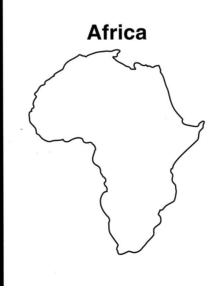

South America

The World

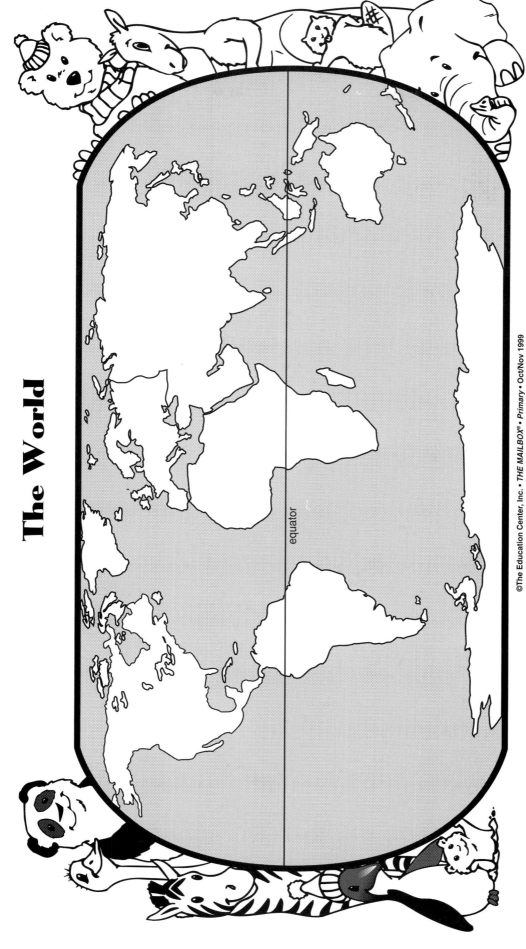

equator

North America	Antarctica	Asia	Europe	South America	Australia
Pacific Ocean	Arctic Ocean	Indian Ocean		Atlantic Ocean	Africa

©The Education Center, Inc. • *THE MAILBOX®* • *Primary* • Oct/Nov 1999

Note to teacher: Use with "X Marks the Spot" on page 191 and "Continent Quest" on page 192.

A World-Class Tour

1 Zebras live in **Africa,**
   Cheetahs and elephants, too.

2 **Australia** is down under,
   Home of the kangaroo!

3 Clap your hands for **Asia!**
   It's the largest one.

4 **Antarctica** is covered in ice.
   The penguins sure have fun!

5 **North America** is where I live.
   It's where I work and play.

6 In **Europe** you'll find England,
   Where the queen rules every day.

7 **South America** is home to Brazil.
   It's the largest country there.

8 The world has seven continents,
   And I've just named them with great care!

The Power of Perseverance

Perseverance generates success—in school, in a career, and in life itself! The books in this collection feature characters who overcome obstacles and rise above adversity through the power of their own perseverance. Inspire your youngsters to practice perseverance with these delightful tales and the activities that accompany them!

book reviews and ideas by Lisa Leonardi

A person shows **perseverance** when he or she continues toward a goal until it is finished, despite obstacles or discouragement.

PERSEVERANCE POINT

Trail Guide to Perseverance Point

Amazing Grace
Written by Mary Hoffman
Illustrated by Caroline Binch
Dial Books for Young Readers, 1991

Grace loves acting out the exciting parts of all sorts of stories. So when Grace's teacher announces that the class will be performing the play Peter Pan, *Grace knows exactly which character she wants to play! However, Grace's enthusiasm turns to self-doubt when her classmates tell her she doesn't fit the part. Thanks to the gentle guidance of family members, Grace learns the importance of believing in herself and in pursuing her dream.*

Amazing Resa!

Along with winning the part of Peter Pan, Grace earns the support and approval of her classmates. Remind students that Grace wants to play Peter Pan because she loves to dance and perform. Next review the obstacle that Grace faces (Grace is a black girl and her classmates have always seen Peter Pan as a white boy), and help students understand that this obstacle is not related to how well Grace dances or performs. Then have students describe how Grace pursues her goal and reaches it (she convinces herself that she can do it, she practices for the audition, etc.). Next have each student copy and complete the following sentence on one side of a large star cutout: "If Grace can play Peter Pan, I can _____." Then have each child turn her star over, write "Amazing [student's name]," and illustrate the sentence she wrote. Invite students to share their goals with the class and describe how they plan to achieve them. Collect each child's cutout, hole-punch it, and suspend it directly above her desk from a length of monofilament line. Then sit back and watch your youngsters reach for the stars!

Cyrus the Unsinkable Sea Serpent
Written & Illustrated by Bill Peet
Houghton Mifflin Company, 1982

After being called a sissy by a shark, Cyrus, a friendly and kindhearted sea serpent, sets out to prove just how rough and tough he can be. However, his plan to stir up some commotion in the ocean changes when he realizes that a doomed ship needs his help. A series of disastrous events puts Cyrus's goodwill to the test, but the kindly sea serpent refuses to give up until the ship safely reaches the shore.

At the conclusion of this unsinkably funny story, have each youngster make a replica of Cyrus as a reminder of his perseverance. Give each student a light green construction paper copy of page 200. Instruct him to cut out the two patterns and glue them together to make a serpent. On each section of the serpent, a student writes one way Cyrus helped save the ship from the perils of the sea. On the back of her project she writes a sentence that tells what Cyrus's actions taught her about perseverance. Then, using the thin lines as guides, she accordion-folds the serpent to make it self-standing. Now that's a very pleasing *and* persevering sea serpent!

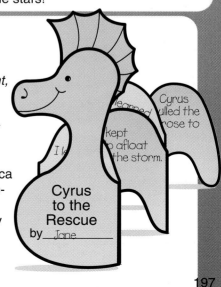

Cyrus pulled the nose to

Kept afloat the storm.

Cyrus to the Rescue by Jane

Brave Irene

Written & Illustrated by William Steig
Farrar, Straus & Giroux, Inc.; 1988

When Irene's mother suddenly falls ill and can't deliver the gown she's sewn for the duchess, Irene offers to make the journey herself. Her trip is full of surprises, which begin with a full-blown blizzard! Although her troubles are as deep as the fallen snow, Irene refuses to allow her determination to get buried. After persevering through a twisted ankle, becoming lost, and getting covered in snow, Irene manages to deliver the gown just in the nick of time!

Although Irene faces many challenges during her journey, she overcomes each obstacle she encounters. Ask students how they would feel if confronted with the challenges Irene faces. Help them understand that Irene shows perseverance by refusing to give up. Next invite students to share how they persevere when the going gets tough. List their suggestions on the chalkboard. Then challenge students to put these perseverance strategies into practice with this goal-setting project! Give each child a white six-inch circle, a white six-inch doily, and two 2" x 6" paper strips. A student writes a goal he wants to achieve in the near future on the white circle. On the doily he writes his name and glues his school picture. Then he chooses his two favorite strategies from the chalkboard and copies each one on a paper strip, leaving a margin at each end. He glues one end of each strip to the back of the circle, and then he cuts a notch in the unattached end of each strip as shown. To complete his project he staples the doily atop the white circle. Suggest that each child display his perseverance project where it will remind and encourage him to work toward his goal!

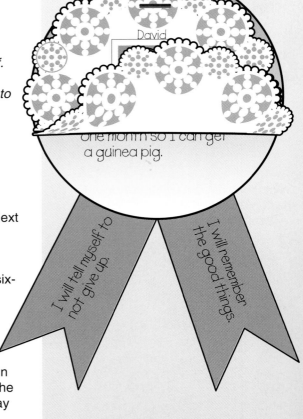

David

one month so I can get a guinea pig.

I will tell myself to not give up.

I will remember the good things.

A Picture Book of Helen Keller

Written by David A. Adler
Illustrated by John and Alexandra Wallner
Holiday House, Inc.; 1991

This engaging look at the life of Helen Keller is a picture-perfect example of the power of perseverance. Left blind and deaf from an illness at the age of 1 1/2, Helen Keller refused throughout her life to let her physical limitations interfere with her goals. Her accomplishments were extraordinary and her actions brought immeasurable hope to millions of others who, like herself, faced challenges that seemed unconquerable.

Medal of Generous Perseverance for Kurt

For her outstanding public service, President Lyndon B. Johnson awarded Helen Keller the Presidential Medal of Freedom, the nation's highest civilian honor. Discuss with students how amazing this accomplishment was, knowing the physical challenges that Helen faced each and every day. Next pair students and ask each child to tell his partner about a time that his perseverance benefited others. After each partner shares his experience, have the students make perseverance medals for each other. To make a medal, a student writes "Medal of Generous Perseverance for [partner's name]" on a five-inch star cutout. Next he glues the star to a five-inch construction paper circle. On the other side of the circle, he writes a sentence describing how his partner's perseverance helped others. Then he hole-punches the top of the circle, threads a length of yarn (or curling ribbon) through the hole, and securely ties the ends. Ask each child to tell the class about his partner's positive actions before he presents the medal to him to wear around his neck.

Thank You, Aunt Joy!

Uncle Jed's Barbershop
Written by Margaree King Mitchell
Illustrated by James Ransome
Aladdin Paperbacks, 1998

Living in the segregated South in the 1920s, Sarah Jean's Uncle Jed was the only black barber in the county. He always talked about owning a barber-shop, yet no one believed he ever would. Twice he came close to having enough money to open his own shop, but Sarah Jean's operation and the Great Depression put his dream on hold. Through his strong drive and determination, Uncle Jed turns his dream into a reality on his 79th birthday.

PERSEVERANCE POINT

It took many years before Uncle Jed's dream came true, but he never gave up! Talk with students about the setbacks that Uncle Jed experienced and ask them to share what they learned about Uncle Jed from his actions. Help students realize that while Uncle Jed's dream was very important to him, he did not let it interfere with the love he felt for his family. He also chose to not dwell on his misfortunes. Tell students that people who recognize persever-ance in others are more likely to reach their own goals. Why? Because they can learn from the examples that others set, just like Sarah Jean learned from her Uncle Jed! Then ask each student to design a construction paper thank-you card for one person whom she admires for his or her perseverance. Suggest that in her card she thank the person for setting such a fine example and explain how the person's actions are helping her pursue her own dreams. Imagine how the recipients of these cards will feel when they realize the influence of their positive actions!

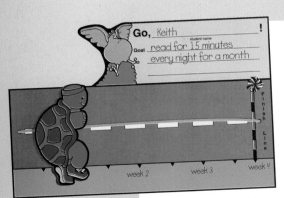

Go, Keith !
student name
Goal read for 15 minutes every night for a month

week 2   week 3   week 4

The Tortoise and the Hare
Adapted & Illustrated by Janet Stevens
Holiday House, Inc.; 1985

When quick-moving Hare challenges slow-moving Tortoise to a race, everyone sees Tortoise as a worthy opponent except for himself. With the encouragement of friends, Tortoise agrees to the race and trains for the big day. And in the end, Tortoise proves that hard work and perseverance bring reward—and in this case it's crossing the finish line before Hare!

Tortoise achieves his goal one step at a time. Challenge students to achieve school-related goals in a similar manner with this goal-setting project! To begin, each child writes his name on a tagboard copy of page 201 and then he writes his school-related goal on the provided lines. Next he divides his goal into two, four, or eight steps and labels the small triangles accordingly (see the illustration). After he colors the racetrack and turtle patterns, he cuts them out. Then he hole-punches the racetrack at each black dot, threads a two-foot length of yarn through the holes, and ties the yarn ends at the front of the project, keeping the yarn taut. Finally, he tapes the turtle to the yarn, atop the knot. Each time he achieves one step of his goal, he moves his turtle forward along the racetrack. When a student moves his turtle across the finish line, lead the class in giving him three cheers for meeting his goal! Provide extra copies of the reproducible and encourage students to repeat the activity as often as desired, setting a new goal each time.

Pattern

Use with *Cyrus the Unsinkable Sea Serpent* on page 197.

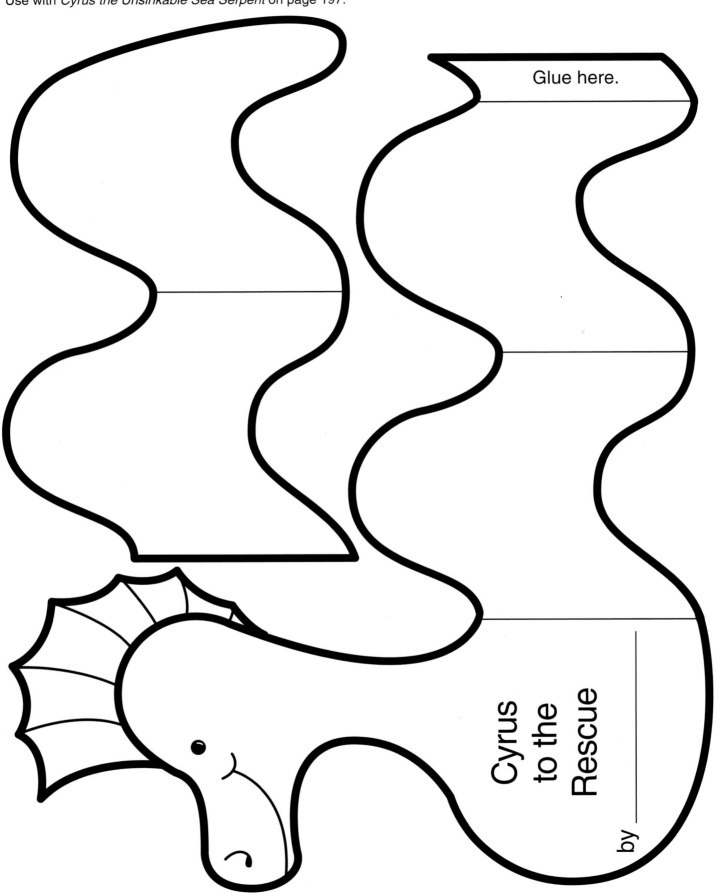

Glue here.

Cyrus
to the
Rescue

by _____

Go, _____ !

student name

Goal _____

Finish Line

©The Education Center, Inc. • *THE MAILBOX®* • *Primary* • Oct/Nov 1999

Note to the teacher: Use with *The Tortoise and the Hare* on page 199.

Native Americans of the Plains

Hundreds of years ago buffalo roamed freely on the Plains of North America where untold numbers of Native Americans lived and hunted. Use these activities to introduce students to the native people of the Plains, their customs of the past, and traditions that carry on today.

by Vicki Mockaitis Dabrowka—Gr. 2, Concord Hill School, Chevy Chase, MD

Pinpointing the Plains

The Plains of North America stretch from the Mississippi River to the Rocky Mountains and from Canada's Saskatchewan River to central Texas. It is a vast region of flat prairies and gently rolling hills. As you show students this area on a U.S. map, explain that the native people who lived here long ago endured extremely cold winters, intense summer heat, droughts, sudden dust storms, and plenty more. Invite students to contemplate how they coped with these conditions. Then have each child complete the mapping activity on page 206.

Two Distinct Regions

Long ago the wide-reaching plains were home to more than 30 Native American nations. While each had its own unique culture, belief system, and language, the environment determined the homes and food supply of the people. Use a Venn diagram to reveal the two distinct regions of the Plains and to explore the similarities and differences among the native people who lived there. Draw and label a diagram that resembles the one shown. In each section, list the provided information and discuss it with the class. Next have each child copy the diagram onto a large sheet of drawing paper and add desired artwork. Suggest that students keep these projects handy so they can continue to add facts throughout their study.

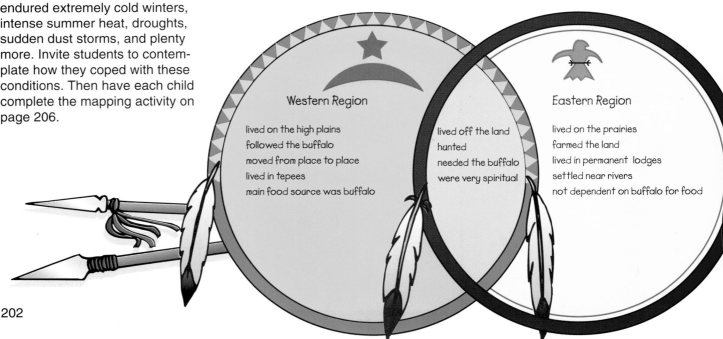

Western Region
lived on the high plains
followed the buffalo
moved from place to place
lived in tepees
main food source was buffalo

lived off the land
hunted
needed the buffalo
were very spiritual

Eastern Region
lived on the prairies
farmed the land
lived in permanent lodges
settled near rivers
not dependent on buffalo for food

High Plains and Prairies

Use this informative chant to reinforce the way of life on the western high plains and eastern prairies of the North American Plains. For added fun, engage students in clapping a rhythmic background beat during the chant.

High Plains and Prairies
The people of the high plains long ago
Hunted and followed the buffalo,
Moving their tepees and arrows.
A need for food kept them on the go.

Off to the east, where the prairies were,
Planting and hunting did occur.
Big earth lodges did not stir.
These people stayed right where they were.

Homes on the Plains

Native Americans of long ago used materials from their environment to build homes that best suited their needs. Enlist your youngsters' help in converting a classroom table into a representation of the Plains. To do this, have each child make one of the Native American homes described below. Display the completed projects on a large classroom table covered with brown paper—tepees to the west, earth lodges to the east. Invite students to add grass, leaves, buffalo fashioned from construction paper, and other elements of the environment to the display.

Tepee

The tepee, which was both permanent and mobile, was a practical dwelling for the hunters of the western Plains. To erect a tepee, a framework of long, straight poles (tied together near the top) was set upright and covered with buffalo hides sewn together and decorated with traditional painted designs.

To make a replica of a tepee, a student uses crayons or markers to decorate a tan construction paper copy of the pattern on page 207. Then she cuts out the pattern and glues the tab to the straight edge so that a cone shape results. When the glue is dry, she makes an entrance flap by cutting a slit in the bottom edge of the tepee and folding back the paper. Then she glues a few toothpicks in the small hole at the top.

Earth Lodge

The most common dwelling to the east was the earth lodge—a large, circular structure with a square smoke hole at the top and a covered porchlike structure, or *vestibule,* at the entrance of the lodge. Each permanent home housed 30 to 40 people. A lodge was built by erecting a large wooden framework and then covering it with layers of branches, grass, and earth.

To make a replica of an earth lodge, precut a small square hole in the bottom of a Chinet® bowl. A student inverts the prepared bowl, trims away the outer rim, and cuts an opening for the vestibule. Keeping the bowl inverted, he sponge-paints it using brown tempera paint that contains a bit of glue. Next he presses dried grass, torn bits of paper, or small pieces of unraveled twine atop the painted surface. Then he adds another layer of paint. Last he rolls a brown paper rectangle into a cylinder, inserts it into the opening of the lodge to create a vestibule, and uses glue or tape as needed to secure it in place.

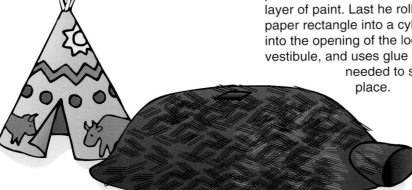

Signs of Communication

The Plains of North America were home to numerous groups of Native Americans, which meant that many different languages were spoken there. As a result, the people of the Plains often used sign language to communicate. Today sign language is still a very important part of Native American culture and tradition, even though spoken language is more often used. Set aside time for students to communicate using traditional Native American sign language. To do this, distribute student copies of the communication card on page 207, pair the youngsters, and challenge partners to silently communicate with each other using the provided gestures. Then bring the class together to discuss the challenges of this type of communication. Later make available *Native American Sign Language* by Madeline Olsen (Troll Associates, Inc.; 1998). This slim paperback offers more than 100 traditional signs for students to learn and use.

A Taste of the Plains

Buffalo was hunted and eaten by all native people of the Plains. It was the main food source on the western Plains, where the land was unsuitable for farming. Wild berries and roots were harvested across the Plains. To the east where the land was fertile, crops of corn, squash, beans, and pumpkins also provided nourishment. Native Americans dried their food to preserve it for year-round eating. For a taste of the Plains of long ago, provide samples of jerky, dried berries, pumpkin seeds, and popcorn for students to eat.

As students enjoy a taste of the Plains, read aloud *Heetunka's Harvest: A Tale of the Plains Indians* by Jennifer Berry Jones (Roberts Rinehart Publishers, 1998). In this beautifully illustrated retelling of a Sioux legend, a greedy woman learns a hard lesson about selfishness.

The Sky Dog

When the horse appeared on the Plains of North America in the 1500s, the lives of the people living there greatly improved. Hunters no longer traveled on foot. Instead they chased down buffalo herds on horseback. More captured buffalo resulted in more food, clothing, and other supplies (see "Buffalo Fact Box" on this page). The horse, respectfully called Sky Dog, Holy Dog, Sacred Dog, and many other names by Native Americans, was believed to be a sacred gift from the Great Spirit.

To further inform students of the importance of the horse, read aloud *The Gift of the Sacred Dog* by Paul Goble (Aladdin Paperbacks, 1984). Then give each child a portion of modeling clay from which to mold a horse shape. While students work, consider reading aloud another enchanting tale from the Plains, such as *The Mud Pony* retold by Caron Lee Cohen (Scholastic Inc., 1992). Invite students to display their clay creations on your tabletop reproduction of the Plains (see "Homes on the Plains" on page 203).

Buffalo Fact Box		
No part of a buffalo was wasted!		
meat	=	food
bones	=	tools, weapons, pipes
intestines	=	cord
hooves	=	jewelry, glue, utensils
horns	=	cups, spoons
hides	=	clothing, moccasins, homes
hair	=	rope, padding

The Vision Quest

One tradition among the people of the Plains was for a boy coming of age to learn of his calling in life during a *vision quest*. At this time, he set out alone, without food or water, for a specific location. Here he prayed that his future be revealed. Tomie dePaola's book *The Legend of the Indian Paintbrush* (PaperStar, 1996) artfully describes this quest through its main character, Little Gopher. Read this story aloud and then challenge students to recall how and why Little Gopher was encouraged to celebrate his unique talents. Next invite students to talk about their special talents or interests. For a thought-provoking follow-up, have each child tear from a brown paper grocery bag a shape that resembles an animal hide. Then ask him to paint on this paper a picture that reflects a special talent or interest. When the paintings are dry, have each child use a marker to sign the bottom of his work. Then display the projects on a bulletin board titled "Painting Our Futures."

The Powwow

The powwow is the oldest North American celebration. Today it continues to be an important expression of togetherness among not only those whose ancestors lived off the Plains, but for all Native Americans. Each year in cities and towns across the United States and Canada, Native Americans from far and near gather to celebrate their culture and share it with non-Native American visitors. Read aloud chosen titles from "Powwow Reading." Next gather students together and ask each child to share one thing he learned about the Native Americans of the Plains. Then, in the tradition of a modern-day powwow giveaway, scatter wrapped candy around the classroom and invite students to collect the candy for eating!

A Reminder About Native American Studies

As you teach about Native American people and their cultures, remember that good information, common sense, thoughtfulness, and sensitivity are your best guides. Always differentiate between the past and the present. Avoid activities that perpetuate stereotypes, such as role-playing or the choosing of "Indian" names. Constantly ask yourself how you are increasing your students' knowledge of these rich cultures and ways of life. And always respect the sacred nature of objects and practices associated with Native American cultures. If you are unsure whether an activity is appropriate, the best thing you can do is consult a Native American for advice.

Powwow Reading

Celebrating the Powwow
Written by Bobbie Kalman
Includes photographs
Crabtree Publishing Company, 1997

Rainy's Powwow
Written by Linda Theresa Raczek
Illustrated by Gary Bennett
Rising Moon, 1999

Powwow
Written & photographed by
    George Ancona
Harcourt Brace Jovanovich,
    Publishers; 1993

*Drumbeat...Heartbeat:
A Celebration of the Powwow*
Written & photographed by
    Susan Braine
Lerner Publications Company,
    1995

A Home on the Plains

Color the map.
First color where the Native Americans of the Plains once lived.
Then color the rest of the map. Use the map key.

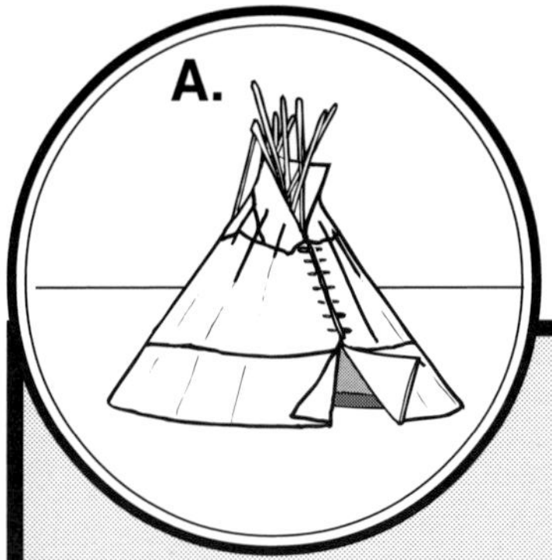

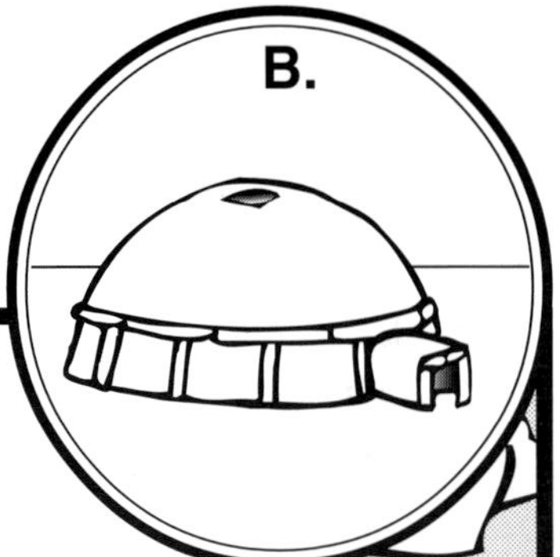

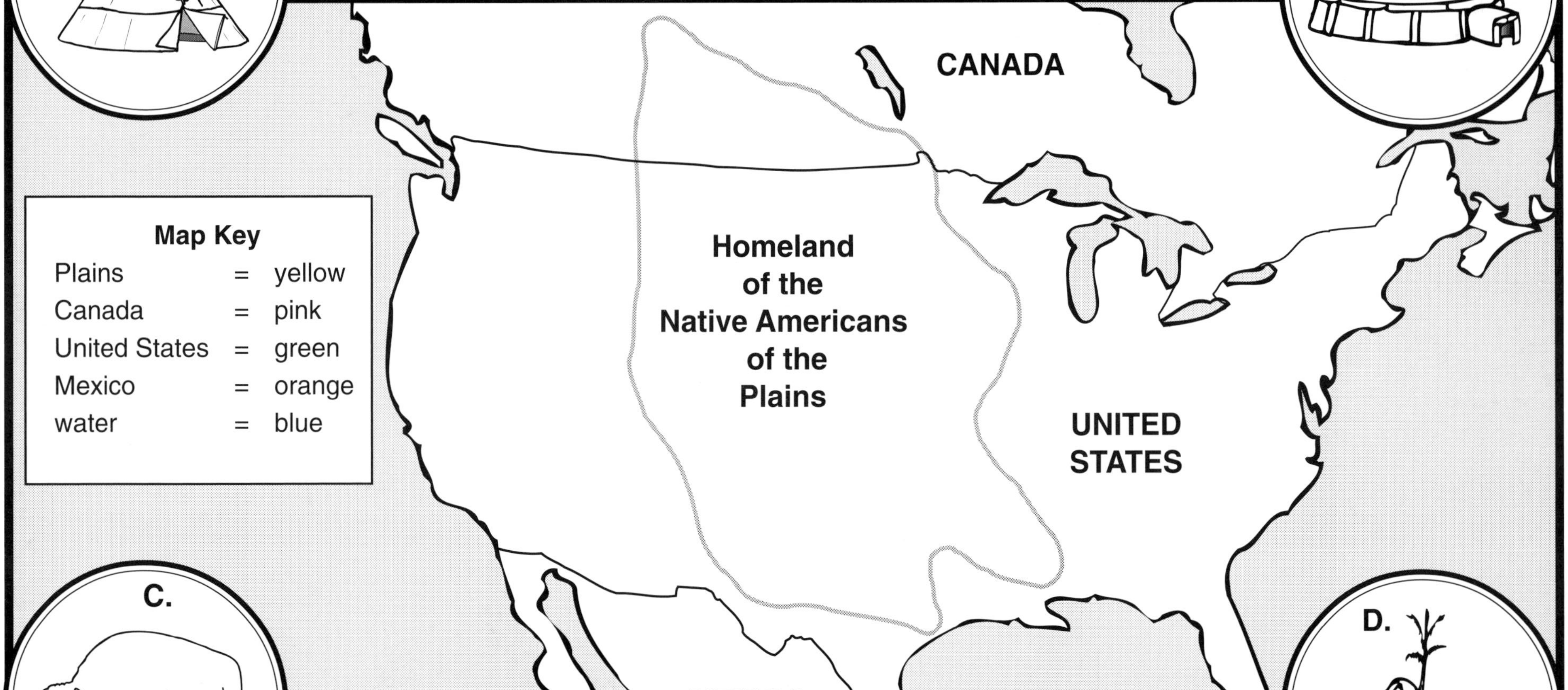

B.

D.

CANADA

UNITED
STATES

Homeland
of the
Native Americans
of the
Plains

MEXICO

Map Key

Plains	=	yellow
Canada	=	pink
United States	=	green
Mexico	=	orange
water	=	blue

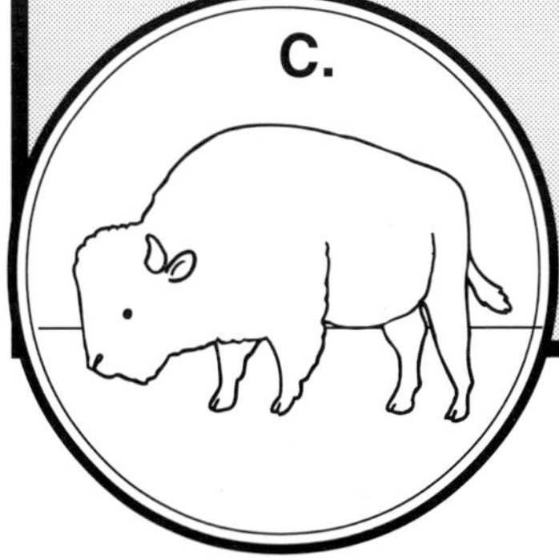

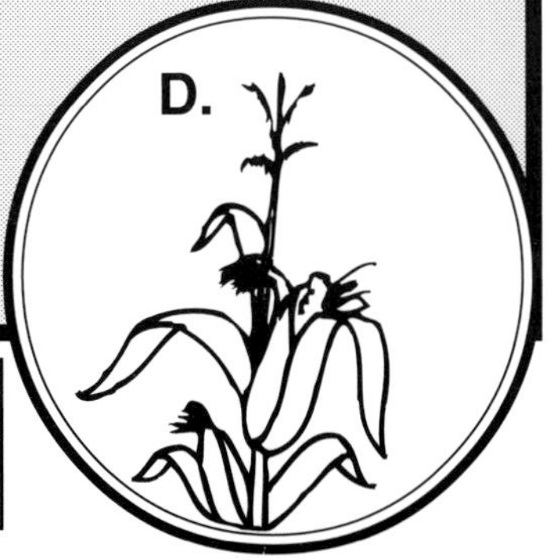

A.

C.

Bonus Box: The item in each circle shows something about the Native Americans who lived on the Plains long ago. Color the pictures. Then choose two of the pictures and on the back of this paper tell how you think they are alike.

©The Education Center, Inc. • *THE MAILBOX® • Primary • Feb/Mar 2000*

Note to the teacher: Use with "Pinpointing the Plains" on page 202.

Pattern and Communication Card

Use pattern with "Homes on the Plains" on page 203 and "Cool Comets" on page 167.

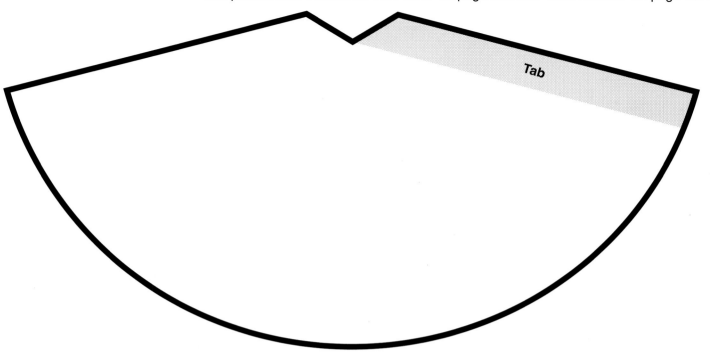

Tab

Use card with "Signs of Communication" on page 204.

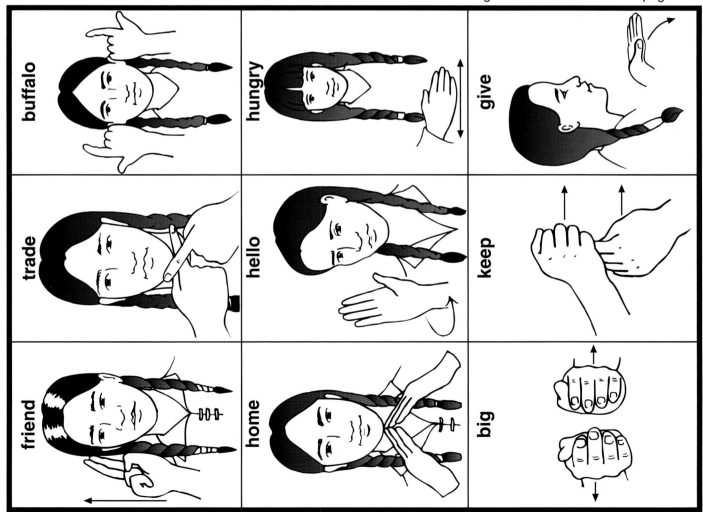

Rx for Earth

Whether you're celebrating Earth Day this April or you're simply looking to give students a healthy dose of environmental awareness, this collection of earth-friendly activities is just what the doctor ordered!

ideas contributed by Njeri Jones Legrand

Explaining Earth Day

Environmental concerns brought about the first Earth Day on April 22, 1970. Its founder, former Senator Gaylord Nelson, wanted people across the country to learn what was happening to the earth's environment. He also wanted to give people a chance to share their ideas for healing the earth. More than 20 million people across the United States participated in the first Earth Day. Today Earth Day is celebrated around the planet by people who care about the future of the earth.

In celebration of the 30th anniversary of Earth Day— April 22, 2000—have each child personalize, color, and cut out a white construction paper copy of the Friend of the Earth certificate on page 212. Tape each child's project atop his desk as an exhibit of his commitment to the earth's environmental future.

Lending a Hand

Spotlight your students' suggestions for improving the environment at this eye-catching display. Mount a large earth cutout and a banner that reads like the one shown. (For a 3-D effect, tuck or tape crumpled newspaper behind the earth cutout before mounting it.) Have each child trace one hand on colorful construction paper, cut along the outline, and then write an earth-saving tip on the resulting shape. After each student reads her tip for the class, tape her cutout to the display. Encourage students to prepare additional cutouts for the display as they learn more ways to lend the earth a hand.

Pam Church—Gr. 1
Weston Elementary
Schofield, WI

Lend the Earth a Helping Hand!

Earth-Friendly Vocabulary

Generate pages of environmental wisdom with daily doses of earth-friendly vocabulary! For each child, staple three or more pages of blank paper between two covers cut from discarded newspaper. Have each child write "[Student's name]'s Book of Environmental Wisdom" on page 1 and add desired decorations. Each day introduce a different word that relates to the earth or its environment (see "Word Bank" for suggestions). Then have each child write and illustrate in his book an earth-friendly tip that includes the featured word. Each day invite students to share the tips they have written. When the project is complete, arrange for each child to read his book of wisdom to a child in a younger class before he takes it home to share with his family.

Word Bank

air
energy
people
plants
animals
fuel
soil
water
clean
recycle
reuse
litter
preserve
oceans
care
world

See page 54 of this book for another project related to recycling!

Museum of Recyclables

Reinforce the importance of responsible recycling at a student-made museum of recyclables. Obtain a list of recycling guidelines from your community. As a class, review the types of items accepted for recycling and the specifications for each, like bundling catalogs, rinsing containers and removing their lids, bagging newspapers, and so on. Then assign a different small group of students to prepare an exhibit of properly prepared materials for each type of recyclable (aluminum, newspaper, office paper, etc.). Have the groups showcase their exhibits in a designated area of the classroom. Invite each child to take one or more students from neighboring classes (or other friends and family members) on a tour through this one-of-a-kind museum!

Reuse It!

Here's a trash-related challenge that encourages creative thinking and earth-friendly behavior! In advance ask each student to bring to school a clean piece of trash that is nonperishable and odor-free. Remind students that reusing items is an effective way to reduce trash. Then challenge each youngster to determine how her item can be reused! In conclusion, have each child show the class her discarded item, explain its original use, and describe how it can be reused. Now that's a show-and-tell session with an important environmental message!

Saving Energy

Conserving energy is an easy way to contribute to a healthier earth. Tell students that the United States uses more energy per person than any other nation in the world. Entertain reasons for this and then ask students to name different ways they use the earth's energy. List their ideas on a length of bulletin board paper. Next give each child an enlarged copy of the pig pattern from page 42. Have her draw a coin slot near the top of the pig, cut out the resulting piggy bank, and list on the shape three or more different ways her family can save energy. Then ask her to take home her energy-saving plan and challenge her family to put it into action. Every few days invite different students to report to the class the positive results of their energy-saving plans.

1. Keep the front door closed.
2. Watch less TV.
3. Turn off lights in a room that no one is in.
4. Do not hold the refrigerator door open.
5. Be on time for the school bus so my mom doesn't have to drive me to school.

A Rising Temperature

Having a fever is no fun—not even for the earth! Tell students that scientists are concerned that the earth's temperature is slowly rising due to increased levels of carbon dioxide in the air. Explain that this gas enters the air each time a person breathes. It is also produced by factories, cars, power plants, and numerous other man-made sources. Help students hypothesize environmental effects of a hotter earth *(weather changes that result in fewer food crops, decrease in wildlife, flooding caused by melting glaciers, etc.).* Then reveal the good news—plants take carbon dioxide out of the air and put oxygen back in! Discuss with students the important role that plants play in the well-being of the earth. Then, in conclusion, give each child a copy of the prescription form from page 212 and ask him to prescribe treatment for the condition "Rising Temperature." Staple a pack of seeds for planting to each child's work before sending it home!

Healthy Habitats

Nursing the earth's habitats back to health is an important environmental issue to address with students. Visually divide the chalkboard into thirds and label the resulting sections "Air," "Land," and "Water." Ask students to name specific ways these environments become polluted. Write their suggestions under the appropriate headings. Next ask students to name wildlife that lives in each environment. List these suggestions in the appropriate columns, too. Then lead students to the conclusion that pollution impacts the welfare of wildlife. For a fun follow-up, give each child a 6" x 18" strip of light blue construction paper to fold in half two times. Then have him unfold his paper to reveal four boxes. Instruct him to round the corners of the top box, label the four boxes as shown, and then illustrate three healthy and thriving habitats. To complete his project, he flips it over and on the back of each pictured habitat writes one or more tips for keeping it healthy.

Earthly Adoption

To maintain student interest in the environment, propose that they adopt an area of the school grounds for the remainder of the school year. After discussing the responsibility of the commitment, ask each child to complete a copy of the earthly adoption certificate on page 212. Then help the students plan and carry out activities that reflect their compassion for the earth. Activities might include cleaning up litter and debris, planting grass or flowers, and providing earth-friendly wildlife feeders. Plan to photograph the students as they work to make the earth a better place!

Jill Higgins—Gr. 1
Eagle River, AK

Earth Saver Solutions

Wrap up your study of the environment by asking each child to design a quilt patch that shows his dedication to taking care of the earth. To do this, he completes and illustrates each sentence starter on a copy of page 213. He colors the border and the earth character, and then he cuts along the bold lines. Collect the projects and mount them on a bulletin board backed with cut-apart paper grocery bags that have been previously used and then donated for this purpose. Use a marker to draw stitches around each patch. Happy Earth Day!

Heather Godwin—Gr. 1
Kemptown Elementary School
Monrovia, MD

Earth Day Web Connections

The Earth Day Groceries Project, 2000
http://www.earthdaybags.org
This site describes a kid-pleasing project that involves obtaining a supply of paper grocery bags from a local grocer. After students decorate the bags with environmental messages, you return them to the supermarket for distribution on Earth Day 2000!

Earth Day Every Day
http://www.earthday.wilderness.org/
This site is a great resource for Earth Day information. Be sure to check out "Kid's Stuff" and "Teacher's Lounge."

Kid's Domain: Earth Day
http://www.kidsdomain.com/holiday/earthday/
Designed especially with kids in mind, this site includes games, songs, activities, coloring pages, word searches, and more. A brief explanation of Earth Day is also included.

Cyndee Perdue Moore
Danville, VA

Certificates and Form

Use with "Explaining Earth Day" on page 208.

Use with "Earthly Adoption" on page 211.

_____
(name)

is a

Friend of the Earth!

©2000 The Education Center, Inc.

Adopt a Piece of Earth!

I, _____,
(name)

agree to adopt a piece of earth.

I promise to do my best to keep the land healthy and free from pollution.

_____
signature

_____
date

©2000 The Education Center, Inc.

Use with "A Rising Temperature" on page 210.

Get-Well Prescription

Patient: _____Earth_____

Condition: _____Rising Temperature_____

Treatment: _____

_____

_____

_____

_____

_____

_____

To help keep the air clean,
I will

To help keep the water clean,
I will

Designed by _____

To reduce garbage,
I will

To beautify the earth,
I will

Note to teacher: Use with "Earth Saver Solutions" on page 211.

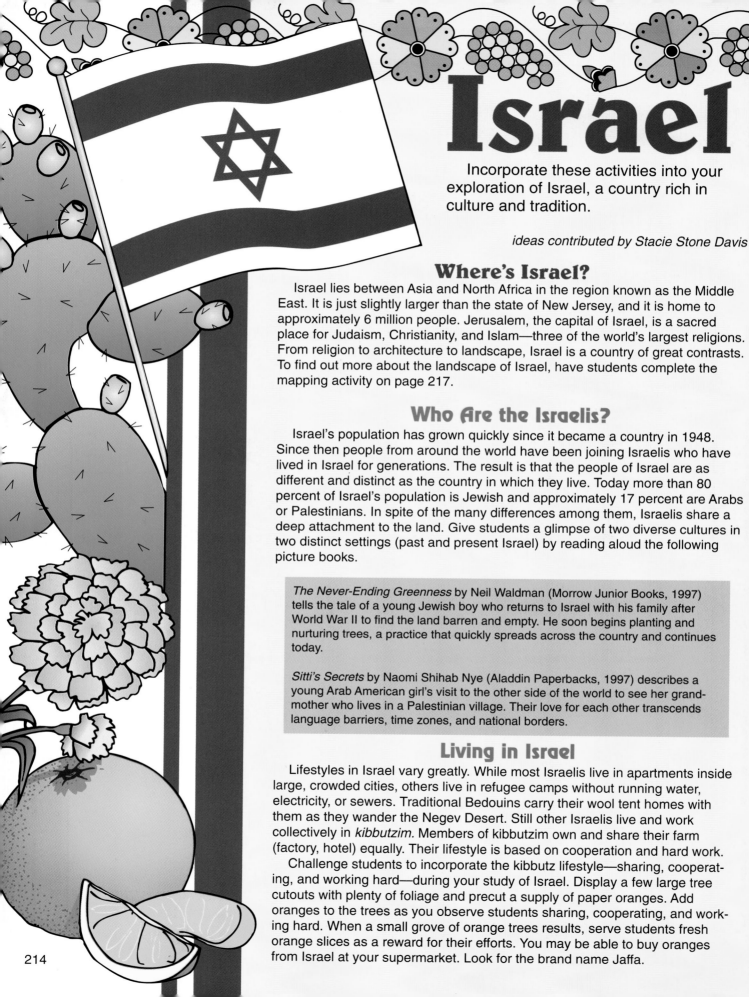

Israel

Incorporate these activities into your exploration of Israel, a country rich in culture and tradition.

ideas contributed by Stacie Stone Davis

Where's Israel?

Israel lies between Asia and North Africa in the region known as the Middle East. It is just slightly larger than the state of New Jersey, and it is home to approximately 6 million people. Jerusalem, the capital of Israel, is a sacred place for Judaism, Christianity, and Islam—three of the world's largest religions. From religion to architecture to landscape, Israel is a country of great contrasts. To find out more about the landscape of Israel, have students complete the mapping activity on page 217.

Who Are the Israelis?

Israel's population has grown quickly since it became a country in 1948. Since then people from around the world have been joining Israelis who have lived in Israel for generations. The result is that the people of Israel are as different and distinct as the country in which they live. Today more than 80 percent of Israel's population is Jewish and approximately 17 percent are Arabs or Palestinians. In spite of the many differences among them, Israelis share a deep attachment to the land. Give students a glimpse of two diverse cultures in two distinct settings (past and present Israel) by reading aloud the following picture books.

The Never-Ending Greenness by Neil Waldman (Morrow Junior Books, 1997) tells the tale of a young Jewish boy who returns to Israel with his family after World War II to find the land barren and empty. He soon begins planting and nurturing trees, a practice that quickly spreads across the country and continues today.

Sitti's Secrets by Naomi Shihab Nye (Aladdin Paperbacks, 1997) describes a young Arab American girl's visit to the other side of the world to see her grandmother who lives in a Palestinian village. Their love for each other transcends language barriers, time zones, and national borders.

Living in Israel

Lifestyles in Israel vary greatly. While most Israelis live in apartments inside large, crowded cities, others live in refugee camps without running water, electricity, or sewers. Traditional Bedouins carry their wool tent homes with them as they wander the Negev Desert. Still other Israelis live and work collectively in *kibbutzim*. Members of kibbutzim own and share their farm (factory, hotel) equally. Their lifestyle is based on cooperation and hard work.

Challenge students to incorporate the kibbutz lifestyle—sharing, cooperating, and working hard—during your study of Israel. Display a few large tree cutouts with plenty of foliage and precut a supply of paper oranges. Add oranges to the trees as you observe students sharing, cooperating, and working hard. When a small grove of orange trees results, serve students fresh orange slices as a reward for their efforts. You may be able to buy oranges from Israel at your supermarket. Look for the brand name Jaffa.

Lots of Languages

Hebrew and Arabic are Israel's official languages, and both appear on Israeli money and stamps. Other languages, including English, are also spoken there. It is not uncommon for Israeli school children to learn three different languages—Hebrew, Arabic, and English! During your study of Israel, teach students the provided words in Hebrew and Arabic. Then have them put the words into practice—using Hebrew words before lunch and Arabic words after lunch, or vice versa!

English	Hebrew	Arabic
hello	shalom	marhaba
yes	ken	na' am
no	lo	la
please	bevakashah	min fadlak
thank you	todah	shoukran

Souvenir Scrolls

There are oodles of interesting facts about Israel, and this hands-on project inspires students to seek out eight of them! Hand out copies of page 218, and have students color each illustration and discover its importance to Israel. Invite students to work together if desired, or lead them through the activity using the answer key on page 313. Then have each student cut along the bold lines and glue strip B to the bottom of strip A. To make a scroll, a student uses markers or crayons to decorate the ends of two empty toilet tissue rolls labeled A and B. Next, he glues each end of his paper strip to the appropriate tube, keeping the illustrations to the inside. When the glue dries, he rolls the paper onto the tubes and uses a large paper clip to hold the tubes together. Last, he ties a two-foot length of cloth or curling ribbon around his project for the trip home!

Camel

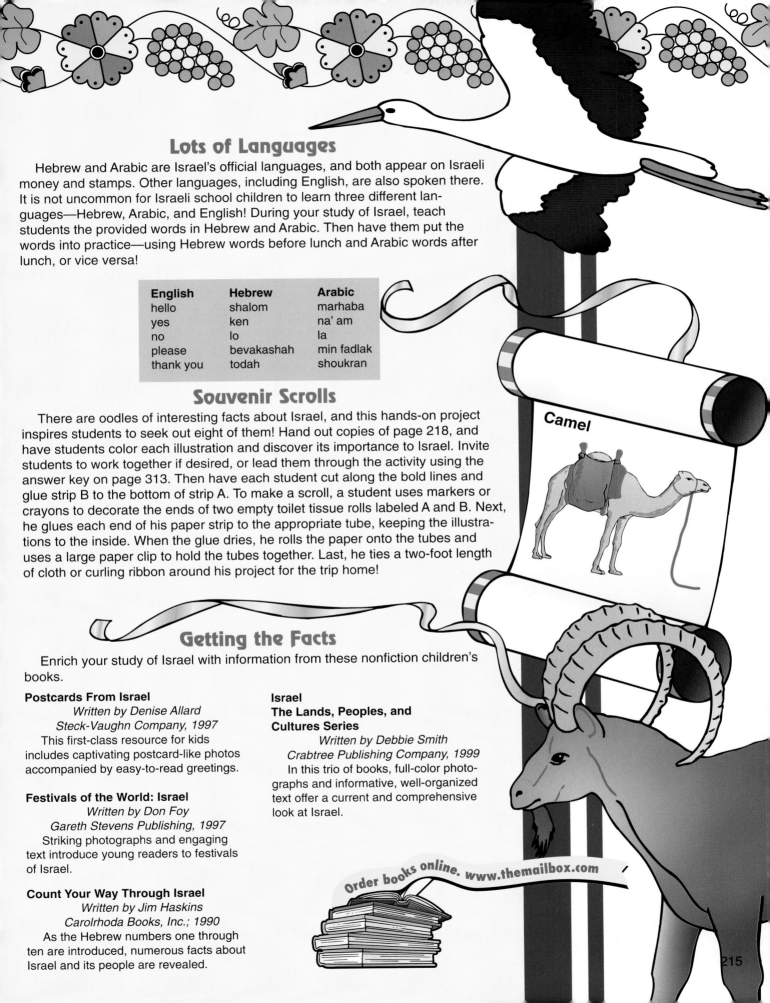

Getting the Facts

Enrich your study of Israel with information from these nonfiction children's books.

Postcards From Israel
Written by Denise Allard
Steck-Vaughn Company, 1997
This first-class resource for kids includes captivating postcard-like photos accompanied by easy-to-read greetings.

Festivals of the World: Israel
Written by Don Foy
Gareth Stevens Publishing, 1997
Striking photographs and engaging text introduce young readers to festivals of Israel.

Count Your Way Through Israel
Written by Jim Haskins
Carolrhoda Books, Inc.; 1990
As the Hebrew numbers one through ten are introduced, numerous facts about Israel and its people are revealed.

Israel
The Lands, Peoples, and Cultures Series
Written by Debbie Smith
Crabtree Publishing Company, 1999
In this trio of books, full-color photographs and informative, well-organized text offer a current and comprehensive look at Israel.

Order books online. www.themailbox.com

Look, No Hands!

Birthday parties are held all over the world, and Israel is no exception! *Bli Yaadaim* (blee yah-DIE-eem), or Without Hands, is a popular birthday party game in Israel and is sure to be a hands-down favorite with your students. To play, group students into teams of four or five players. Have each team form a straight line as the players hold on to an extended jump rope with both hands. Then, on the floor in front of each player, place a paper party hat. On a signal from you, the team players work together to put on their hats—without using their hands! Players may use their feet, heads, arms, wrists, or teeth. However, if a team member uses his hands or drops the rope, his team is disqualified. The first team wearing party hats wins!

Holidays and Festivals

In Israel, hardly a month goes by without some kind of holiday or festival. Explain that most special days in Israel are based on the lunar calendar, which means that the dates of the celebrations change each year. Ask students what they would like the best (least) about this practice. Then teach them the steps to a famous dance in Israel. After all, the best way to celebrate Israeli holidays and festivals is to sing and dance!

The Hora

The hora is danced to any music with two beats per measure. After students have learned the steps, have them form a circle and dance to music!

Dance steps:
1. Step to the left with your left foot.
2. Cross your right foot behind your left.
3. Step to the left with your left foot.
4. Hop on your left foot and swing your right foot across the front of your left foot.
5. Step in place with your right foot.
6. Hop on your right foot and swing your left foot across the front of your right foot.
7. Repeat steps 1–6.

A Taste of Israel

There is a large variety of food and cooking styles in Israel. However, some foods make it to most every table. *Pita,* a flat pocket-like bread, is sold everywhere in Israel. It may be stuffed and eaten as a sandwich or used to scoop up spreads such as *hummous,* a combination of spices and mashed chickpeas. Fresh fruits and vegetables grown in Israel are also common at meals. These include citrus fruits, apples, pears, bananas, avocados, tomatoes, and cucumbers. For a kid-pleasing taste of Israel, ask parent volunteers to prepare and serve pint-size pita sandwiches (one-quarter of a pita), sliced apples and bananas, and lemonade. Delicious!

216

A Sliver of Land

Answer each question about Israel.
Use the map and map key.

1. What four countries border Israel?

   _____

   _____

   _____

   _____

2. What sea borders Israel to the west?

   _____

3. What is the capital city?

   _____

4. What is the tallest mountain?

   _____

5. What body of water is deepest?

   _____

6. What supplies the most fresh water?

   _____

7. Do you think the Dead Sea has fresh water? _____ Explain your answer.

   _____

   _____

   _____

8. Is there a desert in Israel? _____

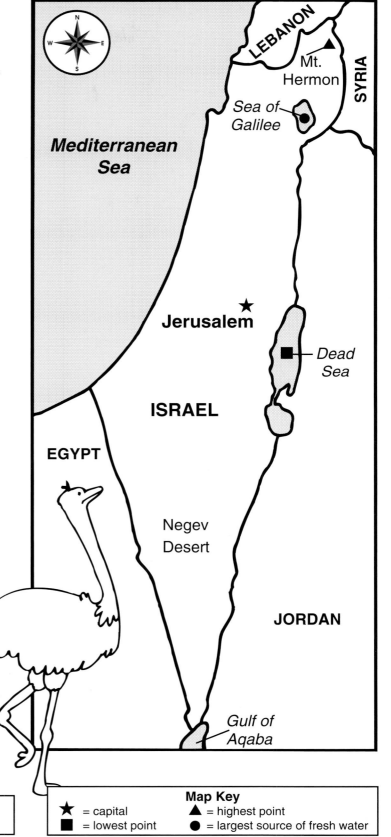

Bonus Box: Color the map. Color all water blue. Then color each country a different color.

Map Key

★ = capital   ▲ = highest point

■ = lowest point   ● = largest source of fresh water

©The Education Center, Inc. • *THE MAILBOX®* • *Primary* • Dec/Jan 1999–2000 • Key p. 313

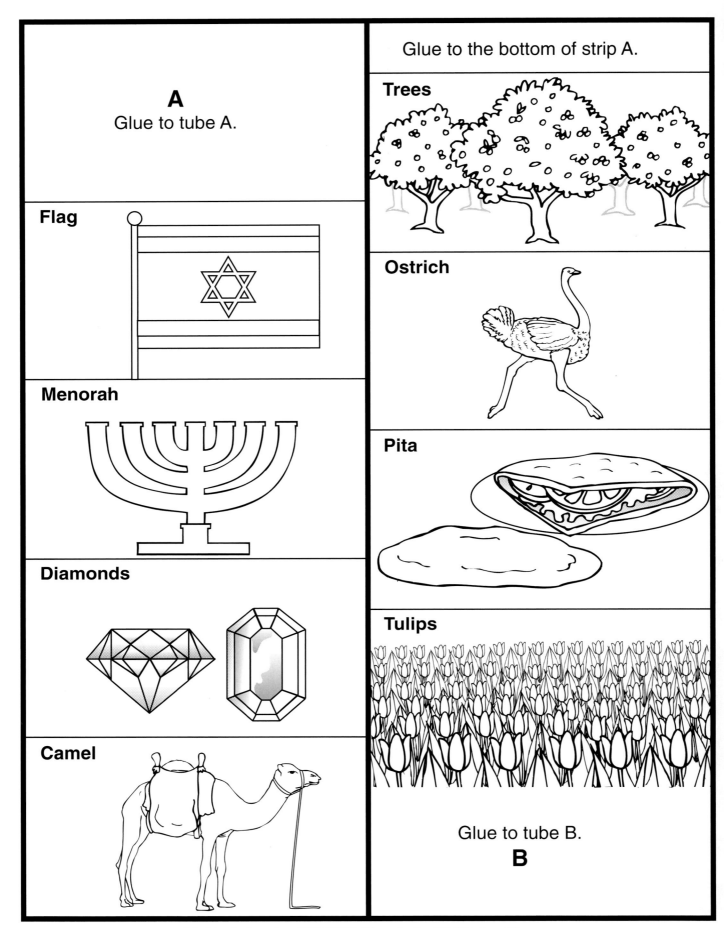

A
Glue to tube A.

Glue to the bottom of strip A.

Flag

Menorah

Diamonds

Camel

Trees

Ostrich

Pita

Tulips

Glue to tube B.
B

SEASONAL UNITS

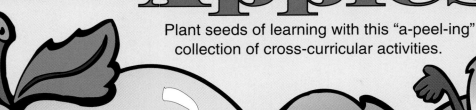

'Tis the Season for... Apples

Plant seeds of learning with this "a-peel-ing" collection of cross-curricular activities.

WRITING
Apple Autobiographies

Students will have a bushel of fun completing this writing activity! In advance label apple cutouts (one for every two students) with get-acquainted questions. Cut each apple shape into four or five pieces and store each puzzle in a sandwich bag. To begin, pair students and give every twosome a puzzle. Students also need pencils and writing paper. Each pair assembles its apple puzzle and reads the question together. Then each child answers the question on her paper in the form of a complete sentence. On a signal from you, the pair rebags its puzzle and passes it to the next twosome along an established route. Continue in this manner until all questions have been answered by all pairs. Ask each student to read her resulting autobiography to the class. You'll learn about your new crop of youngsters and they'll learn about each other!

Jennifer Neimann—Gr. 2
Hempstead Accelerated School, St. Louis, MO

SCIENCE
From Seed to Tree

It's hard to imagine that something as small as an apple seed can grow into a tree! As students handle apple seeds, explain that the hard surface of each seed, called the *seed coat,* protects a baby plant inside. When a seed is planted and watered, its seed coat breaks open and a tiny root grows downward, followed by a stem and leaves *(seedling)* growing upward. The stem of the seedling eventually becomes the trunk of the apple tree! To reinforce this amazing transformation, have each child fold a 3" x 18" strip of drawing paper in half, three consecutive times, and then unfold his paper to reveal eight small boxes. In the first box he illustrates a just-planted apple seed and in the last box an apple-bearing tree. On the remaining boxes he illustrates a succession of stages that occur between the two pictured events. To create a tiny seed booklet—which also has a tree inside—have each child accordion-fold his project and glue it between two identical seed cutouts.

LANGUAGE ARTS
Apple-O

An apple tree only blooms in spring, but you can keep your students' vocabulary skills blooming year-round with this lotto-type game! Write a student-generated list of apple words on the chalkboard. Give each child a copy of page 222 and Apple Jacks® cereal pieces (20 or more) to use as game markers. Have him draw and color an apple or worm in one gameboard space (to make a free space) and then copy a different word from the chalkboard in each remaining space. Announce the game to be played, such as Four Across, Four Down, Four Corners, or Apple-out. Play the game like lotto. A student declares "Apple-O!" when he believes he's won. Play as many games as desired. Then have each child complete the Bonus Box activity as he munches on his game markers.

Frances McCann—Gr. 3
Tabernacle Primary School
Tabernacle, NJ

Psst! Be sure to check out " 'Apple-tizing' Prints" on page 47 of this book and "Apple Decor" on page 298. Most scrumptious!

220

MATH
Seed Estimations

This small-group activity gets to the core of estimation! Ask each group to study a different apple and estimate how many seeds are inside. Then have each group share its estimate and explain the reasoning behind it. Next reveal that most apples, regardless of type or size, contain five to ten seeds. Ask students how this knowledge can be used to estimate the total number of seeds in the groups' apples. After some discussion, have the groups count off by fives and then by tens. Write both numbers on the chalkboard and lead students to conclude that the total seed count should be between these two numbers. Record an estimate from each group, then give each child a napkin and a plastic knife. Slice each group's apple and distribute the slices among the members. Each child uses his plastic knife to remove any seeds from his slice(s). On the chalkboard record a seed count for each group's apple, then total these numbers for a class count. Give the group with the closest estimate a round of applause. Now it's time to eat those apples!

COOKING
Mmm...Mmm...Good!

Top off your apple studies with a tasty snack that's healthful *and* "apple-lutely" delicious! Serve with apple cider, if desired.

Apple Nut Crunch
(makes approximately 24 servings)

Ingredients:
13 small apples, peeled, seeded, and thinly sliced
1 1/3 cups peanut butter
1/3 cup honey
1/3 cup water
1 1/2 cups granola

Directions:
1. Stir honey into peanut butter, then add water and mix thoroughly.
2. Add apples and stir until apples are coated.
3. Spoon mixture into muffin cups lined with foil liners.
4. Sprinkle with granola.
5. Bake at 300° for 30 minutes or until the apples are tender.

Beverly Bippes—Gr. 1
Humphrey Public School
Humphrey, NE

READING
A Bushel of Books

Tempt your students' taste buds with this scrumptious selection of apple literature!

What's So Terrible About Swallowing an Appleseed?
Written by Harriet Lerner and Susan Goldhor
Illustrated by Catharine O'Neill
HarperCollins Juvenile Books, 1996

Apple Picking Time
Written by Michele Benoit Slawson
Illustrated by Deborah Kogan Ray
Dragonfly Books™, 1998

The Seasons of Arnold's Apple Tree
Written & Illustrated by Gail Gibbons
Harcourt Brace & Company, 1984

Albert's Field Trip
Written & Illustrated by Leslie Tryon
Atheneum, 1993

Apple Trees
Written by Dorothy Hinshaw Patent
Photographs by William Muñoz
Lerner Publications Company, 1997

SOCIAL STUDIES
Postcards From Johnny

Who better to help students polish their mapping skills than Johnny Appleseed? As you read aloud a story that outlines Johnny's travels, have student volunteers tape small apple seed cutouts to a U.S. map to show his westward progression. (*Johnny Appleseed* retold by Steven Kellogg [Morrow Junior Books, 1988] is a good choice for this activity.) Then pose map-related questions for students to answer, like "What states are directly north of Johnny's home state?" and "If Johnny had continued westward, what state would he have traveled through next?" Next have each child draw and color a scene from Johnny's travels on the unlined side of a large index card. Then have him turn his card over, imagine that he is Johnny, and write a brief note describing how his travels are going. If desired, also have him copy a make-believe mailing address and render an apple-related postage stamp on this side of the card. Hole-punch the resulting postcards and secure them on a metal ring. Now there's a class publication that students will pick to read time and again!

Dear Nathaniel,
I am living in Ohio. I have planted apple trees across the whole state! I love helping my neighbors. And I love telling tales to the young'uns. I hope you are doing fine, brother. Come see me!
Love,
Johnny

Nathaniel Chapman
123 Apple Lane
Longmeadow, MA 98765

Lisa Striecker—Gr. 3
St. Paul Elementary School
Highland, IL

Apple-O

Bonus Box: Write one word from your gameboard on the line above. In the circle draw and color a picture that shows what the word means. On the back of this paper, write the word in a sentence.

Note to teacher: Use with "Apple-O" on page 220.

The Pick of the Crop

A Book of Apples

by _____

1

_____ is a dark red apple. It is sweet and crisp. This apple tastes good fresh. **(s e l c D i i o u)**

2

_____ is a red apple with yellow or green marks on it. This apple is good to use when baking. **(o m e R u y B t a e)**

3

_____ is a bright red apple. It tastes good fresh. **(c l M t h o s n)**

4

_____ is a golden yellow apple. It tastes good fresh. It is good for baking, too. **(d G l o n e o l c D s e i i u)**

5

McIntosh

Golden Delicious

Rome Beauty

Granny Smith

Delicious

_____ is a bright green apple. This apple tastes good fresh. It is also good for baking. **(r n y a G n m h i S t)**

6

©The Education Center, Inc. • THE MAILBOX® • Primary • Aug/Sept 1999

To the teacher: Duplicate on white construction paper. Instruct each child to write his name on booklet page 1 and the name of an apple on each remaining booklet page. To discover each apple name, the student refers to the work as he unscrambles the letters in the parentheses. Next he reads the sentence and colors the corresponding apple as described. To assemble his booklet, he cuts on the dotted lines. Then he staples the

'Tis the Season for...
Turkeys

Add some extra gobble to the Thanksgiving season with these fine-feathered activities.

VOCABULARY
Turkey Terms

Learning turkey-related vocabulary has never been more "egg-citing"! Trim the top eight inches from a class supply of brown paper lunch bags. Also duplicate eight or more turkey egg patterns from page 226 onto manila paper for each child. Explain that a female turkey, or *hen,* builds a simple nest on the ground and lays from 8 to 18 brown-speckled eggs inside. Next have each child write "hen" and its turkey-related meaning on an egg pattern, cut out the shape, and then decorate it with brown crayon speckles. Give each child a paper bag nest in which to store her egg. Challenge each student to program and decorate seven or more vocabulary eggs for her nest during your turkey investigation.

Be sure to check out "Gobblin' Great Spelling!" on page 10 of this book and "Gobbler Greetings" on page 49!

SCIENCE
A Treeful of Turkeys

As this project takes shape, students learn interesting facts about the nighttime habits of wild turkeys. First have each child use a wide paintbrush to paint a purple watercolor wash on a sheet of art paper. When the projects are dry, ask each child to cut a moon shape and a tree trunk with plenty of branches from construction paper and then glue the cutouts to her painted backdrop. Tell students that a wild animal they are currently studying sleeps in trees like these. When wild turkeys are identified, have each child cut several small silhouettes of snoozing turkeys from black construction paper and glue them perched on the branches of her tree. As students work, explain that a turkey usually sleeps in the same tree night after night. If the tree is really big, an entire flock may be sleeping there!

LISTENING
Hear! Hear!

The ears on a gobbler cannot be seen, but that doesn't mean the bird can't hear. In fact turkeys hear so [well] that it's almost [impo]ssible to sneak [up on] them! This bit of [trivia w]ill surely moti-

[Three Turkeys in a Row — Tommy — Turkeys / Following directions]

[yo]ungsters to be all ears during this listening and following-[direction]s activity! Each child needs a pencil, crayons, and a copy [of "Three] Turkeys in a Row" from page 226. To complete the ac-[tivity, read] a series of oral directions for the students to follow. [Direction]s include "Draw a blue line under the second turkey," ["Color the] tail feathers on the first turkey red," and "Give the [third one a]n orange beak." Collect and check the completed [papers for a]ccuracy or have each child compare his trio of tur-[keys to a cla]ssmate's gobblers.

Note: Write names in the ar[ea...] apple names to the large cutout in order. pages to the large cutout in order.

Colorful Calculations

When it comes to colorful feathers, the *tom,* or male turkey, steals the show! And that's exactly what these math-fact gobblers will do! Give each child a white construction paper copy of the patterns on page 227. A student colors and cuts out the patterns, leaving the circles white. He glues the tail feathers to the turkey and then he writes a different addend from 0 to 9 in each small circle. Next he writes a plus sign and a selected addend in the large circle. Feather by feather, he adds the addend on the feather to the one on the body; then he bends the tip of the feather forward and writes the sum. Check the projects for accuracy. Next pair students and have each child, in turn, orally answer every fact on his partner's turkey. When he answers correctly, his partner gobbles quietly! Students will be eager to trade turkeys with several classmates. Gobble! Gobble!

Ellen Weiss, Fort Lauderdale, FL

Turkey to the Rescue!

Wild turkeys have many talents. They can fly fast—up to 50 miles per hour. They can fly high—clearing the tops of 80-foot trees. They can run fast—up to 25 miles per hour. Wild turkeys also have exceptional eyesight and hearing. And, in the right conditions, a turkey's gobble can be heard from up to one mile away! For a fun creative writing activity, have students incorporate the many talents of a wild turkey into tall tales titled "Wild Turkey to the Rescue!" Ask each child to illustrate his turkey tale before he shares it with the class. Whoa! That's some turkey!

Lip-Smacking Snack

With all the talk about turkeys, your little gobblers are sure to work up quite an appetite. And even though this lip-smacking snack is not authentic food fare for turkeys (like small nuts, seeds, insects, and berries), it's doubtful that you'll hear a single complaint!

For one lip-smacking gobbler:

prepared chocolate icing
1 vanilla wafer
1 Rolo® candy, unwrapped
5 pieces of candy corn
1 chocolate chip
1 red hot candy

Directions:
1. Spread a layer of icing on the vanilla wafer.
2. Holding the wafer on its edge, press the bottom of the Rolo® candy into the icing and then arrange the candy corn as shown.
3. Use dabs of frosting to attach the chocolate chip head and the red hot wattle.

Candi Deal—Gr. 1, Westwood Elementary, Dalton, GA

Turkey Tales

Satisfy your youngsters' cravings for turkey-related literature with these kid-pleasing titles.

Fiction

'Twas the Night Before Thanksgiving
Written & illustrated by Dav Pilkey
Orchard Books, 1990

Sometimes It's Turkey—Sometimes It's Feathers
Written & illustrated by Lorna Balian
Humbug Books, 1994

A Turkey for Thanksgiving
Written by Eve Bunting
Illustrated by Diane de Groat
Clarion Books, 1995

Gracias the Thanksgiving Turkey
Written by Joy Cowley
Illustrated by Joe Cepeda
Scholastic Press, 1998

The Turkey Saves the Day
Written by Shelagh Canning
Illustrated by Doug Cushman
Troll Associates, Inc.; 1997

Nonfiction

All About Turkeys
Written & illustrated by Jim Arnosky
Scholastic Press, 1998

Wild Turkeys
Written by Dorothy Hinshaw Patent
Photographs by William Muñoz
Lerner Publications Company, 1999

Order books online.
www.themailbox.com

Patterns

Use the egg patterns with "Turkey Terms" on page 224.

Use "Three Turkeys in a Row" with "Hear! Hear!" on page 224.

Turkeys
Following directions

Three Turkeys in a Row

Name _____

Grin and... Teddy Bear It!

Pick and choose from this irresistible collection of curriculum-related activities. Just bear in mind that by adding these teddy bear touches to your teaching, a good time is sure to be had by all!

SOCIAL STUDIES
Teddy Who?

So how did the teddy bear gets its name? Ask students to share their ideas on the matter before revealing that it was named after Theodore "Teddy" Roosevelt, the 26th president of the United States! Explain that in 1902 the president, who liked to hunt, refused to shoot a bear because he felt it had been unfairly cornered. When a husband and wife living in New York learned about the president's actions, they decided to make and sell stuffed bears. With the president's approval, they called their creations "Teddy's Bears." Eventually the name was shortened to teddy bear. For a fun follow-up, list the names of several past presidents on the chalkboard and invite students to determine what the teddy bear might have been called if, for example, Harry S. Truman had been the president for whom this beloved stuffed toy was named. Students will have a great time and, in the process, learn the names of several past presidents!

Joan Jones
New York, NY

For more about the history and popularity of teddy bears, read *Teddy Bears* by Arlene Erlbach (Carolrhoda Books, Inc.; 1997).

PHONICS
Teddies in the Tub

Rub-a-dub-dub—there are cubs in these tubs! Students will have plenty of good clean fun at this sorting center. For an activity that reinforces short-vowel sounds, copy the set of three teddy bears and a tub from page 232 on different colors of light-colored construction paper. Label each tub for a different short-vowel sound; then label three different-colored teddies to correspond with each tub. Laminate the patterns for durability and cut them out. For self-checking, label the backs of the patterns in each matching set (one tub and three cubs) with the same symbol. Then store the cutouts in a plastic bag at a center. A student sorts the teddy bears into the tubs and then she flips each set of cutouts to check her work. Bear in mind that these cubs and tubs can be programmed for a variety of sorting skills!

bat   pan   mad

ă

POETRY
Alphabet Bears

Set the stage for plenty of creative expression by reading aloud *Alphabears: An ABC Book* by Kathleen Hague (Henry Holt and Company, Inc.; 1991). In this delightful book, rhyming text and adorable teddy bears introduce the letters of the alphabet. At the conclusion of the book, write on the chalkboard a student-generated list of teddy bear names from *A* to *Z*. Then choose a name from the list (or another name) and model for students how to write a rhyming poem that begins "[Alphabet letter] is for [teddy bear name]…" Have each child copy the sample poem on writing paper and then turn over his paper. Then help each child choose a different name from the posted list and have him write it on the back of his paper. Instruct each child to take home his paper and, with the help of a parent, compose a poem for the teddy bear name he selected.

To make an adorable bear booklet, key the completed poems into a computer and print each one at the bottom of a different page (see the illustration). Have each child illustrate his poem. Then compile the pages in alphabetical order between a construction paper cover titled "Teddy Bears From *A* to *Z*." If students can't bear the thought of not having personal copies of the teddy bear book, consider taking the project to a local printer for duplication.

Susie Shaw—Gr. 1
Harding Avenue Elementary School
Blacksburg, VA

E is for Edwar
A slam-dunking bear,
Who jams with one paw,
And flies through the air.

If is for Freckles,
My furry-faced friend.
He never likes playtime
To come to an end.

ART
Pudding Prints

If the proof is in the pudding, then this multisensory art activity is a sure bet! Give each child a white construction paper copy of the teddy bear pattern on page 233 and a large paper towel. Have each child cut out her pattern and lay it on the paper towel. Then, while students wash and dry their hands, place a large spoonful of chocolate pudding on each child's cutout. Instruct students to fingerpaint their cutouts using the special paint. As students work, have them verbally describe how the special paint feels, looks, sounds, and smells. Next ask students how they think this special paint might taste. Help them identify the paint as chocolate pudding and then suggest that for cleanup they lick the pudding from their fingers! When the projects are dry, have students use wallpaper and construction paper scraps to decorate their bears. For a perfect poetry-writing follow-up, see "Sensory Poems" on page 284 of this book.

Michelle Williams—Gr. 1
Meadow Lane Elementary School
Olathe, KS

COMMUNICATION
Good News!

It's a "bear" fact that good news bears repeating! To spread good news about your students and their teddy bear studies, keep on hand a supply of the form on page 232. Each day complete a form for each of several students. To assure that each child receives a weekly note of praise, program a class set of notes each week. No doubt students will find it quite easy to bear up under this additional positive praise!

LETTER WRITING
Here and There

Where, oh where, is that Travel Bear? For this letter-writing activity, students become armchair travelers! Over the course of several days, arrange for a stuffed bear named Travel Bear (any bear will do) to spend an allotted amount of time with each child. During her time with the bear, a child imagines taking a trip anywhere in the world with Travel Bear in tow. Then, in a friendly letter written to the class, she describes the imaginary trip from Travel Bear's point of view.

To publish the letters, give each child a legal-size envelope on which to illustrate a postage stamp and write an invented return address and the school's mailing address. Then have her cut away the envelope flap, glue the back of the envelope to the center of a 9" x 12" sheet of drawing paper, and decorate the page to reflect her trip with Travel Bear. Fold and tuck each child's letter inside her completed page and bind the pages into a "bear-y" special book titled "Around the World With Travel Bear."

Donna B. Six—Gr. 2
Osceola Elementary
St. Augustine, FL

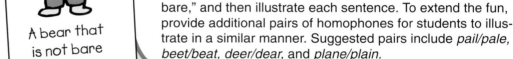

VOCABULARY
A Bare Bear?

Along with providing a good giggle, this quick lesson helps students get their bearings with homophones! Present the homophones *bare* and *bear*. As a class, discuss how the words are similar (pronunciation) and different (spelling, meaning). Next have each child label the left half of a sheet of drawing paper "A bear that is bare" and the right half "A bear that is not bare," and then illustrate each sentence. To extend the fun, provide additional pairs of homophones for students to illustrate in a similar manner. Suggested pairs include *pail/pale, beet/beat, deer/dear,* and *plane/plain.*

Joan Jones
New York, NY

SCIENCE
Teddy Bear Toast

This "paws-on" investigation of primary and secondary colors takes a delicious teddy bear twist! For easy management, prepare a painting center for small-group visitation. Thoroughly mix equal parts of sugar and water in each of three clean and empty margarine tubs. Use food coloring to tint the sugar-water in each container a different primary color. Place the containers at the center along with a class supply of sliced white bread, paper napkins, and several empty containers for mixing colors. Then, for each child visiting the center at one time, provide a clean, thin paintbrush and a container of rinse water. Working atop a napkin, a student paints a teddy bear and other desired decorations on a slice of bread. Encourage each group of students to make additional paint colors by mixing different primary colors in the empty containers. Toast the bread after everyone has taken a turn painting and serve it with milk. As students eat their snacks, invite them to share what they learned about the colors red, yellow, and blue!

Darcy Soule—Gr. 1
Thomas Jefferson Elementary
Newton, IA

MATH
Teddy Bear Estimation

Students may think for a moment that these activities bear a slight resemblance to math, but it's doubtful! Choose four estimation activities that relate to teddy bears. For example, students can estimate the number of Gummy Bears® candies in a jar, the circumference of a teddy bear's belly, the height of a teddy bear, and the number of eyes, ears, or paws in a group of several teddy bears. Present each activity in a different corner of your classroom. Have each child divide his paper into fourths and label each section for a different station. Then divide the students into four groups and rotate the groups through the stations along a predetermined route. Each child records his estimates on his paper. When the students have returned to their desks, enlist their help in counting, measuring, or calculating the answer for each station. Ask each child to compare his estimate to the agreed-upon answer. Now that's math that's bearable!

Joan Jones
New York, NY

WRITING
Teddy Bear Biographies

Every teddy bear has a life story! Tell students that a biography is a true story written about someone's life. Then give each child a copy of page 234 and ask her to write a "bear-y" special biography about her favorite teddy bear (or other stuffed toy). To do this she writes the name of her stuffed toy on the top line and illustrates the toy in the provided circle. Next she writes a corresponding fact in each box. Then she signs her name and writes the date. For added fun, organize a Teddy Bear Tea and invite each child to bring her stuffed toy to school for the special event. Serve teddy bear tea (milk) and Teddy Grahams® crackers. Then ask each child to introduce her stuffed toy and share a few facts from the biography.

READING
Teddy Bear Bookshelf

There are numerous teddy bear books available for your students' reading and listening pleasure. If your bookshelf is missing any of these teddy bear titles, be sure to check them out!

Elmer and the Lost Teddy
Written & illustrated by David McKee
Lothrop, Lee & Shepard Books; 1999

My Friend Bear
Written & illustrated by Jez Alborough
Candlewick Press, 1998
(Also by the same author: *It's the Bear!*
and *Where's My Teddy?*)

The Tangerine Bear
Written by Betty Paraskevas
Illustrated by Michael Paraskevas
HarperCollins Publishers, Inc.; 1997

The Million-Dollar Bear
Written by William Kotzwinkle
Illustrated by David Catrow
Alfred A. Knopf, Inc; 1995

Order books online. www.themailbox.com

231

Patterns and Form

Use the teddy bears and tub with "Teddies in the Tub" on page 228.

Use with "Good News!" on page 229.

Good News Bears Repeating!

For: _____   Date: _____

The good news is _____

_____

_____

A "Bear-y" Special Biography
about

_____

First Memory	**Favorite Place**	**Best Friend**
Best Character Trait		**Favorite Memory**
Only Bad Habit	**Interesting Fact**	**Favorite Activity**

Written by _____   **Date** _____

Leap Into Learning

"Pond-ering" a way to include leap year in your lesson plans? Try these "toad-ally" terrific ideas!

by Amy Erickson

Making Sense of Leap Year

Why does February have 29 days in the year 2000? The answer lies in the earth's orbit. One year equals 365 days; however, it really takes the earth about $365\frac{1}{4}$ days to travel around the sun. Every four years the quarter days are combined and a day is added to February. The year with the extra day is called leap year. Why? No one really knows for sure, though the name may have originated long ago when the English courts did not recognize February 29 and the date was "leaped over" in the records. Share this fascinating information with students, and then give each child a copy of page 236 to complete. (See "Note to teacher" at the bottom of page 236 for programming instructions.)

A "Ribbet-ing" Pattern

Count on this idea to get students thinking ahead *and* exploring number patterns. Write the current leap year on the chalkboard. Then, with input from your students, list below this date in consecutive order the next ten leap years. Ask students to study the numbers and describe any patterns they see. When students identify a number pattern in the ones column, circle each set of repeating numbers (0, 4, 8, 2, 6). Then, with your students' help, continue the pattern by listing additional leap year dates. For more practice with number patterns, have each child write on his paper how old he is on February 29, 2000, and then continue to write the age he will be on each consecutive leap year until he discovers a number pattern!

Clevell Harris

Leap Year Potpourri

These fun-filled language arts activities are sure to have youngsters learning by leaps and bounds!

- To boost vocabulary skills, write a student-generated list of synonyms for *leap.* Then have each child write and illustrate a silly leap year story that includes several of the synonyms.
- Pose this question to students: If a person is born on February 29, when should she celebrate her birthday each year? Have each student write a persuasive paragraph to support her idea.
- Invite each child to design an original birthday card for February 29 birthdays.
- Have each child keep an hour-by-hour journal of how she spends her time on February 29.

Name _____

Pond Pals

Leaping Larry wants to visit Hopping Harry on February 29.
To complete his leap year path, skip-count by 4s.
Write each number in order.

Bonus Box: On the back of this sheet, write a story about a frog that forgot how to leap.

©The Education Center, Inc. • THE MAILBOX® • Primary • Feb/Mar 2000

Note to teacher: Make one copy of this page and program it by writing a desired number on the first lily pad. Give each student a copy to complete.

'Tis the Season for...
Mittens

There's no doubt about it—after you and your students try this cross-curricular unit, you'll be smitten with mittens!

ideas contributed by Vicki Mockaitis Dabrowka and Laura Wagner

WRITING
Warm Up to Winter!

Showcase warm thoughts with this marvelous mitten display! To begin, have youngsters brainstorm ways to keep warm in cold weather, and record their responses on the chalkboard. Then give each student two copies of the blank mitten on page 240. A child cuts out his mittens and places them on his desk so that the thumbs point to each other. On one mitten, he writes and completes the sentence "To warm up on a snowy day…" He illustrates his sentence on the other mitten. Next the youngster glues each mitten onto colored construction paper. He cuts around each shape, leaving a narrow border. Then he tapes one end of a length of yarn at the bottom of each mitten and glues bits of cotton to each cuff. Display the mittens with the title "Warm Up to Winter!" Now that's a handy way to pair writing and illustrating!

To warm up on a snowy day, I drink hot chocolate with marshmallows.

CRITICAL THINKING
"Thumbody" Was Thinking!

Why are mittens designed to keep thumbs free? Challenge students to find out with this hands-on partner activity. First, write on the chalkboard a student-generated list of activities that require the use of hands, such as sharpening a pencil and tying a shoelace. Next give each student pair a mitten and a sock. The twosome chooses three of the activities from the list. Then each partner tries each one—first with the sock on his dominant hand and then with the mitten on his dominant hand. Ask each student pair to share what it discovered. Then invite youngsters to tell why they think mittens have separate thumbholes. Lead students to conclude that thumbs help people grasp objects and make precise movements. When mittens were invented, "thumbody" was really thinking!

PHYSICAL EDUCATION
Snowball Catch

Cooped up inside for recess? Then energize your youngsters with a quiet flurry of activity! Roll together two white socks to create a ball. Ask one student to be the scorekeeper for the first round. Instruct each remaining student to put on a pair of mittens and form a large circle. Explain that for this game, students must be silent—just like falling snow. To play, the students toss the ball to each other as many times as they can without dropping it, while the scorekeeper silently counts the catches. When a student drops the ball, the scorekeeper announces the total number of catches. Then she and the last student who successfully caught the ball switch roles. Continue with additional rounds for a blizzard of fun!

237

MATH
Mitten Math

Mittens and math go hand in hand with these skill-based ideas!

- **Problem Solving:** Give each student four blank mitten patterns (page 240) to cut out. Have her color two red and two blue. Then ask the youngster to use the cutouts to solve this problem: *How many ways can two red mittens and two blue mittens be lined up on a clothesline? Draw pictures or write a list to show as many ways as you can.*

- **Skip Counting:** Invite students to predict how many mitten pairs are needed for a class supply. Then give each student two copies of the small mitten pattern (page 240) to color and cut out. Each student, in turn, glues her mitten cutouts onto a long paper strip and writes the cumulative total of mittens below her pair. Have students compare the final total with their predictions. Then display the strip throughout the season for a handy skip-counting reference.

LANGUAGE ARTS
A Picture-Perfect Retelling

A mitten unit wouldn't be complete without the traditional tale *The Mitten*. Use Jan Brett's enchanting version for this picture-perfect retelling activity. To prepare, visit Brett's Web site at www.janbrett.com/index.html and print from the postcard page an enlarged picture of each character from *The Mitten*. Then copy a class supply of each one. Next read aloud Brett's *The Mitten: A Ukrainian Folktale* (G. P. Putnam's Sons, 1989) and give each youngster a set of character pictures. A child cuts out each picture, mounts it on construction paper, and cuts it out again. Then he tapes a tongue depressor to the back of each cutout to create a stick puppet. Pair students and have each partner take a turn retelling the story. Then, if desired, arrange for each student to retell the tale for a child in a lower grade.

COOKING
Mouthwatering Mittens

Here's a fitting (and yummy!) recipe for your mitten study. To add an extra special wintry touch, serve with hot chocolate. Mmm!

Mouthwatering Mitten Cookies

For one cookie:
a personalized 5" square of foil
3/8" slice of refrigerated sugar-cookie dough*
various cookie decorations (colored sprinkles, mini baking chips, raisins)
ungreased baking sheet

Directions:
1. Working on the foil, gently shape the slice of cookie dough into a mitten shape.
2. Decorate the cookie.
3. Place the project on the baking sheet and bake as directed.

* One roll of dough makes approximately 24 cookies.

Pam Crane

238

You always share.

Carl

Mitten Messages

What better way to celebrate individual differences this winter than with warm fuzzies? On white construction paper, copy a class supply of the blank mitten pattern on page 240. Label one for each child. Remind students that everyone has unique skills and talents. Also explain that complimenting a person on his special gifts is often described as giving the person a warm fuzzy. Then, as you distribute the mitten patterns, ask each student to secretly design a warm fuzzy for the classmate whose mitten he receives. (Make sure no child has his own.) To do this, a student writes a positive note about the classmate on the mitten and then he cuts out the shape. Next he colors the blank side of the cutout and decorates it with cotton. Ask each student to secretly deliver the warm fuzzy to his classmate's desk within a designated number of days. You can be sure each recipient will glow with pride and happiness.

Looks Like Mitten Weather!

Compare temperatures across the United States with this graphing activity. Make a class-size graph and label it with the names of several large cities from across the nation and a series of upcoming dates. Help students locate each city on a U.S. map. Next have them predict which cities might have below freezing temperatures for the featured dates. Draw and color a small mitten shape near the name of each selected city.

Each day, have different students use a newspaper or visit a weather Web site such as http://cirrus.sprl.umich.edu/wxnet to determine the temperature in each city. Have them record the temperatures on the graph and then draw and color a mitten shape in each box that shows a below freezing temperature. After the graph is completed, ask students to analyze the data and compare it with their predictions. Then help them draw conclusions about winter temperatures in different parts of the country.

	Jan. 10	Jan. 11	Jan.12	Jan. 13	Jan. 14
Miami, FL	57°F	60°F	58°F		
Topeka, KS	30°F	29°F	35°F		
New York City, NY	20°F	19°F	19°F		
Dallas, TX	45°F	45°F	47°F		
Seattle, WA	29°F	27°F	26°F		

Wintry Reading

Invite students to cozy up to these mitten-related titles!

The Mitten Tree
Written by Candace Christiansen
Illustrated by Elaine Greenstein
Fulcrum Publishing, 1997

Gabby Growing Up
Written by Amy Hest
Illustrated by Amy Schwartz
Simon & Schuster Books for Young Readers, 1998

A Christmas Star
Written by Linda Oatman High
Illustrated by Ronald Himler
Holiday House, Inc.; 1997

The Woodcutter's Mitten: An Old Ukrainian Tale
By Loek Koopmans
Crocodile Books, USA, 1995

Order books online. www.themailbox.com

Mitten Patterns

Use with the ideas on pages 237–239. Also use the small mitten patterns with "Mitten Matchup" on page 33.

Missing Mittens

Oh, no! The kittens have lost their mittens.
Help the kittens find them.
Read the clues.
Color the mittens.

Puff's mittens have
- a fluffy trim
- stripes
- no dots

Color them red.

Tiger's mittens have
- stars
- a string
- no stripes

Color them blue.

Snowball's mittens have
- stripes
- stars
- no dots

Color them yellow.

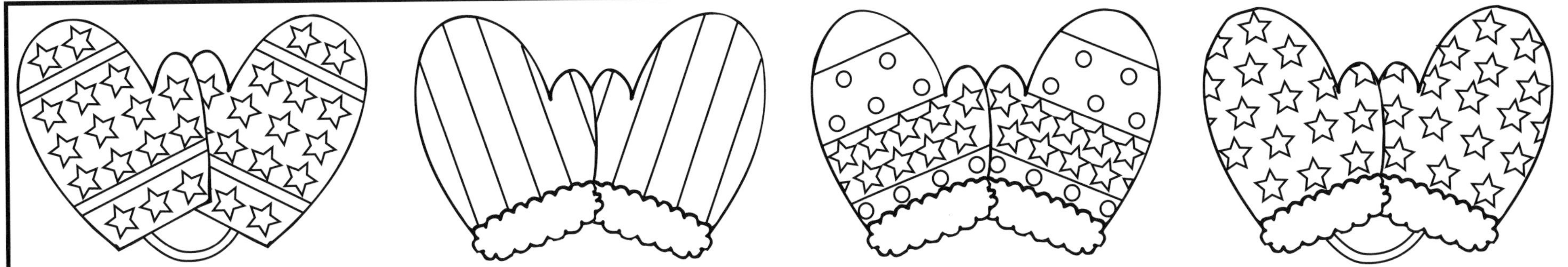

A.

B.

C.

D.

Bonus Box: Color the extra mittens any color you choose. On another sheet of paper, write three sentences to describe them. Think about who might own them. Then draw and color a picture of the owner.

A Man and His Dream

Use these engaging activities to teach students about a remarkable American who dreamed that one day there would be peace and justice for all.

Martin Luther King Jr.

Provide students with a snapshot of the boyhood, adult life, and dreams of Martin Luther King Jr. by reading aloud one or more of the following books:

Happy Birthday, Martin Luther King • Written by Jean Marzollo • Illustrated by J. Brian Pinkney • Scholastic Inc., 1993
A Picture Book of Martin Luther King, Jr. • Written by David A. Adler • Illustrated by Robert Casilla • Holiday House, Inc.; 1991
Martin Luther King Day • Written by Linda Lowery • Illustrated by Hetty Mitchell • Carolrhoda Books, Inc.; 1987

Speaking Out

Dr. King felt that it was his responsibility, or duty, to speak out against violence. Ask students why they think he felt this way. Help them understand that the safety and well-being of the world is everyone's responsibility, and that every person can contribute to making a positive difference. Invite students to share any concerns they have about the world. List their ideas on the chalkboard. Then ask each child to choose one concern from the list and design a poster that speaks out against it. Remind students that when Dr. King spoke out, he always provided peaceful solutions. Ask students to do the same. After each child has presented his poster to the class, showcase the messages around the school.

Festive Timelines

In celebration of Dr. King's birthday (the third Monday in January), have each child make a festive four-event timeline of his life. To make a timeline, fold a 3" x 12" strip of drawing paper in half twice; then unfold the paper to reveal four equal sections. Leaving a half-inch margin at the top of the strip and working in chronological order from left to right, label each section with a different event.

To transform the project into a birthday cake look-alike, accordion-fold the strip and decorate the front of the folded project to resemble a birthday cake. Next cut out four candle flames from scrap paper and glue them to the tops of four 1/2" x 2" construction paper strips to make lit candles. Unfold the timeline and glue one candle to the top of each section, positioning the candles so that when the project is refolded, each one is visible. Now that's a timeline that's even better than a piece of cake!

Happy Birthday, Dr. King!

In 1929 Martin Luther King Jr. was born in Atlanta, Georgia.

In 1953 Martin got married to Coretta Scott.

In 1963 he gave a speech in Washington, DC, about his dream for the future.

In 1968 Martin Luther King Jr. was killed.

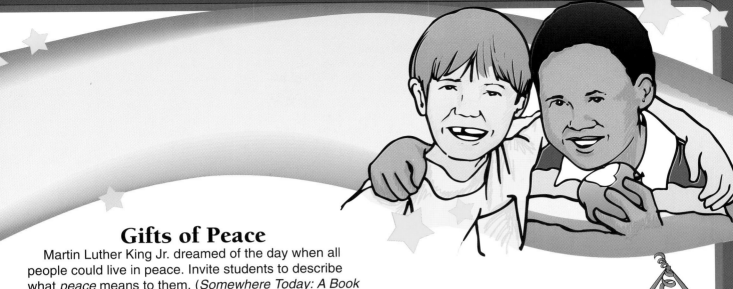

Gifts of Peace

Martin Luther King Jr. dreamed of the day when all people could live in peace. Invite students to describe what *peace* means to them. (*Somewhere Today: A Book of Peace* by Shelley Moore Thomas [Albert Whitman & Company, 1998] is an exceptional book that is perfect for prompting thoughts of peace and reinforcing the concept of nonviolence.) Encourage plenty of discussion and accept all answers. Then, on provided paper, have each child describe and illustrate one gift of peace that she would give the world. Invite each child to share her gift with the class. Then collect the papers and publish them in a class book titled "Our Gifts of Peace."

Our Gifts of Peace

I would give the gift of listening to one another.

Sherry

Footsteps to Follow

When Martin Luther King Jr. graduated from college, he decided to become a minister just like his father. Explain to students that because Martin admired his father so much, he was proud to follow in his footsteps. Ask each student to label a colorful footprint pattern with the name of a person she admires and hopes to grow up to be like. After she cuts out the pattern, have her copy, complete, and illustrate the sentence "When I am older I hope to follow in the footsteps of [name or description of person] because..." Display the completed projects on a bulletin board titled "Footsteps We Hope to Follow."

Grandpa Keller

When I am older I hope to follow in the footsteps of Grandpa Keller because he helps sick kids. He is a doctor.

Keeping the Dream Alive

Dr. King's dream included freedom, peace, and understanding. He dreamed that one day all people would love and help each other. Review Dr. King's dream with the class and challenge students to explain how they can contribute to keeping it alive. Help them realize the impact that their thoughts and actions have on his dream. Next give each child a copy of page 244 and a 6" x 18" strip of red or blue construction paper. To complete the project, a child writes an ending for each sentence and colors the portrait of Dr. King. Then he cuts along the bold lines, positions the pieces on his construction paper in a pleasing manner, and glues them in place. If desired, have each child hole-punch the top of his project, thread a length of curling ribbon through the holes, and tie the ribbon ends. Suggest that each child display his project at home to remind him of the important role that he plays in keeping Dr. King's dream alive!

A Man With a Dream

Martin Luther King Jr.

Dr. King dreamed that all people would love each other and help each other. _____ 1.

He also hoped that people would not fight. _____ 2.

I can keep his dream alive by being nice to others and not fighting. _____ 3.

Learning about Dr. King has taught me that it is good to have a dream. He also taught me that being mean is dumb. _____ 4.

Order books online.
www.themailbox.com

Martin Luther King Jr. Project

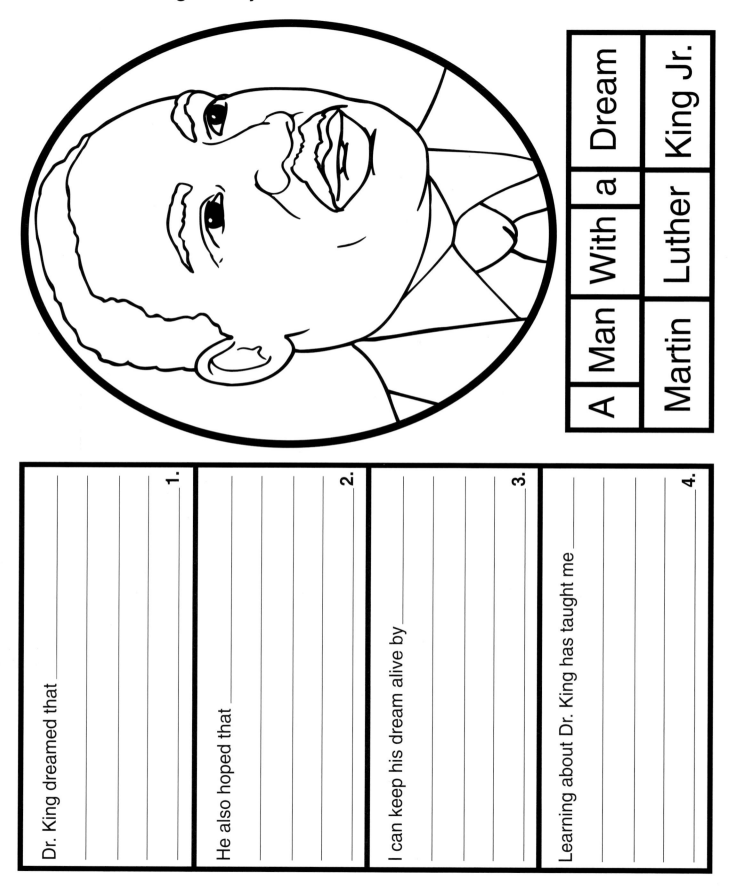

A	Man	With	a	Dream
Martin		Luther		King Jr.

1. Dr. King dreamed that _____

2. He also hoped that _____

3. I can keep his dream alive by _____

4. Learning about Dr. King has taught me _____

Note to teacher: Use with "Keeping the Dream Alive" on page 243.

Black History Month by the Numbers

Harriet Tubman

This clue-filled math activity leads to countless facts about famous Black Americans! And what better time to uncover this information than February, Black History Month? Each day of your study, post a different math problem that has an answer related to a significant fact in black history (refer to "Notable Numbers" below). Provide time for students to solve the problem. At the end of the day, invite volunteers to share their solutions. After verifying the answer, explain the significance of this number in relation to Black History Month. If desired, enlist students' help to find additional number-related facts about famous Black Americans and create corresponding math problems. For more learning fun, modify this idea to introduce or review other desired topics.

adapted from an idea by Laura Covell
St. Joseph Child Development Center, Kansas City, MO

$11-5=6$ $1+2+3+0=6$ $2\times3=6$ $510-504=6$ $2\times4-2=6$ $4+2=6$ $12\div2=6$

Martin Luther King Jr.

Notable Numbers

1: On December 1, 1955, Rosa Parks refused to give up her seat on a public bus. As a result, Parks became a key figure in the Civil Rights movement.

6: On April 6, 1909, Matthew Henson was the first Black American to reach the North Pole. Henson accompanied Robert Peary on the expedition to this site.

8: Mae Carol Jemison orbited the earth in the space shuttle *Endeavour* for 8 days. She was the first Black American woman in outer space.

11: Mary McLeod Bethune was 11 years old before a school was opened near her home and she was able to attend. As an adult, she dedicated her life to the education of blacks and created Bethune-Cookman College.

15: Martin Luther King Jr. was only 15 years old when he entered college. He worked hard to end segregation and promote peace.

17: Duke Ellington was 17 years old when he wrote his first song. He became a great jazz composer who has had a lasting influence on the field of music.

23: June 23 is Wilma Rudolph Day in Tennessee. After overcoming physical disabilities, Wilma Rudolph won three gold medals in the 1960 Olympics track-and-field events.

24: Thurgood Marshall served as a Supreme Court justice for 24 years. He was the first Black American on the U.S. Supreme Court.

26: Rebecca Lee Crumpler was 26 years old when she entered medical school. She became the first Black American woman to become a doctor.

44: Hank Aaron's baseball uniform number was 44. Aaron hit 755 home runs during his career in the major leagues.

100: Basketball player Wilt Chamberlain was the first player to score 100 points in one NBA game. Chamberlain was named the NBA's Player of the Decade for 1957–1966.

300: Harriet Tubman took 300 slaves to freedom using the Underground Railroad. Many years later, a postage stamp was designed in her honor, making her the first Black American woman to have her picture on a stamp.

Mary McLeod Bethune

Matthew Henson

Hearts

Use these sweet cross-curricular activities to celebrate Valentine's Day *and* the holiday's most popular symbol—the heart!

SCIENCE
A "Heart-y" Tune

When it comes to teaching how a heart works, this little ditty and follow-up can't be beat! Explain that a heart is a muscle. The top half lets in blood through tubes called *veins*. Then the blood goes to the bottom half where it is pumped out through *arteries*. Every time a heart beats (60–100 times per minute), it sends blood to other parts of the body. Lead students in the song shown below; then place a bucket of water, a squeak toy, and a supply of paper towels (for drying hands) in a center. Arrange for two students to visit the center at one time. To represent a beating heart, one student holds the toy under the water. He squeezes and releases the toy as his partner slowly counts to 60 (to equal approximately one minute). Then the partners switch roles. With this hands-on idea, students are sure to realize how hard a heart works!

Heather Graley
Eaton, OH

A "Heart-y" Tune
(sung to the tune of "The Farmer in the Dell")

My heart is a muscle.
My heart is a muscle.
It's a pear-shaped muscle
That's the size of a fist.

My blood goes in through veins,
My blood goes in through veins,
Into the atria,
My blood goes through the veins.

Arteries take my blood,
Arteries take my blood,
Out of the ventricles,
Arteries take my blood.

LANGUAGE ARTS
Rebus Writing

Looking for a picture-perfect Valentine's Day card project? Try this! Display a rebus (see the example), and read it with students' help. Explain that a message that uses pictures in place of some words is called a *rebus*. Then have each student make a Valentine's Day rebus card for a loved one. To make her card, a youngster cuts a heart from a nine-inch construction paper square. She colors and cuts out selected patterns from a copy of page 248. Then the student glues them onto her heart cutout, adding words or letters to complete her message. She glues the cutout inside a construction paper card and embellishes the card as desired before delivering it. No doubt students will lose their hearts to this fun-filled style of writing!

Jill D. Hamilton
Ephrata, PA

MATH
The Price of Love

Deliver mouthwatering math practice with this "cent-sational" idea! Draw and label a chart; then write the numbers 1 through 10 as shown. Give each student a paper plate and 20 heart candies. Tell students that each candy represents 10¢. Then have each youngster place two candies on his plate. Explain that two candies represent the cost of mailing one Valentine's Day postcard (20¢). Write this information on the chart. Next, have each student use his candies to determine the postage for each listed set of postcards, in turn, up to six postcards. Record the answers on the chart. Then ask each youngster to study the chart and predict the costs of sending the remaining sets of postcards. Have him use his candies to verify his predictions for each set. Add each answer to the chart; then invite students to snack on their candies. For more fun with valentine postcards, see page 249.

Jill D. Hamilton

Number of Postcards	Cost
1	.20
2	.40
3	.60
	.80

SOCIAL STUDIES
A Legendary Holiday

Get to the heart of Valentine's Day with a class book project! Invite students to share their ideas about the origin of this holiday, explaining that no one knows for sure how it began. Next ask each student to write and illustrate a legend that tells how he thinks Valentine's Day started. If desired, have him mount his legend on a sheet of paper that he has sponge-painted with holiday colors. After each youngster reads his legend aloud, share the age-old legends that are provided. Then bind the students' projects into a class book titled "Getting to the Heart of Valentine's Day."

Age-Old Legends About the Origin of Valentine's Day
- Long ago, the Roman emperor did not allow marriages. A priest named Valentine defied the emperor and married young couples. After Valentine died, the holiday was named for him.
- When a man named Valentine was jailed in ancient Rome because of his religious beliefs, his friends sent him notes. Valentine's Day was later established in his honor.
- Once there was a holiday for Juno, queen of the Roman gods and ruler over marriage. This day was celebrated as a holiday of love.

ART
Zany Heart Zoo

Heart-shaped lions and tigers and bears—oh, my! This zany art activity rounds up lots of creativity. Divide students into small groups and provide scissors, glue, and a selection of colored construction paper. Challenge the students in each group to use heart shapes cut from the provided paper to create a large likeness of an animal of their choice. Display the critters on a wall with the title "Welcome to the Zany Heart Zoo!" Invite students to use colored paper to create zoo scenery, too. For a "pawsitively" delightful extension, ask each youngster to pen a tale about how these hearty critters celebrate Valentine's Day.

Helen Hawkins
Beverly Gardens School
Dayton, OH

CHARACTER EDUCATION
Friendly Thoughts

Everyone knows Valentine's Day is a time to express affection. But deciding *how* to do that can put youngsters in a quandary. Help students solve the problem with this flowery display. First, brainstorm ways to communicate affection to a friend. Then have each student make a construction paper flower with heart-shaped petals as shown. Have him write "I like you" on the center of the flower and a way to express affection on each petal. Display students' projects with the provided poem, and watch confidence in developing friendships blossom!

Martha Kelly
Roanoke, VA

Smile.

Give a Valentine's Day card.

I like you.

Give a compliment.

Share.

Roses are red,
Violets are blue.
Here are some good ways
To say "I like you!"

READING
Books With Heart

Your youngsters are sure to fall in love with these heartwarming and humorous holiday books!

Hearty Har Har: Valentine Riddles You'll Love
Written by Katy Hall and Lisa Eisenberg
Illustrated by R. W. Alley
HarperFestival, 1997

Somebody Loves You, Mr. Hatch
Written by Eileen Spinelli
Illustrated by Paul Yalowitz
Aladdin Paperbacks, 1996

The Valentine Bears
Written by Eve Bunting
Illustrated by Jan Brett
Clarion Books, 1985

Roses Are Pink, Your Feet Really Stink
Written & Illustrated by Diane deGroat
Mulberry Books, 1997

Rebus Patterns

Use with "Rebus Writing" on page 246.

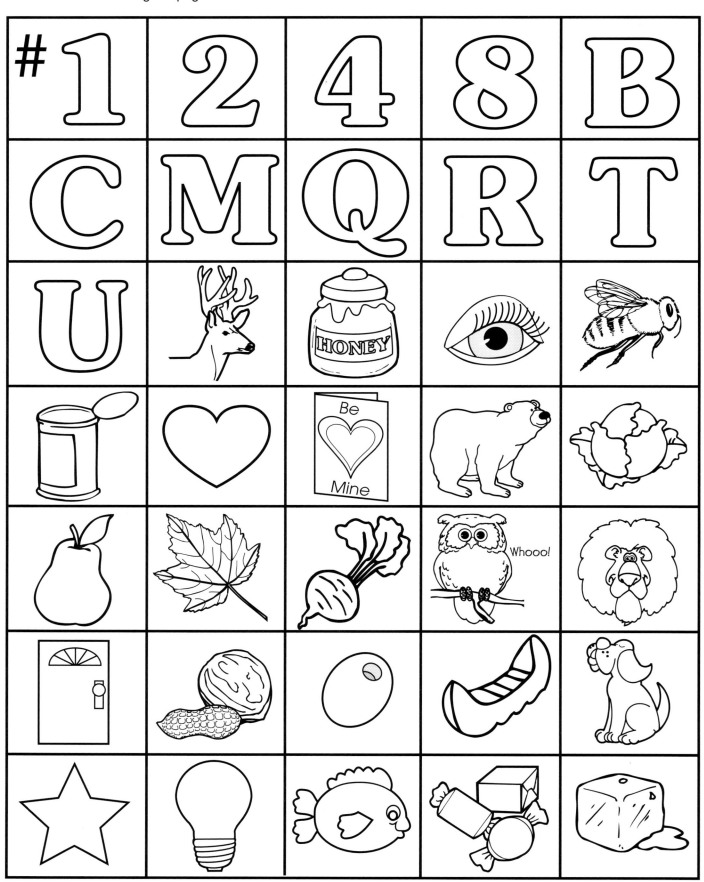

Mail Mix-Up

Sammy Skunk needs your help! He has two postcards to deliver to each house.
Read the delivery clues.
Write the letter of each postcard below the house where it belongs.

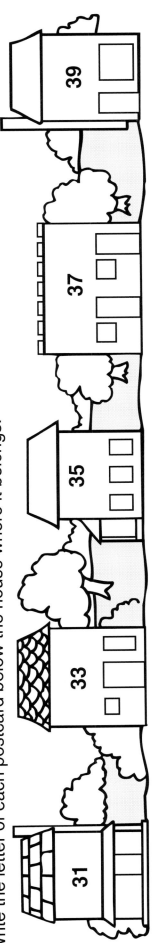

Delivery Clues

The house number for the letter marked:

A has digits that total 10
B is 5 less than 40
C is less than 36
D is greater than 35 and less than 39
E has digits with a difference of 0

F is 6 more than 25
G is an odd number
H is halfway between 30 and 40
I has matching digits
J is one less than 40

Bonus Box: Color the picture. Then, on the back of this sheet, draw and color a valentine for Sammy.

©The Education Center, Inc. • THE MAILBOX® • Primary • Feb/Mar 2000 • Key p. 313

'Tis the Season for... Jelly Beans

Spill the beans about jelly beans with this delicious collection of cross-curricular activities!

ideas contributed by Laura Wagner

SOCIAL STUDIES
A Sweet Invention

No one really knows when, where, or how jelly beans were invented. As each child munches on a few of the candies, point out Middle Eastern countries on a world map. Reveal that most candy experts agree that the candy's jelly center was invented there long, long ago. Next point to France and explain that the process for making the candy's outer shell was invented there. Then show students Boston, Massachusetts, on the map and tell them that it was there, in the year 1861, that the jelly bean was first advertised. For a fun follow-up, pair students and have them use this jelly bean knowledge as they brainstorm a theory for how the jelly bean might have been invented! Ask each pair to share its theory with the class.

Pam Crane

SCIENCE
Five-Sense Investigation

Sweeten your students' observation skills with a five-sense jelly bean investigation! Give each child one jelly bean and a copy of page 252. To begin, ask each child to touch her jelly bean and then write words on her paper that describe how it feels. Invite several students to share what they wrote; then proceed through each remaining sense in a similar manner, saving the sense of taste for last. Then have each child complete the remainder of the activity on her own. "Sense-sational!"

CREATIVE THINKING
Flavors of the Future

It's no secret that jelly beans come in a variety of colors and flavors. This booklet project prompts students to exercise their creative-thinking skills as they recall existing jelly bean flavors and brainstorm new ones. Have each child fold a 3" x 18" strip of white paper in half three times and then unfold the paper to reveal eight rectangles. A student writes a different color of jelly bean at the top of each rectangle and then she illustrates a matching bean at the bottom. For each bean color, she lists possible jelly bean flavors. (Encourage students to collaborate on this part of the project if desired.) When her brainstorming is complete, she glues construction paper jelly bean cutouts (pattern on page 253) to the back of the first and last rectangles. Then she accordion-folds the resulting booklet and titles it "[Student name]'s Book of Jelly Bean Flavors." Now that's a tasty project!

250

Savory Sites

Which United States president loved jelly beans so much he kept them in the Oval Office *and* on Air Force One? Ronald Reagan, of course! In fact it was his desire to serve red, white, and blue jelly beans during his inauguration festivities that prompted the invention of the blueberry bean!

To discover additional information about "the original gourmet jelly bean"® preferred by the former president, take your class online to http://www.jellybelly.com/. Another savory site that features information about jelly beans is http://www.candyusa.org/. Log on today!

MATH
Bunches of Beans

You can count on this estimation activity to provide mouthwatering results! Display a clear container of jelly beans for students to study for the purpose of estimating the number of candies inside. A few days later, have each child write his jelly bean estimate on a copy of "Sweet Estimates" (on page 253). Next pour about one-fifth of the beans into a large zippered bag. Quickly count the beans and announce the total. Ask each child to restudy the container and write a second estimate based on the new information he gathered. Then dispense the jelly beans from the container into four more zippered bags. To count the beans, divide students into five groups and have each group count the beans in a different bag. Combine these counts for a grand total. Have each child write the grand total on his paper and describe a strategy he used during the estimation exercise. Then invite each group to evenly distribute its jelly beans among its members.

Name Jackson

Sweet Estimates
Jelly Beans Estimation

Estimate 1	Estimate 2	Final Count
500	250	173

A strategy that I used to help me estimate was to use the bean count Mrs. Wagner gave us. She only took out 38 beans and I thought she took out 100! I knew my estimate was too high.

WRITING
Jelly Beans in Space

Jelly beans in outer space? It's true! In June 1983 the space shuttle *Challenger* orbited Earth with two firsts on board—jelly beans and America's first female astronaut, Sally Ride. Share this fascinating fact with students; then have them brainstorm places jelly beans have probably never been, like inside a volcano, a shark's stomach, or a pyramid. After each child traces a large jelly bean shape on story paper and cuts out the resulting shape, have him write and illustrate a story that describes the day he takes a bag of jelly beans to an unusual location. Have each child mount his completed story on a 9" x 12" sheet of colorful construction paper and then trim the paper to create an eye-catching border. After each child shares his far-out tale with the class, bind the projects into a class book titled "Jelly Bean Firsts" for further reading pleasure.

Jelly Beans
Five senses

Jelly Bean Investigation

Use your five senses to learn about a jelly bean!
In each box write words that describe the jelly bean you have.

It feels...	It looks...	It sounds...	It smells...	It tastes...
		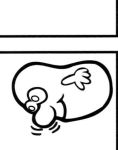		

Write a delicious description of the jelly bean you investigated. Use the words you wrote above.
Draw and color a picture of the jelly bean in the box.

_____

_____

_____

_____

©The Education Center, Inc. • THE MAILBOX® • Primary • April/May 2000

Note to teacher: Use this activity with "Five-Sense Investigation" on page 250.

Pattern and Form

Use the jelly bean pattern with "Flavors of the Future" on page 250.

Use the form below with "Bunches of Beans" on page 251.

Name _____   Jelly Beans
Estimation

Sweet Estimates

	Estimate 1	Estimate 2	Final Count

A strategy that I used to help me estimate _____

_____

_____

_____

_____

"Quazy" About Ice Cream!

Dish up skill review by the scoopful using the activities and reproducibles in this cool and creamy collection.

An Unsolved Mystery

Who invented ice cream? No one knows for certain. One myth suggests Marco Polo first saw ice cream while traveling through China. Another gives credit to a French chef under the employ of Charles I of England. And yet another myth credits a Roman Emperor for stirring up ice cream made from freshly fallen snow, nectar, and fruit. For a fun creative-writing activity, have students step back in time to dream up and illustrate original tales of how ice cream was invented. After students share their work, bind the projects into a class book titled "The Real Scoop! How Ice Cream Was Invented."

Linda Masternak Justice, Kansas City, MO

Creamy Facts

Ice-cream facts from American history are the focus of this booklet project. Distribute copies of the cards from page 258 and have each child personalize the title card. Then read aloud each fact as students color the corresponding ice-cream scoop. To assemble his booklet, a child cuts out the cards, sets the title card aside, and glues the fact cards in chronological order on a 3" x 18" strip of colorful construction paper. When the glue is dry, he folds the first card atop the second card and accordion-folds the remainder of the project. Last, he glues the title card to the front of the project. Now that's a booklet of cold, hard facts!

Linda Masternak Justice

Creamy Facts
by
Jackson

1776
The first ice-cream parlor opens in New York City.

More Frosty Facts

Here are a few more ice-cream-related facts students are sure to enjoy!
- The average American eats about 15 quarts of ice cream per year.
- Over ten percent of the milk produced in the United States is used in making ice cream.
- More ice cream is sold on Sundays than on any other day of the week!
- About one-third of the ice cream sold in the United States is vanilla. Chocolate and Neapolitan rank next in popularity.

A Chilling Discovery!

Sprinkle some science into your ice-cream studies with this two-day experience.

Day One: Ask students what will happen when milk, sugar, and vanilla (ice-cream ingredients) are mixed together and frozen. Note their ideas on chart paper. Then, with their help, prepare one batch of Dreamy Mix and freeze it overnight.

Day Two: Show students the results from the previous day's experiment and have them contemplate what went wrong. Then divide students into small groups and have each group prepare one batch of Dreamy Mix. Place each group's bag of mix in the center of a gallon-size resealable freezer bag, fill the larger bag half full of party ice, add six tablespoons of salt, and then seal the bag and lay it on a dish towel. Ask the members of each group to take turns shaking the bag of ice for the next five to ten minutes. (Have students use the towel to hold the bag, as the bag becomes quite cold!) During this time, ask students how this experiment differs from yesterday's. Note their ideas on chart paper. Last, have each group remove its bag of Dreamy Mix and look inside. Give each group member a plastic spoon to scoop out one spoonful of delicious ice cream!

Dreamy Mix

Mix together the following ingredients:
½ cup whole milk
1 tbsp. sugar
½ tsp. vanilla

Pour into a quart-size resealable freezer bag. Seal the bag.

This Is Why

The Dreamy Mix from Day 1 froze, but it did not make ice cream. To make ice cream, the mix must be shaken (stirred, whipped) as it freezes. Shaking the mixture blends the ingredients and creates tiny air bubbles in it. Approximately one-half of the volume of ice cream is air! The salt is added to the ice because it lowers the temperature of the ice in the bag, creating a colder temperature at which the mixture can freeze.

adapted from an idea by Linda Masternak Justice
Kansas City, MO

A Tasty Test

Who knew that creating a pictograph could be such a tasty experience? In individual bowls, place a spoonful of each of three or four different ice-cream flavors. Give each child a cup of water, a bowl of ice-cream samples, a plastic spoon, and a napkin. List each ice-cream flavor being tasted on a length of bulletin board paper. Then direct students to taste the flavors one at a time, stopping in between each flavor to wipe his spoon clean and take a drink of water. After the final flavor is tasted, have all students wipe their spoons clean. Then, in turn, have each child tape his spoon to the bulletin board paper to create a "licktograph" of favorite flavors. Have the students use the information on the pictograph to determine the most (least) popular flavor and to create and solve a variety of word problems.

Karin Thompson—Gr. 2
Franklin Township School, Quakertown, NJ

Our 2nd Grade "Licktograph"

Graham Cracker Crunch

Raspberry Punch

Triple Chocolate Chip

Banana Split Blowout

Each 🥄 equals one vote.

Far-Out Flavors

Cocoa mocha macaroni? Tapioca smoked baloney? Set the scene for this recipe-writing activity by reading aloud "Bleezer's Ice Cream" from Jack Prelutsky's *The New Kid on the Block* (Greenwillow Books, 1984). Then have each child create an original ice-cream flavor! To do this, she writes her name and the name of her ice cream on a copy of the pattern from page 259. Then she lists the ingredients and illustrates the new ice cream in the box. Next she cuts out her completed project and glues it on a 6" x 8" rectangle of colorful construction paper. Bind the projects into a booklet titled "[Number of students] Far-Out Flavors."

adapted from an idea by Karin Thompson—Gr. 2

Scooter Squirrel's
student

Nutty Crunch
flavor

Ingredients: Peanuts, Walnuts, Pecans, Cashews, Milk, Sugar

Delicious Motivation

It takes students nine weeks to earn these scrumptious sundaes, but you won't hear them complain! Prior to the last nine-week grading period of the year, make a poster and a management chart as shown. Display the poster and tell the class that each week every child has the opportunity to earn one party item for an end-of-the-year ice-cream party. Explain how the refreshments will be earned (by completing homework, displaying outstanding classroom behavior, etc.). Also explain that the refreshments must be earned in order. Update your management chart at the end of each week. (If desired, provide extra-credit opportunities for students who fall behind in earning refreshments.) On the day of the party, each child enjoys the refreshments he has earned! Yum!

Ashley Rebman—Gr. 2
Cresset Christian Academy, Durham, NC

End-of-the-Year Ice-Cream Party!

Week	Party Item
1	napkin
2	spoon
3	bowl
4	scoop of ice cream
5	scoop of ice cream
6	fudge or caramel topping
7	whipped cream
8	sprinkles
9	cherry

Similes From Sundaes

Writing a simile is as easy as eating an ice-cream sundae! Display a list of sundae ingredients (ice cream, fudge topping, nuts, sprinkles, whipped cream, cherry). Ask students to brainstorm words that describe each ingredient, and write the adjectives nearby. Next, give each child a copy of the sundae pattern on page 259. Ask him to choose five adjectives and copy them on the dish. Then have him color the pattern and cut it out. Next, he glues his cutout to one end of a 12" x 18" sheet of drawing paper, titles the page "Similes From a Sundae," and writes five similes on the page, using the adjectives he wrote. Last, he underlines each adjective to match the color of the ingredient it describes. Very sweet!

Kristel Schmidt
Jupiter, FL

Steps to an Ice-Cream Sandwich

1. Fresh milk is delivered to an ice-cream factory.
2. Milk and sugar are mixed together and heated.
3. When the heated mixture cools, flavoring is added.
4. The flavor mixture is chilled. Air bubbles are added.
5. The ice cream is pressed between two cookies.
6. The sandwiches are wrapped, frozen, and taste tested.
7. The sandwiches are ready to be sold.

Cool Sandwiches

What's the coolest sandwich on earth? An ice-cream sandwich! For this sequencing project, a student folds in half a 5" x 8" rectangle of brown construction paper and a 6" x 8" rectangle of white construction paper. She slides the white paper inside the brown paper so that the folds are flush; then she glues the brown paper to the white paper. Next, she carefully reads a copy of the sentence strips from page 258. She numbers the strips from 1 to 7 to show how an ice-cream sandwich is made. Then she cuts out the strips, glues them inside her booklet in sequential order, and titles her work "Steps to an Ice-Cream Sandwich." Last, she closes the booklet and uses a brown crayon or marker to add desired details to the cover. Now that's a booklet that looks good enough to eat!

adapted from an idea by Kathryn Lovell—Gr. 2
Margaret Leary Elementary, Butte, MT

I became friends with Becky.

I learned to count by 5s.

I scored in the basketball game.

We went to the aquarium.

I read my first chapter book.

Juan

A "Scooper" Year!

Students dish up plenty of sweet memories during this delicious activity! Using tagboard templates, each child traces a cone shape onto brown paper one time and a scoop shape onto pastel paper five times. He writes his name on the cone shape. On each scoop he writes a sentence that describes one sweet memory from the school year. Next, he cuts out the shapes and glues them together as shown. Invite each youngster to top off his project with a red paper cherry. Then mount the projects on a bulletin board titled "Sweet Memories From Our School Year!"

Karin Thompson—Gr. 2, Franklin Township School, Quakertown, NJ

Patterns

Use the sentence strips with "Cool Sandwiches" on page 257.

Use the cards with "Creamy Facts" on page 254.

Creamy Facts

by

_____

○ The sandwiches are wrapped, frozen, and taste-tested.

○ The flavored mixture is chilled. Air bubbles are added.

○ Milk and sugar are mixed together and heated.

○ The sandwiches are ready to be sold.

○ When the heated mixture cools, flavoring is added.

○ The ice cream is pressed between two cookies.

○ Fresh milk is delivered to an ice-cream factory.

1776
The first ice-cream parlor opens in New York City.

1813
Dolley Madison serves ice cream in the White House.

1846
Nancy Johnson invents the hand-cranked ice-cream freezer.

1851
Jacob Fussel opens the first ice-cream plant in Baltimore.

1896
Italo Marchiony invents the ice-cream cone.

1904
The waffle cone is introduced at the St. Louis World's Fair.

Use the container with "Far-Out Flavors" on page 256.

's

student

flavor

Ingredients:

Use the sundae with "Similes From Sundaes" on page 257.

'Tis the Season for...
Strawberries

Take students on a stroll down strawberry lane with this handpicked batch of cross-curricular ideas!

ideas contributed by Vicki Mockaitis Dabrowka

ART
Shapely Folders

Since no two strawberries are shaped exactly alike, this folder-making project is full of possibilities! To make a folder (for storing strawberry-related activities), a child folds a 12" x 18" sheet of red construction paper to form a pocket. She uses a black marker to personalize the pocket; then she trims the paper into the shape of a strawberry. After she carefully glues the outer edges of the pocket together, she uses a cotton swab to dab yellow tempera paint seeds on the front of the resulting folder. When the project is dry, she cuts a strawberry cap from green paper and glues it in place.

Gather the student-made folders and laminate them for durability; then carefully slit open each folder pocket using an X-acto® knife. Mount the folders on a bulletin board or secure each child's folder to her desk. Either way you'll end up with a patch of strawberries like no other!

Strawberries grow around the world.

Sharon

SOCIAL STUDIES
Juicy Facts

Stir up additional interest in strawberries with this fact-finding activity! Each day write two comparable sentences on the chalkboard: one that states a fact about strawberries and one that does not. (For ideas, see "Strawberries: Fact and Fiction" below.) Challenge students to use their prior knowledge to suggest which sentence is true. After plenty of discussion, erase the incorrect sentence. Then have each child copy the real fact on provided paper and tuck it inside his strawberry-shaped folder for safekeeping.

Strawberries: Fact and Fiction

Fact	Fiction
One strawberry has about 200 yellow seeds.	One strawberry has no seeds.
A strawberry plant is from the rose family.	A strawberry plant is from the cherry family.
Strawberries grow around the world.	Strawberries grow only in the United States.
In the United States, California harvests the most strawberries.	In the United States, Alaska harvests the most strawberries.
Strawberries are a good source of vitamin C.	Strawberries provide no vitamins.

SCIENCE
The Strawberry Plant

Cultivate interest in the strawberry plant with this informative mobile project! Give each child a white construction paper copy of page 263. Read the title card aloud and have each child write his name on the provided line. Next, read aloud the four illustrated cards, pausing between each one for students to study and color the illustration. Then read aloud the text on the strawberry as students color the artwork.

To assemble his mobile, a child cuts along the bold lines and folds along the thin lines, keeping the text to the outside. He glues the blank sides of the strawberry cutout together, sandwiching one end of a 30-inch yarn length between them. Next, he slides the folded cards onto the yarn so the story is sequenced and then he glues the blank sides of each card together. Encourage students to use their completed mobiles to tell family members about the strawberry plant.

How Does a Strawberry Grow?

Each fruit grows into a juicy red strawberry!

MATH
Smiling Glyphs

These smiling strawberry glyphs are quite informative! Enlarge the strawberry pattern on page 264 by 50 percent; then make student copies on 9" x 12" red construction paper. Each child also needs a copy of the legend "Strawberry Symbols" from page 264, a 4" x 8" rectangle of green construction paper (for the cap), access to construction paper scraps (green, blue, brown, black, gray, pink, and yellow), glue, scissors, markers or crayons, and a pencil. A student cuts out his strawberry pattern; then he uses the legend to decorate it. Post the completed projects and an enlarged version of the legend on a bulletin board titled "Who's Who?" Each day, spotlight a different berry. Help students discover the classmate it represents and then write the child's name on the berry's cap. Too sweet!

LANGUAGE ARTS
Sweet Synonyms

Sweeten your students' synonym skills at this matching center! Use the patterns on page 264 to make an equal number of red paper berries and green paper caps. Match each cap to a berry and then program each set with a different synonym pair. Laminate the patterns for durability and cut them out. For a self-checking center, use a permanent marker to draw the same symbol on the back of each cutout in a matched pair. Store the cutouts in a zippered bag at a center. A student matches a cap to each strawberry; then she flips the matched cutouts to check her work. "Berry" nice!

close

near

WRITING
The Berry Snatcher

Juice up your youngsters' creative-writing skills with a presentation of *The Grey Lady and the Strawberry Snatcher* by Molly Bang (Aladdin Paperbacks, 1996). In this award-winning and wordless picture book, invigorating illustrations show how a clever woman clutching a container of juicy strawberries eludes a "berry" mysterious creature! At the conclusion of the book, ask each child to write either a story to accompany Molly Bang's illustrations or an original tale about the Grey Lady and the Strawberry Snatcher. For added fun, have each child illustrate his tale by drawing or painting on gray construction paper. Be sure to set aside time for students to share their work with the class.

COOKING
Sippin' Strawberries

What do eight strawberries add up to? More vitamin C than one orange! For a quick and nutritional snack, combine strawberries (with caps removed), banana slices, orange juice, and ice cubes in a blender. Blend the ingredients until smooth. Pour individual portions of the fruity drink into beverage cups. If desired, add a flexible straw and one strawberry slice (for garnish) to each cup before serving. Simply delicious!

READING
Picks From the Patch
These strawberry-related picture books are just ripe for reading!

Good Job, Oliver!
Written and Illustrated by Laurel Molk
Crown Publishers, Inc.; 1999

The First Strawberries: A Cherokee Story
Retold by Joseph Bruchac
Illustrated by Anna Vojtech
Puffin Books, 1998

Sweet Strawberries
Written by Phyllis Reynolds Naylor
Illustrated by Rosalind Charney Kaye
Atheneum Books for Young Readers, 1999

The Little Mouse, the Red Ripe Strawberry,
and the Big Hungry Bear
Written by Audrey and Don Wood
Illustrated by Don Wood
Child's Play (International) Ltd, 1990

First Woman and the Strawberry: A Cherokee Legend
Retold by Gloria Dominic
Illustrated by Charles Reasoner
Troll Associates, Inc.; 1998

by _____

©The Education Center, Inc.

How Does a Strawberry Grow?

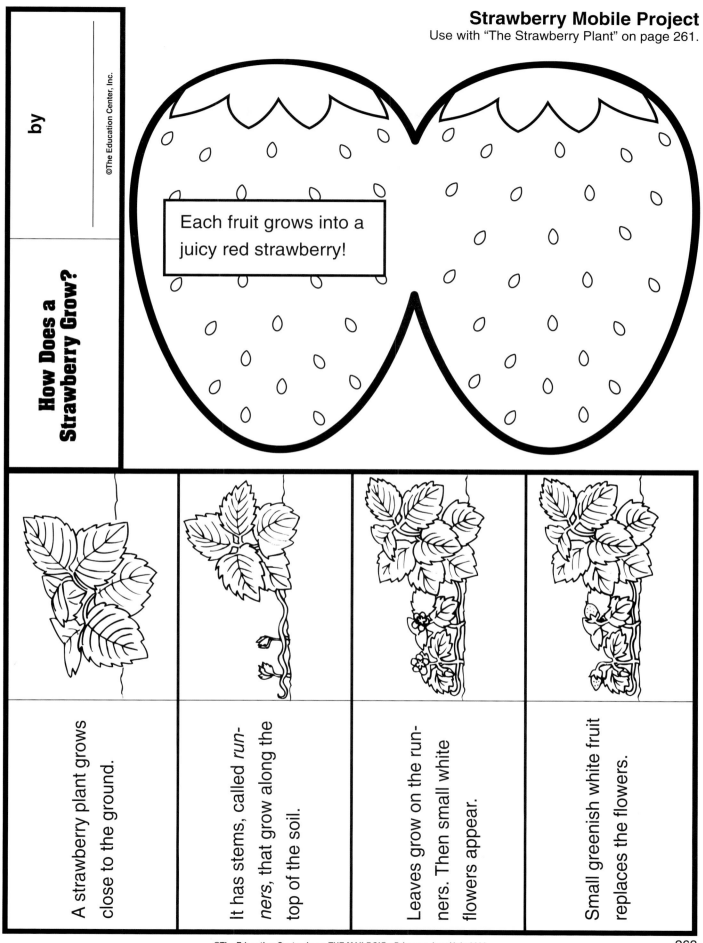

Each fruit grows into a juicy red strawberry!

A strawberry plant grows close to the ground.

It has stems, called *runners*, that grow along the top of the soil.

Leaves grow on the runners. Then small white flowers appear.

Small greenish white fruit replaces the flowers.

Patterns and Legend

Use the cap and strawberry patterns with "Sweet Synonyms" on page 261.
Enlarge the berry pattern to use with "Smiling Glyphs" on page 261.

Use the legend with "Smiling Glyphs" on page 261.

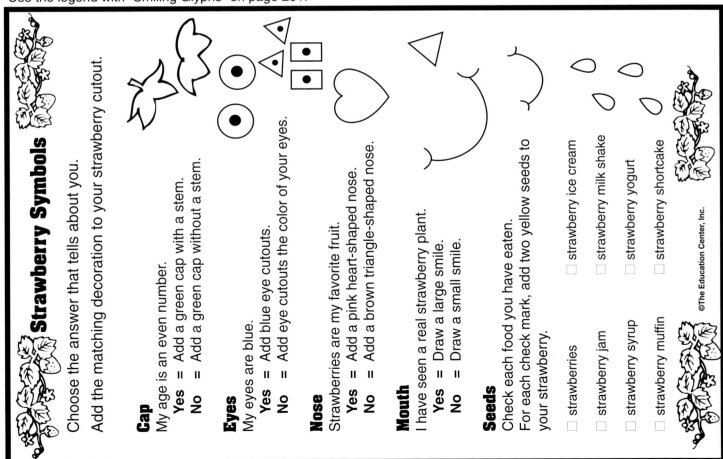

Strawberry Symbols

Choose the answer that tells about you.

Add the matching decoration to your strawberry cutout.

Cap
My age is an even number.
Yes = Add a green cap with a stem.
No = Add a green cap without a stem.

Eyes
My eyes are blue.
Yes = Add blue eye cutouts.
No = Add eye cutouts the color of your eyes.

Nose
Strawberries are my favorite fruit.
Yes = Add a pink heart-shaped nose.
No = Add a brown triangle-shaped nose.

Mouth
I have seen a real strawberry plant.
Yes = Draw a large smile.
No = Draw a small smile.

Seeds
Check each food you have eaten.
For each check mark, add two yellow seeds to your strawberry.

- [ ] strawberries
- [ ] strawberry jam
- [ ] strawberry syrup
- [ ] strawberry muffin

- [ ] strawberry ice cream
- [ ] strawberry milk shake
- [ ] strawberry yogurt
- [ ] strawberry shortcake

©The Education Center, Inc.

Teacher
Resource Ideas

A Blueprint for Open House

It's no secret that open house and parent night procedures vary from school to school. In fact, that's why we think this collection of tried-and-true suggestions from our subscribers is the perfect tool for customizing open house plans. So whether you're breaking new ground or simply looking to remodel, dig in! The sky's the limit!

Guess who?

I have lots of stuffed animals.

My dog's name is Porkchop.

I love macaroni and cheese.

Guess who was here?

A mom who loves her daughter very much.

A mom who sneezes when she smells fish!

Who Sits Where?

Students provide the clues, and parents solve the case! The day of open house, have each child draw her self-portrait and write a few clues about her identity on drawing paper. Help students paper-clip their projects atop their desktags so that their names are hidden from view. Parents study the projects to determine where their children sit during the day, using the desktags to confirm their hunches. For added fun, invite each parent to turn her child's project over and write a message to her child on the back—using clues, of course!

Valdarine S. Kemp, Oakes Field Primary School
Nassau, Bahamas

Slide Show Extravaganza

Most parents would love to know what happens during a typical school day, so why not show them! Photograph students involved in daily activities, making sure that every child is caught on film. Then sequence the slides so that a typical school day unfolds. Preview the slide show with your youngsters and, if desired, write a class-created script for the production. You may not win an Oscar® for your efforts, but you'll definitely receive plenty of praise from pleased parents!

Lori Demlow—Gr. 2, Heritage Lakes, Glendale Heights, IL

The Parent Game

Try this open house icebreaker! Have each parent list his child's favorite food, book, color, song, and place to visit on provided paper. Invite parents to predict how well they think they've done on this little pop quiz; then have them compare their answers with the responses their children gave earlier in the day. Parents are sure to enjoy the activity, and you'll have quickly put the group at ease.

Joyce Sutherland—Gr. 1 , Pecan Grove Elementary
Richmond, TX

Picture-Perfect Parade

These unique get-acquainted projects make an irresistible open house display! Ask each student to bring photographs from home that show him and various family members engaged in assorted activities. Or have students illustrate similar scenes on photo-size rectangles of drawing paper. Then have each child create a full-body self-portrait, like the one shown, on which to exhibit his pictures. Ask older students to pen captions for their pictures, too. After each child presents his project to the class, display it in the hallway outside your classroom door. The result is a picture-perfect parade that's guaranteed to stop open house visitors in their tracks!

Katie Robinson—Gr. 3, Limestone Walters School, Peoria, IL

Choose Your Favorite Fast Food

Burger													
Hot dog													
Pizza													
Taco													
Other													

Graph It!

It's easy to create a kid-pleasing graphing lesson during open house! Make two identical "Choose Your Favorite" bar graphs like the one shown. The day of open house, have each child write his name on a sticky note and attach it to one graph. As parents enter the classroom that evening for open house, ask them to write their names on individual sticky notes and attach the notes to the second graph. Parents are sure to find the graphs interesting, and students will have a ball evaluating and comparing them the following day!

Charlene Afflitto—Gr. 2, Grandview School, North Caldwell, NJ

A "Tree-mendous" Affair

You can count on plenty of enthusiasm when you ask students to be open house tour guides! After you talk with the class about the role of a tour guide, write a student-generated list of open house attractions on the chalkboard. Then have each child list her favorite attractions on a white construction paper copy of a large tree pattern like the one shown—one attraction per leaf. Invite each student to color her itinerary; then have her place it on her desktop for open house that evening. Parents are sure to enjoy and benefit from the guided tour, students will feel "tree-mendous" about their participation, and you'll be thankful for the time you spent visiting with your guests.

Cathy Howlett—Gr. 3, Franklin Elementary, Mt. Airy, NC

A "Tree-mendous" Affair

art center   math center   reading bulletin board

my teacher   discipline chart

my portfolio   classroom library

Welcome to My Classroom!

Family Puzzles

They're not exactly door prizes, but they could be the next best thing for promoting open house participation! On the day of open house, have each child illustrate his family on provided paper. Then have him cut his artwork into a designated number of pieces and store the pieces in a personalized envelope or zippered bag on his desktop. When parents arrive, they'll be eager to piece together the puzzles their children have prepared for them. And you can anticipate plenty of smiles as the family portraits take shape!

Alesia M. Richards—Gr. 1
Redbud Run Elementary
Winchester, VA

Just Hangin' Out!

Give your guests a clear picture of day-to-day activities at this eye-catching display. Photograph each child engaged in a different school-related activity; then mount each snapshot on a T-shirt cutout. Ask each child to write on his cutout (or dictate for you to write) a caption that describes what he is doing in the photograph. Title a bulletin board "Hangin' Out in [grade level]!" and use lengths of heavy string or plastic clothesline and clothespins to suspend the projects.

Sandy Preston—Gr. 2, North Street Elementary, Brockway, PA

Each afternoon we have Buddy Reading. We take turns reading to a friend.

Open House Apples

Apples are for *teachers,* right? So what could be more appropriate than presenting your students' parents with apples at open house? To prepare each apple, wrap it in plastic wrap and then use a length of curling ribbon to secure the wrap at the top. Glue a copy of the poem shown onto a leaf cutout. Hole-punch the leaf, thread the curling ribbon through the hole, and tie the ribbon ends. What a great way to let parents know how much their involvement is appreciated and needed!

Jo Fryer—Gr. 1, Kildeer Countryside School
Long Grove, IL

An apple for the teacher
Is really nothing new,
Except when you remember
Parents are teachers, too!

Customizing Your Raffle

Everyone knows that a raffle is a great way to boost open house attendance. But did you ever consider that a raffle is also a great opportunity to gather information? To customize your raffle, create a raffle ticket that gives parents an opportunity to ask questions (like the one shown) or elicits information from them (such as special interests and skills). Encourage each family attending open house to fill out one raffle ticket. Hold the raffle the following day and award the winner the promised prize. Then read the raffle tickets to follow up on the information you've gathered.

M. J. Owen—Gr. 3, Baty Elementary, Del Valle, TX

The Secret's Out!

Parents will be pleased as punch to learn that the typical response to "What did you do at school today?" should no longer be "Nothing!" During open house, inform parents that you conclude each school day by reviewing the events of that day. This means that with a bit of encouragement every child will have something to share about his day!

Kate Pointkowski—Gr. 2, Spring Hill Elementary School, McLean, VA

One-of-a-Kind Presentation

Patterning your open house presentation after a popular game show is sure to bring rave reviews from parents. For a game of Jeopardy®, create a gameboard by taping construction paper squares labeled with dollar amounts to the chalkboard as shown; then write a different school-related category above each column. To play, parents take turns picking categories and dollar amounts. After each selection is made, announce an answer related to the chosen category and challenge the group to furnish the corresponding question. Keep the game moving right along by giving extra clues when needed. Parents will appreciate your efforts to entertain and enlighten them!

Jeannie Frye—Gr. 3, Alvord Elementary, Alvord, TX

Superstar Students

Propel your youngsters' self-esteems to extraordinary heights with these parent-authored stories. Personalize a copy of the superstar form on page 272 for each child. Send each child's form home with a visiting parent or send it home with the child on the day following open house. A parent describes her child's superstar status, signs and dates the form, and then returns it to school by a designated date. With lots of fanfare, read aloud the parent projects for all children to enjoy. If desired, laminate the keepsake projects before presenting them to the students.

Diane Outlaw, San Antonio, TX

My child, _____, is a **SUPERSTAR** because

_____

_____

_____

_____

Signed _____ Date _____

Child-Centered Survey

Open the door to valuable information when you invite parents to share insights and information about their children. Place a copy of the survey on page 271 on each child's desk and request that parents complete the form during their open house visit. As you collect the surveys, assure parents that you will promptly follow up on any concerns that they have. Label the remaining surveys with the appropriate student names and send them home the following day for parents to fill out and return. In just one evening you'll have sent a clear message that you value and encourage input from parents. And you'll have learned a lot, too!

Ritsa Tassopoulos—Gr. 3, Oakdale Elementary, Cincinnati, OH

High Five Banner

When students lay their eyes on this colorful banner the day following open house, they'll grin from ear to ear! During open house, ask each visitor to add his handprint and an encouraging message to a length of white bulletin board paper that you've provided for this purpose. (To make a handprint, a parent paints colorful tempera paint on his hand before he presses it on the paper.) Display the parent-made project in a prominent classroom location all year long. It will be a great source of motivation for all!

adapted from an idea by Becky Hilbrands—Gr. 3
Remsen-Union Elementary
Remsen, IA

High Fives For You!

Way to go!
Keep smiling!
Keep reading!
Always give it your best shot!
I'm very Impressed!
Kindness counts!
Keep up the great work!
Love you!
What a talented group!
Your hard work shows!
You are amazing!
Thank you for being honest!

Phone Home

Keep an open line of communication between school and home by announcing a phone home plan during open house. Whether you agree to phone home once a month or once a week, parents will be pleased to know that you'll be checking in and giving them an opportunity to express their satisfaction and concerns. Brrring!

Rebecca Abney Roy—Grs. 2–3, Centerfield Elementary
Oldham County, KY

Follow the Footprints

Let colorful footprints guide your open house visitors right to your classroom door! Have each child trace the shape of each of his feet onto colorful paper and then cut out and personalize each resulting footprint. Use the cutouts to create a path from the front doors of the school to your classroom door!

Fran Blaess—Gr. 2
Middletown, RI

Remember When...

Parents are sure to enjoy taking a trip down memory lane! Ask each parent to copy the story starter "When I was in [child's grade level]..." on a sheet of story paper and complete it by writing about a memorable experience from that grade. Provide crayons for illustrations. Collect the projects at the end of the evening. Over the next several days, share a handful of the stories with your youngsters during storytime. When all the stories have been read, bind them and give each child an opportunity to take the collection home to share with his family.

Del Bull—Gr. 1
Jesse Boyd Elementary
Spartanburg, SC

Halloween Party Sign-Up!

Thank you in advance for your generosity.
Please provide enough for 23 students.

Drink

Cups

Nonfood treat
(pencils, erasers, etc.)

Napkins

Baked goods

Candy

Your donation will be confirmed several days before the party.

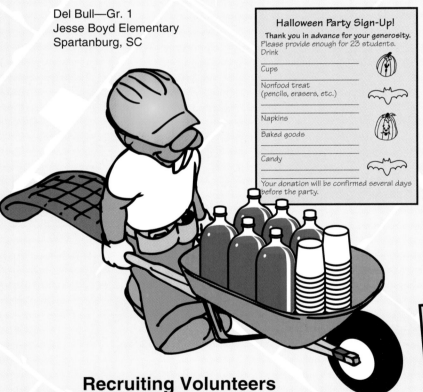

Making Party Plans

The evening of open house is the perfect time to round up donations for upcoming classroom parties. Create a sign-up sheet, like the one shown, for each party. Post the sheets in a prominent classroom location and encourage parents to sign up throughout the evening. As each scheduled party draws near, confirm donations by contacting the parents on the corresponding list. Easy as pie!

Roxanne Ward—Gr. 3
Greenwood Elementary School
Sylvania, OH

I volunteer to tutor individuals or small groups once a week (1–2 hrs.)
1.
2.
3.
4.

I volunteer to donate ingredients or help cook during special projects.
1.   8.
2.   9.
3.   10.
4.   11.
5.   12.
6.   13.
7.   14.

I volunteer to help from my home. Tasks may include cutting, coloring, and gluing.
1.   5.
2.   6.
3.   7.
4.   8.

Recruiting Volunteers

Open house is also the perfect time to recruit parent volunteers. During your presentation, briefly inform parents of your needs and direct them to an area of the classroom where you've posted colorful sign-up sheets that clearly outline a variety of ways in which they can help—at school and from home. Then stand back and watch in amazement as signatures begin to accumulate!

Rebecca Abney Roy—Grs. 2–3
Centerfield Elementary
Oldham County, KY

A B C 🍎 1 2 3 🍎 A B C

Tell Me About Your Child

🍎 My child's name is _____.

🍎 My child's interests and/or hobbies include _____
_____.

🍎 My child's favorite subject(s) is _____
_____.

🍎 My child's special qualities include _____
_____.

🍎 My child approaches learning...

_____with excitement   _____with curiosity

_____with confidence   _____with anxiety

_____with reluctance   _____without interest

🍎 Goals for my child include _____
_____
_____
_____.

🍎 Questions or concerns that I have: _____
_____
_____
_____.

🍎 This survey will be strictly confidential. Thank you for helping make this a great year for your child.

A B C 🍎 1 2 3 🍎 A B C

©The Education Center, Inc. • THE MAILBOX® • Primary • Aug/Sept 1999

Note to teacher: Use with "Child-Centered Survey" on page 269.

Pattern and Form

Use the macaw head and bill patterns with "Magnificent Macaws" on page 47.

bill

head

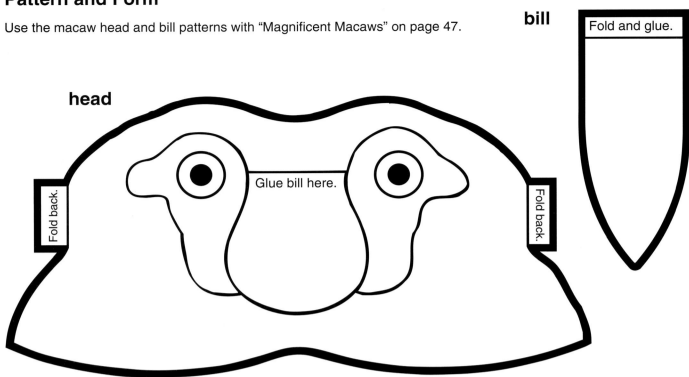

Fold and glue.

Fold back.

Glue bill here.

Fold back.

Use the form with "Superstar Students" on page 269.

My child, _____,

is a

SUPERSTAR

because

_____

_____

_____

_____

_____

Signed _____ Date _____

Putting Last Year's Calendars to Good Use

If you think the perfect place for an outdated calendar is a recycling bin, think again! Generate days, weeks, and months of fun-filled learning by teaming these easy-to-implement suggestions with outdated calendars.

Becky Forsyth—Gr. 3, Palmer School, Walnut Creek, CA
Theresa Weeks, Sweeny, TX

Using Large Calendar Pictures

- Cut each picture into puzzle pieces and store the pieces in a resealable plastic bag along with the preview pictures from the back of the calendar. Invite students to assemble the puzzles during free time.
- Cut the pictures into halves (or quarters) and place all cutouts in one resealable plastic bag for student assembly.
- Have students use the pictures as story- or sentence-writing prompts.

Using Calendar Numbers

- Cut out the numbered rectangles on each calendar grid and store each set of numbers in a resealable bag. Prepare one bag of numbers per child. Or place several bags at a math center for students to use. Have students
    - —sequence the numbers
    - —sort odd and even numbers
    - —use the numbers to count by 2s, 3s, 4s, and 5s
    - —use the numbers to create addition and subtraction problems (10 + 12 = 22, 30 – 14 = 16, etc.)
- Place a calendar grid and a calculator at a center. Have students use the calculator to find the sum of each horizontal (vertical) row of numbers.

Using Calendar Words

- Cut out the names of the months (or days of the week). Store the cutouts at a center. Have students
    - —arrange the names chronologically
    - —alphabetize the names
- Cut out the names of the months (or days of the week). Store the cutouts at a center along with a code that assigns a value to each alphabet letter (a = 1¢, b = 2¢, etc.). Have students calculate the value of each name.
- Cut out the names of the months (or days of the week) and then cut between the letters in each word. Store the cutouts in a resealable plastic bag at a center. Have students use the letters to spell the months of the year (or days of the week).

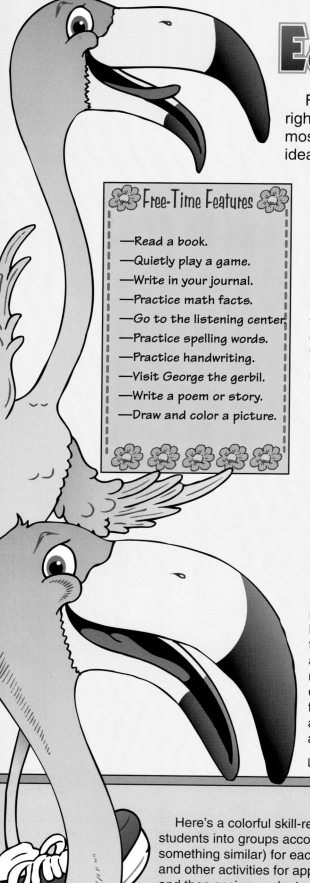

Early Bird Special

For nearly every lesson, there's a student or two who flies right through the assigned work with time to spare. Make the most of your early finishers' free time with this flock of subscriber ideas that include management tips and suggested activities.

Free-Time Features

Spark enthusiasm for learning with a student-generated menu of free-time activities. Remind students that they are all unique, and for this reason they complete assignments in varying amounts of time. Explain that having a list of free-time options helps early finishers use their time wisely and learn as much as possible. Then, with students' input, list on the chalkboard several free-time suggestions that can be completed at any time during the year. Copy the list on colorful paper, add a desired title and decorations, and display the resulting poster in a prominent classroom location. When a student finishes his work early, he selects a free-time activity from the poster. Now that's using time wisely!

Ritsa Tassopoulos—Gr. 3, Oakdale Elementary, Cincinnati, OH

🌸 Free-Time Features 🌸

—Read a book.
—Quietly play a game.
—Write in your journal.
—Practice math facts.
—Go to the listening center.
—Practice spelling words.
—Practice handwriting.
—Visit George the gerbil.
—Write a poem or story.
—Draw and color a picture.

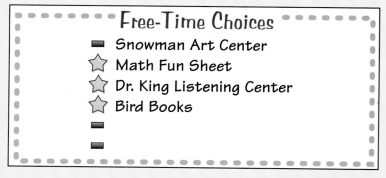

Free-Time Choices
- Snowman Art Center
- Math Fun Sheet
- Dr. King Listening Center
- Bird Books

Day by Day

If free-time choices in your classroom tend to change daily, weekly, or monthly, try this! Title a sheet of poster board "Free-Time Choices" and laminate it. Use a wipe-off marker to list current choices on the chart; then add and remove activities as desired. To further customize the chart, attach small Velcro® strips along the left-hand margin of the chart. Laminate a supply of small cutouts, attach Velcro to the back of each one, and display a cutout in front of each listing. To temporarily eliminate an activity from the chart, remove its cutout. This option is handy when noise level is a concern or when you wish to limit the activities to a specific subject area, like math-related free-time activities during math time, and so on.

LeeAnne Bohleke—Gr. 3, Charlotte Anderson Elementary, Arlington, TX

Color-Coded Options

Here's a colorful skill-related answer to the question, "What do I do now?" On paper, divide students into groups according to their skill levels. Obtain a different-colored plastic crate (or something similar) for each group. Stock each crate with a variety of skill sheets, learning games, and other activities for appropriate skill reinforcement. Position the crates around the classroom and then assign each student a color, making it appear as though the colors have been randomly assigned. When a youngster has free time, she completes an activity from the appropriate crate. To offer time on the computer, drop a card (or two) labeled "Ten Minutes of Computer Time" into one crate; then boot up the classroom computer with an appropriate learning game or activity.

Heather Fischer—Gr. 2, Prairie Heights Elementary, Dwight, KS

Customized Collections

Do you have a small group of students who routinely seek free-time activities? Try this! Personalize a shoebox (or other desired container) for each child. Inside each box place a copy of a learning log like the one shown and several activities that you think the owner of the box will enjoy. Ideas for activities include a topic to research, an Internet site to explore, a magazine to read, and a critical-thinking puzzle. When a student completes an activity from his box, he records it on his learning log, and then he passes the activity (if appropriate) and his related work to you. Routinely add new activities to the boxes and respond to the comments on the students' learning logs.

Carol Ann Perks—Gifted, Grs. 1–5
Comstock Elementary, Miami, FL

Name: Frank

FREE-TIME LEARNING LOG

Date	Activity	What I Learned	Teacher Comment
Jan. 10	I read a magazine.	I learned that some big snakes only eat once a year.	Wow! I didn't know that! Ms. P.
Jan. 11	I did a puzzle.	I learned that the puzzle was very fun!	I'm glad! Ms. P.
Jan. 12	Research project	I'm learning about pythons! I hope you like my report.	I'm looking forward to your report. Ms. P

Monthly Booklets

Students love this free-time activity because it's fun for them to do. Teachers love it because skills are reinforced and it's easy to implement! Each month, have every child personalize a construction paper folder and title it "Bonus Pages." Each day or two place copies of a different fun-to-complete skill sheet at a free-time center. In another location, provide a completed copy of the page(s) for students to check their work by. A student with free time takes a copy of the page to his desk. When he completes the activity, he checks his work against the provided answer key, and then he stores the page in his folder. At the end of the month, help each student staple his free-time work inside his folder before he takes it home to share with his family.

Janet Finley Landry—Gr. 3
Kim Cosgrove—Gr. 3
Wren Hollow Elementary
Ballwin, MO

Theme Crates

Providing students with additional resources and activities relating to recent and current themes of study is a great solution to the free-time dilemma. Label a large plastic crate for each theme. Stock the crate with theme-related books, magazines, games, hands-on activities, and so on. And the learning goes on!

Jennifer Hass—Resource Teacher, K–6
Western Coventry Elementary
Coventry, RI

Spare-Time Story Starters

Keep students on the "write" track with this free-time selection. Cover a clean and empty ice-cream bucket with colorful paper, and then label the bucket "Spare-Time Story Starters." Write a different story starter on each of a number of cutouts. Place the cutouts in the prepared bucket and store the bucket and a supply of story paper near a bulletin board titled "Just Published!" A youngster who has free time selects a story starter. After he writes and illustrates a story, he displays his work on the bulletin board. Feature a new supply of story starters each month. Write on!

Amy Ekmark—Gr. 1, Eastside Elementary School
Lancaster, CA

Math Challenges

This free-time math activity has three kid-pleasing options. Place three trays at a math center. Fill the first tray with blank paper, label the second tray "Problems to Solve," and label the third tray "Problems to Check." Position a fourth tray labeled "Finished Papers" near your desk. A student with free time may take a blank sheet of paper, create a page of problems for a classmate to solve, and then place the paper in the "Problems to Solve" tray. Or she may complete a paper from the "Problems to Solve" tray and place it in the "Problems to Check" tray. Another option is to correct a paper from the "Problems to Check" tray and then place the completed paper in the "Finished Papers" tray. So many options and so much math. Now that adds up to a great free-time opportunity.

Karen Lee Koroluk—Grs. 2–3
St. Dominic Savio Elementary
Regina, Saskatchewan, Canada

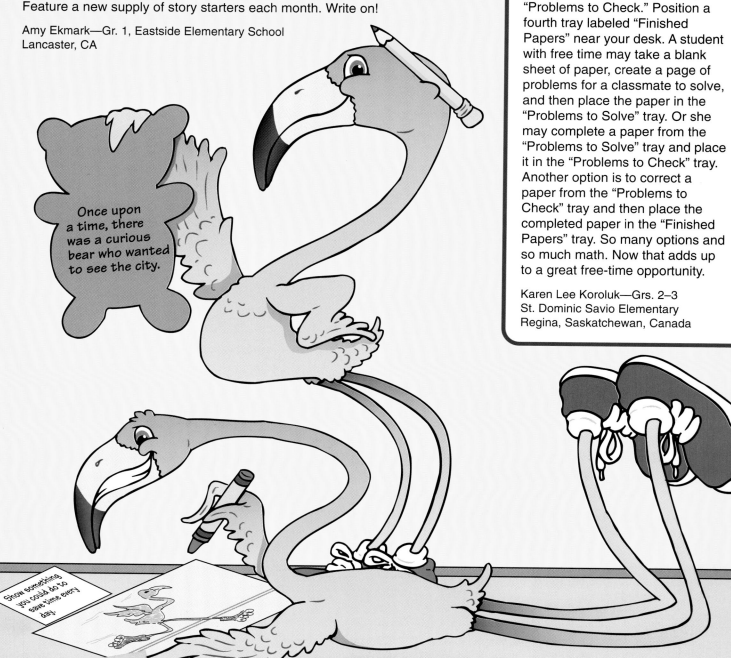

Once upon a time, there was a curious bear who wanted to see the city.

Show something you could do to save time every day.

275

Picture Prompts

...e sure to think that this free-time choice is strictly for fun, and that's just fine! Label each of ...ards with drawing prompts that encourage creative thinking. Suggestions include "Illustrate ...om might look to an ant" and "If you could go anyplace for one day, decide where it would ...nd color a picture of that place." Store the cards in a decorated container and then place the ...g paper, pencils, crayons, and markers at a center. An early finisher chooses a card and ...ponse. Encourage older students to write a sentence or two of explanation on the back of ... that's a picture-perfect way to put extra time to good use!

...Teacher, Fredericksburg Academy, Fredericksburg, VA

Company's Coming!

Once a week, or whenever a classroom visitor is expected, get the classroom in order with the help of your early finishers. List housekeeping tasks on the chalkboard. When a student has extra time, she writes her name beside one task to alert her classmates that it is being taken care of. After she completes the task, she erases it along with her name. In no time at all your classroom (and the chalkboard!) will be wiped clean!

Becky Forsyth—Gr. 3
Palmer School
Walnut Creek, CA

Teacher Timesaver

When student papers begin to pile up around your desk, offer this free-time alternative. Give an early finisher a class list, a set of completed papers, and a Hi-Liter® marker. Have him highlight the student name on each paper and check it off the list. Scan the list to see who has turned in the assignment and, if necessary, determine the owners of no-name papers. You'll save precious time, and the early finisher will feel proud to have helped you out!

Lisa Strieker—Gr. 3
St. Paul Elementary
Highland, IL

Mail Call!

Encourage written communication from students with this extra-time activity. Place a mailbox or a mailbox-type receptacle in a prominent classroom location. Label it with a fictitious address such as the one shown, and place a container of large, lined index cards nearby. When a student has extra time, he illustrates the blank side of a card to resemble a postcard. Then he divides the lined side of the card in half. On the left half, he writes a message to you. On the right half, he writes your name and the posted address, then illustrates a stamp. He places the card in the mailbox and, if necessary, raises the flag. At the end of the day, remove the mail and lower the flag. Acknowledge each child's correspondence with a verbal thank you or, as time permits, with a written response.

Debby Ohlson—Art Teacher, Fredericksburg Academy, Fredericksburg, VA

Ms. Ohlson
16 Learning Lane
Teacher Town, VA

Special Delivery

Meeting Special Needs

Place Value Cards

Do you have students who have trouble understanding place value? If so, reteach the concept with place value cardholders. To prepare one cardholder, label four library pockets as shown. Glue them onto a 6" x 15" poster board strip, leaving slightly more space between the first two pockets. Then insert a comma as shown. Program four blank 3" x 5" cards for each numeral from 0–9. Label the top half of each card as shown. Store the cards in a resealable plastic bag.

To use the cardholder, name a one- to four-digit number. Have a student show the number by placing the appropriate cards in the correct pockets. Or give a student a written numeral and have him display it in his holder. Then ask him to read the number aloud, referring to the pocket labels as needed. What a nifty way to pocket plenty of place value practice!

Kim Pratt—Gr. 3, Shirley Hills Elementary School
Warner Robins, GA

Step and Say

Step right up! Try this motor activity with youngsters who need extra help developing phonemic awareness. On your classroom floor, place five masking tape strips approximately 12 inches apart to create a path as shown. Ask a student to stand at one end of the path. Call out a word that has five or fewer syllables. Then, as you both slowly segment the word (saying it syllable by syllable), the student takes one step on the path for each syllable. Repeat the activity, saying the word more quickly. Continue with a desired number of additional words.

For more phonemic awareness practice, try these variations:
- To actively involve the entire class, ask students to say and clap each syllable of a word while one youngster walks the path as described above.
- Have a student take one step on the path for each sound, or phoneme, in a word (add more masking tape strips to the path as necessary).
- For a desktop version of this activity, give each student several small manipulatives. Have him line up the manipulatives across his desk. Then ask him to "walk" his fingers along the line of manipulatives as he says a word.

Janie Gray—Special Education
Ridgeway Elementary, Severn, MD

in-de-pen-dence

Coloring Guide

With this handy tip, coloring within the lines will be a breeze for youngsters who have visual-motor difficulties. To prepare one duplicated picture to be colored, outline each part of the picture with a thick line of white glue. Allow the glue to dry, then have the youngster color as usual. The raised lines created by the dried glue will clearly define each section to be colored.

Cathy Collier—LD Teacher, Southeastern Elementary
Chesapeake, VA

Special Delivery

Meeting Special Needs

Answers That Stick

Do you have students who have trouble completing math skill sheets because of fine-motor difficulties? If so, here's a solution that's sure to stick! Obtain a set of circle stickers such as the color-coding labels available in office supply stores. To prepare a skill sheet for one student, program a set of stickers with answers, interspersing the correct answers with several incorrect responses. To complete the skill sheet, the student solves each problem, identifies the sticker with the corresponding answer, and then adheres it to the answer space. It's as easy as 1, 2, 3!

Jennifer Wrzyszczynski—Special Education, Grs. 1–3
Greenwood School
Jacksonville, FL

Sticker Safe

With this approach, practice and reward are a winning combination for youngsters who have weak auditory memories. Cover an empty box and its lid with colorful paper. Draw, label, and cut out a construction paper combination lock; then mount it on the box. Make a tagboard dial and use a brad to attach it to the box as shown. Decorate the resulting safe as desired; then place an assortment of stickers inside and replace the lid.

Recognize individual student successes by inviting each deserving youngster, in turn, to visit the safe. Recite a series of numbers of your choice for the safe combination (vary the series for different students as appropriate). Have the youngster repeat the combination, say it again as he turns the dial to the corresponding numbers, and then remove the lid and select a sticker. To maintain interest, periodically stock the safe with different treats such as seasonal pencils or decorative pencil toppers.

Julie Cole and Carrie Riebel—Speech and Language, Grs. K–6
Marmaton Valley Elementary, Moran, KS

Sunny Papers

Help students who have low self-esteems focus on their achievements with this sunny approach to correcting papers! To mark a completed paper, use a yellow highlighting marker to draw a line through each correct answer and a circle beside each incorrect answer. Reteach the targeted concept(s) as necessary, and have the youngster correct any errors. Then use a pen to draw a smiley face in the yellow circle beside each correction. What a cheery way to provide feedback!

Ginger Becker—Gr. 2
Marion Elementary School
Marion, KS

279

Special Delivery

Meeting Special Needs

Robert G.
Spelling Test
6-16-00

Red List

1. get
2. come
3. could
4. people
5. now
6.
7.

Savvy Spelling Tests

Here's a simple and sensitive way to dictate different levels of spelling tests. Randomly assign each list of weekly spelling words a neutral name such as the name of a color or a shape. To administer the weekly tests, have each student prepare her test paper as usual and label it with the appropriate list name. Then, alternating between the word lists, dictate the spelling words, prefacing each one with its corresponding name. The list names alert a student to which words she should write, and no one feels singled out for having a different spelling list!

Kendra K. Hamby—Gr. 2, Clark Elementary
Franklin, IN

Desktop Page Finder

This tip minimizes the frustration felt by youngsters who have difficulty locating specific book pages. For each child, make or purchase a desktop number strip that features numbers from 1 to 100 (or higher). Laminate the strips and tape one on each student's desktop. When you ask a child (or class) to turn to a specific book page, use a wipe-off marker to highlight the corresponding number on the student's number strip. As he searches for the correct page, he refers to the strip to determine if he should turn the pages in his book ahead or back. When he locates the page he is searching for, he wipes his strip clean.

Jennifer Wrzyszczynski, Special Education, Grs. 1–3
Greenwood School, Jacksonville, FL

1	2	3	4	5	6	7	8	9	10	11	12	13	14	15	16	17	18	19	20	21	22	23	24	25
26	27	28	29	30	31	32	33	34	35	36	37	38	39	40	41	42	43	44	45	46	47	48	49	50
51	52	53	54	55	56	57	58	59	60	61	62	63	64	65	66	67	68	69	70	71	72	73	74	75
76	77	78	79	80	81	82	83	84	85	86	87	88	89	90	91	92	93	94	95	96	97	98	99	100

Stamp of Success

Do you have students who struggle to write math answers because of fine-motor difficulties? Try this alternative! Ensure that the problems on an assigned skill sheet have ample space for answers. (If necessary, cut apart a copy of the page and reposition the problems on one or more sheets of paper before duplication.) Then give a student a copy of the page, a set of number stamps, and a stamp pad. After solving a problem, the youngster stamps his answer on his paper. Now that's increasing student independence by the numbers!

Lori Franz—Grs. 1–2
Butterfield Elementary, Tucson, AZ

WRITE ON!

Write On!

Ideas and Tips for Teaching Students to Write!

Summer Snapshots

Summer memories become picture-perfect with this back-to-school writing project. Have each student illustrate a favorite summer event on one side of a large white index card. Encourage her to illustrate the entire side of the card so that her work resembles a postcard photograph. On the opposite side of the card have her write a note to the class in which she introduces herself and describes the illustrated event. While the students are working, ask each child to sign the front or back of a large index card titled "Summer Snapshots." Invite each child to share her project with the class. Then collect the cards and hole-punch the top left-hand corner of each one (including the autographed card). Secure the cards on a metal ring for further reading enjoyment.

Sharon MacQueen—Gr. 3, St. Zachary School, Des Plaines, IL

Who's There?

This get-acquainted writing activity induces plenty of grins and giggles! Begin by sharing a few of your favorite knock-knock jokes or reading aloud selected jokes from *1000 Knock Knock Jokes for Kids* by Michael Kilgarriff (Ballantine Books, 1990). Then challenge each child to use his first or last name to write knock-knock jokes. For the best results, display a format like the one shown for students to copy and complete. Be sure to set aside time for students to share the jokes they've written with their classmates—or even another class. Knock, knock. *Who's there?* Ima. *Ima who?* Ima sure your youngsters will love this writing experience!

Jill Hamilton—Gr. 1, Schoeneck Elementary, Stevens, PA

Abloom With Color

Color words are the key to spouting this big book of blossoms! Ask students to imagine a colorful flower garden or show them a picture of one. Then write a student-generated list of color words on the chalkboard. Working in small groups or pairs, have the students use art supplies like crayons, markers, scraps of tissue paper and construction paper, and glue to create colorful flowers on 12" x 18" sheets of white construction paper. Next ask each group to copy and complete the following sentence about its flower (or dictate for you to write): "[color word] flower, [color word] flower, what do you see?" Collect and stack the projects; then add a page to the bottom of the stack that you've programmed "I see a colorful flower garden looking at me!" Compile the pages into a class book titled "Our Big Book of Blossoms." Read aloud the big book and share the final page with great fanfare. Then invite each child to draw and color a flower on the final page to create a must-see flower garden! You can count on this class book being read time and time again!

To increase the difficulty *of this activity,* ask students to incorporate additional adjectives in their flower descriptions.

Karen Cook—Grs. K–1, McDonough Primary School, McDonough, GA

Write On!

Ideas and Tips for Teaching Students to Write!

My Pumpkin Seed

I planted my pumpkin seed and I watered it. The next morning a big green vine poked out of the ground. So I watered the vine. That is when I heard a very deep voice. It said, "If you water me with diet cola, I can grow magic pumpkins!" I almost fell over! Each day I poured a can of diet cola on the vine. And in one month I had four magic pumpkins! The first pumpkin told jokes. The next pumpkin helped me with my homework. The third pumpkin turned green peas into gumdrops. The last pumpkin gave me a magic seed to plant next year!

by Sofie Ray

Magic Pumpkin Seeds

Paper plates and pumpkin seeds are just what you need to sprout a bumper crop of creative writing! Each student lays a pumpkin seed in the center of a paper plate, lightly pencils a circle around it, and sets the seed aside. Then he pretends that his seed is magic and writes a story about it on his paper plate, without writing inside the circle. Next he erases the circle and glues his pumpkin seed in the empty space. After each child shares his work with the class, bind the stories into a class book. To do this, paint the bottoms of two paper plates with orange tempera paint. Hole-punch the top of each painted plate (when dry) and each student project. Use a length of green curling ribbon to secure the student projects between the painted covers and then curl the ribbon ends. Also tape a green paper stem inside the back cover, near the top. Now there's a pumpkin that's packed with the impossible!

Lisa Strieker—Gr. 3, St. Paul Elementary School, Highland, IL

Twigatops

My dinosaur discovery is a Twigatops. He is very nice. He eats lots of grass. He looks like a big fat bush. I wish I had a Twigatops in my backyard. That would be really cool!
by Gene W.

"Invent-a-saurus"

Looking for some "dino-mite" writing inspiration? Try this! Have each child cut out a tagboard dinosaur pattern. Then have her take home her cutout and invent a new type of dinosaur by decorating the cutout with a chosen item. For example, a Cottonasaurus might be covered with cotton, a Twigatops adorned with twigs, and a Stamposaurus rex embellished with canceled stamps. Set a date for the dinosaur projects to be returned. Then schedule writing time for students to pen paragraphs about their prehistoric creatures. Display each child's projects together on a bulletin board titled "Priceless Prehistoric Discoveries!"

Mary E. Maurer, Caddo, OK

Lost in the Leaves!

"Be-leaf" it or not, students' sentence-writing skills begin piling up during this activity! Each child chooses an object that could be lost or hidden in a pile of leaves. Then, keeping the object's identity a secret, he writes five clues about it on a 9" x 12" sheet of drawing paper. As the students write, move around the classroom reading their sentences. Star each complete sentence and leave a fall-colored leaf pattern for the writer. When a child collects five leaf patterns, he cuts out each one. Next he turns over his paper and illustrates his mystery object near the center of the blank page. Then one by one, he lays his leaf cutouts atop his illustration, taping only the stem of each leaf to his paper (see illustration). He also titles his work. Have each child in turn hold his project so that his classmates can view the leaf pile and he can read aloud his clues. After reading each clue, he entertains two guesses. If his mystery object isn't identified, he folds back one leaf. He continues until the hidden object is identified or revealed.

Anne Hott, Washington County School, Hagerstown, MD

Lost in the Leaves!

Clues

★ 1. It is bigger than a quarter.
★ 2. It is smaller than a pancake.
★ 3. You cannot eat it.
★ 4. It is a toy.
★ 5. It has string in the middle.

Write On!

Ideas and Tips for Teaching Students to Write!

Sensory Poems

This kid-pleasing approach to writing poetry makes perfect sense! Select a topic that students are familiar with, like a gumdrop. Then ask them what they think a gumdrop looks like and list their ideas on the chalkboard under the title "Looks Like." Repeat the exercise for each of the following titles: "Feels Like," "Sounds Like," "Smells Like," "Tastes Like." Accept all suggestions and encourage plenty of creativity. To write his poem, a child chooses his favorite idea from each list and writes the ideas on his paper in the format shown. Then he adds a title and decorates his work as desired. Using this easy-to-follow format, students can pen poetry about a variety of topics!

Heather Disharoon—Grs. 1–2, Dawson County Primary School, Dawsonville, GA

Oh, What Fun!

Unique holiday celebrations unfold when students spotlight their families' favorite traditions. For this project, each child copies "Oh, what fun it is to…" near the top of a white seven-inch oval and illustrates a favorite holiday tradition in the remaining space. Then, on a 4" x 6" sheet of writing paper, she describes the tradition she has illustrated. Next she folds a 6" x 18" strip of colorful construction paper in half. Keeping the fold at the top, she glues the oval cutout to the front of the resulting card and her written work inside it. Provide time for students to embellish their work with markers, crayons, and construction paper decorations. For added sparkle, have each child squeeze a thin trail of glitter glue around the oval on the front of her work. Display the projects for all to see on a bulletin board titled "Oh, What Fun!" Happy holidays!

Tina Fox-Henderson—Gr. 2, Christiansburg Primary School, Christiansburg, VA

Wintertime Writing

You can count on students warming right up to this cold-weather writing activity! Ask students to brainstorm words and phrases that remind them of winter. Write their ideas on the chalkboard. Then have each child copy and complete the sentence "Winter is…" on 3" x 5" writing paper, referring to the class generated list as desired. Next have him color a white construction paper copy of the mug of cocoa pattern on page 288 and cut it out. To complete his project, he glues his writing on the mug and a few white pom-pom marshmallows floating in the cocoa. Set aside time for students to share their writing with their classmates over cups of real cocoa!

Fara Singer—Gr. 1, Public School 2 Queens, Jackson Heights, NY

Write On!

Ideas and Tips for Teaching Students to Write!

Silly Jill Day
My holiday will be named Silly Jill Day. It will be on January 5. That is my birthday. School will be closed. Everyone will eat fish, french fries, and ice cream. People will act silly and tell jokes all day long!

February 17, 2000

Dear Tooth Fairy,
How are you? I hope you are finding lots of teeth. I have been taking very good care of my teeth. I am brushing a lot. I am eating crunchy foods. I am trying to eat less sugar. I think I will have a tooth for you soon. It just started to wiggle!

Your friend,
Robbie

am as fast as a cheetah!

Holiday Hoopla
Begin this kid-pleasing writing activity by reviewing with students the history behind a popular holiday celebration like Valentine's Day or St. Patrick's Day. Then have each student contemplate what a holiday designed especially in *her* honor might be like. Ask each child to choose a name for her holiday, decide when it would be celebrated, and select foods and activities for the special day. Then have her write and illustrate a paragraph that names and describes her holiday. Display the completed projects on a bulletin board titled "Hip, Hip, Hooray for *OUR* Holidays!"

Jill Hamilton—Gr. 1, Schoeneck Elementary, Stevens, PA

Dear Tooth Fairy
February is National Children's Dental Health Month and that makes it the perfect time to write friendly letters to the tooth fairy! After a review of the five parts of a friendly letter, have each child write to the tooth collector. Encourage students to describe in their letters the good dental health habits they are practicing and inform the fairy about any teeth they will soon have ready for her. Display a pillow at the front of the room and have each child tuck his completed letter under it. Before students arrive on the following day, remove the letters and tuck a class supply of sugarless gum under the pillow. Sprinkle glitter around the pillow for added effect. Students will be all grins!

Beth Jones—Gr. 2, Stevensville Public School, Niagara Falls, Ontario, Canada

Similes Made Simple
An introduction to similes is as easy as pie when it's coupled with an oral reading of Audrey Wood's *Quick as a Cricket* (published by Child's Play [International] Ltd). At the conclusion of the book, have students brainstorm adjectives that describe ways they feel or look. Write their ideas on chart paper. Then select two or three adjectives from the list and demonstrate how to write each one as a simple self-describing sentence *(I am brave.)* and a self-describing simile *(I am as brave as a lion.)*. Next have each child select an adjective from the class list and write and illustrate a self-describing simile on provided paper. No doubt your students' success at writing similes will have you feeling as proud as a peacock!

Kim Wachtel—Gr. 1, Sacandaga Elementary School, Scotia, NY

Write On!

Ideas and Tips for Teaching Students to Write!

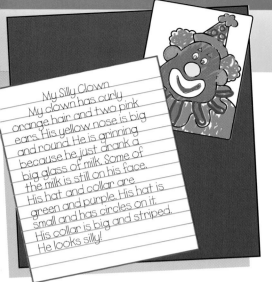

My Silly Clown
My clown has curly orange hair and two pink ears. His yellow nose is big and round. He is grinning because he just drank a big glass of milk. Some of the milk is still on his face. His hat and collar are green and purple. His hat is small and has circles on it. His collar is big and striped. He looks silly!

One-of-a-Kind Clowns

Do you believe that clowning around can enhance descriptive writing? You will at the conclusion of this activity! Have each child complete a copy of page 289. Encourage him to color his clown creatively and list four descriptive words for each clown part. Then provide plenty of time for students to write their paragraphs. For a fun follow-up, collect the students' completed papers. Tape the clown portraits to the chalkboard and then read the paragraphs to the class. Ask a different child to match each description to a clown. No funny business here, just descriptive writing at its best!

Susan M. Stires—Gr. 3, Sam Houston Elementary, Wichita Falls, TX

Colorful Prose

To introduce this poetry-writing activity, give each child a sheet of paper and a colorful marker (crayon, colored pencil). Ask her to think about the color of her marker and then use it to list phrases that describe the feelings, ideas, or objects she associates with its color. Next use student-contributed phrases to write a color poem (like the one shown) for the class. Then instruct each student to pen an original color poem using phrases from her brainstorming. To publish her poem, she mounts her final draft on construction paper in the color of her poem topic. Showcase the projects on a bulletin board titled "Colorful Poetry."

Sue Lorey, Arlington Heights, IL

Red

Red is
A juicy apple
Rudolph's nose
Tomato Soup
And my face when I cry

Red is
Scary when it is blood,
A stoplight,
My first bike,
And a rose that smells really good.

That is what red is to me.

by Mira Stovall

Sweet Stories for Mom

Mem Fox's well-loved picture book *Koala Lou* (Harcourt Brace & Company, 1994) provides the inspiration for this writing activity. As you read aloud this story of a mother koala and her cub, place special emphasis on the mother koala's refrain: "Koala Lou, I DO love you!" Next ask each child to think of a sweet expression that he likes to hear his mother (or another significant woman) say to him. Then have him write and illustrate a story that incorporates the expression he chose. Explain that the story can describe a special time that has already happened or one that he hopes will happen. Moms are sure to cherish these Mother's Day surprises.

Marsha Portnoy—Grs. K–5 Reading, Village Elementary School, Syosset, NY

Nicholas

Sweet as Sweet Potato Pie
My grandma loves me a lot. I love her a lot, too. I like it when she tells me I am sweet as sweet potato pie. One day she was sick. I made her a card. Then I picked her some flowers. They were the little ones that grow in her yard. She hugged me tight. She told me I was as sweet as sweet potato pie!

Ideas and Tips for Teaching Students to Write!

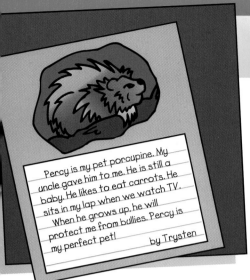

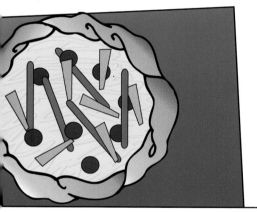

Pet Paragraphs

Paragraph writing is easy to "purr-fect" when pictures of possible pets provide writing inspiration! Each student selects a pet by cutting out a picture of an animal from a discarded magazine. As a prewriting activity, he names the pet and lists details about it. Then he uses his ideas to write a paragraph about his new pet. To assemble his work he glues his cutout and paragraph on construction paper as shown. Bind completed projects into a class book titled "Perfect Pets and Paragraphs!"

adapted from an idea by Diane B. Rinehard—Gr. 2, Beechgrove Elementary Independence, KY

Pizza With Pizzazz!

Any way you slice it, this tasty activity teaches students how to use commas in a series! Write a student-generated list of favorite foods. Then write a silly pizza-related sentence on the chalkboard that lists four favorite foods as toppings. For example, "Hope likes ice cream, strawberries, spaghetti, and cream corn on her pizza." Explain that when a sentence contains a list of three or more items, commas are used to separate the items in the list. Ask each child to write several sentences that list silly pizza toppings. Then have her copy her favorite one on provided paper and use construction paper scraps, glue, and crayons to decorate a brown paper circle to resemble the pizza she described. For a 3-D crust, she rolls brown paper towels and glues them around the edge of her pizza. Display the projects with the title "Pizzas With Pizzazz!"

Sharon L. Brannan—Gr. 2, Holly Hill Elementary, Holly Hill, FL

Fasten Those Seat Belts!

No doubt students are daydreaming about summer vacation. So why not use their dreams as fuel for a writing activity? Ask each child to pretend he is in charge of planning a five-day road trip for his family. Have him pen a story that tells *when* the trip will begin, *who* is going, *where* they are going, *why* they are going, and *what* they will do during the trip. Then have him color a white construction paper copy of page 290, cut out the car, and glue it to the top of his story as shown. Display the completed projects with the title "Our Seat Belts Are Fastened!"

Cheryl Stein—Gr. 2, Hankinson Elementary School, Hankinson, ND

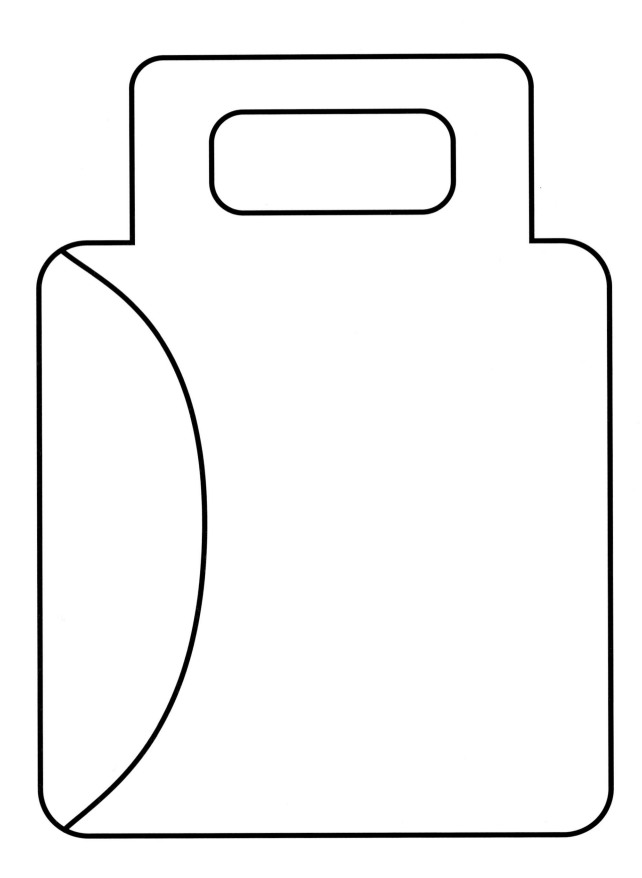

Name _____

A One-of-a-Kind Clown

Color the clown.
Study each clown part listed below.
On the lines write words that tell about it.

hat _____

hair _____

nose _____

ears _____

mouth _____

collar _____

Use a sheet of writing paper.
Write a paragraph that describes the clown.
Be sure to use some of the words you listed!

©The Education Center, Inc. • THE MAILBOX® • Primary • April/May 2000

289

Note to teacher: Use with "One-of-a-Kind Clowns" on page 286.

Pattern

Use with "Fasten Those Seat Belts!" on page 287.

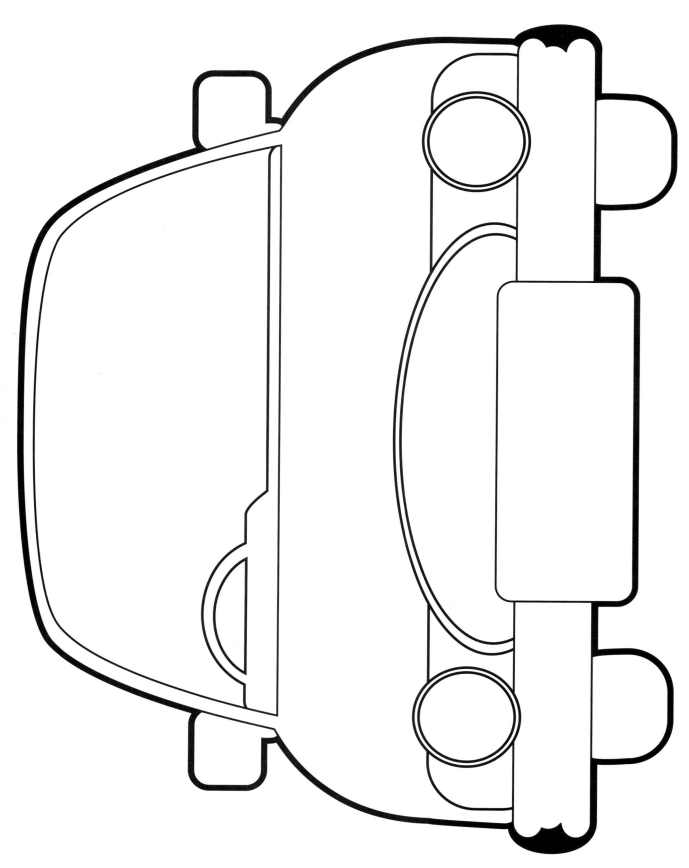

LIFESAVERS

Colorful Reminders

Colorful apple cutouts are just what you need to monitor classroom noise. Post a red apple to signal a quiet work time. Post a yellow apple when a moderate level of noise is acceptable. If any noise level is OK, post a green apple. Students respond to the colorful cues and that means you'll receive a bushel of cooperation!

Janica Peppard—Gr. 1
Pine Tree Academy
Freeport, ME

All Smiles

Taking attendance is a snap with this cheery chart! Visually divide a sheet of poster board to suit your needs and make a supply of happy face cutouts. Laminate the chart and cutouts. For easy reprogramming, tape name cards in place. Attach Velcro® dots to the chart and to the backs of the cutouts. Display the chart and then store the cutouts in a container nearby. Each morning a student adds a happy face to the chart to show that she's present. Each day before dismissal, a volunteer returns the cutouts to the container. If desired, supply special cutouts for students to use when they leave the room for bathroom breaks or special classes.

Kathleen Gillin—Gr. 2, Cold Spring School, Doylestown, PA

Jared	Adriana	Jace	Gina	Jordan
☺	○	○	○	○
Cecilia	Nicholas	Matthew	Cohen	Thomas
○	○	☺	○	○
Gregory	Stephanie	Alexander	Amelia	Sonya
○	☺	○	☺	○
Patrick	Tyler	Austin		
○	○	☺	○	○

Showcasing Student Work

Finding extra classroom space to display student work just got easier! Hot-glue individual clothespins to poster board stars. Use Velcro®, Sticky-Tac, magnetic tape, or masking tape to mount the stars on closet doors, file cabinets, windows, walls—any location that's within a youngster's reach and is suitable for displaying papers and projects. Have each child clip a sample of his finest work to a different star. Invite students to update their all-star displays as often as they wish. Everyone's a star!

Cindy Fingerlin—Gr. 3
Eisenhower School
Parlin, NJ

Justin

1. sheep   1
2. apple   2
3. shoe   1
4. basketball 3

Math Bags

Do you spend precious minutes of math time distributing and collecting manipulatives? Try this! Personalize a large zippered bag for each child. Every week or so, stock the bags with the manipulatives students need for the next several math lessons. Store the bags in a designated container and distribute them as needed. Or ask each child to store his math bag inside his desk. Every minute saved is one more minute of math instruction!

Kimberly Baker—Gr. 1, Skyview Elementary, Richardson, TX

By the Number

Score big with this classroom management tip. In the corner of each child's desktop (or table space) tape a card labeled with a numeral from 1 to 4. If student desks are arranged in groups, vary the numbers in the group. Use the numbers for a variety of tasks. For example, ask "fours" to collect math manipulatives or "threes" to line up first. Ask every "two" to pair with a "one" and so on. The possibilities are innumerable!

Lia Caprio—Gr. 3, Ingleside Elementary, Norfolk, VA

LIFESAVERS...
management tips for teachers

Popcorn Payoff

Good behavior pops up everywhere with this positive approach! On your desk display a large, clear plastic container with a lid. Store a supply of popcorn kernels and a one-fourth cup measurer nearby. Each time the class receives a compliment, ask a student volunteer to measure a quarter cup of kernels and pour them into the class container. When it's full, pop the good-behavior kernels in an air popper and serve the tasty snack to the students for a job well done!

Kristin Peluso and Julie Boris—Gr. 1
Clyde C. Cox Elementary
    School
Las Vegas, NV

Lesson Plan Lists

Stick with this idea and you'll know at a glance if you have the supplies you need for each day's lessons. As you plan for the upcoming week, label one sticky note per school day. Attach the notes to the corresponding lesson plan page or to an inside cover of your planbook. On each note, list papers to duplicate, supplies to gather, and so on. Cross off the tasks as you finish them. When an entire list is completed, toss it and feel twice the satisfaction—your list is gone and your preparation is complete!

Tiffany L. Gosseen
Hopkins, MO

Record-Keeping Calendars

Tracking students' work habits just got easier! Make a construction paper folder for each child and mount a duplicated calendar page on the front of it. Each day have students store their completed assignments inside their folders. Every afternoon remove the contents of each child's folder. If an assignment is missing, note it in the calendar space for that day. If all work has been completed, stamp the space with a seasonal stamper. At the end of the month, document each child's work habits in your gradebook; then send the folders home. A parent is sure to appreciate this visual record of his or her child's monthly work habits.

Kellie Provost—Gr. 3, Arroyo Mocho Elementary, Livermore, CA

Center Selections

Here's an easy way to avoid overcrowded learning centers. Write the name of each classroom center on a poster board circle like the one shown. Along the edge of each circle section, draw one or more rectangles to show how many students can work at the center at one time. Laminate the resulting center wheel and display it within students' reach. A student clips a personalized clothespin in an empty rectangle on the center wheel and then visits the corresponding center. When she leaves the center, she removes her clothespin. It's a snap!

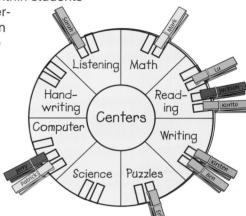

Mary E. Hoffmann—Gr. 2
Camp Avenue Elementary
North Merrick, NY

The Silent Check

Save precious teaching time by keeping class reminders to a minimum. List frequent reminders on the chalkboard, such as "Name on paper," "Desk clear," "Feet on floor," and "Ready to listen." Then begin activities with a silent check. Read aloud the expectations that apply, pausing after each one. If a student has fulfilled it, he makes a large check mark in the air. Students are so eager to "check off" their positive behaviors that they complete each reminder on the spot!

Lu Brunnemer—Gr. 1
Eagle Creek Elementary, Indianapolis, IN

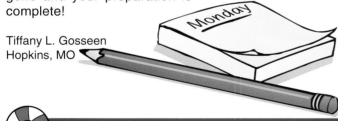

LIFESAVERS...
management tips for teachers

"Class-y" Behavior

An element of chance makes this seasonal plan for reinforcing classroom behavior extra appealing. For the month of December, display a large paper wreath. Have each child cut three holly berries from red paper and write her initials on each one. Collect and store the berry cutouts in a designated container. Each time the class receives a behavior-related compliment from you or another adult, remove a cutout from the container. Ask the student whose initials appear on the berry to glue the cutout to the wreath. Then present the child with a holiday sticker or another small treat. You'll enjoy outstanding classroom behavior and create an eye-catching holiday decoration!

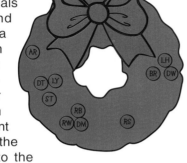

Jolene DuBose—Gr. 2, A. T. Mahan Elementary School
Keflavik, Iceland

Schoolwide Memos

If your school saves paper by sending home schoolwide memos with just the oldest child in each represented family, try this! Attach a colorful sticker dot to the desk of each child who is to receive the paperwork. Then send home schoolwide memos with students who have the dots on their desks. Distributing papers by the dots definitely saves time!

Kelly Hanover—Gr. 2, Saint Edward School, Racine, WI

Sticker Rings

Save time and minimize clutter by organizing your sticker collection on metal rings. Hole-punch the top of each sticker sheet as you sort the sheets by theme, holiday, or other desired criteria. Then bind each group of stickers onto a separate ring. Your days of sifting through miscellaneous stickers are over!

Heather Volkman—Grs. 1–2
Messiah Lutheran School
St. Louis, MO

Follow-up Folder

Providing individualized instruction just got easier! Keep a file folder labeled "Follow-up Needed" on your desk. When a child's completed work indicates that he needs additional help with a skill, file his paper in the folder. Each time you have a few free minutes, select a paper from the folder and meet with the corresponding youngster. Spare minutes quickly become teachable moments!

Gina Marinelli—Gr. 2
Bernice Young Elementary
Burlington, NJ

Scheduling Tip

Get a clear picture of when individual students attend special classes with this tip. Clip a sheet of clear plastic over each page of your current week's plans and then use a colorful wipe-off pen to program the plastic with desired information. (See the illustration.) Each week transfer the plastic sheet to your current plans and update as needed. A quick glance reveals who is exiting when, as well as when the entire group will be together. A substitute teacher is sure to appreciate this helpful approach.

Darcy Keough—Gr. 1
Doolittle School
Cheshire, CT

Computer Lab Queries

Implement this three-step approach to answering computer-related questions and there's an excellent chance students will use it throughout the school day! Ask that during lab time each child try first to answer his own question. If he cannot, he asks a classmate for help. If his question is still unanswered, he displays a bright orange card (or something similar) to request help from the teacher. Along with fostering a user-friendly lab, you'll boost the self-esteem of your students!

Cori Collins—Computer Teacher K–5
St. Mary, St. Margaret Mary, and St. Gabriel Schools
Neenah-Menasha, WI

LIFESAVERS...
management tips for teachers

Paper Trail Notebook

Here's a simple system for tracking assorted parent correspondence from field trip permission forms to conference slips to requests for supplies. Prepare a class list (or two), leaving blank space at the top of each list for a title. Keep a supply of the lists in a notebook at your desk. To track returned correspondence, appropriately title a class list and then mark out each child's name as you receive her paperwork. Circle the name of any student who forgets her paperwork and follow up with her. If your record keeping reveals that select students routinely need reminders, address the issue with the youngsters and their parents.

Nancy Long—Gr. 1
Washington-Wilkes Primary School, Washington, GA

Letter-Perfect Lineup

Try this letter-perfect lineup tip! Program a class supply of clothespins with the letters of the alphabet (add selected blends or digraphs if you have more than 26 students). Every Monday dispense the clothespins, making sure the line leader for the week receives clothespin A. During the week, students line up alphabetically by their assigned letters. The following Monday, collect and redistribute the clothespins. It's as easy as A, B, C!

Christine Schirmer—Gr. 1
Van Zant Elementary School, Marlton, NJ

Golden Behavior

March is the perfect month to implement this behavior management plan! Display a small black pot and keep a supply of plastic gold coins (or something similar) handy. Each time the class demonstrates exceptionally positive behavior, deposit a coin in the pot. When the pot is full, reward students with a bounty of praise and a class treat or privilege. How's that for a pot o' golden behavior?

adapted from an idea
by Christine Schirmer

Silent Signal

Monitoring independent workers just got easier! For each student, laminate a red poster board flag like the one shown and use Velcro® to attach it horizontally to the side of his desk. When a youngster needs assistance, he alerts you by turning his flag upright. Now there's an idea that really delivers!

Michele Curlings—Gr. 1
Oak Grove Elementary School
Lexington, SC

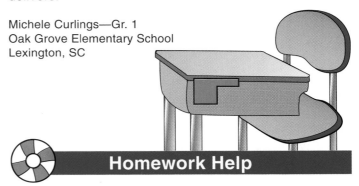

Homework Help

Taking a weekly approach to homework assignments benefits students and you! On Monday send home a form like the one shown that lists the homework assignments for the week. Then, on Friday, collect the students' homework along with their parent-signed assignment sheets. Students (and their parents) appreciate the flexibility of this approach, and you'll find that you spend less time checking homework. In addition, you have a ready-to-file record of each child's weekly homework efforts.

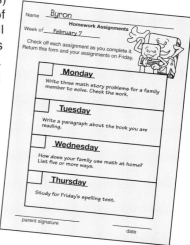

Angela Story—Gr. 2
Cedar Road Elementary
Chesapeake, VA

Handy Holders

Do you have students who spend valuable learning time searching their desks for needed supplies? Try this! Use clear packing tape to attach a plastic cup to the side of each child's desk. Suggest that students store frequently used supplies like pencils, erasers, and glue sticks inside. Imagine the minutes that will be saved!

Stacey McKee, Franklin Smith Elementary
Blue Springs, MO

LIFESAVERS...
management tips for teachers

 ## Go "A-head" and Write

Create a quiet environment during independent writing time with an eye-catching hat. When you wear the hat, everyone writes quietly. When you remove the hat, students may ask questions, share their writing with partners, or edit with peers. Now that's using your head!

Shari Abbey—Gr. 3
Abilene Elementary
Valley Center, KS

 ## Special Assistant

Promote positive classroom behaviors with a daily-assistant program. Each day watch for an undisclosed behavior. At the end of the day, reveal the behavior, report sightings of it, and select a child who repeatedly displayed it to be your special assistant the following day. Make an effort to reward each child's positive behaviors before the end of the year. Happy students, great behavior, and a little extra help for the teacher—that's a Grade-A plan!

Pam Rawls, Harpeth Valley School, Nashville, TN

 ## Compliment Chain

Recognize and reward your students' outstanding behavior with a compliment chain. Keep a supply of construction paper strips handy. Each time your class receives a behavior-related compliment from a staff member, parent volunteer, or other adult, add a link to the chain. When a predetermined number of links is earned, reward students with a popcorn party or another desired treat or privilege.

Jennifer Norman—Gr. 1
Maplewood Elementary
Ocala, FL

 ## Papers for the Teacher

This timesaving tip helps the school day start smoothly! Rather than gathering assorted paperwork from students as you greet them each morning, ask youngsters to place the papers they have for you in a designated basket. Or go a step further and have them sort the paperwork into individual baskets labeled with specific categories, such as "Notes From Parents," "Homework," and "Permission Slips." Then, as time allows, address the paperwork in order of importance.

Barby Punzone—Gr. 3, Public School 205, Brooklyn, NY

Hallway Manners

Here's an upbeat way to quickly settle your troop before leading it into the hallway. When the class is lined up, sing each line of the cadence call shown, pausing for students to repeat each line after you. This military-style chant readies your brigade to march through the hall with pride!

Amy Kallelis
Cold Spring Elementary
Doylestown, PA

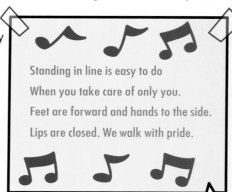

Standing in line is easy to do
When you take care of only you.
Feet are forward and hands to the side.
Lips are closed. We walk with pride.

 ## Random Responses

Keep students tuned in and ready to participate with a customized card deck! Personalize one index card per child and label two more cards "Wild." To use the card deck (for class discussions, large-group reviews, etc.), shuffle it, and then draw cards one by one, calling upon the corresponding students. When a Wild card is drawn, the student who answered the previous question answers again or chooses a classmate to answer. Regularly shuffle the deck to keep everyone tuned in! It's a great deal of fun!

Sister Maribeth Theis—Gr. 2, Mary of Lourdes Elementary, Little Falls, MN

OUR READERS WRITE

Our Readers Write

Caught Being Good!

This catchy chant promotes community within the classroom and helps refocus the class for the next task at hand. To establish a beat and ready the students, alternate between clapping your hands and patting your thighs. Students join in and then begin the chant on your cue—pausing to hear which student you call upon and sitting quietly while he responds. Students enjoy sharing the good deeds of their classmates and occasionally catch a teacher being good, too!

Hey, class! What do you say?
Who have you caught being good
  today?

Hey, [student's name]. What do you
  say?
Who have you caught being good
  today?

Laura Dickerson—Gr. 1
Seawell Elementary School
Chapel Hill, NC

Desktag Tip

Save time and money by laminating back-to-school desktags and using a wipe-off marker to program them. You can have desktags in place when the students arrive, yet you have the flexibility to reprogram them with preferred nicknames. And if a student is a no-show, you can reprogram her desktag for a student who just registered that morning. Then either permanently program the desktags that afternoon or cover the wipe-off programming with lengths of clear book tape (allowing you to later wipe away the programming and reuse the tags).

Luella Brunnemer—Gr. 1
Eagle Creek Elementary
Indianapolis, IN

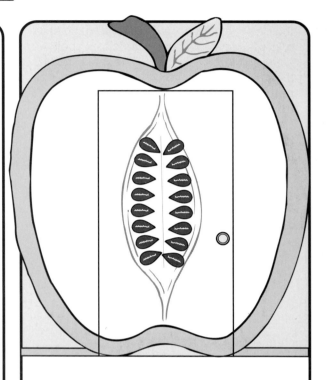

Apple Decor

When students set their eyes on this "a-peeling" door decoration, you'll hear a chorus of ohs and ahs! Cover the door and an area of wall space around it with white paper. Mount a red apple-shaped border around the door, trim away unwanted white paper, and attach a paper leaf and stem. Personalize a seed cutout for each child. Mount the cutouts on the door and then use chalk or crayon to add apple core details. Wow! What an awesome apple!

Joyce R. Welford—Gr. 2
Sandra Smith—Teacher Assistant
Leakesville Elementary School
Leakesville, MS

Toothy Tote Bag

Make the event of losing a tooth even more special with a toothy tote bag! Pack a canvas bag (or other carrier) with two or more tooth-related books, a small photo album, and a tooth-shaped writing journal. When a student loses a tooth, take a candid Polaroid® picture of him for the photo album. Then seal the child's tooth inside an envelope and send it home in the tote bag. A child shares the contents of the bag with his family members and then with their help, writes and dates an entry in the journal. Ask the child to return the tote bag—minus his tooth, of course—the following school day.

Kay Young—Gr. 1
Mt. Vernon Elementary
Clermont, GA

First-Day Photo

Snap a class photo on the first day of school, and you're sure to capture miles of smiles! Feature the snapshot in your first weekly newsletter, and you'll earn rave reviews from parents. After all, one picture is worth a thousand words!

Jan McManus—Gr. 2, St. Clement School
St. Bernard, OH

Hurrah for Grandparents!

National Grandparents Day is the first Sunday following Labor Day, yet any day is perfect for recognizing these fine folks! For this presentation, students form two rows facing their audience. Selected students in the back row hold individual letter cards that spell the word GRANDPARENTS. The class recites the first stanza of the provided poem. Then as each additional line of the poem is read from cue cards, the student who holds the corresponding prop raises it high above his head. When the performance is finished, the message is clear. Grandparents are grand!

> We're thankful for so many things
> Today and through the year.
> We'll name some of them just for you
> And show you who's *most* dear.
>
> **S**ugar, sports, and Saturdays;
> **T**eachers, trust, and time;
> **N**eighborhoods and nutty jokes;
> **E**verything that chimes.
>
> **R**eading, rain, and root beer;
> **A**steroids, aunts, and art;
> **P**izza, pups, and parents;
> **D**oughnuts by the cart.
>
> **N**ursery rhymes and nature;
> **A**nything that's new;
> **R**ainbows, rocks, and wrestling;
> **G**randparents just like you!

Rachelle Williams—Gr. 3, Central Elementary
Plainfield, IN

Double Desktags

Two desktags are better than one, and here's why! Sometimes it's difficult to clearly view a desktop tag from a distance. So by placing a second tag on the side or front of a desk, classroom visitors can read student names more easily. In addition, if the second desktag is backed with magnetic tape and you have a magnetic chalkboard, students can use these tags for class graphs, class lists, and so on. Better get a second set of desktags made on the double!

Candi Barwinski—Gr. 2
Fleetwood Elementary School
Fleetwood, PA

Desktop Sticker Collections

Between the folds of these nifty desktags, students find the perfect place to store treasured stickers! Label and then laminate a desktag for each child. Fold the desktags in half and secure the bottom half of each one to the appropriate student's desk. Inside attach some Velcro® so the tag will lie flat. Sh! There's a sticker collection inside!

Isabel Pardo—Gr. 1, Bowman Foster Ashe School, Miami, FL

Marshmallow Toes

Here's a tasty first-week activity that leaves a lingering impression about acceptable hallway behavior. To begin, have each child use her five senses to investigate a large marshmallow. (Emphasize that marshmallows are soft and noiseless.) Next instruct every child to nibble off each corner of a large graham cracker. Then have her nibble away a section near the middle of the cracker to create a shape that resembles a footprint. Finally, have each child use peanut butter to attach five mini-marshmallow toes to the footprint. As the students eat their snacks, ask them to imagine softly walking down the hallway on marshmallow toes. Then invite them to practice these soft steps each time they enter the hallway.

Misti Craig—Gr. 1, Campbellsville Elementary
Campbellsville, KY

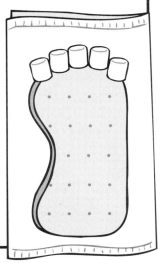

School Map

This first-day activity familiarizes students with their school, and it shows them that a map represents a real place! Post a simple map of the school on a bulletin board. Ask students to name important places around the school, and list their ideas on the chalkboard. Next take the class on a walking tour of the school. Be sure to visit each important place and take an instant picture there. When the tour is over, enlist your students' help in mounting the pictures around the edge of the school map and using lengths of yarn to connect the photos to their corresponding map locations.

Jennifer Alexander—Gr. 2, Stocks Elementary
Greenville, NC

Weekly Quotes

Keep parents informed *and* entertained with an easy-to-publish weekly edition of classroom news! Near the end of each day, gather student quotes about the day's events and write them on a dated form like the one shown. On Friday add a note from you and then make a copy for each student. Have each child describe or illustrate her favorite event of the week on the newspaper she's taking home. Extra! Extra! Read all about the week!

Christine Schirmer—Gr. 1
Van Zant Elementary School
Marlton, NJ

Classroom Quotes
for the week of
September 13, 1999

Monday	Tuesday
Shelby said, "Today was really fun because we had art. We used marshmallows to print apples!" Jackson said, "I love school!"	"I like learning about magnets," said Nathan. "I'm going to tell my mom I attract dirt and repel soap!"
Wednesday	Thursday
Friday	Picture of the Week
Note from Ms. Schirmer	

Off the Wall

Incorporating classroom furnishings and supplies into first-day lessons is a fun way to introduce students to their new surroundings. Have students sort attribute blocks by shapes or Unifix® cubes by colors. Read aloud a fiction and a nonfiction book from the classroom library, and ask students to use the classroom clock to answer time-related questions. Use a globe or map to review the continents and oceans of the world, and refer to the birthday display to create a class graph of student birthdays. This introduction to the classroom is sure to make students feel right at home!

Pamela Reifsneider—Associate Teacher
Newtown Friends School
Newtown, PA

Disposable Smocks

How do you transform a large plastic shopping bag with handles into a disposable paint smock? Cut away the bottom of the bag! To slip on the smock, a child pulls it over his head, poking his head through the main opening and his arms through the handle holes. When the smock comes off, it goes directly in the trash!

Theresa Zule—Teacher Aide K–2
Easton Primary School
Easton, KS

Meet the Class

Instead of sending home the interest inventories that your students complete on the first day of school, collect and publish them in a three-ring notebook. For durability, insert the students' papers into plastic page protectors. Also include a photograph of each student with his interest inventory, if desired. Then arrange for each child to take home the notebook so he can introduce his family to his new classmates. Each time a new student joins your class, update the notebook and then invite him to take it home for the evening so he can quickly get to know his new classmates!

Lynn Lupo-Hudgins
Austin Road Elementary
Stockbridge, GA

Three Class Rules

One, two, three! Take this approach to identifying class rules, and three is all you need! Begin by asking students to brainstorm possible class rules. List their suggestions on an overhead or on the chalkboard. When the list is much too long for anyone to remember, suggest grouping the rules into categories. Three positively stated categories that will include most rules are "Be kind," "Stay safe," and "Follow directions." Lead students to this discovery and then post the class-created rules in a prominent location. Positive results are sure to follow!

Cheryl A. Wade—Gr. 2, Golden Springs Elementary School, Anniston, AL

Year-Round Border

Do you have a year-round display that needs your students' touch? Try this! On the first day of school, review with the class the themes and topics you will teach during the year. Then have each child decorate a scalloped section of bulletin board border with pictures, numbers, and/or words representing the themes and topics in which they are most interested. Keeping the border on display year-round reminds students of what they've learned and what they have to look forward to!

Trisha Owen—Gr. 3, Libbey Elementary School
Wheatland, WY

Individual Audiotape

How does a blank audiotape become a reading portfolio and a Mother's Day gift? Read on! Every month, record a sample of each child's oral reading on her personal tape. For May's recording session, ask every student to read aloud a special passage or poem for her mother or another chosen adult. Then have each child tuck her audiotape inside a handcrafted holiday card for her special loved one!

Kimberly A. Packard—Gr. 1, St. Bartholomew Catholic School, Philadelphia, PA

Melrose Park School
Mrs. Michelle Lechel
Room 10
school: 123-123-1234
voice mail: 100-100-1000

Please feel free to call me with any questions or concerns that you may have regarding your child's education.

Customized Business Cards

To make it easy for parents to contact you, use a computer to customize a business card especially for their use. Include your name, the name and phone number of your school, and an email address and/or voice mail number where messages can be left. Print the information on blank business cards purchased from a local office supply store. (The cost for 100 cards is about $7.00.) To create magnetic cards, attach the cards to precut business card magnets (also available from office supply stores). It's an inexpensive way to encourage parents to stay in touch!

Michelle Lechel—Gr. 2, Melrose Park School
Melrose Park, IL

Day by Day

Keeping a daily account of classroom events is a snap when the entire class participates! Designate a different student reporter for each school day in a month, making sure that students have equal opportunities throughout the year. Near the end of her assigned day, a reporter completes and illustrates a provided sentence about the day. Mount the completed projects around the classroom. Then, once a month, chronologically organize the projects from the previous month and bind them into a class book. Imagine the fun you'll have at the end of the school year reviewing these monthly publications of picture-perfect memories!

Kay Young—Gr. 1, Mt. Vernon Elementary, Clermont, GA

On the 22nd day of September, my class played a really fun math game.

Birthday Graph

Here's a first-day activity that teaches and pleases students! Display a large bar graph titled "Birthday Graph." With your students' help, list the 12 months of the year on the graph. Next have each child write her name and birthdate on the graph for the correct month and lightly color the corresponding square. Pose questions about the completed graph for students to answer. Then, after a review of monthly abbreviations, have each child label a 9" x 12" sheet of one-inch graph paper for a birthday graph and then color the spaces to correspond to the posted graph. Students will be proud to share these first-day projects with their families, and you'll feel good about the concepts you've covered!

Pamela Williams—Gr. 3
Dixieland Elementary
Lakeland, FL

Jan.						
Feb.						
Mar.						
Apr.						
May						
June						
July						
Aug.						
Sept.						
Oct.						
Nov.						
Dec.						

Birthdays on Display

Birthdays are in the bag at this festive display! Recycle a dozen different gift bags and add some colorful tissue paper to each one. Cut out 12 large construction paper gift tags and label each one for a different month. Write each child's name and birthdate on the appropriate tag. Attach the tags to the bags with colorful ribbon. Display the gift bags on a bulletin board or wall, adding the title "Happy Birthday to You!"

Sharon Kirk—Gr. 3, Oak Mountain Elementary
Birmingham, AL

Binding Class Books

Bind class books in a jiffy with the help of plastic cable ties (available at hardware stores). Simply hole-punch the project and then thread a cable tie through each opening and lock it—leaving plenty of room for the pages of the book to be turned. Snip off any excess plastic at the end of each tie and the class book is ready to read!

Suzanne Gerczynski—Gr. 1
Glen Burnie Park Elementary
Glen Burnie, MD

Daily Vowel Review

Reviewing a vowel sound a day increases knowledge and builds vocabulary! Each morning, as part of your morning routine, hold up a word card that contains a single vowel sound. On a count of three, have students say the sound; then have them confer with classmates seated near them to choose another word that contains this sound. List the suggested words on the chalkboard and discuss how they are similar. Encourage students to suggest new words for repeated vowel sounds and their vocabularies will grow right before your eyes!

Karen L. Simms—Gr. 1, Lyter Elementary School
Montoursville, PA

Names That Teach

The next time you name cooperative groups, choose names that teach. For example, to teach vowel letters, choose the group names A, E, I, O, U and Sometimes Y. Or to reinforce shapes, choose names like Squares, Ovals, Circles, Rectangles, and Triangles. For additional learning, write or illustrate each group name on individual cards—one card per group member. Then tape a card in the corner of a group member's desk. What's in a name? A lot!

Karla Campagna—Gr. 2
Northwestern Primary School
Darlington, PA

Holiday Treat Bags

Deliver first-class treats to students in these nifty treat bags. To make a pair of treat bags, seal a business-size envelope and then cut it in half. For decorative edges use paper edgers. Then, keeping the sealed flap to the back of each bag, use markers, rubber stamps, and stamp pads to decorate the fronts of the treat bags as desired. Place a handful of wrapped candies inside each pouch, or slide a large plastic-wrapped cookie inside. Happy holidays!

Erin Hoffman
Brecknock Elementary
Shillington, PA

Story Writing Express

Keep students on the "write" track with a locomotive spotlighting beginning story-writing elements. Prepare or purchase tagboard cutouts of an engine and three train cars. Program the cutouts as shown. Introduce and display the engine first, explaining that a main character and a story setting must be chosen before a story can get rolling. Then display the three train cars in sequential order, explaining each story part as you go. Encourage students to refer to the locomotive whenever they write stories. All aboard the Story Writing Express!

Pat Urbach—Gr. 1, B. A. Kennedy Elementary, Prairie du Chien, WI

Word Wheel

Put a new spin on sight words with a recycled Rolodex® card file. Type each word from the Dolch list of the 250 most commonly used words (or another desired list) on a self-sticking label. Remove the alphabetized dividers from the card file and then stick each prepared label on an individual card. There you have it. A word wheel with plenty of appeal!

Marni Krams—Special Education, Royal Palm Elementary
Lauderhill, FL

Weekly Reflections

This end-of-the-week writing activity is a winner! Every Friday have each student write and date a personal evaluation of his past school week in a "Weekly Reflections" journal. Then, either collect the journals and pen a positive response to each child's entry, or send them home so parents can read and respond to their youngster's writing. The weekly evaluations motivate students to do their best throughout the week, and the adult-written replies are wonderful self-esteem boosters for students!

Judy Wetzel—Gr. 2, Woodburn School
Falls Church, VA

Kindness Counts

Promote random acts of kindness with a R.A.K. cube. Cut the top from an empty tissue cube. Have students brainstorm different ways to be kind to others and list their ideas on chart paper. Then copy these ideas onto individual paper strips and deposit them in the prepared cube. Periodically remove a paper strip from the cube, read aloud the act of kindness that's listed, and encourage students to put it into action. A few days later, invite the class to talk about the benefits of sharing this act of kindness with others. No doubt students will agree, R.A.K.s are A-OK!

Janet Finley Landry—Gr. 3
Wren Hollow Elementary, Ballwin, MO

Individual Paint Palettes

Take the pain out of class painting projects with individual paint palettes! Give each child a five-inch square of leftover laminating film. To disperse paint, squeeze dollops of desired tempera paints directly on the palettes. When it's time for cleanup, allow the paint on the palettes to dry before removing it (it crumbles easily). Presto! The palettes are ready to be reused!

Charlotte Cross—A.R.T.S.
Fletcher Elementary, Fletcher, OK

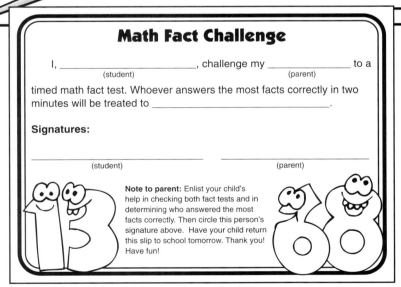

Math Fact Challenge

I, _____, challenge my _____ to a
        (student)   (parent)

timed math fact test. Whoever answers the most facts correctly in two minutes will be treated to _____.

Signatures:

_____   _____
       (student)   (parent)

Note to parent: Enlist your child's help in checking both fact tests and in determining who answered the most facts correctly. Then circle this person's signature above. Have your child return this slip to school tomorrow. Thank you! Have fun!

Durable Bookmarks

These easy-to-make bookmarks are clear winners with kids! Use a paper cutter to cut laminating film leftovers into slightly oversized bookmark shapes. Trim each shape with paper edgers to create a decorative edge, and then press a colorful sticker at the top of the shape. The bookmark is ready to use!

Pat Kourt—LMS
Thomas-Fay-Custer Unified Schools
Thomas, OK

Math Fact Showdown

Here's a homework assignment students request time and again! Send each child home with two identical copies of a timed fact test and a Math Fact Challenge like the one shown. A child and parent fill out the challenge, take the test, and then determine who answered the most math facts correctly. Ask each student to return the completed challenge sheet the following school day. Learning math facts quickly becomes a top priority!

Maria Smith, Bess Race Elementary, Crowly, TX

Reading for Dominoes

Here's a surefire way to motivate students to read science-related books—or any type of books for that matter! Place a handful of dominoes on one arm of a balance scale. For every book a student reads, he writes the title, author, his favorite part of the book, and his name on a large index card. Then he places the card on the other arm of the scale. When the index cards outweigh the dominoes, reward the students for their reading efforts. Each time you repeat the reading challenge, increase the domino count!

Sherry Rogers—Gr. 2, Cooper Elementary, Superior, WI

Freckle Juice
by Judy Blume

My favorite part is when Andrew goes to school with blue freckles.
Patrick O.

Workin' on Subtraction!

Singing this little ditty will definitely keep students motivated to memorize their subtraction facts. Sing to the tune of "I've Been Working on the Railroad."

I've Been Workin' on Subtraction

I've been workin' on subtraction,
All the livelong day!
I've been workin' on subtraction.
I need to know my take-aways.
Yes, you can use a calculator,
But I need to know them all by heart.
And pretty soon before you know it,
I'll be subtraction smart!

Elizabeth Almy
Greensboro, NC

Snowy Desks

Chances are, your youngsters' desktops could use a good scrubbing. Take a few minutes to let it snow dollops of foaming shaving cream on your youngsters' desktops! Then read aloud *The Snowy Day* by Ezra Jack Keats (Viking Press, 1981) and have students use their fingers to imitate the main character's snow-related actions. By the conclusion of the tale, the desktops will be sparkling clean and ready to wipe down. Now that's a literature connection with good, clean results!

Melissa Beasley—Chapter 1
North Columbia Elementary, Appling, GA

Two by Two

Everyone steps up to help make this counting activity a wintertime favorite! Pair students and ask each partner to take a turn standing on black paper while his partner traces around his shoes. After the students cut out their shoe outlines, glue each pair on a long length of white bulletin board paper. Trim the paper to resemble a snowy path and label the project for skip-counting by twos. Then display it along the bottom of a hallway wall. Encourage students to quietly count by twos as they tiptoe alongside the snowy path!

Barbara Lynch—Gr. 1
College Point, NY

2   4   6   8   10   12

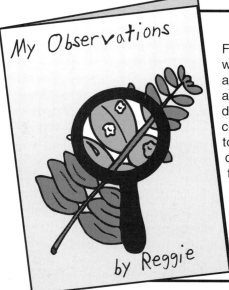
My Observations
by Reggie

Observation Is Key!

Fine-tune your youngsters' observation skills with this journaling activity. Give each child a construction paper booklet of blank pages and have him personalize the front cover as desired. Then, every week at a designated center, display a different item for students to observe. Each day a student writes and dates an observation in his journal. Set aside time at the end of the week for students to compare, contrast, and discuss the notes they've taken.

Kym Sitz—Gr. 2
Academy Elementary School
Little River, TX

100 Words

Promote literacy with this 100th-day display! Write 100 high-frequency words on individual cards. Display the cards in the hallway so that the number 100 is formed. Nearby post the challenge "Can you read these 100 words by the 100th day of school?" No doubt youngsters will be up for the challenge *and* ready to read!

Laurie Wojslawowicz—Grs. K–3
Literacy Specialist
Agassiz School, Cambridge, MA

Candy Land

Candy Land

Peppermint Road

Candy Cane Lane

Gumdrop Blvd.

Chocolate Drive

Map Key

street

house

river

Candy Land

Peppermint Road

Candy Cane Lane

Gumdrop Blvd.

Fudge

Corner

Chocolate Drive

Map Key

street

Sweet Map Skills

This 3-D mapping activity is a perfect way to display the gingerbread houses your students make each year! On a five-foot square of paper indicate the streets of a village called Candy Land. Replicate this information on an open map reproducible like the one shown and make student copies. Embellish the larger project with decorations that include a lake, railroad tracks, a river, a bridge, and several 3-D trees. Then arrange the gingerbread houses on the map. Next hand out the map reproducible. Ask each child to design a map key that corresponds to the larger map and to create a map of the village. Who knew map skills practice could be so sweet?

Linda Valentino—Gr. 2
Minisink Valley Elementary School
Slate Hill, NY

Snap and Clap Spelling

Add this snappy review to your bag of spelling tricks! To begin, announce a spelling word. Students orally spell the word in unison, snapping their fingers after calling each letter. Then they clap their hands and say the word. Continue in this manner, increasing the pace as desired, until all spelling words have been snapped and clapped!

Misty Bridges-Clark—Gr. 3
East End Elementary
Little Rock, AR

Season's Readings!

Each day during December give students a heartfelt holiday gift by sharing with them the joy of reading. On a bulletin board, showcase a large holiday tree cutout, the provided poem, and the title "Gifts of the Season." Then, for every day you plan to read aloud, gift wrap one book. Stack the gifts on a table beneath the display. Each afternoon ask a different child to unwrap one gift from under the tree and show it to the class. Then read aloud the chosen book for your youngsters' listening pleasure.

Kristin McLaughlin—Gr. 1
Daniel Boone Area School District, Boyertown, PA

Gifts of the Season

Choose a book
and open its cover.

A wonderful gift you
will discover!

Q and U

Here's an effective way to reinforce that *q* is almost always followed by *u!* Make a class set of necklaces like the ones shown, labeling half of the cards "q" and the other half "u." Give every child a necklace to wear for the day. Each time students line up, have them stand according to the *q* and *u* rule. Lining up has never been more educational!

Judi Lesnansky—Title I
New Hope Academy
Youngstown, OH

First-Class Scroll

A spiffy scroll of letters is sure to be well received by a child who's recently moved away or missed several days of school due to illness. Have each child write a letter to the classmate on provided paper. Tape the letters end-to-end, roll the resulting length of paper into a tube, and tie it with a length of ribbon. Package the scroll for mailing or hand-deliver it. Now that's a special delivery!

Kelly A. Lu—Gr. 2
Berlyn School
Ontario, CA

Fly's-Eye View

Bring a bird's-eye view into focus with this literature-related mapping activity. Read aloud Jim Aylesworth's *Old Black Fly* (Henry Holt and Company, 1995), which gives a rollicking account of a family in hot pursuit of a fly. Then have students imagine that a distant relative of the old black fly has landed on the classroom ceiling. Ask each child to draw the classroom from the fly's perspective. Invite that old black fly back into your classroom as needed for further mapping fun.

Brigid Lund
Plymouth, MN

Dear Dad,
I need a paper towel tube by Tuesday.
Love,
Jerome

It's in the Bag!

The next time a child needs to replenish a school supply or you're requesting that students contribute to a class project, try this! Have each child write a short note to his parent(s) on the outside of a folded paper sack that, when unfolded, can be used to carry the needed supply to school! These unique requests really deliver!

Janice Keer—Grs. 1–2
Irvin Pertzsch School
Onalaska, WI

Soaking Up Knowledge

Get students absorbed in learning with this clever idea! Show the class a dry, natural sponge. Then place the sponge in a shallow container of water and have students observe it soaking up the water. Tell them that just as the sponge soaks up water, their brains can soak up knowledge. Showcase the sponge and container for a constant reminder of this analogy. Then conclude each day by inviting students to share the knowledge they've soaked up!

Jo Fryer—Gr. 1
Kildeer Countryside School
Long Grove, IL

SLURP!

Ketchup Day

What in the world is Ketchup Day? A day to catch up, of course! Keep a plastic bottle of unopened ketchup in your closet. Periodically display the container and proclaim a designated amount of time for catching up on incomplete work. Students who are all caught up may participate in quiet free-time activities. Isn't it amazing how a bit of ketchup can increase the appeal of just about anything?

Jo Fryer—Gr. 1

BILL'S
Squeeze
Ketchup

Helping Verbs

Need a hand teaching some of the most common helping verbs? This song, sung to the tune of the "Mickey Mouse Club March," is sure to help!

Helping Verbs
Have, has, had,
Is, am, are,
Be, being, and been.

Helping verbs, helping verbs.
Helping verbs, helping verbs.
Forever, ever keep them in our
Minds, minds, minds.

Come along and join our verbs and
Sing our language song.
Have, has, had,
Is, am, are,
Be, being, and been.

Debra Kain—Gr. 2
Sewell School
Sewell, NJ

Fairy-Tale Follow-Up

Wrap up a study of fairy tales with this kid-pleasing project. Have each child secretly choose his favorite tale and then create a collage that characterizes it. To do this, he cuts out pictures from discarded magazines and glues them on a sheet of construction paper. Showcase the students' projects on a hallway bulletin board and invite passersby to guess which tales they represent.

Mary A. L. Boardwine—Library Media Specialist
Montvale Elementary School
Blue Ridge, VA

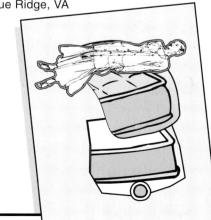

Good News Checklist

Keeping a good news checklist assures that you regularly acknowledge the positive behavior of all students. Make it a practice each day to write and send home notes recognizing different students for their positive traits. As you complete each child's note, check off his name. A quick glance at the list reveals whose positive traits have been overlooked and need to be noted right away!

Ellen Muscato
South Elementary School
Castle Rock, CO

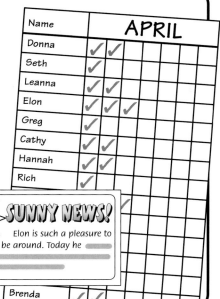

Name	APRIL		
Donna	✓	✓	
Seth	✓		
Leanna	✓	✓	
Elon	✓	✓	✓
Greg	✓		
Cathy	✓	✓	
Hannah	✓	✓	
Rich	✓		
Brenda	✓	✓	
Peter	✓		

SUNNY NEWS!
Elon is such a pleasure to be around. Today he

Cool Paint Tray

An ice cube tray is perfect for dispensing assorted colors of tempera paint to small groups. Four students can easily share one paint tray. For cleanup, rinse the tray and place it in a dishwasher for a thorough cleaning. Since the trays are stackable, storage is a snap as well!

Victoria Cavanagh—Gr. 1
Troy Hills School
Parsippany, NJ

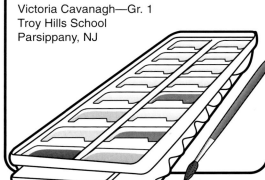

Earth-Friendly Request

The next time you send home a parent newsletter, introduce a new column titled "Good Junk." In the column, request routinely discarded items—like empty shoeboxes and cereal boxes, colorful plastic tops from dried-up markers, used envelopes and cards, and so on—that you can put to use in the classroom. Parents appreciate the opportunity to contribute, you receive needed supplies, and students reap the benefits of everyone's earth-friendly behavior!

Maureen Jannetta—Gr. 1
Holy Name School
Providence, RI

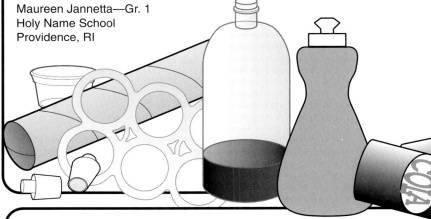

Priority Folders

Need help convincing students that completing unfinished work is top priority? Try this! Give each child a manila folder to title "Top Priority!" and decorate to his liking. A child files all unfinished work in his folder and attempts to complete each top-priority assignment during free time. Any work remaining in his folder at the end of the day becomes homework. These folders work like a charm!

M. J. Owen—Gr. 3
Baty Elementary
Austin, TX

Basic Fact Hunt

Practicing basic facts just got "eggs-tra" fun! For each child, place a list of unsolved math facts inside a plastic egg; then add a coupon for a homework-free night inside one of the eggs. Hide the eggs while the students are away from the classroom. To begin the activity, ask each child to find and bring one egg to his desk. Then, on a signal from you, have all students open their eggs. Congratulate the child who found the egg containing the coupon; then have the students copy and answer the math facts on provided paper. Repeat the activity daily until the Easter bunny disappears for another year!

Heather Graley—Gr. 3, Columbus, OH

6 x 7 =
4 x 3 =
0 x 2 =
2 x 5 =
8 x 6 =
5 x 4 =
3 x 7 =

May Day Surprises

These sweet May Day reminders are easy to make and certain to please! A child fashions a flower from a four-inch square of construction paper, cuts one or more leaves from green construction paper, and glues the leaves to the flower. Then he carefully pokes the stick of a Tootsie Roll® Pop into the flower center and slides the paper flower along the stick until it meets the wrapped candy. Plan for each child to make at least two blooms—one to give away and one to eat!

Sheri Bradley—Gr. 2
Falling Creek Elementary
Richmond, VA

Spelling Puzzlers

Add some spark to spelling practice with this large-group activity. Copy the weekly word list onto a transparency, and then cut the transparency into individual word cards. To begin, display three or more words on an overhead, making sure all but one share an attribute, such as the same number of syllables or the same ending sound. Students study the words and determine which word doesn't belong. Repeat in a like manner using different groupings of words. Most likely students won't recognize this activity as spelling, and there's no harm in that!

Renee Mason—Grs. K–3
Fairlawn Elementary
Santa Maria, CA

Oral-Reading Choices

Choices for oral reading? You bet! Before a child begins to read, have him announce whether he'll be reading a sentence, a paragraph, or a page. A shy or unsure child will be less likely to fear oral-reading practice and more likely to gain confidence through a series of successful reading experiences. As an added benefit, students quickly learn the definition of *sentence* and *paragraph*!

Jane Clarke—Gr. 3, Thomas Sumter Academy, Camden, SC

Forever Bouquet

This picture-perfect Mother's Day card makes an everlasting keepsake! Pool resources with another teacher or two and purchase a lovely spring bouquet. Then photograph each student holding the flowers. To make her card, a child copies the provided poem on the outside of the construction paper card, tapes her photograph inside, decorates the card to her liking, and signs it. How nice!

Michelle Gagne and Deanna Nadeau—Gr. 1
Montello Elementary School
Lewiston, ME

Dear Mom,

I will love you forever,
And forever you will be
The most wonderful mother.
You mean everything to me.

I thought of buying you flowers
In the usual way,
But I knew you would prefer
A FOREVER bouquet!

Happy Mother's Day
Love, Donna

Pocket Change

All it takes is a pocketful of change to cash in on math skills! Give each child a paper pocket and a matching set of coin manipulatives. Then present a series of oral story problems that can be solved using the manipulatives. For instance, "Leon has 34¢ in his pocket when he goes into the candy store. When he leaves he only has 14¢. How much money did Leon spend?" Now there's a hands-on math experience that's a wise investment!

Suzy Wagness—Grs. 1–2
Holy Rosary School
Duluth, MN

Cookbook for Mom

Cooking up this one-of-a-kind cookbook is a laugh a minute! Each child writes a recipe for the most delicious food his mom (or another significant woman in his life) makes. Type the completed recipes and make a class set of each one. Then collate the copies and bind them into individual books that students can give their moms. A good laugh will be had by all!

Alice Bertels—Special Education
Crestview Elementary
Topeka, KS

Schoolwide Insect Poll

In your school, which insects are students' favorite and least favorite? Send students in search of the answers! Arrange for each class to be polled by different students, making sure each child participates. Then, as a class, compile the collected data on a graph and determine the five favorite and five least-favorite insects. Top off the investigation by having students report the results of the poll during schoolwide morning announcements. Don't be surprised if students immediately start bugging you to poll the school again!

Ashley Rebman—Gr. 2
Cresset Christian Academy
Durham, NC

Luscious Ladybugs

Whether you're studying insects or following up Eric Carle's *The Grouchy Ladybug* (HarperCollins Juvenile Books, 1996), these luscious ladybugs are sure to be a hit! Each child uses a craft stick to frost a chocolate cupcake with red icing; then she uses her stick to draw a line through the middle of the frosting to form two wings. She positions two chocolate chip eyes and several colorful spots (M&M's® candies) before she gently pokes two thin black licorice antennae into place. Yum!

Linda Bobbs—Substitute Teacher
Penn Trafford and Greensburg Salem
   School Districts
Jeannette, PA

Lily Pad Review

Sight-word review is just a hop away with this easy plan. Use a wipe-off marker to label several laminated lily pad cutouts with sight words. Mount the cutouts on the inside of your classroom door. As students wait in line at the door or pass through it, have them read the words you point to. Reprogram the lily pads when desired. Sight-word recognition will improve by leaps and bounds!

Antoinette McCoy—Gr. 1, Woodside Elementary, River Vale, NJ

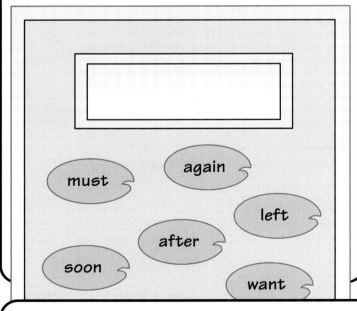

Colorful Evaluations

This colorful approach to assessing students' journal writing highlights the positive! As you read each child's journal entry, use a highlighting marker to draw lines through words that reveal extraordinary spelling or a knowledge of vocabulary. Or highlight capital letters and punctuation marks to reinforce their usage. Yellow, pink, or blue—the color of marker doesn't matter. What does matter is your positive response!

Hilda Fields—Gr. 1
Georgetown Elementary
Savannah, GA

Test-Taking Checklist

Asking students to glance over their finished tests means different things to different youngsters. Take the guesswork out of this step by providing a checklist to use after completing the test. Write the checklist on the chalkboard or staple a copy of it to each child's test. Students appreciate knowing exactly what they are looking for, and there's a good chance a few test scores will improve in the process!

Diane Afferton—Gr. 3
Afton School
Yardley, PA

Picture-Perfect Nouns

Here's a picturized noun review! Ask students to cut out pictures of people, places, and things from discarded magazines. Then, on each of three or four sentence strips, a student writes a different sentence that features pictures instead of nouns. Display the completed projects for all to read!

Patty Knott—Gr. 3, Tabernacle Elementary School, Tabernacle, NJ

Pretty Pens

Create a bouquet of writing motivation using floral tape, silk flowers, and inexpensive writing pens! Trim the stems of the silk flowers to a desired length and then tape a flower stem to each writing pen as shown. Next, cover the outside of a clean and empty juice container with green paper and store the pens inside. Place the bouquet of pens at a writing center and watch your youngsters' interest in writing blossom!

Landria Williamson
Copperfield Elementary
Austin, TX

Rock Song

Introduce this little ditty, and students will have no trouble remembering the three different kinds of rocks!

Kinds of Rocks
(sung to the tune of "Are You Sleeping?")
Metamorphic, metamorphic,
Igneous, igneous.
Then there's sedimentary.
Then there's sedimentary.
These are rocks, kinds of rocks.

Carol I. Smith—Grs. 3–4
Westland Academy
Fredericksburg, VA

Nifty Word Sorts

Easy to make and fun for kids best describes this hands-on activity. Keep several copies of a 16-box grid handy. To make a word sort, program a copy of the grid with words that reinforce a desired objective. Then photocopy the grid as needed. A student cuts out the boxes, sorts the words as directed by you, and then reads aloud each resulting group of words for a classmate.

Kathy L. Kersul—Grs. K–5 Reading Specialist
Limerick Elementary
Royersford, PA

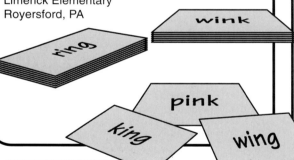

A Journal a Day

Wrap up the year with this journal-a-day writing program! Ask each child to donate a 9" x 12" spiral notebook. Label the first page of each notebook with a different writing topic; then tape a class list to each front cover. A student receives a different journal each day. He crosses his name from the class list, and then he writes in the journal on the provided topic. For added writing motivation, read two or three journal entries aloud each day. When the writing project is complete, display the journals in the classroom library for further reading enjoyment.

Becky Shelley—Gr. 1
Anderson Elementary
Anderson, MO

Writing Topic
Write about a time that you felt very, very proud.

The Time Is...

Try this ears-on approach to reinforcing time-telling skills! Throughout the day, repeatedly set a kitchen timer for different increments of time. Each time the bell rings, everyone in class looks at the class clock and reads aloud the time shown. Your youngsters' time-telling skills will quickly become music to your ears!

Claudia Taylor—Gr. 2
St. John the Baptist
Buffalo, NY

Science Trays

Here's a timesaving tip for hands-on science experiences! In advance of each activity, organize the supplies each small group needs on a nonbreakable serving tray. It only takes a minute to distribute the supply trays, which means students have more time for making hands-on discoveries. Cleanup is a snap as well!

Pam Kucks, Glenwood, NJ

Visions of Summer

Here's an activity that's perfect for the final week of school! Invite students to name their favorite summertime activities. List their responses on the chalkboard. Next, have each child choose his favorite activity from the list and illustrate himself doing it on a 4" x 6" index card. Enlist your youngsters' help in arranging the cards to form a pictograph of summertime activities. Then pose a series of graph-related questions for students to answer.

Elizabeth Searls Almy, Greensboro, NC

Reading the Room

To create enthusiasm for this reading idea, ask students to estimate how many words are displayed on a specific classroom wall. Remind students that all words are to be considered, even those found on posters, charts, and student work. Ask each child to record his estimate in a small booklet of blank pages that you've provided for this purpose. Then challenge him to read the wall of words over the next several days, awarding himself one point for every word he reads. Set aside time at the end of the allotted time for students to reveal what they discovered. Then repeat the activity for each remaining classroom wall. By the time the room is read, your youngsters' reading and estimation skills will be in tip-top form!

Susan Hopkins—Gr. 2
Piru Elementary
Piru, CA

Sailboat Sandwiches

What's delicious, nutritious, and educational? Sailboat sandwiches! Have each child complete a provided activity on one side of a white construction paper triangle. Then give each child half of a plastic straw and a hot dog bun that contains nutritious sandwich fixings. To make his sailboat sandwich, he tapes one straw end to the back of his triangle and inserts the other end into the sandwich. Now that's smooth sailing!

Theresa Tomasello
Point Royal Daycare Center
Foxboro, MA

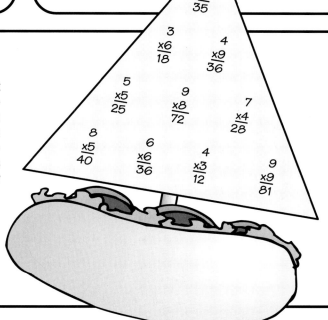

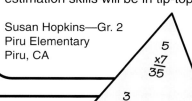

Dear Marie,
Here's a picture you can treasure.
Teaching you has been a pleasure.
It's the end of the year,
And we must part.
Always know you are in my heart!

June 2000
Ms. Cooper

One-of-a-Kind Keepsakes

Use your computer to create a precious memory of the school year for each student and her family! On decorative computer paper, print a personalized copy of the provided poem for each student along with a current picture of the child. The resulting one-of-a-kind keepsake will be cherished for years to come!

Dee Dee Cooper
Monterey Elementary
Monterey, LA

Math Night

Before the school year comes to a close, invite students and their parents to school for an evening of math-related fun. Make available a variety of math games for your guests to play, including several computer games. Talk with parents about enjoyable ways to reinforce math skills during the summer months. A fun time is sure to be had by all, and you'll have paved the way for plenty of summertime math reinforcement.

Anita DeLaTorre—Gr. 2
Hutton School
Chanute, KS

ABCs of Summer

Students have a ball playing this end-of-the-year game! Use a permanent marker to label an inflated beach ball with the letters of the alphabet. To play, seat students in a circle on the floor and toss the ball to one student. Holding the ball, the child calls out the letter nearest his right thumb and a summer word that begins with (ends with, contains) that letter. Then he tosses the ball to a classmate who has not yet taken a turn. Play continues until all students have participated.

Catherine Broome—Gr. 1
Melbourne Beach, FL

Many Thanks

The next time you prepare a thank-you note for a guest speaker or field trip host, fill it to the rim with thankfulness! Copy and sign a class-created letter of thanks on a form similar to the one shown. Then display the letter at a center along with a supply of colored pencils or fine-tipped markers. Have each child sign her name in an empty box. In any remaining boxes, draw a symbol such as a heart, an apple, or a smiley face. Very nice!

Todd Helms—Gr. 2
Pinehurst Elementary
Pinehurst, NC

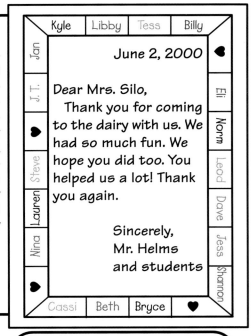

Gift of Appreciation

Express your heartfelt appreciation to parent volunteers with this gift-giving idea! Purchase one apron per volunteer (about $3.00 each when purchased at discount or dollar stores). Use fabric markers and a variety of templates to draw a large heart and assorted geometric shapes (one per student) on each apron. Copy the provided greeting in the heart and sign and date it. Then have each student autograph a geometric shape. What a wonderful way to say thank you!

Theresa J. Casey—Gr. 1
Chukker Creek Elementary
Aiken, SC

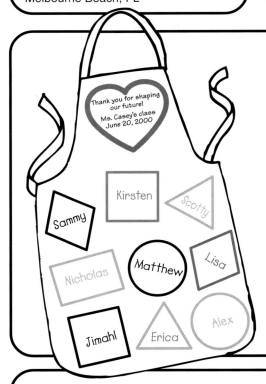

Favorite Things

Add a couple of steps to a favorite end-of-the-year writing activity, and the result is a unique keepsake for kids! This year as you read the paragraphs students pen about their favorite memories from the school year, keep an ongoing list of the named events. Then type the list on your computer, title it "Our Favorite Things From the Past School Year," and print student copies onto colorful computer stationery. There you have it! A quick and easy reminder of a fun-filled year!

Sara Gallenstein—Gr. 2
Loveland Miami Elementary School
Maineville, OH

Certificates of Achievement

There will be milewide smiles when you present these certificates of achievement to students! Personalize a certificate like the one shown for each child, then sign and date it. Around the edges of the certificate, press reward stickers that recognize the child's accomplishments. (Sunshine Label is one excellent source for stickers. Call 1-208-524-2042 to request a catalog.) Students will be bursting with pride over their achievements from the past school year!

Cindy Barber—Gr. 1
Fredonia, WI

312

Answer Keys

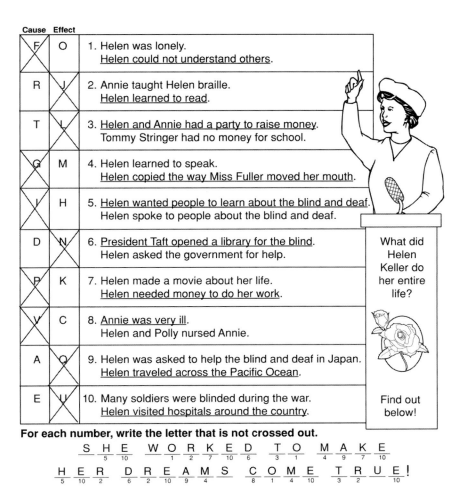

Cause	Effect	
F̶	O	1. Helen was lonely. Helen could not understand others.
R	J̶	2. Annie taught Helen braille. Helen learned to read.
T	L̶	3. Helen and Annie had a party to raise money. Tommy Stringer had no money for school.
G̶	M	4. Helen learned to speak. Helen copied the way Miss Fuller moved her mouth.
I̶	H	5. Helen wanted people to learn about the blind and deaf. Helen spoke to people about the blind and deaf.
D	N̶	6. President Taft opened a library for the blind. Helen asked the government for help.
P̶	K	7. Helen made a movie about her life. Helen needed money to do her work.
V̶	C	8. Annie was very ill. Helen and Polly nursed Annie.
A	Q̶	9. Helen was asked to help the blind and deaf in Japan. Helen traveled across the Pacific Ocean.
E	U̶	10. Many soldiers were blinded during the war. Helen visited hospitals around the country.

What did Helen Keller do her entire life?

Find out below!

For each number, write the letter that is not crossed out.

S H E   W O R K E D   T O   M A K E
5 10   1 2 7 10 6   3 1   4 9 7 10

H E R   D R E A M S   C O M E   T R U E !
5 10 2   6 2 10 9 4   8 1 4 10   3 2   10

Page 217
1. Egypt, Jordan, Syria, Lebanon
2. Mediterranean Sea
3. Jerusalem
4. Mt. Hermon
5. Dead Sea
6. Sea of Galilee
7. No. Because the Dead Sea is deeper and bigger than the sea that supplies the most fresh water.
8. Yes

Page 241

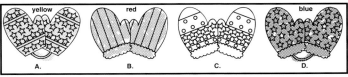

Page 218
Accept all reasonable answers.

Flag: Israel's flag shows a blue Star of David.
Menorah: It is the official symbol of Israel.
Diamonds: Israel exports these to other countries.
Camel: Camels are used for transportation in the desert.
Tree: Orange trees grow in Israel.
Ostrich: This animal lives in Israel.
Pita: This is a popular kind of bread in Israel.
Tulips: Israel grows lots of tulips for export.

Page 249
31: F, C
33: I, E
35: B, H
37: A, D
39: G, J

Index